William Sandys, Andrew Forster

The History of the Violin and Other Instruments Played on with the Bow from the Remotest Times to the Present

William Sandys, Andrew Forster

The History of the Violin and Other Instruments Played on with the Bow from the Remotest Times to the Present

ISBN/EAN: 9783741173462

Manufactured in Europe, USA, Canada, Australia, Japa

Cover: Foto ©Angelika Wolter / pixelio.de

Manufactured and distributed by brebook publishing software (www.brebook.com)

William Sandys, Andrew Forster

The History of the Violin and Other Instruments Played on with the Bow from the Remotest Times to the Present

THE

HISTORY OF THE VIOLIN,

AND OTHER INSTRUMENTS PLAYED ON WITH THE

BOW FROM THE REMOTEST TIMES

TO THE PRESENT.

ALSO, AN ACCOUNT OF THE PRINCIPAL MAKERS, ENGLISH AND
FOREIGN, WITH NUMEROUS ILLUSTRATIONS.

BY WILLIAM SANDYS, F.S.A.

AND

SIMON ANDREW FORSTER.

"Omnium rerum principia parva sunt, sed suis progressionibus
usa augentur."—*Cic. De Fin. Bon. et Mal.*

LONDON:
JOHN RUSSELL SMITH,
36, SOHO SQUARE.
ADDISON AND LUCAS, 210, REGENT STREET.
1864.

PREFACE.

HAVING for many years past been in the habit of making collections respecting (among many other things) violins and instruments played on with the bow, we have ventured to lay the result of our labours before such portion of society as may feel an interest in the subject; and, as the taste for music has of late years so much increased, we may hope this may not be a small portion. Our work should strictly have been called, "Collections towards the History of the Violin," as we ourselves have not only been obliged to omit many things connected with this history, to avoid making the book too bulky and too expensive, but are fully aware that there must be many facts connected with it with which we have not been fortunate enough to meet. We may observe here, that what we have omitted, would only have been additional illustrations, or evidences in support of what we have already stated in the work, and we should be well pleased if any one competent to the task, and with better opportunity and leisure than we have had, would undertake the History in a more enlarged and important shape. In the meantime we trust this work may be received in the kindly spirit in which it is offered to the musical world. Throughout a long extent of time we have been thrown in the society of many professors (some of the highest talent and genius) and amateurs, and among both have numbered some of our dearest friends, and we would willingly consider our book as a slight mark of regard and affectionate memory to those dear friends departed before us, and of esteem and brotherhood to those still remaining; and we must be allowed to express our satisfaction at having the permission to inscribe it to the Wandering Minstrels.

We have stated nothing without authority, though we have not in every instance given it, it seeming scarcely necessary, as all the important ones are given, and we shall be happy on application to supply the particulars of any others in our possession. The index will refer to several, but this is itself only intended to enable the reader to find the principal subjects, as many perhaps as may be requisite, but is by no means presented as a complete index.

In every case where practicable we have referred to the original authorities, and have taken every care to have the illustrations accurate. The lithographs of the Viol da Gamba are taken from excellent photographs of the instrument by Mr. Robert C. May, of Sloane Terrace. We have read with attention and derived information from the numerous works of the well-known author, Mons. Fetis, as far as they relate to the subject of our work, and, in common with all lovers of music, must express the obligation we are under to him for his interesting publications; and have to thank Mons. Vuillaume, the celebrated French maker, for a copy of "Antoine Stradivari." We have also, especially, to give our

thanks to that distinguished writer, Mons. de Coussemaker, for the interest he has shown in our undertaking,
and the leave he has kindly given us to copy or trace all
or any of the illustrations to his valuable "Essai sur les
Instruments de Musique au Moyen Age," in "Annales
Archeologiques." We have been able to introduce some
original letters of Haydn, which we think will be of
interest.

We have endeavoured to give our opinion of the origin
of the bow impartially, and if any differ from us we
would gladly hear their proofs and reasons, our object
being to get at the truth. The origin of many well
known things is difficult of proof—

> "Felix qui potuit rerum cognoscere causas."

CONTENTS.

x CONTENTS.

HISTORY OF THE VIOLIN.

CHAPTER I.

SMITH says, at the commencement of his "Harmonics," that "Sound is caused by the vibrations of elastic bodies, which communicate the like vibrations to the air, and these the like again to our organs of hearing." "For instance, the vibrating motion of a musical string puts others in motion, whose tension and quantity of matter dispose their vibrations to keep time with the pulses of air, propagated from the string that was struck." The sound of the violin, and instruments of that class, arises from the vibrations of the strings produced by the friction of the bow communicating with the air, the power being increased by means of the two vibrating plates of the instrument, generally called the back and the belly, connected with each other by the sound post, and with the strings by means of the bridge.

The greatest care is necessary in the construction of these instruments; to ensure the proper elasticity of the vibrating plates, to settle the model or form of the body, the position of the sound-holes; and, in fact, the whole structure is the result of long experience and skill. The

pitch depends on the length, thickness, and tension of
the strings, and the quality, on the shape, proportions,
and materials of the instrument; and, also, on the purity
of the strings, and the power, taste, and talent of the
performer; the difference between the delightful tones of
a performer of the first class, and the twang of a crowdero vile, being such that we can scarcely realize them as
proceeding from the same instrument.   By one we are
soothed until for a time the cares of the world are forgotten, whilst the other seems to rasp against the nerves,
and scrapes us to the quick.   We are here speaking of
the majority of mankind, for there are some few who
seem insensible to the charms of music; and among
these, even excellent good people, quite unfit for "trea-
sons, stratagems, and spoils," but probably defective in
organization.   King George III. said to Madame D'Arblay (then Miss Burney), that Lady Bell Finch once
told him that she had heard there was some difference
between a psalm, a minuet, and a country dance, but
they all sounded alike to her.   On the other hand,
there have been excellent musicians who have been excellent in little else.   The celebrated Lord Chesterfield
told his son that fiddling "puts a gentleman in a very
frivolous and contemptible light, and brings him into a
good deal of bad company, and takes up a good deal of
time which might be much better employed."   Considering, however, the nature of Lord Chesterfield's advice to
his son in some other respects, we may discard him as
any authority.   He would probably have approved of
the Gentoo Law, which prescribed that the king or rajah
should not always be employed in dancing, singing, and
playing on musical instruments.

Curious effects have been produced on animals by
music.   Fetis mentions a dog, which had such a dislike

to the sound of a violin, that he began to howl in antici-
pation as soon as he saw it touched. He gives an account
of a lizard, which would come out of an old wall, where
he had established a domicile, on hearing the adagio to
Mozart's quartett in C, but would not pay the same compliment to any other piece. The little reptile's musical
taste must have been limited as well as scientific. The
same remark may apply to the pigeon mentioned by Mr.
John Lockman, as cited by Hawkins, which would fly
down from his dove-house, and perch on the parlour
window, to hear Handel's air of " Spera si, mio caro,"
played on the harpsichord, and return when the tune was
finished. Lenz, in his anecdotes of animals, relates one
of an elephant, who paid no attention to the performances
of an orchestra in his vicinity, until they played " Char-
mante Gabrielle," when he appeared much pleased,
keeping time with his trunk, and was particularly
attracted by M. Duvornais, who played the horn.
Vigneul Marville, whose real name was Noël Bonaven-
ture d'Argonne, and who lived in the latter half of the
seventeenth century, in his " Mélanges d'Histoire," &c.,
and Bonnet, in his " Histoire de la Musique," give some
examples. On hearing a trumpet marine, a dog sat on
his hind legs, like a monkey, fixing his eyes on the performer, and remained so for more than an hour. An
ass continued to eat his thistles with sublime indifference.
Domestic poultry seemed to pay no attention, while the
smaller birds around sang in rivalry as if they would
burst. Cows stopped, looked up a little, and then walked
on. A hind raised her ears, and seemed attentive. A
horse raised his head from time to time while feeding;
and horses generally are attracted by the sound of the
trumpet, and other warlike instruments; we have seen
them attentive to the sound of a gong. A cat seemed

to pay no attention to the trumpet marine, and looked as
if he would give all the instruments in the world for a
mouse. Cats, however, are capricious, for while some
that we have known have remained stretched on the rug
in a state of the utmost indifference to the sound of the
violoncello, others have shown the greatest objection to
it (perhaps the fault of the performer), particularly to
those notes producing what is called the wolf. A gentleman frequently practising on the instrument, observed
that if those notes often occurred, the cat then reposing
on the rug became restless, and gave indications of dis-
pleasure, but if he dwelt on the note the animal would
look up at him with anger, and if he persisted would
begin to growl, and finally spit and hiss, and run away
in violent indignation. There is a singular but well
authenticated anecdote related of an officer of the regiment of Navarre, confined in the Bastille for six months
for having spoken too freely of M. de Louvois. He
was allowed the use of his lute, but on beginning to play
he was surprised to see the mice come out of their holes,
and the spiders descend from their webs. The intendant
of Madame de Vendôme assured M. Bonnet that he
had tried the same experiment himself with a violin, and
that within a quarter of an hour a great number of
spiders had descended towards his table. Playford, in
his "Introduction to the Skill of Musick," says, that as
he was once travelling near Royston he met a herd of
about twenty stags following the sounds of a bagpipe and
a violin, walking on while the music was played, but
stopping when it ceased; and in this manner they were
brought from Yorkshire to Hampton Court; a dance
that beats Kempe's "nine daies morris daunce" from
Norfolk.

One of the most ludicrous anecdotes, however, of the

power of music, is that related by Howell, in a letter
to Sir James Crofts, 6th September, 1624, where he
calls it a pleasant tale of Sir Thomas Fairfax, of a soldier with his bagpipes, who, after a weary walk in Ireland,
sat down to enjoy his frugal meal of bread and cheese.
While so employed, two or three gaunt and hungry
wolves approached, and the soldier, somewhat dismayed,
first threw them a bit of cheese, and then a bit of bread,
till his stock was exhausted, but the fierce animals still
seemed unsatisfied, and approached nearer. The soldier
then took up his bagpipes in despair, and treated the
animals with some choice bits on this ancient instrument,
on which they turned tail, and trotted off, howling in
unison. "A plague on it," says the soldier; "if I had
known you loved music so well, you should have had it
before dinner."

It may seem to those but imperfectly acquainted with
the subject that not much can be said respecting the
history of the violin. Fiddles were played on, they
suppose, some time back, perhaps by the Greeks and
Romans; they have heard of Nero playing the fiddle
while Rome was burning, and have been told that the
best fiddles are called Cremonas, and, indeed, even in
the present day, some have asked whether Cremona is
the name of a maker or a performer.

In truth, however, the history of the violin—meaning
thereby stringed instruments played on with a bow—is a
subject of great difficulty, and the origin, like that of
many other well known things, seems lost in obscurity,
especially the commencement of the use of the bow.
Considerable labour and attention are required to give
even a reasonable account; and, though we do not seek
to rival the research and perseverance of Father Ocampo,
who began his intended history of the emperor Charles V.

with the Creation, and after thirty years' labour was surprised by death, when he had only reached the time of
the Sabine War, yet we have honestly endeavoured to
give such a chronicle as may prove useful and interesting
not only to the musician but to the general reader, so
that we may not be asked, as Ariosto was by the Cardinal
d'Este, "Dove diavolo avete pigliato tanto coglioncric?"

Jean Rousseau, the great violist of his age, in his
"Traité de la Viole," 1687, seeking to prove the antiquity and excellence of his instrument, says, that as
Adam was acquainted with all arts and sciences, and the
viol is the most perfect instrument, if he had any instrument, it must have been that. We may, however, refer
to Jubal as the father of all such as handle the harp
(*i.e.* the kinnor) and organ; or, in the quaint words of
Capgrave, "Jubal, he was fader to alle hem that singe
in the orgoun, or in the crowde."—"He was fynder of
musick, not of the very instrumentis which be used now,
for thei were founde long after."

The words translated into harp and organ in the Old
Testament may probably be considered as representing
the stringed and wind instruments, and though the
learned Kircher describes the kinnor, or harp, as something like a dulcimer with thirty strings, he cannot be
relied on. Peter Walker may as well be taken for an
authority for ancient fiddles, where, in his "Life and
Death of Three Famous Worthies," referring to the destruction of Sodom and the surrounding country by fire
and brimstone from heaven, while the wicked people
were enjoying "fulness of bread and idleness," he says,
"their fiddle strings and hands went all in a flame; and
the whole people in thirty miles of length, and ten of
breadth, as historians say, were all made to fry in their
skins." Kircher describes several others of the ancient

Jewish instruments, as supposed by him, mentioning that
some were played on with a bow, but there is no authority for this. Rousseau, eager to prove the antiquity of
the viol, refers to Kircher's description of the neghinoth,
as being similar to it, having three gut strings, and played
on with a horse-hair bow; and Baptiste Folengius considers the nablum, or psalterium, to have been the same
as the viol. The passage in the old play of "Lingua"
may be considered of equal authenticity.

> " 'Tis true the finding of a dead horse-head
> Was the first invention of string instruments,
> Whence rose the gitterne, viol, and the lute."

Numerous musical instruments are mentioned in the
Old Testament, and in the early times, as now, the Jews
were skilled in the science; but it would be foreign to our
purpose to enter into any account of these instruments,
as there is no proof, or even a probability, of any of them
having been of the violin or bowed class. It is true, according to our version, Isaiah says, speaking of the feasts of
Israel, "the harp and the viol, the tabret, and pipe, and
wine, are in their feasts;" and Amos speaks of the
melody of viols, and says, "they chant to the sound of
the viol, and invent to themselves instruments of music
like David;" but the word viol was only used by the
translators as the name of an instrument known to them,
to express the Hebrew word *nebel*, of which instrument
nothing distinctly was known.

The kinnor, translated harp, was probably like the
portable harp, or lyre, used by the early Egyptians and
Ninevites, to which we shall presently refer; and thus
David could play on it, even while dancing before the
ark, and the Jewish captives could readily hang it up by
the waters of Babylon.

Julius Bartoloccius, cited by Gerbert, in his valuable

work, " De Cantu et Musicâ Sacrâ," mentions among
the instruments of the Hebrews the viola, or chelys, and
many other stringed instruments, but he makes no advance in identifying them ; and as, amongst other instruments, he mentions the "spinettæ," the integrity of his
list cannot much be depended on. He divides the instruments into three classes, and thus describes what he calls
fidicina : "Secundi generis sunt omnia instrumenta quæ
chordis seu nervis instructa, digitis vel pinnis vel etiam
plectris in harmonicos motus artificiose incitantur, et
sonum suavem reddunt; ut sunt, citharæ, testudines,
theorbæ, nablia, harpæ, lyræ, viola seu chelys, sambucæ,
pectides, pandoræ, clavicymbala, clavichordæ, spinettæ,
barbita, aliaque his similia, et omnis generis citharæ
vulgo chitarre."

The Eastern nations had, probably, from an early
period stringed instruments, but principally of the lute or
guitar class. There is no early record or representation of
the use of the bow ; and when it does appear, it may have
had its origin from a more frequent intercourse with the
Western and Northern countries. We do not, therefore,
look for the introduction of the bow from the East, though
we may be indebted remotely to the ancient Egyptians,
as hereafter mentioned, for an instrument that, with
some modification, may have afterwards become one of
the earliest bowed instruments. The bowed instruments
most in use in the Eastern countries were generally made
of a cylinder of sycamore, or other suitable wood, or
sometimes a cocoa-nut, hollowed out and polished, a
prepared skin, or a slip of fine satin-wood, being placed
over the cavity. The neck was very long and slender,
and the strings two or three in number, with a bridge ;
the bow of bamboo and hair. Varieties of these are still
in use in India, Persia, Arabia, China, and other coun-

tries. Captain Saris, who was at Japan in 1613, says the ladies played on an instrument like the theorbo (a species of lute), but having only four strings, which they fingered very nimbly with the left hand, having an ivory plectrum in the other.

Several early instruments of the East are named, varying in number of strings and details, as the serinda, omerti, rouana, and ravanastron, and others; the latter, according to the exaggerated Oriental tradition, having been invented by Ravona, king of Ceylon, 5000 years before the Christian æra.

The Indian mythology has some curious legends about music, which may be seen more at length in Creuzer's "Religions de l'Antiquité," vol. i. Hanouman, a faithful follower of Vishnu, was a skilful musician, and the inventor of one of the four systems of Indian music that keeps his name. He with his lyre, and Crichna with his flute, conducted the dance of the spheres, the stars, the months, and the seasons, accompanied by the raguinis, and other musicians of the court of India. Saraswati was the goddess of music, and her son Naesda invented the lyre. The six ragas who presided over the six musical modes were also her children, and each of these had thirteen assistants of an inferior class, so that there were eighty-four modes of the Indian mythological system of music connected with their astronomy, namely, six primitive and seventy-eight derivative. The power of these ancient modes, called the ragas, was very great, placing Orpheus quite in the background. A celebrated musician once sang that called the night raga, before the Emperor Akber at mid-day, and caused night within the sound of his voice. Another raga had the quality of destroying by fire any one who sung it; but the same emperor, notwithstanding, compelled an unfortunate vocalist to sing it, when, although every precaution was taken, and he was plunged up to the neck in the river Jumna, the flames burst out and destroyed him. A female singer was more happy, for in a time of famine from want of rain, she sung the rain-producing raga, and seasonable showers followed and revived the parched rice crops.

Many have seen the anecdote given by Olaus Magnus, of Eric, king of Denmark, who was excited to madness by the performance of a celebrated musician. First he produced grief, then joy, and then fury, to such an extent that Eric destroyed some of those who endeavoured to restrain him. We can only say that we have seen this account in the work of Olaus, and that Kircher believed it. However, he also believed the story of the magic piper of Hammelin, who in the year 460, in revenge at not being paid for piping away the mice of the place, piped away all the boys from four to twelve years of age, and disappeared with them in the side of a hill. Verstegan says the year was 1376, and that the boys were 130 in number, of whom one who was lame escaped by lagging behind. Kircher must be right, for he had seen the hill, and a picture representing the fact.

The fancy of the music of the spheres is not confined to India—

> " The music of the spheres,
> So loud it deafens mortal ears,
> As wise philosophers have thought,
> And that's the cause we hear it not."—*Hudibras.*

The celebrated astronomer Kepler, had a fanciful notion about this music of the spheres, making Mercury the treble, Venus and the Earth the counter-tenors, Mars the tenor, and Jupiter and Saturn the basses. If he had lived to this time, he might have established a very imposing choir with the numerous additional planets.

Stringed and bowed instruments are mentioned by travellers in many countries, but they are generally of a simple, and often of a rude form, and to none can we look for the origin of our violin. The Tatars, the modern Greeks and Egyptians, even the Africans have them. Bowditch, in his " Mission to Ashantee," describes one used by the natives from the interior, made from a calabash, with a deer-skin at the top, having two large sound-holes, one broad string made of cow-hair, and the bow strung with the same material. Layard mentions the Bedouins who attended him chanting verses to the monotonous tones of a one-stringed fiddle, made of a gourd covered with sheepskin. Prince Youssoupow also, in his " Luthomonographie," relates having met with travelling orchestras of Persians, Turks, and Armenians, in which there were instruments of the violin class, but without its tone or regular form, being commonly made of half a gourd, or sometimes hollowed wood covered with a piece of bladder, having three or four strings. The prince is in favour of the Eastern origin of the violin, thinking it was brought to Spain by the Moors in the eighth century, but whatever instruments they had were probably more of the guitar or lute kind. Du Halde refers to a kind of violin with three silken strings, in China, used by the common people ; and Sir Joseph Banks saw one in Iceland of a clumsy form, with four copper strings and frets ; this, however, might have been adopted from Norway or Sweden. Sir Edward Belcher mentions those of the Asiatic Esquimaux, and their skill on violins of their own manufacture.

The Arabs, besides their lute, or guitar, or mandolin, of which Laborde, in his somewhat fanciful " History of Music," mentions a species having no less than a hundred frets, and the neck of which must, therefore, have rivalled

that of the giraffe, had a bowed instrument that may
have been similar to one frequently named by the old
poets and romance writers.   This was the rebab, or
rebec, with two or three strings, which is supposed by
some to have been brought into Europe by the Crusaders;
but as at the time of the Crusades the viol had been for
a very long time well established in England and many
parts of the Continent, it is more probable that the Sara-
cens adopted it originally from the Crusaders. Monsieur
Fetis, whose extensive musical research is well known,
considers that the bow was not derived from the East,
but from some of the Northern people, from whom it
travelled southward, and passed into the East at a very
early date.

The Russian peasants have a rude sort of violin without any inward curvatures, called the goudok: it has
three strings, of which the first is touched with the finger,
while the other two are sounded at the same time by a
short, clumsy bow.   They have also an instrument of
the guitar kind, called the balalaika, with two or three
strings and a very long neck, which is mentioned by
Laborde, and also by De Passenans in " La Russie et
l'Esclavage," 1822.

Neither the Greeks or Romans appear to have any
authentic representations of a bowed instrument; they
had principally different kinds of lyres and flutes, together
with the ancient syrinx or Pan's pipes, now degraded
into a common street instrument, and indeed, seldom
heard at all. Mersennus and other writers of the middle
ages, use the word barbiton for instruments of the fiddle
class, but the barbiton that Anacreon complains of, as
preferring love-strains to singing of Atreides and Cadmus,
was a species of lyre, the ode being addressed to his lyre.
We should have said Anacreon, or whoever wrote the

poems generally attributed to him, as modern progress supposes them to be of a later date; just as Babrius supplants our old friend Æsop. Horace also mentions the barbiton.

The epigonium and magadis have been named as the originals of the viol and violin, but the former appears to have been of the lute or harp class, having forty strings, and an instrument called the simicon had thirty-five; while, as to the magadis, according to the Supplement to Montfaucon, it is not even agreed what the instrument was; whether a flute, or of the guitar class, and if so, whether it had twenty strings or less—that the pectis was the same as the magadis, and the dicord the same as the pectis; but that the matter was altogether uncertain. Apollodorus says it was the same as the psalterium. Some further particulars will be found in "Musonii Philosophi Opus de Luxu Græcorum," in the eighth volume of Gronovius's "Thesaurus," including the scindaphos, pariambos, clepsiambos, lyrophœnicion, spadix, phorminges, trigona, chelys, cithara, lyra, "et alia fortasse quamplurima, quorum investigationem aliis relinquamus." A representation is given in the Supplement, of the dicord, and also of a cithara, taken from an old Roman sculpture, which seems to have eight strings, though there are but five screws. It is like the old viol in shape, and has no appearance of frets, bridge, or finger-board, but is not adapted to the use of the bow. Anacreon mentions playing on a magadis with twenty strings (this puts an end to the flute question), and in another ode names the pectis, which has been translated cithara. Aristotle also calls these the same instruments. Montfaucon gives a representation of a procession of Isis taken from an old sculpture, where one of the figures —probably a priestess—is playing on a large triangular

or harp-shaped instrument, having twenty strings, held
under the right arm, on which she plays with a plectrum,
and which may have been a magadis. He has also a
representation of Apollo (supposed to have been intended
for Nero), with a lyre in his left hand and a long plectrum in the right.

There are numerous representations of the plectrum
used with the ancient lyre and lute, many of which, with
the authorities, may be found in Montfaucon, and in
Millin's "Galerie Mythologique."   In the latter work
there is a figure of Polyphemus in a state of musical and
jealous excitement, holding an enormous lyre, made of
the trunk of a tree with two branches, having four strings,
and played on with a plectrum. Among the fictile vases
in the British Museum, there is a figure of Anacreon
playing on a lyre with seven strings, which has a plectrum attached to it by a string, and is played on with
the right hand, while the fingers of the left hand touch
the strings; the instrument is somewhat like the lyre
du Nord, referred to hereafter.

Some supposed old Roman sculptures or medals are
mentioned with representations of something like a
violin, but these are not considered genuine.   The
following is Spence's account of the detection of some
that were once considered proofs of the early use of the
bow, commencing with the figure of Apollo in the Grand
Duke's Tribuna at Florence, supposed by Addison to
have been genuine, but proved by Winckelman to be
comparatively modern.   "The little figure in the Tribuna, with a musical instrument like a violin, is left
rough and unfinished by the artist, particularly the
violin and the stick to play on it.   It is held as we hold
our violins."   Mr. T. — Spence adds, "I have met but
with two figures besides this with the modern violin.

One of them is in a relievo on the death of Orpheus, in
the University at Turin ; and the other is a statue either
of Orpheus or Apollo, in the Montalta Gardens at Rome.
It is unlucky that all three have something to be said
against them.   That at Florence is an unfinished piece,
and perhaps not quite indisputable ; that at Turin of a
very bad taste, or of a low age; and in that at Rome,
the fiddle at least is evidently modern."   Mr. Singer,
the editor of "Spence's Anecdotes," from which these
extracts are taken, being part of the valuable "Library
of Old Authors" published by Mr. J. Russell Smith,
thought that Mr. T. was probably Mr. Townley, (who,
in his account of some ancient gems, mentions a curious
figure of a centaur, with a whip in his hand to lash
himself!)

Rousseau refers to an account given by Achilles Tatius
of a banquet, where a youth came forward with a cythara,
on which he first played with his fingers, and then used
a bow, and sang to it: also to a description of Orpheus
by Philostratus in the time of Nero, who supports the
lyre on his thigh, striking the strings with his left hand,
whilst his right holds a bow.   Rousseau uses the words
violo and archet, but the Latin words are cythara and
plectrum, which do not warrant his translation ; nor can
we agree with him in his application of a quotation from
Ovid's third book "De Arte Amandi"—

> " Nec plectrum dextrâ cytharam tenuisse sinistrâ
>   Nesciat arbitrio fœmina docta meo."

The plectrum and cythara here neither mean a viol or a
bow, but the former was occasionally long, such as that
represented by Montfaucon in the figure of Apollo before
mentioned.   In the early ages of Christianity, the word
cythara was frequently used to designate any stringed

instrument; as, cythara Barbara, cythara Teutonica, cythara Anglica (which seems to have been a harp).

Hawkins cites Nichomachus Gerasenus, who in his account of stringed instruments A.D. 60, does not name the bow. Blanchinus, in his history of the instruments of the ancients, gives a figure called the chelys (a term in after-times applied to the viol class) or, as he adds, "seu lyra Mercurii reformata." It is of the lute kind, and has neither bridge, sound-holes, neck, or finger-board, and is played on with a plectrum.

If, however, these nations, whose languages and customs were instilled into us during our eight years' residence at our venerable old school at Westminster, had not violins and bows, they forestalled us in the appointment of a coryphæus or conductor, who kept time either with his foot, armed with a wooden or iron sandal, or with his hands, having shells or bones of animals in them to increase the sound. How would a modern audience like such a conductor, performing thus a sort of sabotier dance, or rivalling the " bones " of the American minstrels?

With our comparatively simple system of notation, it seems scarcely credible how the complicated and cumbrous system of the Greeks could ever be properly understood; it must alone have proved a great check to anything like rapid execution, from want of capability to express such passages. Or, if once such execution had been attempted and introduced, the necessity of the case would have advanced the notation. Their characters, though comparatively few at first, and formed from the letters of their alphabet, increased so much that they were obliged to vary the position of these letters in various ways, and to introduce numerous arbitrary signs, every mode requiring a new arrangement; and in the time of Alypius, 115 B.C. the characters amounted to

more than 1600. A very laboriously constructed table
of them may be seen in the first volume of Laborde's
History. The Romans also used the letters of the
alphabet. It is, however, foreign to our purpose to do
anything more than refer slightly and occasionally to the
systems of notation, as it would require a volume with
numerous illustrations to treat the subject properly.

CHAPTER II.

THE Egyptians were musical from the earliest times, but their usual stringed instruments appear to have been the harp and lyre, or of that class. They are repeatedly found in their sculptures, and Sir Gardner Wilkinson, in his " Ancient Egyptians," mentions a harp as old as Osirtasen I. who was the Pharaoh of Joseph, and therefore lived about 1700 years before our Saviour. The harps were generally of a portable shape, the strings varying in number from four to twenty-two, and made of what is commonly called catgut. They were occasionally made of costly materials and richly ornamented, and sometimes were played on with a plectrum; but there is no appearance of any bowed instrument. Burney gives a figure of an instrument of the guitar class, with a long neck and two strings, sculptured on a broken obelisk supposed to have been brought from Heliopolis by Sesostris, but this does not appear to have been played on with a bow. Rousseau, however, in his enthusiasm for the viol, says the Egyptians had one with one or two horsehair strings, played on with a bow strung with similar materials; it had a long neck, and was supported on the ground by an iron rest. As before mentioned, he thought Adam might have played on the viol, and he might therefore have deduced its descent through Noah to the Egyptians. He does, however, give its travels

from Egypt to the Greeks, then to the Italians, then to
the English, who first composed and played pieces of
harmony for the instrument; from them it passed to the
Germans and Spaniards, and finally, as he says, to the
French, to whom it owes its perfection.

Passing by Rousseau's theory, which has not the proof
of any Egyptian viol to support it, the Egyptians had an
instrument with considerable affinity to the crwth, and
to which we shall presently refer again, wishing first to
make a few observations on the musical instruments on
the sculptures at Nineveh made known to the world by
the skill and enterprise of Mr. Layard. Some of these
are supposed to be at least as old as any mentioned by
Sir G. Wilkinson, and among them there is no appearance
of the bow. There is the representation of a very ancient
one on an engraved scarabæus, where it is called a nable
or guitar, and there are figures of a portable lyre or
harp struck by a plectrum. In one bas-relief from
Konyunjik there is a representation of musicians going
to meet the Assyrian conquerors—three men carry harps
with many strings; another has a stringed instrument
like the modern sautour of the Egyptians, with a number
of strings stretched over a hollow case or sounding-
board; the strings are pressed with the fingers of the
left hand, and struck by a small wand or hammer in the
right; there are also four women playing harps.

The Egyptians and Ninevites, as before observed,
had in the earliest ages an instrument somewhat similar
to the crwth, which was not played on with a bow,
but sometimes with a plectrum, sometimes only with
the fingers; the strings varying from three to thirteen
(Fig. 1). When the tide of population flowed westward
and northward, the descendants of Japhet took this
crwth-shaped instrument with them, and in very early

ages were established in our country. The bow, we

consider, was afterwards intro-
duced or invented here, for we
find here the earliest trace of
it, and none of any antiquity in
the East.   The wand or plectrum was an approach to the
bow; the beating on the tight-
ened strings inducing the experiment of the effect of friction, and thus lending to its use.

Long before the time of
Cæsar there were inhabitants in
our land who had made considerable progress in the arts
and learning of the early ages,
as the Celtic records remaining prove; and the earliest of

FIG. 1.

these show their love for music. It is supposed by
scholars of high repute, that Ireland and the south-
western parts of England were in very early ages
peopled from the peninsula of Spain, where the Phœ-
nicians had formed a colony or settlement; and many
parts of the south coast may have been probably peopled
from the opposite coast of Gaul.   In other parts, settlers
came over from Scandinavia and Germany—for the first
visit of the Saxons or Northmen was long previous to
Hengist and Horsa—and they appear to have had at an
early age an instrument of the fiddle or viol class.

The crwth of the Britons resembles to a considerable
extent the Egyptian and Ninevite instrument before referred to, and was well known to the Continent in very
early times.   Venantius Fortunatus, Bishop of Poitiers,
who lived about the end of the sixth century, says—

" Romanusque lyra plaudat tibi, Barbarus barpa,
  Græcus Achilliaca, chrotta Britanna canat."

The chrotta must have been known on the Continent
as a British instrument long before this, or it would
scarcely have been so distinguished by a foreign author.

Notker, in the ninth century, says that the rotta (or
chrotta) was derived from the psalterion—the ancient
psalterion, as he even at that early time calls it. This
instrument had some similarity to the Egyptian or Ninevite instrument before referred to, and was sometimes
of a triangular form, sometimes square or rectangular,
with occasional varieties of form. Notker says that the
ancient psalterion had ten strings, and that the form,
the Greek delta (Δ), had a mystical signification; but
after it became in use by common or secular performers,
they added strings to it, and made the shape more convenient (by rounding the angles), and called it the rotta,
thus changing the mystical form of the Trinity. The
mysticism, however, of the form, probably only existed
in the imagination of Notker, and the passage is in an
article " In Symbolum Athanasii." This rotta, as appears from the lines just quoted, was known long before
Notker, but we have cited him as an authority for its
derivation from the ancient psalterion. In a letter from
Cuthbert, cotemporary with Bede, to Lullus, successor
of St. Boniface, Archbishop of Mayence, written about
755, he says, " Delectat me quoque cytharistam habere
qui possit cytharizare in cythara quam nos appellamus
rottæ, quia citharam habeo et artificem non habeo."
M. Fetis considers this to have been the cithara Teutonica, formed from the rounded psalterion ; and with
him Mr. W. Chappell, whose opinion on everything
connected with music is entitled to much attention,
concurs. M. de Coussemaker, to whose learned " Essai

sur les Instruments de Musique au Moyen Age," we are
much indebted, and with whom M. Bottée de Toulmon
agrees in his "Dissertation sur les Instruments de
Musique employés au Moyen Ago" (Mémoires de la
Société Royale des Antiquaires de France, vol. xvii. p.
95), considers that the rote was derived from the chrotta
or crwth in the following manner :—It was found after
a time (and after the introduction of the bow) that the
hand was embarrassed in its movements by the shape of
the instrument, as the bow must necessarily have struck
several strings together. To obtain greater facility, the
external parts surrounding the neck, which had been
introduced, were removed, and the shape became gradually something like the bass-viol, and played in the same
way, between the legs, or on the knee. The rote, then,
according to this opinion, was a modification of the
original chrotta or rotta, and this does not seem inconsistent with the derivation of the early instrument given
by Notker, and Gerbert gives two representations of the
cythara Teutonica (Figs. 2 and 3) from MSS. of probably about the eighth century, though he considers one
to be older. From the epithet "Teutonica," they were
evidently instruments derived from or belonging to the
northern countries, and similar to the chrotta Britannica,
and not at this time played on with the bow. The word
cythara seems to have been used by the early writers as
a general expression for many classes of stringed instruments: the cythara Anglica, for instance, was a harp,
another example of a northern instrument. Cassiodorus,
in the sixth century, includes among stringed instruments,
and which he says were struck with a plectrum, " species
cithararum diversarum."

These instruments, including the ancient psalterion,
were not viewed by the Churchmen with favour for

ecclesiastical use. In the Council of Cloveshoe, 747, it
was decreed that "ex monasteriis citharistæ aliique
fidicines expellerentur;" and St. Jerome says, "fidicinas
et psaltrias et hujusmodi chorum diaboli quasi mortifera
sirenarum carmina proturba ex ædibus tuis." The

Cythara teutonica

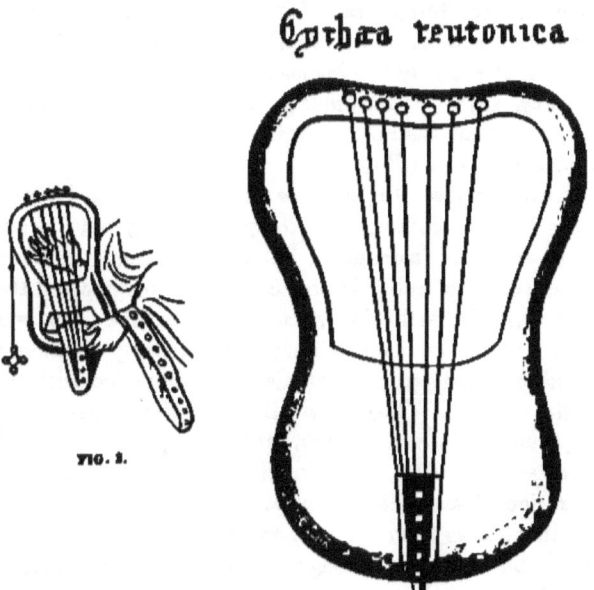

FIG. 2.

FIG. 3.

Abbot Amalarius, in the early part of the ninth century
as cited by Gerbert, referring to the expression required
in singers, says—implying the absence of any instruments,—"Nostri cantores non tenent cymbala, neque
lyram, neque citharam manibus, neque cætera genera
musicorum, sed corde. Quanto cor maius est corpore,
tanto Deo devotius exhibetur, quod per cor fit, quam
per corpus, ipsi cantores sunt tuba, ipsi psalterium, ipsi

cithara, ipsi tympanum, ipsi chorus, ipsi chordæ, ipsi organum, ipsi cymbala." John of Salisbury, in the twelfth century, writing on the use of music in churches, says: "Sumite psalmum, date tympanum, psalterium iocundum cum cithara." In an old French Bible of the same date, the third verse of the 149th Psalm is rendered, "Loent-il son noun en crouth, si chantent-il à lui en tympan et psaltruy." Thomas Aquinas, in the thirteenth century, says, "Instrumenta musica, sicut citharas et psalteria, non assumit ecclesia in divinas laudes, ne videatur iudaizare."

Although the rotta, rota, or chrotta, was thus derived, according to Notker, from the psalterion, yet it did not supersede that instrument, but they gradually differed more from each other in shape, and the rote adopted the bow, while the psalterion, about the fifteenth century, was known as the dulcimer. They are frequently mentioned together in old writers, and also in conjunction with the vielle, or viola. The pseudo-Bede mentions together the organum, viola, and cithara, atola, and psalterium; and Constantinus Africanus, in his work "De Morborum Curatione," says that soft music should be played before the invalid, as from the campanula, vitula, rota et similibus; and Sanutus, amongst other sweet music, names "violæ, citharæ, et rotæ."

Gerson, of a later date (about the fourteenth century), whom we also cite from the valuable work of Gerbert, in reference to the passage in the Psalms, "*laudate eum in chordis et organo*," says, "Chordæ secundum glossas positæ sunt pro quibuslibet instrumentis, aliis a psalterio et cithara quæ chordis sonat (*sic*) repercussis, sit viella, sit symphonia, sit lyra, sit rota, sit guiterna," &c.; and in another part he says, "Canticum cum pulsu fit tripliciter; aut in rotatu, ut in symphonia; aut tractu aut retractu, sicut in viella aut rebella; sive cum impulsu vel impulsivo quodam tractu cum unguibus vel plectro, cum virgula, ut in cithara ot guiterna, lituo, psalterio quoque et tympano, atque campanulis." In these passages he refers to the rota as a bowed instrument, and to the psalterion as not being bowed.

Many examples may be given from the ancient poets and romance-writers to the same effect, of which we will cite a few, and they may also be taken to show the use of the instruments, the vielle, or viol, and the gighe; and to prove that the vielle, gighe, rote, psalterion, and symphonie, or chyfonie, and rubebe (rebec), were different instruments. In the Roman de Brut, about the end of the twelfth century, we find—

> "Lais de vieles et de rotes,
> Lais de harpes et de fretiaux,
> Lyres, tymbres, et chalumiaux,
> Symphonies, salterions,
> Monocordes, tymbres, corrons."

In another part, relating the skill and talents of the celebrated king Blegabres (or Blæthgabreat, as he is called in the version of Lazamon), who flourished, according to Stow, 104 A.C., was the god of jongleurs and singers, and played on every instrument, he is thus described:—

> "Blegabres regna aprés li,
> Cil sot de nature de cant,
> Oncques nus n'on sot plus, ne tant.
> De tos estruments sot maistric,
> Et de diverse canterie;
> Et mult sot de lais et de note,
> De vièle sot et de rote,
> De lire et de salterion,
> De harpe sot et de choron,
> De gigho sot, de symphonie.
> Si savoit assés d'armonie.

> De tous giex sot a grant plenté ;
> Plein fu de debonnaireté,
> Por ce qui il ont de si bons sens,
> Disoient li gent à son tens,
> Que il ert dex des jugléors
> Et dex de tos les chantéors."

In or about the thirteenth and fourteenth centuries
there are numerous examples. From the "Estoire de
Troie le Grant," Roquefort, "De la Poesie Françoise,"
&c. quotes :—

> " N'orgue, harpe, ne chyfonie,
> Rote, vielle, et armonie,
> Sautier, cymbale et tympanon,
> Monocorde, lire et coron,
> Ses sont li xii instrument
> Que il sonne si doucement."

Also from " Roman de la Poire,"—

> " Et si i ot à grant planté
> Estrement de divers mestiers,
> Estives, harpes, et sautiers,
> Vieles, gygues, et rotes,
> Qui chantoient diverses notes."

In a romance by Guiraud de Cabrera, the following
instruments are mentioned together :—

> " L'us menet arpa, l'autre viula,
> L'us flautella, l'autre aiula ;
> L'us mena giga, l'autre rota."

In the " Romance of Cleomades,"—

> " Plenté d'estrumens y avoit ;
> Vieles et salterions,
> Harpes et rotes et canons
> Et estives de Cornouaille."

Guillaume de Machault, of the fourteenth century, in
" Le Tems Pastour," has a very long list of instruments :—

> " Mais qui véist après mangier
> Venir menestreux sans dangier

> Pignez et mis en pure corps.
> Là furent meints divers acors
> Car je vis là tout en un cerne
> Viole, rubebe, guiterne;
> L'enmorache, le micamon,
> Citole et le psaltarion;
> Harpes, tabours, trompes, nacaires,
> Orgues, cornes plus de dix paires;
> Cornemusea, flajos et chevrettes,
> Douccines, simbales, clochettes,
> Tymbre, la flaute Brehaingne
> Et le grand cornet d'Allemaingue,
> Flajos do Saus, fistule, pipe,
> Muse d'Aussay, trompe polite,
> Huisines, eles, monicorde,
> On il n'a qu'une seule corde,
> Et muse de blet, tout ensemble;
> Et certainement il me semble
> Qu'oneques mais tele mélodie
> Ne fut onequea veue ne oye."

In the "Prise d'Alexandrie," by the same author, many of the same instruments are mentioned together, among which are the following which relate to our subject:—
"Vielles, rubebes et psalterion, gingues, rotes, monocorde, chifonie."

Eustace Deschamps, in his poem on the death of Machaut, introduces together,—

> "Rubebes, leuths, vielles, syphonie,
> Psalterions, treslous instrumens coys,
> Rothes, guiterne, flaustres, ehalemie."

In the "Romance of Sir Degrevant," of about the fourteenth century, printed by the Camden Society, it is said,—

> "He was flayre mane and ffree,
> And gretlech yaff hym to gle,
> To harp and to sautré,
>   And geterne ffull gay;
> Well to play in a rote."

In a note, a passage from an unpublished poem by

Lydgate is given, where the following instruments are named,—

> " Harpys, fythels, and eke rotys,
> Wel accordyng with her notys,
> Lutys, rubibis, and geterns,
> More for estatys than taverns:
> Orguys, cytolys, monacordys."

Here we have the word fythel introduced.   Gower says,—

> " Ho taught her, till she was certene
> Of harpe, citole, and of riote,
> With many a towne, and many a note."

And Chaucer's " frere,"—

> " ———— Certainly he had a merry note,
> Wel coude he singe and plain on a rote."

Very long before the time of these latter examples the rote had received various modifications and improvements in form, and the bow had been introduced.   M. de Coussemaker has given the figure of a rote or crwth of the eleventh century, with three strings, and played on with a clumsy bow (Fig. 4).   This has quite the character of the old crwth, and the method of using the fingers is shown.   Another, given by him from the Cathedral of Amiens, of the thirteenth century, with six strings, has also many of the distinctive

FIG. 4.

marks of the crwth; and the similarity of the sound-holes to the modern ones will be observed (Fig. 5).

Carter, in his "Ancient Sculpture," gives the figure of an angel playing a crwth, in Worcester Cathedral, of about the twelfth century, under part of the seats of the choir. It has five strings, a tail-piece, and two sound-holes; no neck, no bridge, the left hand being placed through the hole at the lower end to manage the strings. The bow is short, and in form like the modern double-bass bow; it is a characteristic example, but in this instance the instrument was held like the viol (Fig. 6).

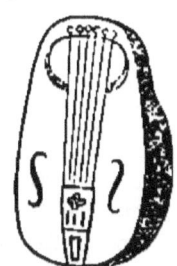

FIG. 5.

FIG. 6.

The word crwth was occasionally used for the violin and viol down to a recent time, and is still so applied in some parts of the country, most commonly to the violoncello, or bass-viol, as it is also called. A curious example may be given from a work not likely to be much known to our readers; an old Cornish drama of the date probably of the fourteenth century, called "Ordinale de Origine Mundi." The ancient Cornish language was akin to the Welsh, both having the same origin, and this extract will show that the words "crowd" and "fylh" were applied to different instruments. King David is giving directions to his minstrels—

" Whethong menstrels ha tabours
    trey-hans harpes ha trompourn
        cythol crowd fylh ha savtry
    psalmus gytirens ha nakrys
    organs in weth cymbalys
        recordys ha symphony."

Thus translated by the able editor, Mr. Edwin Norris—

> " Illow, minstrels, and tabours ;
>   Three hundred harps and trumpets ;
>   Dulcimer, fiddle, viol, and psaltery ;
>   Shawms, lutes, and kettle drums ;
>   Organs, also cymbals,
>   Recorders and symphony."

The crwth was of early date in Scotland, as well as in England and Wales, and an instrument of this nature was among the ornaments on the outside of Melross Church, founded in 1136.

Dauney, in his "Ancient Scottish Melodies," quotes from an old poem called the "Houlate," 1450, where are mentioned—

> " The psaltry, the citholis, the soft atharift,
>   The croude and the monycordis, the gythornis gay ;
>   The rote and the recordour, the ribus, the rift," &c.

Edward Jones, in the "Relics of the Welsh Bards," gives a poetical description of the crwth, written in the fifteenth century by Gruffydd Davydd ab Howel, with a translation. It agrees very much with that given by Daines Barrington, to which we shall presently refer. It is said that Bishop Morgan, in his translation of the New Testament into Welsh, printed in 1567, translated "vials of wrath" by crythan, that is, crwds or fiddles. Hawes, in his "Pastime of Pleasure," of nearly the same date, thus describes the attendants of Dame Music :—

> " There sat dame Musyke, with all her mynstrasy ;
>   As tabours, trumpettes, with pipes melodious,
>   Sakbuttes, organs, and the recorder swetely,
>   Harpes, lutes, and crouddes right delycyous ;
>   Cymphans, clarycordes, eche in theyr degro,
>   Did sytte aboute theyr ladyes mageste."

We find the word crowd used for fiddle by the dramatic writers of the seventeenth century. For instance, in

"The Old Law," by Middleton, fiddlers are introduced
to play at an expected wedding, a ceremony where they
were always in requisition : Gnatho, the servant, says :
"Fiddlers, crowd on, crowd on ; let no man lay a block
in your way; crowd on, I say!" The wedding being
broken off, the unlucky fiddlers are sent off without their
fee : "Case up your fruitless strings, no penny, no
wedding." In Marston's "What you will" they are
mentioned in a somewhat disparaging way :—

> "—— Now the musicians
> Hover with nimble sticks o'er squeaking crowds,
> Tickling the dried guts of a mewing cat."

Their constant resort to convivial meetings is frequently
alluded to, as—

> "The fiddler's crowd now squeaks aloud,
> His fidlinge stringes begin to trole ;
> He loves a wake and a wedding cake,
> A bride-house and a brave May-pole."
>
> *Cupid's Banishment,* 1617.

Ben Jonson and Drayton each name the crowd, as an
instrument to dance to ; and Sir W. Leighton, in "Teares
or Lamentations of a Sorrowfull Soule" (1613), where a
curious list of musical instruments is given to sound the
praises of the Almighty, mentions crowdes and vialls.
In the "Diary of John Richards," printed in the "Retrospective Review," published by Mr. J. Russell Smith,
there is an entry on 5th July, 1699, of Mr. Mallerd
coming to finish Jack's crowd, and taking away his own
bass-viol to mend. This crowd was no doubt a fiddle, as
part of Jack's outfit in 1700, on going to Wimborne
School, was "1 violin." We are inclined to think that
during our Westminster æra, a fiddle would have led a
sad life amongst our three hundred companions ; we
have heard, however, of one or two now of distinguished

rank who boldly persevered, but personally remember
no musical attempts, excepting some half-dozen flutes
and flageolets, in a greater or less state of perfection;
we confess to two joints of one of the former. We must
not omit some notice of Hudibras's Crowdero, said to
have been one Jackson, formerly a milliner, who lost a
leg in the service of the Roundheads, and was obliged to
get a precarious livelihood by fiddling from one tavern
to another.

> " I'th' head of all this warlike rabble
> Crowdero march'd expert and able,
> *   *   *   *
> A squeaking engine he applied
> Unto his neck on north-east side,
> *   *   *   *
> His warped ear hung o'er the strings,
> Which was but some to chitterlings :
> His grizly beard was long and thick,
> With which he strung his fiddle-stick ;
> For he to horse-tail scorn'd to owe
> For what on his own chin did grow."

After this digression on the application of the word
crowd to the violin, we must return for a short space to
the ancient crwth, which appears to have continued in
use in Wales until a comparatively recent time. Daines
Barrington, in 1770, says that the only person that could
then play on it was John Morgan of Newburgh in
Anglesey, then aged fifty-nine years; but Bingley, in
his account of North Wales, says he heard an old bard
play on the instrument at Carnarvon in 1801. We have
given a figure of one from Mr. Barrington's account in
the third volume of "Archæologia" (Fig. 7). It has
six strings placed in a peculiar way, with a flat bridge,
so that the bow must have struck several together, and
prevented any extent of execution. The bridge is curious,
as one leg goes through the sound-hole to the back of

FIG. 7.

D

tho instrument, thus serving also for a sound-post. There is no proof, however, of this example having been of ancient date. It is stated to have been thus tuned :—

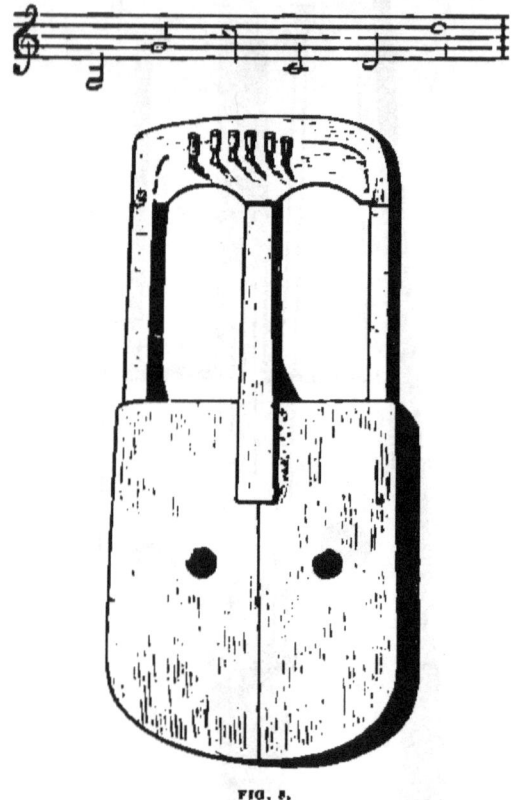

FIG. 8.

We have only been able to meet with one existing specimen, which by the kindness of Charles W. G. Wynne, Esq. we have had an opportunity of examining and of giving a drawing. The wood is worm-eaten and in tender condition, showing apparently greater age than the date of the ticket, and rendering it not improbable that it might have been only repaired at that time. It has no bridge, or tail-piece, or strings at present. It is 22 inches in length (about that of a violin), 9½ in width, and 2 in depth at the deepest part; the finger-board being 10¼ inches long. It is a curious and interesting relic (Fig. 8). The following is a copy of the ticket:—

maid in the paris of
anirhengel by Richard
Evans Instruments maker
In the year 1742.

CHAPTER III.

HE names fiddle, or fythele (fydele), among the Anglo-Saxons, and fidula with the Latin writers, are of very early date; by some of the latter, the "cithara sive fidula" is classed with "vulgaris musica." Isidore, Bishop of Seville in the seventh century, uses the word cithara as a general name for stringed instruments, stating there were several sorts, as psalterium, lyra, barbiton, &c. Some have derived the Latin word vidula, or vitula, from vielle, but we do not see why it should not be derived direct from fythele. Mr. Wm. Chappell, in his valuable and interesting work on the "Popular Music of England," one that while it shows the research of its author, places our country in a high position in the early history of music, derives vielle from fythele in the following manner. The Normans, finding the Saxon ꝺ or *th* not easy to pronounce, were in the habit of adapting it to their own pronunciation, and thus changed the word fythele to viele, or vielle, omitting the objectionable letters; but whether this derivation be correct or not, the term fydyll or fithele also continued in use. In the legendary life of St. Christopher, written about the year 1200, it is said the king "loved melodye of fithele, and of songe;" and in the version or edition of Lazamon's "Brut" (a work of the thirteenth century) by Sir F. Madden, the fythele

is named among the instruments of the accomplished
Blæthgabreat :—

> " Ne eude na mon awa muebel of song
> of harpe & of salterian :
> of fidele & of coriun
> of timpe and of lire."

We have already referred to the lines of Lydgate—

> " Harpys, fithelos, and eke rotys,
> Wel according to ther notys."

In " The Vision of Piers Ploughman," of the middle of
the fourteenth century, the word is again introduced,—

> " I am a mynstrall," quod that man,
> " My name is Activa Vita ;
>
>   *   *   *   *
>
> . . I ken neither taboure ne trompe,
> Ne telle no gestes,
> . . ne fithelen
> At festes, ne harpen."

And in " Octouian Imperator," where the rote and
psalterion are mentioned together :—

> " Ther myghth men here menstraleye,
> Trompys, taborus and cornettys erye,
> Rowte, gyterne, lute, and sawtrye,
> Fydelys, and other mo :
> In Parys grot melodye
> They maden tho."

The admirers of Chaucer will remember that the
Clerk of Oxenford would rather have—

> " Twenty bookes, clothed in black and reed,
> Of Aristotil and of his philosophie,
> Then robus richo, or fithul, or sawtrie."

In the present day wiser scholars than he have proved
that a clerk may love his " fithul" without neglecting his

"philosophie." Queen Guenever, of scant fame, had at
her revels, as appears in the "Romance of Launfel,"—

" . . . menstrales of much honours,
         Fydelers, cytolyrs and trompours."

While Sir Thomas on his visit to the Fairy Queen finds
harp and fidul, getorn, santry, lute, and rebybe, and "alle
maner of mynstralcy." So Sir Thomas was very well
pleased for a time, as may be seen in Halliwell's "Fairy
Mythology," which contains much interesting matter.
Many other examples might be given, if necessary, in
further proof of the frequent use of the word; we shall
bring forward some of them by and bye for a different
purpose. One or two references may be made to more
sober writers, as Geoffrey de Vinesauf, about the year
1200, who, after mentioning "somniferæ cytharæ," immediately afterwards introduces "vitulæ jocosæ." Gerbert adds, "Vitulæ an violæ? quæ passim inter instrumenta musica medii ævi censentur." John de Garlande,
in his vocabulary of the middle of the thirteenth century, has the word vidula amongst his musical instruments; and we are told that Isabella, Queen of Edward
II, had in her train, amongst others, two poor musicians,
"vidulatores," to play before her. The fiddle of these
early times, however, was the viol and not our modern
violin.

In the "Nibelungen Lied," of the twelfth century, a
celebrated warrior and minstrel is introduced, named
Volker; his fiddle-bow, or videl-bogen, appears to have
been a powerful weapon of offence; and he is called
videlære. A short but amusing account of Volker, and
some other ancient musical worthies, as Swemmel and
Werbel, "court fiddlers and minstrels" to King Etzel,
will be found in "A Few Notes on the Fiddle," by the

accomplished antiquary Mr. William J. Thoms, published
in No. 47 of the "Musical World," where, however, he
finishes by leaving his friend Volker in the lurch, admitting him to be a myth. As we, in common with
all who have the pleasure of knowing him, must hold his
learning and wit in high estimation, and, as in these "Few
Notes" he says, "No catalogue of fiddlers can be complete in which there does not appear the name of Lewis
van Vaelbeke as a player and maker," we must state from
his information that Lewis, or Lodewyk van Vaelbeke,
of Brabant, who died at Antwerp in the very beginning
of the fourteenth century, was an eminent "vedelare,"
and, on the authority of a rhyming chronicle, written by
Nicolaus Clerk, was the first to stamp or beat time.
Mr. Thoms humorously commences his translation of the
lines applicable to Van Vaelbeke thus :—

> " About this time departed slick,
> That good fiddler Lodewyk ;"

and finishes thus—

> " He was the first to find and show,
> To stamp or beat the manner how,
> Just as we hear it practised now."

We cannot, however, on the authority of the extract
given—and with the highest respect for the translator—
admit the name of Vaelbeke as a maker, without further
authority, and Mr. Thoms himself allows the obscurity
of the phrase cited for the purpose. We have already
shown that beating time was known to the Greeks.

Johannes de Muris, about the fourteenth century,
would seem to distinguish the vielle from the fiddle as a
variety. In describing the class of instruments he calls
chordalia, he says, "Chordalia sunt ea, quæ per chordas
metallinas, intestinales vel sericinas exerceri videntur,

qualia sunt cytharæ, viellæ et phialæ, psalteria, chori,
monochordum, symphonia seu organistrum et his similia."
In "Promptorium Parvulorum" (about 1440), fydyll
and fyyelo (viol) are Latinized, viella, fidicina, vitula;
while crowdo is called chorus.

The viol, or viello on the Continent, was the name
most commonly used for instruments of this description,
and viol, indeed, has descended to the present time, while
vielle, about the fifteenth century, became applied to an
instrument the parent of our hurdy-gurdy, which was
originally called the organistrum, and symphonie, or
ciphonie.   This was clearly a different instrument from
the rote, being frequently mentioned at the same time.
The celebrated Blæthgabreat played on the rote and the
symphonie, and in the " Romance d'Alexandre," quoted
by Ducange (voce *rota*) " Rote, harpe, vielle et gigue et
ciphonie," appear together.   In that curious composition,
" Les Deux Troveors Ribauz," of about the thirteenth
century (which may be found in " Œuvres de Rutebeuf,"
i. 335-7), being a dispute between two trouveres, or
minstrels, as to their qualifications ; one of them says to
his opponent,—

> " Sez-tu nule riens do citole,
> Ne de vide, ne de gigue ?
> Tu ne ses vaillant une figue."

To which the answer is,—

> " Ge te dirai que je sai faire:
> Ge suis juglères de vicle,
> Si sai de muse et de frestele,
> Et de harpe et de chifonie,
> De la gigue, de l'armonie,
> De l'saltcire, et en la rote
> Sai-ge bien chanter une note."

He then goes on to say he can raise spirits, and perform

feats of magic, which are foreign to our purpose; the
extract, however, shows the symphonie and rote to have
been different, as well as the vielle and the gigue.   This
symphonie is also mentioned as the lyra mendicorum,
and a figure of it is given by Mersennus and other
writers, proving its similarity to the hurdy-gurdy. Happily this instrument is now very rarely heard in our
streets since the departure of blind Sally of Westminster
notoriety, whom many of our readers may remember; a
slight suspicion of it only occasionally occurring in the
hands of some wandering Italian boy.

In a MS. of the fourteenth century at Ghent, referred
to by M. de Coussemaker, there is the figure of an instrument to which no name is attached, said to have been
invented by one Albinus.   The
celebrated Alcuin, who died in
804, travelled on the Continent
under that name, and was skilled
in music, having written a treatise
on the subject, although it is not
now extant.   It may not, perhaps,
be assuming too much to consider
him the Albinus referred to.   The
instrument is somewhat of guitar-
shape, and has four strings marked
c, g, d, c.   There are considerable
inward curvatures, but no bridge
or finger-board; the tail-piece is
broad, and there is a semi-lunar
sound-hole on each side (Fig. 9).
On a capital of the eleventh or

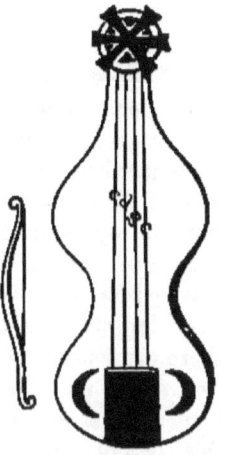

FIG. 9.

twelfth century, from Boscherville, stated to be in the
Museum at Rouen, there are eleven figures playing
on different instruments, while a twelfth is tumbling.

One of the instruments (Fig. 10) is held on or between  the knees of the performer, and, though of smaller size, is not unlike the viol da gamba in shape. It has four strings, and four semi-circular sound-holes, but no appearance of a bridge or finger-board. The absence, however, of some of the details of an instrument, either in sculpture or paint- ing, must not be taken as a proof in all cases that the parts omitted did not exist ; they might have been omitted by the artist either from want of knowledge of the instrument, or because he thought such details unnecessary. It might also be possible, in some cases, that a layer of hard wood was applied, as in the present guitars, to avoid the indentations that would take place in soft wood from constant use.

FIG. 10.

In the porch of Notre Dame de Chartres of the twelfth century, is a representation of a curious instrument of this class (see Fig. 11, from Potier's " Monumens Français," vol. i.). It is not unlike a cumbrous violoncello in shape, but the apparent heaviness may be the effect of the sculpture. The bridge in particular is thick, and deeply grooved for the strings, which are three in number and very large. The tail-piece is much ornamented, and there are four sound-holes, two of quatrefoil shape, and two much like the modern ones, but with both ends turned the same way. There is another instrument of this class of the same date, mentioned by M. de Cousse- maker, from a marble statue in the Museum at Cologne. The body is rather longer than usual, it has three strings, and two wide sound-holes. This, with the examples 9 and 10, are of the class considered by M. de Coussemaker to be rotes, or viols of large size, and Potier's example is similar.

Shaw, in "Dresses and Decorations," gives an example of the thirteenth century from Arundel MS. 157, which has three strings and two round sound-holes (Fig. 12); the bow is much like the modern violoncello bow, but is held underhanded.

Another variety was called the rebec, sometimes the ribible or rebelle, and rubebe. It seems originally to have been of a trapezoid form, and afterwards oblong, with the angles cut, and had two or three strings. Roquefort says it was a sort of bastard violin, or "violin champêtre," and was a favourite among the rustic classes, but fell into disuse in the sixteenth century—probably in con-

FIG. 11.

sequence of the introduction of the violin proper about this time. Laborde, in his "History," gives engravings of persons playing on the rebec, and on the violin, as he calls it, with three strings, of the thirteenth and fourteenth centuries; but the figures are evidently modernized, and little reliance can be placed

FIG. 12.

on the early part of his history. He mentions the figure of the celebrated Colin Muset at the porch of St. Julien des Menestrier at Paris, of the date of 1240, playing on a rebec or violin ; but the hospital of St. Julien and St. Genès (who was a Roman mime martyred in the time of Dioclesian, and adopted as the patron saint of his profession) was founded by the Corporation of Minstrels about the year 1330, and the figure called Colin Muset by Laborde, is by others said to have been King Chilperic, or St. Genès himself. The church referred to was destroyed in the time of the French Revolution. The instrument is mentioned by Aimeric de Peyrac in the thirteenth century, and is frequently named in the fourteenth century. It was played on by Absolon, Chaucer's parish clerk, who appears also to have been a distinguished dancer.

> " In twenty maners he coude skip and daunce,
> After the scole of Oxenforde tho,
> And with his legges casten to and fro;
> And pleyen songes on a small rubible."

The instrument is named with the Idle Apprentice in the " Cook's Tale."

A gay young clergyman of the time of Edward II. when he goes out—

> " He putteth in his pawtener
> A kerchyf and a comb,
> A skewer and a coyf
> To bynd with hys loks,
> And ratyl in the rowbyble
> And in non other boks
>   No mæ."

Gerbert quotes Gerson of the fifteenth century, who names the viella, the rota, and the rebolla (that is, the rebec) together as bowed instruments. We have given a figure of one, which seems characteristic of the class, from a picture attributed by M. de Coussemaker to Hemling of the fifteenth century, where an angel is represented playing on it (Fig. 13).

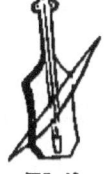

Henry VIII. had three rebecs in his band, as well as two viols; and the same instruments appear in the bands of his three children, his successors. The three performers in the band of Henry VIII. in the seventeenth year of his reign, were John Severnake and John Pyrot, who had forty shillings monthly wages each, and Thomas Evans, who had only six shillings and eight pence. Severnake seems to have been continued in the three following reigns. In the privy purse expenses of Henry VIII. 1531, there is an entry of xx' " paiede for a Rebecke for great guilliam ;" a considerable sum, taking into account the difference in the value of money; it is unlucky that the name of the maker is not mentioned. There is a rebec mentioned in that valuable record, the " Northumberland Household Book," 1512, who had 33s. 4d., and it forms one of the " mynstrasy " of Dame Musyke, before mentioned.

FIG. 13.

Jerome de Moravia describes the instrument as having two strings, tuned by fifths, and extending from C (Ut grave) to the D octave, but it could not rise higher, proving that the shift was not then known: however, it frequently seems to have had three strings. Towards the sixteenth century it declined in favour, and became more particularly the instrument of the lower classes on the Continent, and was used to accompany the rustic dances. Artusi mentions it in 1600, together with the viol, the bastard-viol, and the violin, and many other instruments. It was evidently considered of an inferior rank in France in the seventeenth century, as in regulations made in 1628 and 1648, all minstrels not properly admitted as masters, are forbidden to play any violin except that with three strings, or the rebec, and it gradually got into disuse. M. Hersart de la Villemarqué, in the introduction to " Barzaz-Breiz populaires de la Bretagne," names it as in use there among the wandering minstrels, " bardes mendiants."

The rebec, as well as other varieties of the viol, occasionally had a head carved at the end of the neck, where the scroll now is, and generally a grotesque or fanciful one. Rabelais distinguishes Badebec, the mother of Pantagruel, by her likeness to one :—

> " Elle en mourut la noble Badebec
> Du mal d'enfant que tant me sembloyt nice
> Car elle avoyt visaige de rebec."

In an inventory of King Charles V. in the middle of the fourteenth century, several instruments are particularized, having carved heads, one with the head of a lady, another of a lion, &c.

Another variety, the gigue, is frequently mentioned in the thirteenth and fourteenth centuries, and is supposed to have been derived from the ancient form of the viol, which was originally of something like pear-shape ; that is, like the half of a pear, cut through longitudinally, and was made of one piece ; it gradually became of an oval shape, and the neck was detached. What was called the gigue, retained very much the old shape ; the back, however, becoming gradually rounded, the neck still being a prolongation of the body. It generally had three strings, and continued in use till towards the latter part of the sixteenth century, and occasionally was even of later date. It would seem to have been of German adoption, as the word geige is the German name for a viol or violin, and the performers were sometimes called "guguéours d'Allemagne." It was probably the instrument used in some of the curious early dramatic performances of Gros-Guillaume, Gautier Garguille, and Turlupin (or the comic actors who assumed those names), which were a strange medley of singing, recitation, and dancing. Something like them was afterwards introduced in England, and hence the name jig may have arisen. The three celebrated actors just mentioned met with a melancholy end after a successful career for fifty years. Gros-Guillaume was imprisoned for imitating the grimaces of some well-known magistrate, who was stupid enough to exercise his power to punish him. The

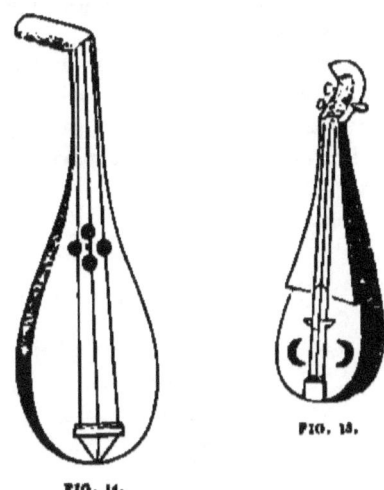

FIG. 15.

FIG. 14.

unfortunate man died from shame in consequence, and his two friends are said to have died from sympathy.

One of the figures of the elders at the cathedral at Amiens, of the thirteenth century, has in his hands a gigue with three strings and two sound-holes, but with

no appearance of a bridge or distinct finger-board.
M. de Coussemaker describes one from the Cathedral
at Mans, of the fourteenth century, where the head is
thrown back; it has three strings, with the sound-holes
placed in a peculiar manner, and the shape is elegant,
but there is no appearance of a bridge (Fig. 14). In
the same century, the top of the instrument was frequently rounded, and was not unlike the modern scroll.
Martin Agricola, 1545, gives characteristic figures of
four of these instruments, of different sizes; Discantus,
Altus, Tenor, and Bassus. They have three strings,
bridge, tail-piece, and two crescent-shaped sound-holes.
The peculiar shape will be seen from the representation
of the Descantus (Fig. 15).

As we have before observed, the several instruments
before referred to were distinct from each other, and are
frequently mentioned together in the same passages of
the early English and French romance writers.

CHAPTER IV.

HAVING shown the probability of the introduction or invention of the bow in this country in connection with the crwth or instruments of that class, and referred to the very early use of the instrument generally known as the viol, and also the absence of proof of the prior use of the bow elsewhere, we think we may fairly claim the origin of it for our own country. We were peopled in very early ages, and, although some of our ancient chronicles give rather fabulous accounts of the first settlers, yet they are generally not devoid of some foundation, however perverted and exaggerated the facts may have become. The Druids, in the time of Cæsar, were a learned body, and skilled in the arts of their age, which, from many of the existing Celtic remains, had made considerable advance. Some antiquaries, of deep research, believe they can see glimpses amongst our oldest remains or monuments of the past, of a state prior to the Druids, whether connected with the serpent worship, or with what else, is foreign to our purpose. The great antiquity of our island as an inhabited country is undoubted, and the early use, therefore, of the musical instruments of which it is our earnest wish to give a just and impartial, and we hope also an interesting account, though the undertaking may be difficult. We may observe that in our

E

very early history there are references to and statements
of visits to the neighbouring continent, and after the
arrival of the Romans there are many instances of emi-
gration there, and on one occasion a kind of colony was
established in Britanny, where there are still many marks
of resemblance to the Celtic portions of our country.
King Alfred even sent a mission to the far East; and on
all these occasions some of our arts and customs would
be carried over to, and, to some extent, be adopted by,
the countries visited.

The more ancient form of the viol, as before mentioned,
appears to have been of pear shape, that is, like a pear
divided longitudinally; but it afterwards became of a
more oval shape, and subsequently inward curvatures,
more or less defined, were introduced, and the instrument
in time became much in form like the modern violin,
though of heavier make; but this was after the lapse of
centuries. Before the inward curvatures were introduced, the rounded sides must have interfered with anything like execution, and checked the action of the bow,
which, from the form of some of these instruments, must
have struck several strings together. As increased execution, or the desire for it, occurred, the sides would be
curved inwards to meet the necessity, and frets were
afterwards introduced to guide the fingers. These curvatures would also facilitate the holding of the larger
instruments between the knees. The strings varied from
one (but this is very rare, and we only find it in Gerbert's
example) to six, but rarely more. At first there was no
detached finger board, but the neck was an elongation of
the body of the instrument; the sound-holes were generally two, but there are examples with four; there was a
bridge varying in size and position, and usually a tail-
piece of some sort. There are instances of two bridges,

but these are quite exceptional, and probably arise from some error in the representation, as they would seem to be unmanageable.

The earliest representation we have been able to find is that in the learned work of Gerbert, " De Cantu," &c., plate 32, taken from a MS. supposed to be of the eighth or ninth century, and called " Lyra." It is of pear shape, and has but one string, but there are two semi-circular sound-holes, with a small bridge between them; the neck, although in shape like an elonga-tion of the body, yet from the mark of division across it might have been of a separate piece (Fig. 16).

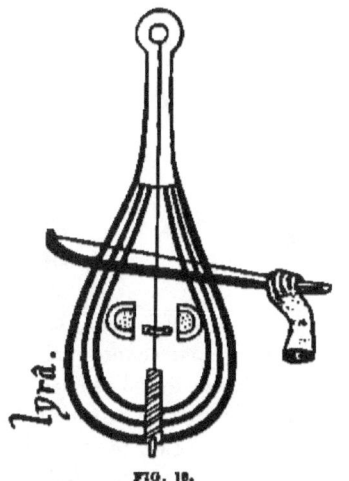

FIG. 16.

The Cotton MS. Ti-berius, c. vi. of the tenth century, contains repre-sentations of several an-cient instruments similar to those given by Ger-bert, and De Cousse-maker, but the most interesting one for our purpose is that of the performer on the viol, who is accompany-ing a juggler playing with three balls and three knives, and rivalling our modern wonders in this line. The figure has been often produced before, but we think it necessary to insert it here as a very early and distinct specimen (Fig. 17). It is of pear shape, with four strings, two round sound-holes, and a tail-piece, but with no appearance of bridge or finger-board. The

bow is somewhat of the form of our modern double-
bass bow. The performer looks
as serious as the man who does
Punch in the streets, looking at
his companion's skill as the mere
means of procuring a dinner.

FIG. 11.

In Gori's "Thesaurus Vete-
rum Diptychorum," there is a
representation, supposed to have
been taken from a MS. of the
ninth century, of David playing
on a sort of lyre, and four
musicians with him; one playing an organ, one a trumpet,
one on four bells, and the
fourth on a viol with three
strings, and two crescent-shaped
sound-holes, a finger-board, and,
apparently, a tail-piece, but no bridge. It is of oval, or
nearly circular shape, and the bow something between
the double-bass and violoncello bow. Ledwich describes,
among the figures in the crypt at Canterbury Cathedral,
a grotesque figure playing on the viol, which he ascribes
to the time of Alfred, but this crypt is not considered
to have been older than the twelfth century, and the
figure, therefore, is somewhat more recent than those in
Peterborough Cathedral, to which we shall soon refer.
The viol is mentioned in a "Treatise on Music," formerly attributed to the Venerable Bede, but now supposed to be of later date, by one who may be called
Pseudo-Bede.

From the earliest Anglo-Saxon times the viol and its
congeners appear to have been well established instruments at all festivals and social meetings, and so continued

downwards during the successive changes of dynasties,
until superseded by the more lively violin. Played by
the violars, frequently associated with jougleurs and minstrels, at the courts of the kings of the eight Saxon
kingdoms, which we are instructed in youth to call the
Saxon Heptarchy—afterwards at those of the Normans
and their successors—in the bowers of the fair Saxon
and proud Norman dames—at the country gatherings
and fairs—and in the halls of the barons, where, as
Whistlecraft (Frere) says—

> " They served up salmon, venison, and wild boars,
>   By hundreds, and by dozens, and by scores,
>   *   *   *   *
>   With mead, and ale, and cider of our own,
>   For porter, punch, and negus were not known."

To be sure these barons, notwithstanding their encou-
ragement of minstrelsy, were sometimes troublesome
neighbours ; one would occasionally have a grand *battū*.
when—

> " . . . omne vicinagium destruebat,
>   Et nihil relinquebat de intacto,
>   Ardens mulinos, casas, messuagia,
>   Et alia multa damna atque outragia," &c.

We have before observed that the instrument was frequently called the fythele. In Strutt's " Manners and
Customs," there is a figure from a
MS. in the Bodleian Library, of the
twelfth century, of a performer on
the viol of an oval shape, having
five strings, without any appearance
of sound-holes, bridge, or finger-
board, but with a tail-piece (Fig. 18).
FIG. 18.

The tail-piece in some instances may have been attached
to the belly in the same manner as in our guitar, and
therefore have partially served for a bridge. There is a

curious variety of the instrument, stated to be of the
end of the eleventh century, given in that richly em-
bellished work, Shaw's "Dresses and Decorations," from
additional MS. 11,695. It is of long oval shape, with five

FIG. 19.

strings; the neck is, perhaps, separate, and
it has no bridge or sound-holes. It seems
to have been of large size. The screws are
placed in a singular manner at the top (Fig.
19). The bow is very much curved. Figures
of about the same date, playing on the usual
oval-shaped viol, were on the door of the
ancient church of Barfreston, Kent, and on a
frieze at Adderbury Church, Oxfordshire, and
in other places, some of which of a later date
we shall mention afterwards.

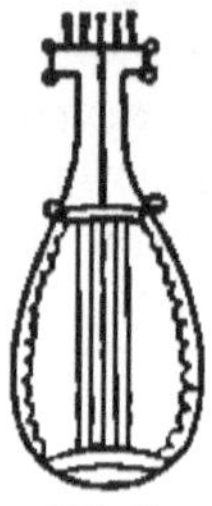

We must not omit to notice one well worthy of honour
—Rahere, the king's minstrel, who founded St. Bartholomew's Hospital in 1103, and whose name is still attached
to a small street in the neighbourhood.   He is said to
have kept company with fiddlers who played with silver
bows; but our authority, "The Pleasaunt History of
Thomas of Reading," is not convincing as to this latter
fact.   He appears, however, to have been a man of wit,
and to have been jester as well as minstrel, to Henry I.
and this before the court jester degenerated into the
mere buffoon.   He was one of the first known as "joculator regis;" not the first, as has been stated, for William
the Conqueror had one who was probably on one occasion during his wars the means of saving his life. Berdic,
joculator regis, is also mentioned in Domesday Book, as
of the time of Edward the Confessor.

There are some very curious representations of the
viol and other instruments painted on the interior of the
roof of the fine old cathedral at Peterborough, which we

have seen, and are fortunate enough to possess a copy of
the coloured engraving of it by Mr. Strickland, by
whose permission we will introduce some of the figures.
This roof is considered to be of the date of 1194, or
a little earlier, when the work was completed by Abbot
Benedict, who presided from 1177 to 1194. The ceiling
was retouched a little previous to 1788, and repaired in
1835, but the greatest care was taken to retain every
part, or restore it to its original state, so that the figures
even where retouched are in effect the same as when
first painted. One is a grotesque figure playing on a

FIG. 21. FIG. 22.

viol with three strings and four sound-holes (Fig. 20,
frontispiece); another is a crowned figure, perhaps to
signify a royal minstrel, playing on an instrument with
four strings and two sound-holes (Fig. 21); a third is a
female figure having the instrument on her lap with four
strings and four sound-holes (Fig. 22). Each figure on
the roof is placed in a separate lozenge-shaped ornamental compartment, differing occasionally in the style
of ornament, and in the colour of the ground. We have
represented that belonging to number 20. The instruments have inward curvatures at the sides, and are not

very unlike the modern violin in shape. There is an
appearance of finger-boards and tail-pieces, but none of
bridges. Other female figures are represented playing
on the psalterion or dulcimer, and the symphonic, the
parent of our hurdy-gurdy. Grotesque figures in paintings and sculpture were not uncommon about this time,
and many may be found in old manuscripts and in the
wood carvings of ancient churches. There is a curious
representation on the Peterborough roof, of an ass playing on the harp, which may have some reference to the
singular celebration of the Feast of the Ass, wherein
part of the service was called "Asinus ad Lyram;"
but it would occupy a chapter by itself to enter even
slightly upon this interesting subject, and the numerous
varieties of the Feast of Fools. In "Monnaies des
Fous," &c., mention is made of the figure of an ass on
the old tower at Chartres, playing on a stringed instrument, which, from the account given, appears more like
a harp than the vielle, but the figure had the name
of "l'âne qui vielle."

In France, as in England, music was encouraged from
an early period, having been introduced, as appears most
probable, from the north; and the performers frequented
the courts of the kings, from Clovis downwards. There
is a St. Arnold, who was a "joueur de violon," that is
the viol, in the ninth century. In the midst of the
changes of the French monarchy and their constant
warfares, petty and great, and notwithstanding the uncertain tempers of their royal and noble patrons, the
minstrels kept their ground. And a difficult task they
must sometimes have had. Take Sismondi's account of
one, rather a quiet one, towards the end of the eleventh
century, Philip I. "Cependant, comme il n'avait point
de volonté, il n'éprouvait point de contrariétés; comme

il ne faisait jamais la guerre, il n'était point battu; et
comme il ne formait pas de projets, il ne les voyait
jamais échouer : sa vie domestique était prospère, et sa
santé résistait à sa longue intempérance."

Instruments played with the bow do not appear to
have been numerous on the Continent before the
eleventh century, but increased in number and variety
towards the middle of it. The form at first was conical
or pear-shaped, having the body and neck formed of one
piece; but soon assumed a more oval shape, with the
neck and body separate. There is said to be a representation of an ancient French king in the church of
Notre Dame, with a bow in one hand and a viol in the
other, of about the last date; but there is some doubt
whether this is Chilperic or Robert, who commenced
the building in the tenth century; Montfaucon says it
was the former. There is a curious figure of a performer
on the viol on a medallion of the eleventh century at
Boscherville. He holds it artistically under the chin,
and appears to be singing at the same time, though his
aspect is somewhat lacrymose, as if he
were attempting for the first time the
studies of the Paganini of the period.
The instrument apparently has four
strings, and is of oval shape, but has
neither bridge, sound-holes, or finger-
board in the representation. We have
referred before to the figures on a capital
at Boscherville of the twelfth century;
one of these is playing on a sort of viol
of oval shape, having two semicircular
sound-holes, but without any appearance

FIG. 23.

of bridge or finger-board (Fig. 23). M. de Coussemaker considers this instrument to be a gigue.

As far back as the thirteenth century we find the
figure of a monochord of a rectangular, oblong, and
narrow form, and taller than the performer; from this
was probably derived that curious instrument, the
trumpet marine. There was also an instrument somewhat smaller, having two strings, called the diacord or
dicord.

The profession of a jougleur or trouvère of early
times, was by no means an easy one, and comprised not
only skill on several instruments, but juggling, sleight of
hand, and many similar qualifications. We have already
referred to some of these in our extract from "Les
Deux Trovéors Ribaux."

Colin Muset, the celebrated minstrel of this date,
according to Laborde, even exceeded the usual musical
qualifications; but the song given by him as one of
Muset's, is evidently modernized, and we will give but
one verse, concluding with the bard's modest estimation
of himself.

> " Il chante arec flûte ou trompette,
>   Guitarre, harpe, flageolet,
>   Tambourin, violon, clochette ;
>   Il fait la basse et la fausset ;
>   Il invente vielle et musette :
>   Pour la manivelle ou l'archet,
>   Nul n'égale Colin Muset."

But even the great Colin Muset had sometimes to
complain of neglect from the great. He thus speaks of
one who had paid him nothing for his minstrelsy :—

> " Sire quens j'ai vielé
>   Devant vos en vostre otel ;
>   Si ne m'avez riens donné,
>   Ne mes gages acquitez,
>   C'est vilanie."

A great improvement had taken place in musical

notation by the time of the eleventh century, and the
name of Guido d'Aretin is well known for his exertions
in this respect, and indeed, as is frequently the case in
such matters, he has more credit given to him than he is
entitled to ; some of his supposed discoveries having been
previously known. For a considerable time prior to such
date, notation was by what were called neumes ; whence
Ducange says, " Neumare est notas verbis musicè decan-
tandis superaddere." These neumes were arbitrary
characters or accents, several in number, which superseded the letters previously in use, and were placed over
the words to be sung, a separate value, or power, or
pitch, being attached to each. Gerbert gives a table of
forty, with their names. At first, until about the end of
the ninth century, there were no lines or indications of
clefs, and there being no guide, it was difficult to assign
the value with any accuracy, and people differed as to
the relative pitch. About the tenth century a horizontal
line, either black or red, was placed over the words,
which marked the place of a fixed note, and the place
of the neumes over or under this line distinguished the
quality of the note much better than had previously
been the case. A song of the twelfth century on the
battle of Fontanet or Fontanay, with notation in the
style of the neumes, without the horizontal line, is supposed to be one of the earliest examples of secular music.
Afterwards, two lines were used, one red, which had the
letter F at the commencement, and the other yellow or
green, which had C. Subsequently two other lines were
added ; one between the two former ones, and the other
either above or below them ; the letters at the head of
the principal lines being the origin of the clefs of our
modern notation. The notes were named, ut, re, mi, fa,
sol, la, from the commencing syllables of the lines of a

Latin hymn, of which the corresponding musical notes were each a tone higher than that of the preceding syllable. They were afterwards called C ut, D re, &c. Howell, in one of his letters, October 7, 1634, mentions that the Germans, who were then great drinkers, would sometimes drink a health musically to each of the six notes, comprising them, together with the reasons for drinking, in the following hexameter :—

UT RE levet MIserum FA tum, SOL itesque LA bores.

The lines were afterwards increased to five: indeed, there are some ancient pieces of music with many more; but still much—especially of the ecclesiastical music—continued to be written with four. In the twelfth century, the grave square notes still to be seen in the old church music, came into general use; those gradually improved in appearance, and became less in size, as they became the representatives of greater celerity, until now they have reached that extreme railway speed and complication of figure scarcely to be managed in many cases but by musicians of the highest skill and practice, of whom, happily, we have many.

CHAPTER V.

N the twelfth and thirteenth centuries, the representations of the viol differ much; the strings vary from two to six, but three and five are the usual numbers. Some have inward curvatures more or less defined; the majority have bridges; there is seldom any appearance of a detached finger-board, and the sound-holes are usually two, sometimes four, and occasionally there is one like that of the guitar. As before observed, the defects in the details may sometimes arise from omissions in the delineations.

Potier, in "Monumens Français," vol. i. says there are no representations of the viol before the tenth century, but frequent examples after the eleventh. M. de Coussomaker says the oldest representation is on a sculpture at the door of the church of St. Aventin, in the environs of Bagnères, of the eleventh century. Gerbert's representation, however, and that in Cotton MS. are older. Potier gives several examples of the twelfth century; some from the porch of St. Denis. A king, said to be David, who is often named when the identity of the monarch is doubtful, holds in his right hand a viol with five strings: the body is oval and somewhat of a guitar shape, with two sound-holes, and apparently a bridge, but no separate finger-board. The bow is short, and

like that of the double bass. There are two other
instruments very similar, one of which has but three
strings, but by way of compensation has four large sound-
holes, two in each division. He gives representations of
two viols of the same date from a MS. in the Bibliothèque Impériale, one of which is of oval shape, with
five strings, and one large round sound-hole like the
guitar in the centre. The other has inward
curvatures, four strings, and two small sound-
holes (Fig. 24). They both appear to have
bridges, but no distinct finger-boards.

M. de Coussemaker, in his learned and interesting account of ancient instruments so frequently referred to, mentions a viol of the
twelfth century, on a window at the royal chapel
of St. Denis. It is of a long oval shape, much
more so than usual, with six strings and two
large semi-circular sound-holes. There is no bridge, and
what we should call the tail-piece is in the middle of the
body, and the strings seem to be fastened to each end of
it. The bow is like that of the double bass, a common
form in these times (Fig. 25). There is also a grotesque
figure of Neptune of the same date playing on a viol
with three strings, and two semicircular sound-holes, with
a kind of tail-piece, but no appearance of a bridge or
separate finger-board (Fig. 26).

In Cotton MS. Nero. D. i. of about the same date,
there is a viol which shows the distinctive oval shape,
having the neck and body of one piece. It has two
semicircular sound-holes, with four strings and a tail-
piece, but no appearance of a bridge (Fig. 27). There
is a figure like this in the left hand of one of the elders
in the Cathedral of Amiens (Fig. 28). Other representations of about the same date and much of the same

character may be found in MSS. at the British Museum and elsewhere, of which it does not seem necessary to multiply examples, and this remark will apply to subsequent times. We may observe that Jerome de Moravie, in his

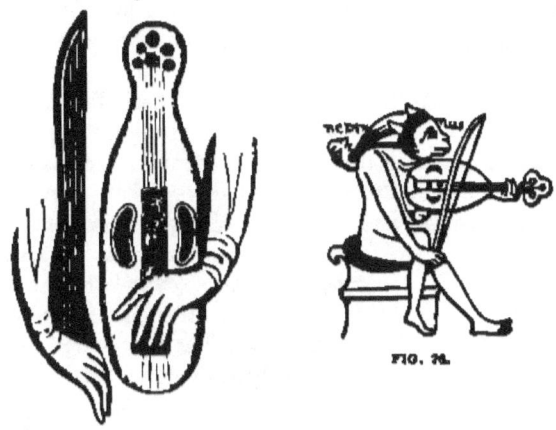

FIG. 25.   FIG. 26.

treatise on music, of the thirteenth century, mentions the vielle amongst instruments having four or five strings.

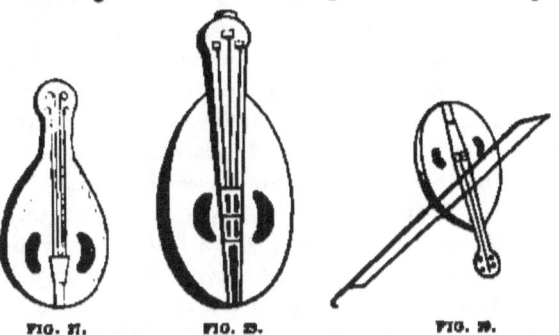

FIG. 27.   FIG. 28.   FIG. 29.

Among the sculptures at what is called the Musicians' House at Rheims, of the thirteenth century, there is a figure playing on an oval-shaped instrument with three strings, and two sound-holes nearly in the shape of ears. The attitude of the performer is very easy, and the bow is iron and of light construction, almost appearing to be an addition of more modern date. We have given a representation of the instrument and the bow (Fig. 29).

Burney notices an antique enamelled basin found near Soissons, which he states to be of the ninth century ; but it is now considered to be of the thirteenth, and has been described both by Potier and de Coussemaker. Amongst other musical figures, it has two, apparently females, playing on the viol ; one of the instruments has three

strings, with two sound-holes and a bridge, while the other has apparently only two strings, but four sound-holes and two bridges, though what is called a second bridge was probably only to denote the end of the finger-board, as two bridges would be objectionable in many respects (Fig. 30).

FIG. 30.

Towards the end of the thirteenth century the convex sides of the viol became by degrees indented, or more or less curved inwards, to give freer scope for the bow, though much time elapsed before the present finished form was arrived at, and many trials made, and failures experienced.

Catgut strings, as they are generally called, though now made from sheep, are of very great antiquity, as they were used for the harp of the ancient Egyptians. In the thirteenth century the sale of strings must have been a matter of some importance, and recognised as an article of trade, for in an old poem of this date called ."Du Mercier," which may be considered as a sort of trade-song by a mercer, amongst other articles to entice customers, he says—

"J'ai bones cordes à violes."

If the prices had been affixed it would have been more interesting.

About the same time, in an account of Paris under Philippe le Bel, 1292, being the particulars of a tax of 100,000 livres levied on the inhabitants, there is probably the first notice of any makers of instruments, namely, "citoleours 4," being strictly makers of citoles, a species of guitar; but no doubt they were also makers of the different sorts of viols, just as the term "luthiers" was applied afterwards not only to makers of lutes, &c., but also of viols and violins. There is another maker, however, who is still more defined, "Henri aus vièles," or Henry, the maker of viols, who may be considered the first of his art on record.

The representations and notices of the viol or vielle, and instruments of that class, are numerous in the fourteenth century. It was a favourite instrument with the minstrels, and the name of one is handed down as Arnold le Vielleux, and another in the service of the Emperor Conrad IV, called Jouglet, was distinguished as a performer. In an account of the Dukes of Burgundy from 1362 to 1481, there is an entry of musical instruments, from which it appears that the Duchess had two Spaniards, performers on the vielle or viol, called Juan de Cordova, and Juan Fernandez, of whom the former was blind. In the wardrobe accounts of Edward II, who was not sparing in his expenses, there is a payment of 5l. to "Robert Daverouns, violist of the Prince of Tarentum, performing his minstrelsy in the king's presence, of the king's gift at Neuburgh;" a great sum

F

in those days, probably equal to 70*l.* or 80*l.* at present.
On the marriage of his sister Margaret, minstrels came
from all parts, foreign as well as English, 426 in number,
to whom 100*l.* were given in reward. We have already
mentioned Queen Isabella's vidulatores. Edward III.
in his band of nineteen musicians, had a fiddler (*i.e.*
violist) with the pay, like his companions, of 12*d.* a day.

The sound-holes were usually two, semi-circular or
ear-shaped, and placed nearly as at present; the strings
varying from three to six. The instrument had now
generally inward curvatures, more or less decided.
There is not always the indication of a bridge, or
detached finger-board, but, as before observed, the
absence or imperfection of details cannot always be
taken as proof of the state of the instrument. M. de
Coussemaker gives a representation of one of the fourteenth century, the body of which does not differ much
in shape from that of the modern violin. It has three

double strings, though the screws appear to be four, a rounded bridge, and
two semi-circular sound-holes, but no
distinct finger-board; and the top of
the neck, or what would be our scroll,
is turned at right angles (Fig. 31). He
gives the representation of another from
the Royal Library at Brussels, without
curvatures, and with four strings that
pass through a series of teeth with
which the bridge is provided; it has a
finger-board, and two sound-holes.

FIG. 31.

Polier has given a figure of an in-
strument of the fourteenth century, with three strings
and a bridge, but no separate finger-board; the neck,
if it may be so called, is large, and of a lozenge shape,

found in the early forms of the instrument, but at this time going out. It has two sound-holes, and the bow like the double-bass bow (Fig. 32). D'Agincourt, in his "History of Art," has a representation from a painting by Barnabas de Modena, 1374, of the crowning of the Virgin by our Saviour in Heaven, where several figures are introduced playing on musical instruments. Amongst them is the viol, having five strings, with two semi-lunar sound-holes and a tail-piece, but no bridge or finger-board: the bow-hand has great ease in its position, and

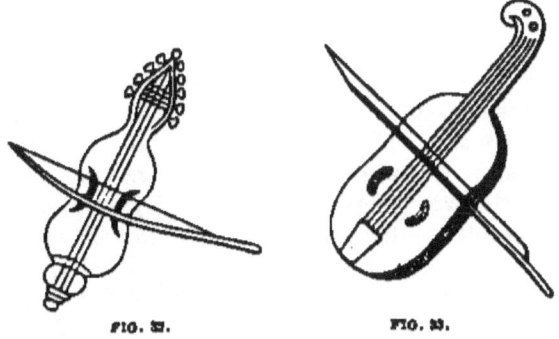

FIG. 32.　　　　　FIG. 33.

the bow is very like that known as the Corelli bow (Fig. 33). A small pair of double drums is introduced, placed on the back of one angel, and played on by another; also the musette or bagpipes.

The viol may frequently be found in the sculptures in our cathedrals and old churches. Carter has given some representations from Ely Cathedral of the early part of the fourteenth century. One appears to have five strings and a tail-piece, but with no appearance of bridge or sound-holes; the other has more the form of what has been called

FIG. 34.

the rebec, without inward curvatures, but the details are very imperfect (Figs. 34 and 35). The superb screen in York Cathedral, separating the nave from the choir, has numerous figures of angels playing on musical instruments, and the viol among them. In Exeter Cathedral there is a small fabric of stone projecting from the north wall of the nave, of about the middle of the fourteenth century, supported by a cornice, and called the minstrels' gallery. The front is supported by thirteen pillars, dividing it into twelve niches, each containing an angel playing on a musical instrument, and among these is the viol. It is the custom for the choristers to go to this gallery on Christmas Day and sing a hymn. Carter represents the figure of an angel on the lower tier of the screen at the west front of this cathedral, playing on a pear-shaped viol. Minstrel galleries, with figures playing on musical instruments, are likewise mentioned at the cathedrals of Winchester, Lincoln, and Worcester. Dibdin, in his "Bibliographical Tour," gives engravings of what he calls "Drolleries at Strasbourg Cathedral," of about the date 1370; one of these grotesque figures is playing on a sort of pear-shaped viol, with apparently four strings, and two ear-shaped sound-holes, but no other details.

The *báton* of the conductor is comparatively a modern introduction into our orchestras, and many of us still remember the tap of the leader in our concerts, for which the *báton* has now been successfully substituted. It had, however, been known long previously on the Continent, and in a list of the orchestra of the Opera at Paris, in 1713, there appears at the head, "the Batteur de Mesure," with a salary of 1000 livres. The cantor's staff was known many centuries back in our ecclesiastical establishments, and in those on the Continent, and the custom is still preserved in many parts. Pugin, in his "Glossary of Ecclesiastical Ornament," gives an engraving of a highly decorated one, and describes others at St. George's, Windsor; York, St. Paul's, and Lincoln, naming at the latter cathedral "two staves of wood, having upon them little plates of silver, with branches of vines." Gerbert mentions some singers having silver wands and staffs about the sixteenth century.

There is a curious story or gossip about a *bâton de chantre*, related in "Annales Archéologiques," iii. 266-7, which may not be generally known. When Napoleon I. was crowned, he intended, in order to have all the adjuncts as complete as possible, to carry in his hand the original sceptre of Charlemagne. It was resuscitated for the purpose from the treasures of the Abbey of St. Denis, and was to be repaired and put in order for the ceremony; most unexpectedly, on removing the old velvet with which it was covered, there appeared the date 1394, which the Committee of Antiquaries, to whom the matter had been intrusted, saw was inconsistent with the time of Charlemagne; and there was not only this date, but also an inscription, from which the following is an extract, proving the supposed sceptre to be simply a *bâton de chantre* :—

> " Qu'il fut gardé,
> Et en grans fentes regardé,
> Car pour loyaulte maintenir
> Le doibt chantre en la main tenir."

What was to be done? De Non was consulted, but he desired that the discovery should be kept secret. The *bâton* was dressed up, and converted into the sceptre of Charlemagne (just as upon occasion a common working grub is converted into a queen bee), and performed its appointed part in the imposing ceremony.

The troubadours were accompanied by violars, or performers on the harp, or viol, or instruments of that class, and were frequently skilful performers themselves. Indeed Thibaut, Count of Champagne, towards the beginning of the thirteenth century is said to have taken up the study of the viol, to console himself in an unsuccessful attachment for Queen Blanche, the mother of Saint Louis, and became a skilful performer. We must, however, refer those who wish to learn more of the history of this distinguished race, from William, Count of Poitiers downwards, to Hawkins's "History of Music," and more especially to Raynouard, "Choix des Poésies Originales des Troubadours," and Fauriel, "Histoire de la Poésie Provençale," where many of the chanzos, sirventes, &c. will be found. The romantic histories connected with Châtelain de Courcy, Jauffred de Radel, Guillaume de Cabestaing, and others, afford curious examples of the manners of their age. The last-named of these troubadours, as is known to those versed in these chronicles, fell violently in love with Sermonde, the wife of Raymond of Roussillon; but the husband, instead of approving of this choice, slew the poet, and, having taken out his heart, had it served up at table before his wife, who, when she became informed of the fact, threw herself out of window and was killed. Her friends and those of Guillaume, assisted by other troubadours, took upon them to ravage the lands of Raymond, and destroy his castle; after which praiseworthy act they buried the unfortunate lovers in one grave. The husband was certainly a little brusque in his treatment of de Cabestaing, but we cannot help thinking that all the sympathy is not due to the lovers. Jauffred de Radel was still more

romantic; he fell violently in love with the Countess of
Tripoli from mere description, and induced his friend
Bertrand d'Allamanon to accompany him to the Levant
in 1162, but fell ill during the passage, and, on his
arrival at Tripoli, just lived long enough to see the
countess, express his passion, and then die. In the
"Conte of Aucassin and Nicolette," Nicolette having
been made captive, is discovered to be the daughter of
the King of Carthage, and she wishes to return to Aucassin to avoid being married to a rich pagan king.
The difficulty is how to escape, but at last she contrives
to manage this in the garb of a minstrel: "Elle quist
une viole, s'aprist à vieler, et elle s'embla la nuit, si
s'atorna à guise de joglior;" and having thus arrived
safely in Provence, "si prist sa viele, si alla vielant par
le pays, tant qu'elle vint au castel de Biaucaire."

CHAPTER VI.

THE minstrels are so connected with the practical part of music, that a short notice of them appears requisite in a work of this nature, even at the risk of repeating in part what may be found elsewhere; but we hope, also, we may add some particulars that may not be generally known. The distinguished antiquary, Mr. Thomas Wright, F.S.A., has a chapter on minstrels and jougleurs in his interesting "History of Domestic Manners."

In the early times of our country the king's bard, or harper, was an officer of high rank, and enjoyed many privileges; the king's minstrel was also an officer of distinction at the Saxon and Norman courts. The story of Taillefer, at the time of the Conquest, is well known; jumping on shore one of the foremost of the invaders, singing the war-song of the celebrated Rollo, and dying like the fabled swan, with a song in his mouth. We have no particular account of any such officer in the reigns immediately succeeding the Conquest, though every one, even without the benefit of a competitive examination, as fully believes the story of King Richard and Blondel as he does those relating to the bold Robin Hood, Little John, and Scathlock, or Scarlett, with Maid Marian, and that unlucky Bishop of Hereford. In the forty-first of Henry III, however, we find a payment of

4*l.* 7*s.* paid to Henry Abrinces, the king's versifier, by
some called his jester, who received 6*d.* a day. If there
may be some doubt as to his being a minstrel as well as
a poet, we may at any rate consider him as a sort of
proto-poet-laureate. He offended, on some occasion,
Master Michael Blaumpayne, the humorous Cornish
poet, who abused him in some very personal satirical
lines. At the installation feast of Ralf de Born, Prior
of St. Augustine, Canterbury, 1309, the minstrels present were paid 3*l.* 10*s.* for their reward. Edward II.
during his father's life was evidently fond of convivial
society, and payments are found to William Fox, and
Cradoc his companion, for singing before the prince and
other nobles; generally 20*s.* each time. After he succeeded to the throne, several minstrels are named, and
on the occasion of the marriage of Elizabeth, daughter
of Edward I. to John, Earl of Holland, every king's
minstrel received a fee of 40*s.*; and one at least, named
Robert, was in the habit of receiving regular pay. Ja-
nino le cheveretter, or bagpiper, at one time had 40*s.*
given to him, and at another 20*s.* The bagpiper, however, seems to have been in repute in these times, for in
the reign of Edward III. Barbor the bagpiper had licence
to go beyond the seas to visit the schools of minstrels,
with 30*s.* for his expenses; and Morlan the same leave,
with 40*s.* This was, no doubt, to enable them to see if
any advantages were to be derived from the study of
the Continental style of play. The musette, a very
ancient instrument, was popular on the Continent, and,
judging from the tone of the modern instruments, it is
softer and more melodious than that of the common
bagpipe. During the festivals on the crowning of Pope
John XXIII, about 1410, the Marquis of Ferrara brought
with him fifty-four knights, all clothed in scarlet and

blue, attended by five trumpets, and four companies of
minstrels, each with different instruments ; and, on the
morrow of his coronation, the Pope was attended during
his procession by thirty-six bagpipes and trumpets, and
ten bands of minstrels playing on musical instruments,
each band consisting of three performers. In that curious
poem, " The Vows of the Heron," about 1338, where
some strange examples of the vows of the knights, and
even of the ladies, may be seen, Robert of Artois has the
heron brought in between two dishes of silver, and com-
pels two players on the viol, and one on the guitar, to
introduce it—

> " Entre deux plats d'argent fu li hairons assis ;
> Deux maistres de viele a quens Robert saisis,
> Avec un quisstronous, accordant par devis ;"

afterwards they fiddle very sweetly,—

> " Et li dois menestral vielent douchement ;"

but subsequently, at his command, they have to come
out *fortissimo*—

> " Il fait les menestreux de viele efforchier."

Many entries are found of payments to minstrels, and
frequently large ones, considering the difference in the
value of money, but generally the recipient is only called
minstrel, and his particular instrument is not named.
In the eleventh of Edward III, John de Hoglard, minstrel of John de Pulteney, was paid 40s. for exhibiting
before the king at Hatfield and London ; and Roger the
trumpeter, and the minstrels his associates, for performing at the feast at Hatfield, for the queen's delivery, had
no less a sum than 10l. presented to them. At the feast
of St. George at Windsor, in 1358, connected with the
celebration of the Order of the Garter, the early history

of which will always be interesting, whether connected
with the Countess of Salisbury or not, Haukin Fitz-
Libbin and his twenty-three fellows, the king's minstrels,
had for their good services 16*l.*

During the compulsory visit of John, King of France,
here, after the battle of Poictiers, from 1357 to 1360,
there are several entries in his accounts of payments to
minstrels. In one case there is a payment of four nobles
to go and see some instruments for the king, and on
another occasion two nobles to buy a harp. The largest
appears to be forty nobles, or 13*l.* 6*s.* 8*d.* to the minstrels
of the King of England, the Prince of Wales, and the
Duke of Lancaster, who played before the king on the
feast of St. John, June 24, 1360. There is, however, an
unlucky note in the margin of the original account, implying that this money was not paid, though for what reason
does not appear. Payments to minstrels appear in the
time of Richard II, who was better suited to the luxuries
of a court than the cares of a crown. There are similar
payments in the time of Henry IV, among which there
is one to William Byngley, the king's minstrel, of
2*l.* 6*s.* 8*d.* to purchase apparel for his person, probably
for a sort of livery.

When Henry V. went over to France he was accompanied by several minstrels, Rymer mentions fifteen, and
among them was one Snyth Fydeler; their wages appear
to have been 12*d.* a day. They played for an hour
morning and evening at the king's head-quarters, and
on the eve of the battle of Agincourt, though the English were fatigued and oppressed with hunger, and
expected death on the morrow, yet they played on their
trumpets and various other instruments throughout the
night, and confessed their sins with tears, numbers of
them taking the sacrament. A song on the battle of

Agincourt is the oldest English song known with music. There is an order in the first of Henry VI. to pay several minstrels by name an annual pension of 100s. each, of whom the first seven had accompanied his father to France; and in the twelfth year of his reign there is an order for a payment which for procrastination may match any of modern times, being one to the representative of the representative of the man who earned it more than fourteen years previously. It is a payment of 10l. to Henry Jolipas Clerk, executor of Joan, wife of John Clyff, a minstrel, the executrix of the same John Clyff, who had gone over to France in the third year of Henry V. with seventeen other minstrels, at the rate of 12d. a day, and with whom certain jewels had been lodged as a security.

In the twenty-third of Henry VI. there were liberal payments made to some foreign minstrels, who came over to witness the state and grand solemnity of the coronation of the Queen, and make a report of the same abroad. Five minstrels of the King of Sicily had 10l. each, and two of the Duke of Milan 5 marks, or 3l. 6s. 8d. each; liberal payments, no doubt remembered on making the report. Edward IV, who in the early part of his kingly career alternated with Henry VI, according as the white or red rose was triumphant, paid by the hands of Thomas Vaughan 20l. to the heralds and minstrels on the day of the creation of the Lord the Prince at Westminster, in the eleventh year of his reign. Some unlicensed minstrels apparently gave trouble in his time, and got access to great houses and feasts under the pretence of being king's minstrels, which induced him in 1469 to grant a charter to Walter Halliday (a name which appears among the minstrels of Henry V.) as marshal, and seven others, establishing, or as some

called it, restoring a fraternity or guild, to be governed
by a marshal and two wardens, empowering them to
regulate the profession of minstrels, but it did not prove
of much benefit, and they contrived to lose their reputation by the time of Elizabeth. In her reign, 1581, we
find Thomas Lovell, in his "Dialogue betwene Custome
and Veritie concerning the use and abuse of Dauncing
and Mynstralsye," abusing the minstrels for not singing
godly songs, and proceeding,—

> " . . . He that cannot gibe and jest,
>　　Ungodly scoff and frump,
> Is thought unmeet to play with pipe,
>　　On tabret or to thump.
> The minstrels doo with instruments,
>　　With songs, or els with jest,
> Maintain themselves, but as they use,
>　　Of these naught is the best."

Henry VII. was a careful man, and may come under
Sydney Smith's definition of being fond of his specie, if
not of his species. In all his travels and progresses he
was met at different towns by minstrels, waits, and other
musicians, each town of note having then its own set.
There are numerous payments made to them, but in
general, less than 20s. For instance, the waits of Northampton had 13s. 4d. in reward, while those of Coventry,
Sandwich, and Canterbury, had but 10s., and those of
Dover only 6s. 8d. Even the minstrels who played in
his ship, the *Swan*, that took him from Sandwich to
Calais, were only paid 13s. 4d. for their performance,
notwithstanding they had to brave the perils and incon-
venience of the sea. Of the more regular performers,
Pudesay, the piper in bagpipes, had but 6s. 8d. for his
performance, whilst 5l. were paid to three string minstrels for wages; and in a subsequent entry, 15s. is
given to one for a month's wages. In 1501, a sum of 2l.

is paid to the " Princesse stryngmynstrels at Westm' ;"
but in February, 1495, there is a most liberal payment
of 30l. to the Queen of France's minstrels, it being politic
to pay foreign performers of this class well.

Henry VIII. was fond of show and entertainments
during the first twenty years of his reign, and not only
encouraged minstrelsy, but was himself a good musician,
and a gallant sort of personage ; many payments to
minstrels are therefore found in his accounts. In later
times he suffered from an *embarras de richesses* in respect of his wives, and amused his leisure hours with
polemical studies, ultimately becoming fat, argumenta-
tive, and ill-tempered, with the inconvenient power of
cutting off his opponent's head, as well as crushing his
argument. As his size increased, minstrelsy decreased,
and faded for the want of royal patronage.

In the " Northumberland Household Book," it is stated
that my lord is accustomed to give yearly to every earl's
minstrel, when they come to him yearly 3s. 4d., but if
they come only once in two or three years, then 6s. 8d.
The gift to his own minstrels, when at home on New
Year's Day, was 20s. for playing at his chamber door,
being 13s. 4d. for himself, and 6s. 8d. for his lady, when
she was at her lord's finding ; also 2s. for playing at
Lord Percy's, and 8d. at each of the younger sons. In
the " Archives of Canterbury," 1523, there is an entry
on the 1st of July of 6s. 8d. paid to the king's minstrels ;
and in the twenty-second year of his reign, eighteen
minstrels are appointed to the household at 4d. a day,
most of them, from their names, appearing to be Italians.
There is an anecdote of a famous player on the shalme,
among the minstrels of Cardinal Wolsey, when he was
in France in 1527. He was much admired by the
French king ; but, as Stow rather quaintly says, whe-

ther from extreme labour of blowing, or from poison (as some judged) he died within a day or two after playing all night, without resting, to the French king and others who were dancing. There does not appear to have been much necessity for presuming poison in this case.

There was a corporation of minstrels formed in Paris in the early part of the fourteenth century, which was of high repute, and possessed great power. An interesting account of it may be seen in "Bibliothèque de l'Ecole des Chartres," 1841-2, tom. 3, pp. 377-404, and vol. iv. pp. 524-48. It flourished till about the middle of the seventeenth century, when it began to decline, though orders were made for its government from time to time down to the eighteenth century.

Previous to this corporation, and towards the end of the twelfth century, many minstrels and players on instruments were accustomed to frequent Paris, and we find among the king's minstrels performers on the trumpets, timbales, and psalterion, being paid 3 sous a day, and their apparel and board. A sum of 60 sous is given by order of the king to Plumion, to buy "une flute dyvoire." In the middle of the thirteenth century, the minstrels enjoyed many privileges, and amongst them, that of exemption from a certain toll levied on entering Paris, provided they sung the couplet of a song to prove their right. Hence the expression, " Payer en gambades, et en monnoie de singe," as they frequently had monkeys with them, who exhibited their accomplishments in part payment. In the thirteenth century they had so increased, and were of such consequence, that they gave name to "La rue aus Juglécurs," afterwards " Rue des Ménetriers," and in modern times, " Rue Rambuteau." At the time of the tax in 1292 before referred to, there were sixty-three persons assessed in this street.

In the year 1321, thirty-seven minstrels, at the head
of whom was Pariset, monestrel le roy, who was a player
on the "naquaires," or "tymbales," (and at one time
had 60 sous given him to get some timbales made), applied to have some statutes or regulations granted under
the sanction of the Prefect of Paris, and eleven were
granted them, by which they obtained a monopoly, that
enabled them to control the practice of their profession,
and to send away all strange minstrels. Among the
names affixed to these statutes are Johannot l'Anglois,
and Adeline, fame G. l'Anglois.

In 1330 or 1331, they founded the hospital of St.
Julian, and St. Genès already referred to. It took its
rise, like our own Royal Society of Musicians, from the
charitable feelings of two of the profession. These are
said to have been Jacques Grave de Pistoye, otherwise
called Lappe, and Huet le Guette, who were moved with
compassion on seeing a poor paralytic woman, called
Fleurie de Chartres. She became one of the first patients
of the hospital, where she remained till her death. There
were several figures of angels in the church playing on
various instruments; and at the entrance were two sta-
tues, that of St. Julien on the left, and of St. Genès on
the right, in the costume of a minstrel, playing on a viole
with four strings. Laborde calls this figure Colin Muset,
who, however, was of later date. The viol, or vielle, was
a favourite instrument among them. In the account of
the appointment of masters or governors of the hospital
in October, 1343, the names appear of Jehan le Vidaulx
(player on the viol), and Guillaume de la Guietarne, with
others, who chose Henriet de Mondidier and Guillaume
Amy, "fleuteurs," masters and governors.

Among the minstrels who came to France in 1274
with Mary, daughter of Henry III. Duke of Brabant, on

her marriage with Philip III. of France, was Adenez le
Roi, or Le Roi Adenez, king of arms to the duke, who was
an excellent poet also, and may have been king of the
minstrels; but at all events Charmillon, who was chosen
as such king in 1295, is one of the earliest on record,
Robert, king of the minstrels to Louis X, being twenty
years later. Jean Poitevin was "roi des menestriers"
of France in 1392, and one called Hennequin Poitevin
held that title in 1409, and at the same time we find
mentioned "Jehan de Tonnelaur joueur de personnages
du roy," who is probably the earliest comedian of the
king mentioned, and " Gracieuse d'Espaigne menestrelle
de la royne," also has a gift made to her. Jean Farcien
the elder is said to have been king of the minstrels in
the early part of the fifteenth century, probably succeeding Poitevin; he was a performer on the viol. We
are not going to give a chronological list of these distinguished characters, but merely to name a few. There
was one called Nyon, commonly known as La Foundy,
who was remarkable for his skill on the violin; he was
made king of the violins, and died in 1641, having
abdicated however some years previously. In the time
of Louis XIII. in the first half of the seventeenth century, there was an able performer called Constantin,
who held this office and died at Paris in 1657. He was
succeeded in his lifetime by Guillaume Dumanoir in
1630, and after him came Guillaume Dumanoir the
second, who resigned in 1685. No successor was appointed to the office until 1741, when Guignon, remarkable for his execution, was installed, but subsequently
getting into disputes with his fellow-musicians, he found
the office so troublesome that he resigned it in a few
years, and in 1773 it was suppressed altogether.

Charles IX. of France granted by letters patent in

1570, to Jean Antoine de Baïf and Joachim Thibaut de Courville the power to form an academy of music. Among the rules there was one admirable one which might be advantageously introduced in our times, particularly in amateur musical conversaziones, namely, that none of the auditors should talk, or make any noise while there was any singing; we beg to add in defence of the instrumental performers, also while there was any playing. We should, however, call the attention of concert-givers to the observations supposed to have been made by a Chinese, as reported by Abbé Arnaud, in "Variétés Littéraires:" "Vos concerts, surtout s'ils sont un peu longs, sont des exercices violens pour ceux qui les exécutent, et de vrais supplices pour les personnes qui les écoutent."

CHAPTER VII.

IN the fifteenth century we meet with the names of some makers. The viol is represented with four or five strings, and frequently has inward curvatures, the old oval shape gradually becoming obsolete. The bridges and tail-pieces occasionally are wanting, which may be merely an omission in the representation, and frets are shown in some of the figures. The term viello seems now superseded by viol, the former term being applied to an instrument like our modern hurdy-gurdy. The sound-holes, with occasional exceptions, became much like those in present use. Potier gives a representation of an instrument with three strings, and a bridge, having a large perforated sound-hole like the guitar, the head being bent back at a considerable angle : it has no inward curvatures, and the bow is much like that of the double-bass (Fig. 36). There is a figure given by M. de Coussemaker of a viol of this century from a painting by Hemling, which has five strings, with two sound-holes much like our modern ones reversed, with a tail-piece and finger-board ; it also has frets, but no appearance of a bridge, and is of guitar shape (Fig. 37). Another has inward curvatures, with four strings

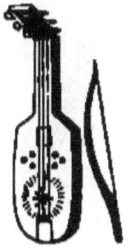

FIG. 36.

fastened like those of the guitar, with a large round
sound-hole in the centre, the head is a little reversed,
with the pegs at the side as at present. D'Agincourt
has a representation of a fresco painting of this age by
Melozzo da Forli (the inventor of foreshortening,) at the
staircase of the Palazzo Quirinale, where the figure of
an angel is introduced playing on a viol with five strings,
but there are no details. In the Minstrels' Pillar, at St.
Mary's Church, Beverley, of the time of Henry VI, one
of the five figures is playing on a viol of oblong shape
with four strings and a short tail-piece; but no bridge,
detached neck, or finger-board are shown in Carter's
delineation (Fig. 38). In

the same church, over the
column, are several figures
playing on musical instruments, and among them an
angel with a long oval or
nearly pear-shaped viol with
three strings; another male

FIG. 37.   FIG. 38.

figure with a large or tenor viol something in shape of a
long modern tenor with angles rounded off; it has five
strings, but no details are given of either instrument,
except two small sound-holes in the last (Fig. 39).

FIG. 39.   FIG. 40.   FIG. 41.

Strutt has given several representations of musical instruments from the "Liber Regalis" of the time of Richard II. of which we have reproduced four (Figs. 40, 41, 42, 43).

There was a curious application of a musical performance in the early part of this century, arising from one of those eccentricities which occasionally vary the common routine of life: it took place on the death of Louis Cortusio, a lawyer at Padua, who

FIG. 42. FIG. 43.

died in 1418; he directed by his will that all the minstrels of the city should be invited to his funeral; fifty were to walk with the clergy, some before and some after the body, filling the air with the sound of lutes, viols, flutes, hautbois, trumpets, tambourins, &c., and chanting as at Easter. Each performer was to have a demi-écu for his trouble; and the body was to be carried by twelve young girls engaged to be married, each of whom had a sum of money by way of portion; they were to sing joyous songs, and the whole ceremony was to be conducted in the same cheerful manner. Any of his relations who wept at his funeral were to have no share of his property, and he that laughed most was to have the largest share. It is not recorded that the tears were abundant; but as his family grieved for the loss of his money, if they did not mourn for him, they disputed the will; however, the Paduan Court of Probate confirmed it. This hilarious funeral reminds us of an amusing French proverb, where, in a country place, the mayor and magistrates are in expectation of a visit from some living great personage, a great event in the chronicles of their town, and also the passage through of the body of a deceased dignitary. Councils are held, committees appointed, honorary secretaries installed; arrangements made to meet the living hero with songs, dances, and garlands of flowers, and the dead with overwhelming grief and sorrow, crape and cypress. Everything is rehearsed and the actors are perfect, or consider themselves so; but by some unlucky confusion, both the living and dead celebrities approach the town unexpectedly from different quarters at the same time. Away fly the magistrates, committee-men, honorary secretaries and all, eager to show their loyalty, and recite their speeches; but more eager than discreet, a sad blunder is made; all the songs, dances, and garlands, are bestowed on the dead, while the living grandee is met with every mark of the profoundest grief and woe, much to his disgust and astonishment.

Deviations from common forms, like those directed by Louis Cortusio, are not, however, confined to any age or time. The late Mr. Knill, who died in 1811, bequeathed some property to trustees, in order that every five years a matron and ten maidens, dressed in white, should walk in procession with music from the market-house at St. Ives in Cornwall, and dance round a granite pyramid erected by him, singing some lines in chorus.

The term fiddler is frequently found in the accounts of this time, as on February 17, 1497: "To the Quenes fideler in rewarde, 1l. 6s. 8d." A female performer, however, is very shabbily paid on November 2, 1495: "To a woman that singeth with a fidell, 2s." In the Scottish accounts, as given by Daunay, similar entries appear, as, 1490: to Benat, 18s., and to "ane oder fydlar," 5s. In 1496: "To the tua fitholaris that sang Graysteil to the king," 9s.

Fetis mentions two "luthiers," or makers of lutes and

other instruments, in the first half of the fifteenth century, namely, Jean Ott of Nuremberg, and Hans Frey of the same place, who was father-in-law of Albert Durer. The term "luthier" was, and still is, applied to makers of violins and other bowed instruments, and we may therefore reasonably suppose that these two "luthiers" made viols as well as other instruments. There was, however, a maker of this date, of whose instruments there can be no doubt. One of his viols was exhibited at Koliker's, in Paris, in the early part of the present century. The neck had been changed, and it was strung with four strings like a violin. It was of a high model, and had no tail-piece, but instead of it, an ivory nut at the bottom, with four holes for the strings. The quality of tone was low and sweet, and it had a ticket with the inscription, "Joan Kerlino, 1449." This maker is considered to have been the founder of the school of makers at Brescia, and is said to have been originally from Britanny.

About this time there was an improvement in the notation of music. Thomas of Walsyngham, in the beginning of the century, says that a new character called the crotchet had been introduced, but mentions the five characters, large, long, breve, semibreve, and minim; stating that musicians should remember there should be no division beyond the minim. Square or quadrate notes had been invented by John de Muris, in the middle of the previous century.

The introduction of printing improved the character of musical notation, and the increased requirements of music, and advancement in powers of execution would cause an extension of the signs. The first specimen of music printing is said to have been by Franchinus Gafurius, at Milan; and Jean Froschouer, at Augsbourg, engraved characters for plain-chant and music, on wood, towards the end of the century. Hawkins states the first music printed in England to have been in the "Polychronicon" of Ralph Higden, by Wynkyn de Worde, in 1495, and strange-looking it is. By the middle of the following century, however, characters were gradually introduced, approaching somewhat in form to those in modern use. Conrad Paulman, who was born blind, and died in 1473, is said to have invented the lute tablature, and to have excelled on all instruments.

Louis XI. was treated with a strange concert of music about this time. Having asked his master of music, the Abbé de Baigne, to give him a concert of pigs, the abbé assembled a number of those peculiarly unmusical animals, of different ages and sizes, and with variety of intonation, it is to be presumed, carefully selected, and placed them in a tent, having in front a table like the keyboard of a pianoforte. As the keys were touched they moved certain pins, which pricked the unfortunate pigs, who grunted and squeaked accordingly; we suppose there must have been somewhat too much sostenuto. This Louis was not much of a man of jokes, except in his own peculiar way, and some of his recorded amusements were not of a harmless description. According to Brantôme and others, he caused his brother the Duc de Guienne to be poisoned, as he feared he might become troublesome, and his crime was accidentally made known to his domestic fool in the following manner. The king was praying to his "bonne patronne," in the presence of his fool, who, he thought, was too imbecile to attend to or to understand him : "Ah ! ma bonne dame, ma petite maistresse, ma grand' amie, en qui j'ai eu toujours mon reconfort, je te prie de supplier Dieu pour

moi, et estre mon advocate envers luy, qu'il me pardonne
la mort de mon frere que j'ay fait empoisonner par ce
mechant abbé de Sainct Jean d'Angely," &c.   The fool
was less imbecile than his master had fancied, and repeated the whole matter for the edification of the king
and his court at dinner-time.

CHAPTER VIII.

IN the sixteenth century we arrive at the æra of the Amatis, and find the violin in its present form, when the details received the most careful attention, and everything connected with the instrument was calculated on scientific principles, and it possessed the power and tone which, after a lapse of 300 years, have not been surpassed. Many experiments have been made, to some of which we shall refer hereafter, in change of form and detail, material and disposition of strings; but none with any effect or improvement; more frequently, indeed, the reverse. Some alterations have been made in strengthening the centre, mostly of the upper vibrating plate; and a stronger sound-bar has been applied to resist the increased tension of a higher pitch; and trials have been made without any sound-posts or bars, and with short tail-pieces, and varied positions and number of sound-holes, but there has been no permanent or essential change since the latter part of the sixteenth century.

The violin is stated to have been first referred to in Zacconi's " Pratica di Musica," 1596, where it is mentioned with a compass precisely of the present extent, without the shift; but the instrument was known in our country, and in use in the royal band, prior to this date, and some of the Amatis also were previous to it.

The viol was still in great repute, and it was by slow
degrees that the superiority of the violin was allowed ;
and this after skilful performers in the succeeding century,
whose powers of execution were in advance of their
time, had shown the increased facility afforded by the
younger instrument, and the brilliancy of tone and
sprightliness of effect of which it was capable, combined
with sweetness, of less monotonous character than that
of the viol. The viol had now from three to six strings,
and a French player named Mauduit, of the time of
Henry IV. of France, is said to have added the sixth
string, but it appears to have been previously in use.
It had frets—occasionally six or seven—to guide the
fingers, made of small pieces of gut-string dipped in
warm glue, and tied round the neck at proper intervals ;
sometimes they were inlaid in the neck or finger-board,
and slightly in relief, and the practice was carried down
to a comparatively recent period.

Franchinus Gafurius, before mentioned in connexion
with music-printing, in "De Harmonià Musicorum
Instrumentorum," 1518, has a plate showing the connexion of harmony with the celestial bodies, &c. There
is a figure playing on a sort of viol, with the neck
turned back, having four strings, but
no bridge or sound-holes ; the bow
something like that of the double-bass
(Fig. 44). We have before observed
on the probability of the absence of
details, even of the bridges, arising
occasionally from the omission of the

FIG. 44.

artist. Carter has a representation of a sculpture on the
outside of St. John's Church, Cirencester, of the beginning
of this century, where there are several figures playing on
instruments ; one has an oval viol, with four strings and

a tail-piece, and four round sound-holes, but no appear-
ance of a bridge (Fig. 45). Potier
describes a handsome instrument of
the larger size of this class from a MS.
of the sixteenth century. It has four
strings, and the scroll is curved nearly
into a semi-circle, having a boldly
carved head at the top; the sound-
hole is round, and perforated like that
of a guitar, and there is no appearance of a separate finger-board or

FIG. 45.

bridge, though this would appear to be necessary on
looking at the formidable bow (Fig. 46).

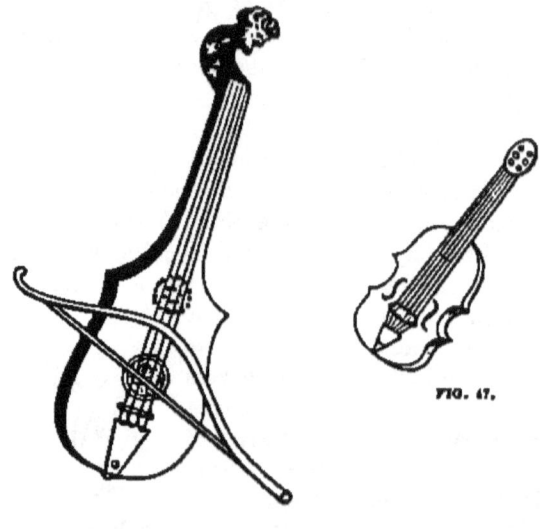

FIG. 46.

FIG. 47.

The celebrated printer John Oporinus, at Basle, about
1530, had for his device, Arion, sometimes standing on

the dolphin with a small three-stringed instrument held reversed in his left hand, and the bow in his right; and sometimes playing on a large viol with six strings, which approaches the modern tenor in form (Fig. 47). Christopher Froschouer, a printer at Zurich of about the same date, also has a viol in some of his title-pages. In the several representations of the " Dances of Death " of this age, the figure of Death is occasionally represented playing on the viol and other instruments, while leading on his victims with grim satisfaction to their fate.

Mersennus gives a description of a bass-viol in the time of Charles IX. which was large enough to contain a young page inside, who sang the treble of some ravishing airs, while the performer, Granier, played the bass part on the huge instrument, and at the same time sung the tenor, thus completing the trio. There is a very large contre-basse represented in a picture of the " Marriage of Canaan," by Paul Veronese, which has nine strings and is apparently about nine feet high; but we must allow for pictorial license.

Martin Agricola, in " Musica Instrumentalis," 1545, on the back of his title-page represents the Fraw Musica, a smartly dressed female, playing on an instrument of the guitar class. In one corner of the engraving is an instrument of the bass-viol kind, with four strings and frets, a bridge, and a tail-piece, with considerable inward curvatures, and two semi-lunar sound-holes under the two outer strings; it has no appearance of a separate finger-board, and the bow is like a double-bass bow. He describes four instruments of different sizes, but all of the same unsightly shape: they are called respectively descantus, altus, tenor, bassus, each with four strings, a large round sound-hole in the centre, like that of the guitar, reaching from side to side, and two crescent-shaped sound-holes facing each other in the upper part

of the instrument, and frets, of which the discant and bass have six, and the others seven; the head is turned back, the curvatures are very abrupt and deep, and extend down half the instrument; there is no appearance of bridge, or tail-piece, or detached finger-board; the bow, as usual, is like that of the double bass. Our figure is that of the discantus (Fig. 48). We have already given the figure of the gigue from the same work. He describes the following as the method of tuning a quartett of viols with four strings:—

FIG. 48.

while for grand viols with five strings, and the bass with six, the tuning is thus:—

The Italian viols, according to Ganasi del Fontego, 1542, had six strings and seven frets, and were tuned thus:—

Rousseau, in his Treatise, written in the seventeenth century, says that the first viols used in France, meaning the class of instrument on which he was a celebrated performer, had five large strings, the bridge placed low and below the sound-holes, and were tuned in fourths from C down to E, and in figure were like what he calls the bass-violin. The viol afterwards, he says, became more like the violin in form, and a sixth string was added, when he describes the tuning as D, A, E, C, G, and D. . After this a seventh string, A, was added by his master, St. Colombe. There were four sizes, answering to the four classes of voices; basse, taille, haute-contre, and dessus. Sometimes also a contre-basse was added.

The French tuned the taille a fourth higher than the bass, the haute-contre a fourth higher than the taille, and the dessus a fourth higher than that. Jerome de Moravia, three centuries before this, gives three different methods of tuning the vielle, but as the description is long and somewhat complicated, we did not think it necessary to insert it.

Luscinius, in 1536, mentions and gives a figure of a chelys or bass-viol, with nine strings and frets, with sides much curved in, and very similar to the figure given from Agricola; also the monochord, the rebec, the viol da gamba, the vielle or lyra mendicorum (that is, the hurdy-gurdy, to which the name vielle was now applied), and the violin or treble viol; but this is an instrument with three strings only, and more properly, perhaps, the gigue. Laborde gives a drawing of a large instrument of the double-bass class, with numerous strings, invented by Jean Doni, called the amphicordum or accord, which must have been very puzzling to play on, and was probably little more than an experiment.

The term chelys is introduced into the somewhat pompous introduction of a curious poem called, " Canum cum catis certamen," in which every word begins with the letter C. -

> " Cattorum canimos certamina clara canumque,
> Calliope concede chelyn ; clarisque Camœnæ
> Condite cum cytharis cælso condigna cothurno
> Carmina."

Hucbald, the well-known writer on music in the ninth century, wrote " Ecloga de Laudibus Calvitii," which, besides a Prœmium and some lines at the end, as " Clausula Carminis," has twelve chapters, each beginning with " Carmina clarisonæ calvis cantate Camœnæ," and consisting of ten lines, every word beginning with C. There is a very rare work, " Carmen contra clypeum Cyclopum concordiam," by John Nasus, a Franciscan monk, about 1580. Other pieces are known, every word beginning with P, as, " Pugna Porcorum," and also with other letters.

Several fine performers on the viol are mentioned at this time, as, Alphonse della Viola, Alessandro della Viola, and Giovan-Battista del Violino (probably a violin-player). Granier was one of the finest players of his age, and died about 1600. He was attached to the court of that singular character Queen Marguerite, who, after the assassination of her husband, Henry IV, lived in a strange mixture of pleasure and devotion, luxury and literature, music, dancing, and charity ; and, according to Dreux du Radier, entertained a passion, when past the age of fifty, for Comine, her master of music, who was called, apparently in consequence, " le Roi Margot." The celebrated female fool of the French court, Mathurine, whose folly in her later years was probably to some extent assumed, and under cover of

which she made a large fortune, had a son called Blanc-
Rocher, who was an admirable player on the lute. When
Henry IV. was stabbed by Jean Chastel, in 1594, he at
first thought the act had been committed by Mathurine,
who was in the carriage with him, and cried out, "Au
diablo soit la folle; elle m'a blessé!" but from her
presence of mind she mainly contributed to the capture
of the real criminal. The celebrated Zwinglius was an
amateur performer, admitting to Faber, who had objected
to his love of music, that he had learned to sing to the
chelys, fidicula, tibia, and other instruments, and de-
fended the art.

Claudio Monteverde, of Cremona, dwelling therefore
among the Amatis, in the end of this century, was not
only a distinguished performer on the tenor viol, but
also a composer, and we shall have to refer to him again.
Vincentio Galilei, the father of the great astronomer,
was an able writer on music, and in 1582 names the
viola da braccio, which he says was called the lira not
many years previously, the viola da gamba, and the
violono, but not the violino, which must, however, have
been known before his time. He attributes the invention,
erroneously, as we consider, to Italy.

Francis I. of France is said to have been the originator
of a chamber-band, in addition to the music of his chapel,
and to have had violins; but there were musical establishments of this nature in the French court long previously. An anecdote is told of his sending a band of
accomplished musicians to Solyman, the second Emperor
of the Turks, in 1543, who, having heard them three
times, caused all their instruments to be destroyed, and
after making them handsome presents, sent them out of
the country, on pain of death should they return; fear-
ing that his people might become enervated by hearing

H

them, and suspecting that Francis had sent them over for political purposes, and to divert him from the business of war. There is a story of much more recent date, where a band was sent over to some Eastern potentate, and on their first proposed performance, began as usual to tune, when the monarch and his grandees, supposing this to be the commencement of the concert, were so astonished and ear-struck, that they sent the unconscious offenders back again as fast as they could, without waiting for further proof of their skill. Something like this would seem to be alluded to in the " Knight of the Burning Pestle," " They say 'tis present death for these fiddlers to tune their rebecks before the great Turk's grace."

In the time of Henry IV. of France, there was a dispute between his musicians and those of the Cathedral of Notre Dame, as to the right of precedence before him ; when the king decided that they should all sing, but that the musicians of his chapel should begin. He had his band of " vingt-quatre violons du Roi," but they seem only to have been used for dancing.

The statutes of the Corporation of the makers of instruments, players, and professors, which had been confirmed in 1454 by Charles VII, and enlarged by François de Harlay, Archbishop of Rouen, in 1517, were regulated in 1578 by Henry III. Even Charles IX. himself was fond of music, and played on the violin. Poisot, in his " History of Music," recently published, states that he had seen his instrument at the Bibliothèque de Cluny Saône et Loire ; but notwithstanding this taste of the king, the composer Goudimel, the master of the renowned Palestrina, was killed in the massacre of St. Bartholomew's Day, which Charles is said to have

personally encouraged, and to have assisted in : but
Nero himself was a patron of music.

The two following entries from the accounts of the
expenses of Charles, taken from "Archives Curieuses de
l'Histoire de France," are interesting, especially the
latter, as it shows that Cremona was then famous for its
instruments ; and, if the fifty livres tournois formed the
price of one violin, the value would be high even at that
time, as the livre tournois was worth five francs five cen-
times, and fifty would be equivalent to 252½, or probably
about 1200 in present value. Part of the sum, however,
may have been for the expenses of the journey :—

"7 Novembre, 1572. A Baptiste Delphinon, violon
ordinaire de la chambre dudict sieur, la somme de 75
livres tourn, dont Sa Majesté luy a faict don, pour luy
aider a supporter les frais et despence qu'il luy convient
faire s'en allant présentement à Millan, par commande-
ment de Sa Majesté pour faire venir des musiciens pour
son service et plaisir."

"27 Octobre, 1572. A Nicolas Delinet, joueur de
fluste et violon dudict sieur, la somme de 50 livres
tourn, pour luy donner moyen d'achepter ung violon de
Cremonne pour le service dudict sieur."

In the accounts of his successor, Henry III, from 1580
to 1588, violins are mentioned amongst other instruments, and as early as 1550 the name of Pierre de la
Haye, joueur de violon, appears in the register of the
performances of the ancient drama at Bethune. Violins,
and instruments of this class, are mentioned frequently
in the accounts of festivals in the French memoirs of this
age, of which a few examples may suffice. There is an
account given in the Memoirs of Marguerite de Valois,
of a *fête* given at the interview of her mother, Catherine

de Medicis, with her son, King Charles IX. in 1565, at
Bayonne, where several provincial dances were introduced with the appropriate instruments, as, "les Poite-
vines avec le cornemuse, les Provençales la volte avec
les timballes, les Bourguignones et Champenoises avec le
petit hautbois, le dessus de violin, et tabourins de village; les Bretonnes dansans les passepieds et branles-
gais; et ainsi toutes les autres provinces." We think a
history of dancing by some properly qualified person
would prove an interesting, as well as an amusing work,
though we are not prepared to go as far as the Maître à
danser, in "Le Bourgeois Gentilhomme:" "Tous les
malheurs des hommes, tous les revers funestes, dont les
histoires sont remplies, les bévues des politiques, et les
manquements des grands capitaines, tout cela n'est venu
que faut de savoir danser."

According to a song made on the marriage of the
same monarch—

> " Tabourins et trompettes,
> Hautbois et violins,
> D'une haulteur parfaite
> Faisoient tantir leurs sons."

At a splendid *fête* given in 1579, on the marriage of
Margaret of Loraine, the sister of the queen of Henry
III, to the Duc de Joyeuse, several violins were introduced to play the dances, the whole being arranged by
the celebrated Baltazar, or Baltazarini, one of the first
famous violin-players on record. He was *valet de
chambre* and superintendent of music to Catherine de
Medicis, and also the chief of the king's band, and was
commonly called De Beaujoyeulx. After the nuptials of
Margaret, Queen of Austria, with Philip III. of Spain,
at Ferrara, in 1598, and those of the Duke Albert with the
Infanta Isabella, the king's sister, amongst other enter-

tainments a concert was given by the nuns of the Convent of St. Vito, wherein they played on violins and bastard viols, together with other instruments, intermingled with voices.

Having previously given an account of a concert of pigs, we may be allowed, perhaps, to vary our work a little by relating one where cats formed part of the orchestra, before Philip II. of Spain, at Brussels, in 1549. A bear was seated on a great car, at the figure of an organ, which instead of pipes had twenty cats, of different sizes and notes, shut up in small cages, with their tails out, and attached to the register of the organ, so that, as the bear pressed the keys, the tails of the unlucky cats were pulled, and, according to the chronicler, the cats began to squeal "des basses, des tailles et des dessus, selon la nature des airs que l'on voulait chanter, avec tant de proportion, que cette musique des bêtes ne faisait pas un faux ton." We should have suspected, but for this statement, some hanging of the notes occasionally. The description proceeds to state that, at the sound of this feline instrument, monkeys, bears, wolves, stags, and other animals danced about on an accompanying stage; but as from the context it appears that, with the exception of the cats and monkeys, the beasts were represented by children dressed up, we may almost fancy some tampering with the cats, though nothing of the sort is mentioned.

The viol appears in England in the royal bands in this century, as well as the rebec and fiddle, as before mentioned. In the seventeenth of Henry VIII. we find his band consisted of fifteen trumpeters, three lewters, three rebikes, three taberets, one harper, Andrew Newman the waite, two vialls, four drumslades, a phipher, and ten sagbuts; the wages varying from 4*l.* to 33*l.* 6*s.*, the three principal sagbuts alone receiving the highest rate. Nearly similar lists appear in subsequent years. In September, 1532, there is a sum of 3*l.* 7*s.* 6*d.* charged in the Privy Purse expenses, for the livery coats of three of the "vyalls," showing that the members of the royal band were provided with a dress at that time. In 1538 Henry had three "vyalls," named Hans Highbourn, Hans Hossonol, and Thomas Highbourne, at salaries of 33*s.* 4*d.* per quarter; and three years after the number was doubled, their names, as we learn from Mr. Collier's "Annals of the Stage," being Vincent de Venitia, Alex. de Venitia, Albertus de Venitia, Ambroso de Milano, Joan Maria de Cremona, and Antony de Romano, all of them foreigners, and one, it will be observed, from Cremona, now soon to take a distinguished place in the annals of the violin; their salary was 4*l.* quarterly. These performers were accustomed to participate in the New Year's Gifts, then so liberally and regularly distributed; for instance, on New Year's Day, 1542-3, they received from the Princess Mary the sum of 20*s.*, being a larger sum than that given to any others of their own class; many similar examples might be given.

In a curious inventory of the effects of Henry VIII, taken immediately after his decease, there are no less than nineteen "viallos," great and small, and four "gitterons" (guitars), with four cases to them, called "Spanishe vialles;" the catalogue comprises numerous instruments, especially flutes, and finishes with "sondrie Bookes and Skrolles of Songes and Ballattes."

The succeeding monarchs, Edward VI, and Mary and Elizabeth, both of whom were skilful musicians themselves, had bands formed much in the same way as that of their father. The viols in Edward's band, of whom there were eight, were paid, six at the rate of 30*l.* 8*s.* 4*d.*

each, one at 20*l.*, and one at 18*l.* 5*s.* The first notice of
violins by name in the royal bands appears to be in 1561,
when the sum of 230*l.* 6*s.* 8*d.* was paid to them; in the
same year we shall find them introduced in the tragedy
of "Gorboduc." Ten years afterwards the queen had
seven, who received 325*l.* 15*s.* One of the New Year's
gifts given to her in 1577-8, was a viol by Marke Antony;
these gifts were so regulated and graduated, that every
one connected with the court was expected to give one,
down to *Smyth*, dustman, who gave "two boltes of
cameryck." There is an entry in the "Calendar of State
Papers," 1569, of the names of the officers of the queen's
household who were defaulters in payment of the sub-
sidy, and all the musicians appear in this list, which does
not speak well for their position, unless they were returned as defaulters as a matter of favour, for the purpose
of being excused. In the Accounts of the Scotch Court,
given by Dauney, in his "Ancient Scottish Melodies,"
are several entries relating to viols and "fithelars" of
this century, as, in 1503, "To Adam Boyd, Bennet, and
Jame Widderspune fithelaris xlij*." 1505, "To Sir
George Lawederis fithelar, ane fithelar of Striuelin, &c.,
ilk man ix*. xlv*." 1507, Jan. 1. "To divers menstrales,
schawmeris, trumpetis, taubroneris, fithelaris, lutaris,
harparis, clarscharis, piparis," extending to lxix persons
"x*. xj*." In 1538, payments are made "To the foure
menstralis that playis upon the veolis, for their yeirlie
pensioun ij*," and also "To Jakkis Collumboll player
upon the veolis."

The price of a common bass-viol was moderate enough,
for there is an entry in the diary of Philip Henslowe,
"Lent unto Richard Jonnes the 22 of desembr 1598, to
bye a basse viall and other instroments for the companey
xxxx*." In an inventory of Henslowe, of the same

year, arc included a trebel viall, a basso viall, a bandore,
and a sytteren.   In the accounts at Hengrave, in 1572,
there is a charge of 20s. for a treble violin ; and there
seems little doubt but that the violin was now in requisition for dances, except perhaps for the stately pavan, or
others of the grave and ceremonious class.

In an interesting "History of Horsclydown," by Mr.
Corner, F.S.A., to whom we are indebted for a copy,
there is an engraving from an old picture in the possession of the Marquis of Salisbury, at Hatfield, the work
of George Hofnagle, a Flemish artist.   The date of this
picture, which represents a fair at Horsclydown, is 1590.
On the right are some figures dancing ; the musicians
are, on one side a piper or flutist, and two playing on
violins, much of the modern shape, and two other similar
violin-players on the other side of the dancers.

The approach to the present shape of the violin was
probably gradual ; the first makers of violins being also
makers of viols.   Kerlin and Duiffoprugcar preserved
much of the viol quality ; but some instruments of Gaspar
de Salo, especially tenors and double basses, are made
quite in the present shape.   At the time of the "Amatis"
this shape seems to have been completely settled and
perfected.

At the conversazione of the Musical Society of London,
on the 29th of January, 1862, the curious old violin
described in "Hawkins's History of Music," with an
engraving, and stated to have been given by Queen
Elizabeth to the Earl of Leicester, was exhibited.   It is
of the date of 1578, and is of heavy make, the upper
part of the body being much deeper than the lower ;
there is a great deal of ornament and carving about it,
and we should expect the tone would be nasal and
sluggish.   It is now kept at Warwick Castle.   Burney

VIOL DE GAMBA

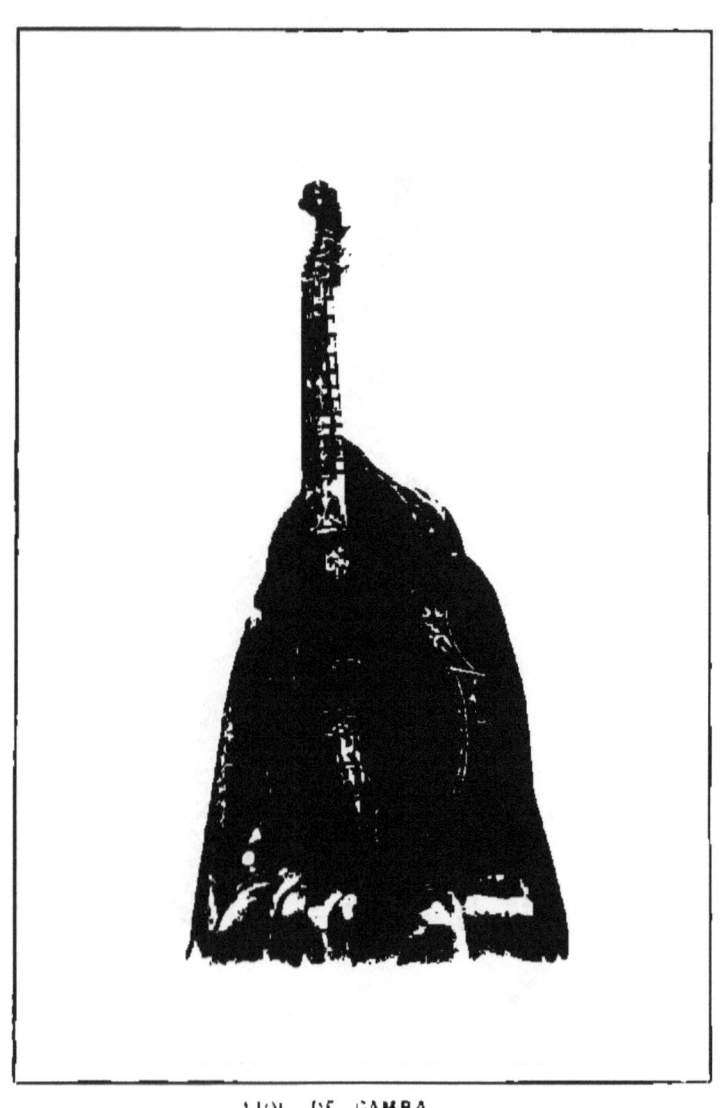

VIOL DE GAMBA

mentions Corelli's violin, then the property of Giardini, after whose death we believe the well-known Mr. Salomon became its possessor; it was made in 1678, and the case is said to have been painted by Annibal Caracci.

One of the writers of this work has in his possession a very handsome viol da gamba of about this date, richly inlaid and ornamented, purchased from the late Mr. John Cawse, the artist, but we have been unable to ascertain the previous owners. The body is about the size of a modern violoncello, and it has frets. It is altogether so fine a specimen of this class of instruments, that we have had photographs, from which our illustrations are taken. (Figs. 49, 50.) When the lamented Prince Consort, on the 16th of April, 1845, being the director for the evening of the Ancient Concert, had some music of the 16th century performed on instruments of that period, some of which were sent over by M. Fetis from Brussels for the purpose, Mr. Cawse lent this viol da gamba, which was played on by Mr. Richard Hatton. In the course of the evening he was desired to attend and show the instrument to the Queen, who examined it carefully, and expressed herself much pleased with it. We may remember that Sir Andrew Aguecheek, amongst other accomplishments, was a performer, "he plays o' the viol-de-gamboys."

Viols, violins, and fiddles, are mentioned in early dramatic works of this age, and in the "Interlude of the Four Elements," in 1510, one character says,—

> " This daunce wold do mych better yet,
> Yf we had a kyt or taberet,
> But alas! ther is none here."

He is answered by another, who proposes to go to a tavern, where they will be sure to find one or two min-

strels.   In that quaint production, " Gammer Gurton's
Needle," our oldest comedy, except " Ralph Roister
Doister," and which is said to have been written as far
back as 1551, Diccon, the mischief-maker between
Gammer Gurton and Dame Chat, says at the end of
the second act—

> " Into the town will I, my frendes to vysit there,
> And hether straight again to see th' end of this gere ;
> In the mean time, feluwes, pypo up your fidles, I say, take them,
> And let your friendes here such mirth as ye can make them."

In our earliest tragedy, " Gorboduc," which was acted
in 1561, we have the first specimen of music between the
acts, the choice of the airs being probably left to the
performers.   There is a dumb-show at the beginning of
each act, taking the place of chorus, and foretelling the
subject of the following division of the play, each accompanied by appropriate music.   At the commencement of
the dumb-show to the first act it is stated, " Firste the
Musicke of Violenze began to play, durynge whiche
came in vppon the Stage sixe wilde men clothed in
leaues."   Previous to the other acts, musical instruments
of different classes are introduced.

In the banquet scene in the " Lamentable Tragedy,
mixed ful of pleasant mirth, of King Cambises," of the
same date, being that alluded to by Shakespeare when
referring to speaking in King Cambises' vein, the king
says :—

> " Me think, mine eares doeth wish the sound
>   of musicks harmony ;
> Heer for to play before my grace,
>   in place I would them spy."

Ambidexter, the vice of the piece, replies,—

> " They be at hand, sir, with stick and fidle ;
> They can play a now daunce called, *Hey, didle didle.*"

He seems to have been hard pressed for a rhyme, but he

is the buffoon of the play, and on his first appearance
comes in dressed with "an old capcase on his hed, an
olde pail about his hips for harnes, a scummer and a
potlid by his side, and a rake on his shoulder."

In Gascoyne's "Jocasta," nearly of the same date, each
act is preceded by a dumb show, accompanied by viols,
cythren, bandores, and other instruments. At the end
of the play of "Wyt and Science," "cumth in foure with
violes and syng, Remembre me, and at the last quere
all make cursye, and so goe forth syngyng." Katherine,
in "Taming the Shrew," calls her supposed music-master
rascal fidler, and twangling Jack; und in the old play
on which Shakespeare is supposed to have founded his,
Valeria, who personates the music-master, exclaims,
" Hold, mistresse, souns will you breake my lute?"

> " *Kate.*   I on thy head, and if thou speake to me,
>   There take it vp, and fiddle some where else.
>   (*She throwes it downe.*)
>   And see you come no more into this place,
>   Least that I clap your fiddle on your face."

In the old play of "Timon" (not Shakespeare's), one of
the hangers-on is Hermogenes, a fiddler, and the fiddle
and fiddling are frequently referred to in connection
with him. In one of the songs during Queen Elizabeth's
royal progresses, being Rowland's song in praise of the
Fairest Beta, by Drayton, about 1590, we find the following collection of instruments:—

> " Sound out your trumpets then from London's stately towers,
>   To beate the stormie winds a-backe, and calme the raging showers.
>   Set to the cornet and the flute,
>   The orpharion and the lute ;
>   And tune the tabor and the pipe to the sweet violons ;
>   And moove the thunder in the ayre with lowdest clarions."

The common fiddlers at this time, if not attached to the
court, or to the establishment of some great person, pro-

bably led a rambling life, inducing too often habits of
intemperance, especially as they frequently had to attend
taverns and social meetings, where, if they possessed
tolerable skill, and were able to sing a good song, their
companionship was courted, especially about Christmas
time.   "Faith, follow fiddlers," says one of the characters in the " Returne from Pernassus," " here's no silver
found in this place; no, not so much as 'the usuall
Christmas entertainment of musitians, a black Jack of
beare, and a Christmas pye."

One of Tarlton's jests is connected with two musicians
(most probably fiddlers) called Fancy and Nancy, who
used with their boys often to visit Tarlton, he being one
of their best friends, at the sign of the Saba, in "Gra-
cious Street."   One summer morning they came to play
him "The Hunt's up," (a tune for playing which
adapted to some political song on the "crowd or fyd-
dyll," one John Hogon had got into difficulties in 1537,)
with other music ; when he came out of his room in his
shirt and night-gown to drink some muscadine with them.
In the meantime, a rogue steps in and steals his apparel,
which seems to be the point of the joke; and many of
these jests are much of the same quality.

Armin, in his "Nest of Ninnies," gives an account of
a mischance that befel a fiddler, in collision with Jack
Oates, the domestic fool of Sir William Hollis.   One
Christmas-time, Oates being out of sorts, his master told
him to go home, as he would get another fool; upon
which Jack began to cry, and went down to the great
hall, where, being strong of arm, he snatched the pipes
out of the piper's hands and broke them over the unof-
fending fellow's head, putting a stop to the dancing. Sir
William was very angry at this, and offered a gold noble
for another fool, on which an unlucky fiddler, who was

present, proposed to take the place, and was approved
of. He was so pleased that he threw his fiddle one way
and broke it, his bow another, and his case another, and
went out to dress. In the meantime Jack returned,
having recovered his good humour, and began his gibes
and jokes, of which an average specimen may be given
in his stating that there was a wench in the hall who had
eaten garlic, and seventeen men were poisoned from
kissing her. His rival, or intended substitute, now entered the room dancing and grimacing, and dressed in
one of Jack's dresses; but the practised fool flew at the
interloper and beat him severely, so that the unfortunate
fellow not only lost his fiddle, but also, as the story says,
the use of his left eye. Those who wish to learn more
of the interesting and curious history of court and domestic fools, will find much entertainment and information in Dr. Doran's work on the subject.

Two celebrated fiddlers, called Out Roaringe Dicke
and Wat Wimbars, are named about this time, who
could make their 20s. a-day at Braintree Fair, a great
resort for these characters. Anthony Now-now, and
Blind Moon, were also well known. The former is thus
introduced in Chettle's " Kind Hart's Dream," 1592:—
" The first of the first three was an od old fellow, low of
stature ; his head was couered with a round cap, his
body with a side skirted tawney coate, his legs and feete
trust vppe in leather buskins, his gray haires and fur-
rowed face witnessed his age, his treble violl in his hande,
assured me of his profession. On which (by his con-
tinuall sawing having left but one string) after his best
manner, hee gaue me a huntsvp: whome, after a little
musing, I assuredly remembred to be no other but old
Anthony Now-now." In some parts of the work the instrument is called a crowd. Anthony Munday is said

to have been the person intended to be ridiculed by
Anthony Now-now, and he obtained his name from
singing a song in which each verse ended with Anthony
now, now ; one verse may suffice for an example :—

> " When is the best time to drinke with a friend ?
> When is the meetest my money to spend ?
>   O Anthony, now, now, now,
>   O Anthony, now, now, now."

The instrument was, however, also admitted into good
society, for Selden's father, who was passing rich with
forty pounds a-year, delighted in the violin, on which he
played well, and would play to his neighbours at Christmas-
time while they danced. Chests of viols were also kept
in many families, as we shall presently describe, and
therefore we may assume that violins were also.

Towards the end of this century publications began to
appear of songs adapted to various instruments, which,
in the succeeding century, were very numerous. In
1558 our acquaintance, Anthony Munday, published
" A Banquet of Daintie Conceits," to sing to the lute,
bandora, virginalls, or any other instrument. In 1593,
William Barley published " A New Booke of Tablature,
containing Instructions to guide and dispose the hand,
to play on sundry Instruments, as the Lute, Orpharion,
and Bandora," &c. John Dowland, the composer of
some excellent madrigals, and himself a distinguished
performer on the lute, whom Fuller calls the rarest musician that his age did behold, published in 1597, "The
First Booke of Songes or Ayres of foure parts with
Tablature for the Lute. So made that all the partes
together, or either of them severally may be song to the
Lute, Orpherion, or Viol de Gambo." In 1599, Richard
Allison published the Psalms of David "in Meter, to be
sung and played on the lute, orpharyon, citterne, or base

violl;" and in the same year Morley printed a work of
still more instrumental character, the "First Booke of
Consorte Lessons," for six instruments to play together,
namely, the treble lute, the pandora, the cittern, the
flute, and the treble and bass viols. At the same time,
Anthony Holborne published a collection of pavans,
galliards, almaines, and other short airs, for viols and
other instruments. William Lawes wrote some fantasias for viols, which it might be curious to compare with
some of our modern fantasias.

There are several payments for strings charged in the
accounts from which we have previously given extracts,
generally called lute strings, but viol and violin strings
may be considered to be included. Some of the payments were large, as for instance: Thomas Lytchfield,
one of the grooms of the Privy Chamber in the time of
Elizabeth, was paid at the rate of 13*l.* 6*s.* 8*d.* a-year for
lute strings; but except in one case, mentioned by Dauney, of 6*s.* paid in 1533 for "one dozen luyt stringis
send to the kinge's grace in Glasgow," we do not find
the actual value of the strings. There was a Custom-
House duty in 1545 of 22*d.* the grose on "Lute Strynges
called Mynikins."

Mersennus says that strings for fiddles and other
stringed instruments were made from the intestines of
sheep; a practice as ancient as the early Egyptians.
Baptista Porta gives some fanciful effects of strings
made from various materials, which we introduce on his
authority, not having had time to try the experiments
ourselves; but will recommend them to any of our
readers having plenty of patience and a good stock of
credulity. Strings made from sheep and wolf combined
produce no music, but jar, and cause discords; while the
sounds of those made from serpents, and especially

vipers, cause women to miscarry. So drums made of
elephants', camels', or wolfs' skins, will frighten horses,
and one of horses' skin is literally a bugbear to the
ursine race, from the antipathy the living animals have
to each other. For a similar reason, Culpepper says
that a cobweb will stop the bleeding of a wound. We
should observe in reference to our recommendation to
make these experiments, that the learned Kircher, in
perfect simplicity and good faith, says, that having seen
the account of Porta, and some similar remarks of
Pythagoras and others, he got two polychords, and
strung one with sheep-strings, and the other with wolf;
but on trying the latter in a sheep-fold, the insensible
animals refused to be frightened, and no breaking of
strings was caused from the antipathy.

The notation of music in the present century is somewhat repulsive to a modern reader, from its angular and
frequently crowded characters; but it was considerably
advanced from former times, and capable of expressing
passages that required much execution; in effect it
comprised our present notation in a ruder form and
without the smaller notes. The first music-printing,
which was from blocks, is said to have been in the works
of Franchinus; and the Germans exhibited much skill
in printing music with letter-press types. There is
some account in Hawkins of musical notes of this time
from Andreas Ornithoparcus, khaw, Wilphlingsederus,
and Lucas Lossius, and he says that music from metal
types was invented by Ottavio de Petrucci, about
1515. Grafton, in the Book of Common Prayer noted,
composed by John Marbeck, and published in 1550,
improved the notes of Higden, and his own characters
were improved by Day in 1560.

Marnef, a printer at Paris in the beginning of this

century, was one of the first who printed the plain-chant in moveable characters with the signs of the ligatures, and about the same time Oglin, at Augsbourg, was the first who printed music from copper-plates; Hautin, at Paris, being the first who engraved music in France. The Ballards had a monopoly there in 1540, which somewhat delayed the improvement, as they used the old characters. Adrian le Roy, an eminent lutenist, was afterwards associated with them, and the type was improved. He published, about 1570, the precepts for the tablature of the lute, an inconvenient method of notation, that was occasionally applied even to the different classes of the viol and violin, and did not wear itself out until a comparatively recent period. Granjon, who formed his notes rounded instead of lozenge-shaped, Attaignant, Guillaume de Bé, Branton, and Sanlecque and his son, were other clever printers of music of this age. For the account of the notes from Gam ut, to E la, from the semiquaver to the large, with all the mysteries of moode, time, and prolation, perfect or imperfect, great or less; with the intricacies of black full, and black void, red full, and red void, we must refer to Morley's "Introduction to Practical Music," 1597, observing, that notwithstanding the various names and characters in his work, they may be readily understood with a moderate degree of attention; and such a study might be as useful—perhaps more so—than the restoration of some of our supposed old ecclesiastical modes, where many of the combinations and sequences sound strange to the modern educated ear, and seem to belong to bygone days; but of which the theory also is very simple, and the knowledge of it to be attained by any one with a moderate knowledge of music in a short time.

I

CHAPTER IX.

N one of the first musical dramas, " L'Anima e del Corpo," 1597, no instruments are mentioned of the viol or violin class, excepting the lira doppia, which has been supposed to be the viol da gamba. In the opera of " Orfeo," 1607, the following instruments were used :— " duoi contrabassi di viola, dieci viole de brazzo, duoi violini piccioli alla Francese," and "tre bassi da gamba." As before observed, the violin was well known both in England nearly half a century previously, and in France before this date, and the use of the term " Francese," does not imply the French origin of the violin, but may show that it was popular, and serve as a distinction from the viols ; and M. Bottée de Toulmon, in his " Dissertation," before referred to, states that he has not been able to find any authorities for the superior claim of the French violin at this time. However, violins were now regularly established in orchestras. In 1634 Stephen Lundi, in his musical drama called " Il S. Alessio," had violins, harps, lutes, theorbes, bass-viols, and clavecins, to accompany the vocal parts. The oratorio " di S. Gio. Battista," by the celebrated Stradella, who was himself a great performer on the violin, was accompanied by two violins and violoncello del concertino, and two violins, tenor and bass, del concerto grosso.

Burney says the first attempt of accompaniments by two violins, tenor and bass, our modern quartett, was in the oratorio "di Santa Cristina," by Federici, in 1676. The orchestras for the compositions of Cavalli, Lulli, and Carissimi (whose "Stabat Mater" is said to have been one of the first pieces in which orchestral accompaniments were introduced into churches), comprised principally violins and viols of different sizes, bass viols, and double bass-viols, called by the Italians violone, in distinction to the violins, which were called by the diminutive violini, the parent name being the viola. The music for the violins was written in the G clef, as at present; and for the viols for the C clef, on the first, second, or third lines, according to the size of the instrument, or soprano, mezzo-soprano, and alto clefs.

In 1637, at Venice, theatrical action, dancing, and the art of dramatic decoration were brought in aid of song and music, and from 1645 operas were occasionally tried in France. In 1671 a theatre was opened in Paris for the lyric drama, under letters patent from Louis XIV, dated the 28th of June, 1669, wherein it was inserted that gentlemen and ladies might sing at the operas without such an act being considered derogatory to their title of nobility, or their aristocratic privileges. Of course whatever Louis said was right; and there is an anecdote of flattery towards him which certainly throws most others in the shade. A preacher, in his discourse before him and his court, made use of the expression, "We are all mortal," a natural remark, considering that Louis himself had descended from a long line of mortal ancestors, and might be expected, notwithstanding his three-score and ten years' reign, to follow them to the grave. However, the incautious preacher found from the looks of some of the courtiers that he had made a blunder, and promptly recovered himself by exclaiming, " Nous sommes tous mortels—ou presque tous."

The viol continued in constant use in England in the seventeenth, as well as in the previous century, together with the violin, and it was common in musical families to have a chest of viols, containing two trebles, a tenor, and a bass-viol, and occasionally there were duplicates of some of the instruments; at Hengrave, for instance, there was a chest of six viols. Sir Thomas More, who was fond of music, kept viols and an organ in his house. Burney gives the following as the mode of tuning a chest of viols, containing three sorts with six strings :—

The bass-viol, or viol da gamba.

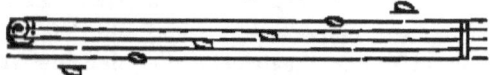

The tenor-viol, or viol da braccio.

The treble-viol.

Cerreto, in his work "Della Prattica Musica," Naples, 1601, has his own portrait on the frontispiece, with an angel at each corner playing on a stringed instrument; two have them of the guitar sort, with five strings and seven frets; the other two have them of the class of viol da gamba, having five strings, with a circular sound-hole in the centre; their necks are long, and one of them has five frets; their forms are like the modern violoncello, with bows similar to double-bass bows. He names four gradations of the viola d'arco, the bass, tenor, alto, and soprano, and gives the compass of the six strings of each, stating that in playing together, the tenor and alto are tuned a fifth above the bass, and the soprano a fourth above them. He gives the names of several Neapolitan performers of the viola d'arco, and the lira, but none on the violin, which, therefore, was apparently of no high repute in Naples at that time. Cerone, a Spanish writer, in "El Melopœo y Maestro," 1613, names as stringed instruments, sistro comun, psalterio, acetabulo, pandura, dulcemiel, rebequina, or rabel, vihuela, violon, lyra, cythara or citola, quitarra, laud, tiorba, arpa, monochordio, clavichordio, cymbelo, and spineta; thus including some of the violin class.

Prætorius, in "Theatrum Instrumentorum," Wolffenbuttel, 1620, gives several curious figures of musical instruments, which may be considered as more particularly representing those then in use in Germany. Among them is the *gross contra-bassgeig*, much like a modern double-bass, with five strings, two S S sound-holes, a bridge, a finger-board, and a tail-piece, somewhat of a fanciful form, no frets, and the scroll like the modern; the bow, also, is similar to the present double-bass bow. The *violone* is much like the violoncello, and has six strings, two S S sound-holes, a bridge, finger-board, tail-piece, scroll like the modern, and six frets; the bow somewhat like a heavy or clumsy violoncello bow. The *Italianische lyra de gamba* is like a thick violoncello, with twelve strings, two S S sound-holes, a finger-board, a tail-piece, a bridge, no scroll, but a flat board, or plate, at the top of the finger-board, in which the screws are fixed; the neck is very short, and there are five frets. The bow is like that of the violoncello, and it would appear from the figure that several of the inner strings must have been struck together. There are three *violen*

de gamba, somewhat in shape like the violone just mentioned, with six strings, a bridge, a finger-board, a tail-
piece, a sound-hole like a crescent, a scroll with a figure
of a lion's head, or something similar at the top, and
each with seven frets.   The *viol bastarda* is also much
of the same shape as the violone, has six strings, bridge,
finger-board, tail-piece, plain scroll, two crescent-shaped
sound-holes, and also a round one above them.   The
Italiänische lyra de bracio is like the *lyra de gamba,*
but smaller, and has only seven strings.   The *geig* is of
long pear-shape, with three strings, bridge, tail-piece, and
circular sound-hole, and very similar to our Fig. 15,

taken from Agricola. The *klein posche*
is a small instrument, somewhat of the
same class, but of oblong shape, and narrow, with the neck apparently detached,
and one S sound-hole at the end of the
finger-board (Fig. 51); we have a similar
one in our possession.   The *discant-geig*
is of violin shape, but with a waving line
in the bouts, four strings, a bridge, a finger-
board, detached neck, S S sound-holes,
tail-piece, and scrolls.   The *rechte discant-geig* is much like the modern violin in every
respect.   The *tenor-geig,* like a modern viola, with
a short neck.   The *bas-geig de bracio,* like a clumsy
shaped violoncello, but with five strings, and a short neck ;
none of the last six instruments have frets.   He gives
the figure of the *trumscheide,* in the shape of a trumpet-
marine, but with four strings ; also the *scheidholt,* which
is a sort of oblong narrow box with three strings (there
are, however, four screws), and seems to have eighteen
frets, with a kind of double-bass bow, and would appear
to be more adapted for experiments than anything else.

FIG. 51.

There are figures of the *schlussel-fiddel*, and *stroh-fiddel*, which are of peculiar shape, and probably were never in general use. One of them has four strings, bridge, &c., but no inward curvatures at the side; the other has four strings, bridge, &c., but has an appendage at the neck, which is too obscure in the figure to be made out. The *alte-fiddel*, or old fiddle, has five strings, though there are ten screws, seven frets, two crescent-shaped sound-holes, and a round one below them, no bridge, and no scroll, but a head-piece turning back; it is much like our Fig. 48, from Agricola. He gives several representations of the varieties of the lute and guitar, harp, and wind instruments.

Mersennus, "De Instrumentis Harmonicis," has numerous representations of the stringed and bowed instruments of his age, the early part of the seventeenth century. He seems to distinguish the violin class as barbiton minor, and the viol class as barbiton major. In describing the first, he says it is much used for dancing, and that the professors of that art used a small one that they could carry in their pocket, called pera, or poche; he has three figures of them, of which we give one (Fig. 52); the others are similar, but of a longer and narrower make, and they all have an additional sound-hole in the shape of a heart, under the notion of thus obtaining more power. The necks are of one piece with the body, and they all have four strings and no frets. This instrument was somewhat akin to the old gigue, and also the precursor of the modern kit. He has figures of two large instruments of the barbiton minor, one of which may be considered as identical with a modern violoncello of very broad model, and the other has the corners at the inward curvatures, very distinct and angular, with the sound-holes larger than in the modern instrument, the neck also is thicker and heavier (Fig. 53). The strings were tuned in fifths, but the

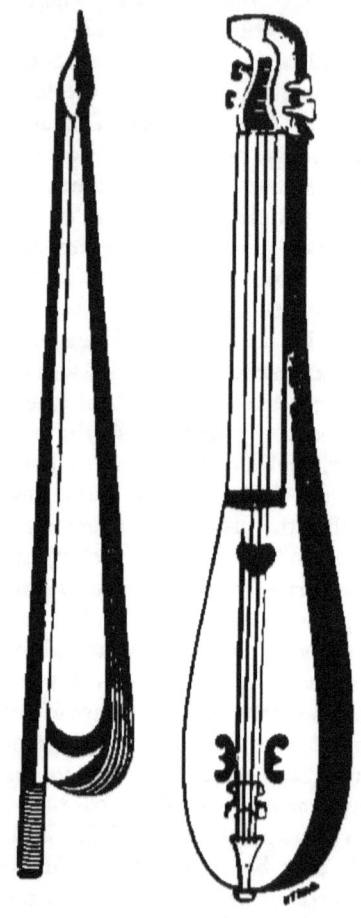

FIG. 53.

lowest string was G, a fifth, therefore, higher than the

violoncello. The representation he gives of another bar-
biton minor, or treble violin, might easily be taken for a modern fiddle (Fig. 54). The sound of this class of instrument, he says, is stronger than that of the barbiton major, or viol; amongst other distinctions he mentions the viols having six strings instead of four, and frets; but these frets appear to have been occasionally applied to the violin; we have given a representation of one of his figures of the barbiton major (Fig. 55). From his account of the fingering of the violin, it would seem as if the shift was not then known; but in

FIG. 54.

describing the barbiton major he says the frets do not exceed eight, which would imply that it was in use. When it was first ventured on it was considered a triumph of skill, and the performer did not attempt beyond the C, or ut, on the first string, and if such a passage was expected, the audience would say softly, "*Gare l'ut;*" if the performer failed he was hissed, but if successful was greeted with bravos and acclamations. Mersennus gives a description with a figure of what he calls the lyre, having eight frets and fifteen strings, of which the bow must necessarily have struck several at the same time. The shape is somewhat unmanageable, being like a violoncello with an additional part at the lower end; probably it was not much in use. He describes the monochord, and that singular instrument, now

FIG. 55.

obsolete, the trumpet marine, the favourite instrument of
M. Jourdain, in "Le Bourgeois Gentilhomme;" also
the lyra mendicorum, like the hurdy-gurdy, which he
says some call the symphony, and the French the vielle.
The principal materials of strings he states were the intestines of sheep and other animals, brass and iron (used
for the clavicymbala), flax, and silk. Rome and other
cities produced the best strings, and some of the larger
ones were composed of from fifty to sixty guts twined
together.

Kircher, in his "Musurgia," 1650, describes and
gives figures of several instruments bearing, as it might
be expected, great similarity to those in the work of
Mersennus, calling the viols and violins by the name of
chelys, and the poche by that of linterculus.

In a curious book, "Symbola Divina et Humana
Pontificum, Imperatorum, Regum," &c. by John Frede-
ricus Hagen, 1666, which contains hieroglyphics of the
popes and monarchs, there are several of the kings of
England; and in that applicable to Henry VIII. is a
large instrument of the fiddle make, with six strings and
frets, but with no distinct finger-board; the head turning
forward. From the description, this is intended for the
pandura, though different in make and in number of
strings from that described by Mersennus, and was not
intended to be played on with a bow. In the accompanying explanation, Henry's usage of his wives is
referred to, and the fact stated that Ann of Cleves, after
her divorce, amused herself by playing on this instrument.

In 1611, Louis XIII. granted several new privileges
to the Corporation of Musicians. Two of the musicians
belonging to this monarch's chapel got into disgrace on
some occasion, and were curtailed of half their appointments. In their distress they applied to Marais, his

buffoon, who devised the following plan to relieve them.
He went with them to dance in a masquerade before the
king, each of them being only half dressed. " What
does this mean ? " said the monarch. " Sire," they
replied, " it is because those who have only half their
appointments, can only go half dressed ! " Louis laughed,
and restored them to favour and to full dress. A story
of somewhat similar class is told of Haydn respecting
his candle overture or symphony (letter B). Prince
Esterhazy having for some reason dismissed all his band
except Haydn; the composer, not liking to part with his
old associates, composed the above piece of music, in the
last movement of which, each performer as he completed
the music allotted to him, put out his candle and quitted
the orchestra, leaving the first violin to play about twenty-
two bars by himself. The Prince was angry at this
curious arrangement, and sent for Haydn to inquire into
the meaning of it. Haydn bowed submissively, and
said he wished to show of what little use one performer
was, and the band were accordingly restored to their
appointments.

Mersennus mentions some of the most distinguished
performers of the seventeenth century, and in referring
to the harmony produced by the twenty-four royal
fiddlers, who consisted of six treble violins, six counter-
tenors, six tenors, and six basses, says nothing could be
sweeter or more pleasing; and as to the players, who
more elegant than Constantine on the treble, more
enthusiastic than Bocan, more delicate than Lazarino
and Foucard, and Leger on the bass ? There is a story
told of this band of twenty-four going round as usual on
New Year's Day, to play to the grandees and officers of
the court, and obtain the gifts of the season in return.
They went to the Marshal Duke de Grammont amongst

others, when, after a little time, he put his head out of window and said, " Combien êtes-vous, messieurs ? " " Nous sommes vingt, monsieur." " Je vous remercie tous vingt bien humblement," says the Marshal to the expectant musicians, shutting his window.

Bocan was the musician selected by Cardinal Richelieu in the following singular scene, related in the " Mémoires de Brienne," and elsewhere. The Cardinal, in the height of his power, had ventured to address the Queen, Anne of Austria, in the language of love. She, disguising her feelings at his boldness, informed him by her confidant, Madame de Chevreuse, that she required as a proof of his sincerity that he should appear before her in Spanish costume, and dance a saraband, never supposing that he, a high Churchman, and occupied with the state affairs of the country, would condescend to such a course. To her surprise, however, supposing that he had succeeded in his suit, he consented, merely stipulating that none should be present except her Majesty and his musician Bocan, who, however, is said to have betrayed him. The queen, notwithstanding, placed her favourite, Madame de Chevreuse, and two of her gentlemen, Vautier and Beringhen, behind a screen. At the appointed time Richelieu entered dressed in a tight-fitting suit of green velvet, with silver bells at his knees and castagnets in his hands, and began his task in sober earnest, until the queen could preserve her gravity no longer, and burst into a fit of laughter, which was repeated by her attendants behind the screen. The Cardinal left the room in great anger, and from that time became the enemy of the queen and her favourite.

Our Queen Elizabeth was fond of dancing, and when advanced in years seems to have used it politically; as Weldon mentions, that when any messenger came to her

from King James, on lifting up the hangings, he was
sure to find her dancing to a little fiddle "affectedly,"
that he might tell James her youthful disposition, and
how unlikely it was he should come to the coveted
throne.

Mersennus names Maugard and Hotman as extraordinary performers on the violin and viol; Rousseau
says they were the first men who excelled on the viol in
France, the former having great science and execution,
and facility of working on a given subject; while the
latter had a beautiful tone. He names also Père André,
a Benedictine, as a perfect master of the instrument,
and Marais as a scientific player; but the best pupil of
Hotman was Sainte-Colombe, who surpassed his master,
and is said, as before mentioned, to have added a seventh
string to the instrument, and to have introduced lapped
silver wires, but this is doubtful, as the same is said of
Marais.

Amongst other players of this age, the most distinguished were Biber, who was also a difficult and fanciful
composer; Michel Angelo Rossi, who played Apollo in
his own opera of "Erminio sul Giardino," 1637, and
proved his title to the name by his sweet and graceful
melody; Marco Fraticelli, who surpassed all previous
performers on the viol da gamba; and Carlo Ambrosio
Lunati, of Milan, commonly called Il Gobbo della
Regina, who went to England in the time of James II.
The celebrated singer Leonora Baroni was also an
excellent player on the theorbo and viol. Pierre Pièche,
who was appointed "musicien et garde des instrumens
do la musique de la chambre du roi," on March 3,
1672, may be named for another reason, connected with
an ancient custom of the French court. Previous to
this time it had been customary to keep dwarfs as well

as fools as court appendages, but the practice was now abolished, and the salary that had been given to Baltzard Pinson, nain, was transferred to Pièche. Ernest Henri Hesse, born in 1676, became one of the best players on the bass-viol in Germany. It is said he went to Paris in 1698, where he stayed three years, and took lessons at the same time from Marais and De Torqueray, unknown to each other. Each boasted of the superiority of his pupil, and they determined to test the merits of their respective scholars at a public concert, when, to their surprise and disappointment, they discovered the identity. Schnittelbach, of Lubeck, about 1660, was a fine performer, and the teacher of Strungk, one of the greatest players of his age. His visit to Corelli is no doubt known to many of our readers. In answer to Corelli's inquiry if he could play, he said he could do so a little, but should wish to hear Corelli, who accordingly gratified him. Strungk then took up the instrument and ran carelessly over the strings, upon which Corelli complimented him, and said that with practice he would make an excellent player. Strungk then altered the pitch of all the strings, and played with such skill that Corelli exclaimed, "They call me Arcangelo, but by heavens, sir, you must be Archidiavolo." Corelli, who was born in 1653, was a fine player himself, with a clear sweet tone ; his celebrated compositions may be studied and practised with much advantage even at the present day. His quiet and retiring behaviour when present at a large assembly where there was much talking, and therefore much interruption, was somewhat different to that of Viotti in a similar position. The latter, when about to play a concerto at the French court, had just commenced, when a cry was raised of "Place à monseigneur le Comte d'Artois!" The usual bustle ensued,

in the midst of which Viotti placed his fiddle under his arm
and walked off, to the great astonishment of the company,
nor would he play in public again for a considerable
time. Corelli, in his case, put his fiddle quietly on the
table, saying he was afraid he disturbed the conversation.

The musician Maugard was an abbé, and formed one
of the band of the Cardinal Richelieu. He played very
finely on the bass-viol, but was deficient in other respects,
and ill-conducted; his forehead was particularly narrow
in shape. He in some way or other offended the Abbé
de Bois-Robert, who, however, professed to be reconciled,
and recommended him to apply to the cardinal for the
Abbaye de Crâne-étroit, which he told him was about
to become vacant. The unconscious victim accordingly
went to his great master to beg the vacant benefice.
The cardinal, suspecting the author of the joke, could
hardly refrain from laughter, but told him he should
have the appointment, which he would no doubt retain
for the rest of his life. Maugard went directly to the
cardinal's secretary, a grave, solemn personage, to
arrange, as he supposed, the formal part with him; but
the secretary, looking at him in a contemptuous manner,
asked him how he dared come about the Abbaye de
Crâne-étroit, which existed nowhere except in his face.
The disappointed abbé then began to suspect the hoax,
and kept out of the way for some time, to escape the
jokes against him.

Corelli's concertos, trios, and solos have been frequently
played in public, until within the last few years, especially
during the existence of the Ancient Concerts; and the
delightful performance of the ninth solo, and in the
eleventh trio of the second set by Lindley and Dragonetti,
will never be forgotten by those who heard them. One
of the last performances in public of the inimitable

K

Lindley was in that trio at the Philharmonic concert.
Torelli's concertos appeared three years before those of
Corelli, and he is therefore called the inventor of the
concerto grosso.   Burney says the first trios for two
violins and a bass, were by Turini, in 1624; and in
1652 Gregorio Allegri published some quartetts for two
violins, tenor and bass.   There were also other writers
for these instruments in different manners.   We may
refer, though the want of competent performers seems
strange, to the anecdote in Mr. Chappell's work from
Corette, that when the Regent Duke of Orleans wished
to hear Corelli's sonatas, he was obliged to employ three
singers, as no performers of sufficient skill could be procured.   Those who know these trios will think there are
some queer passages for the voice.

In Brossard's Dictionary the following varieties of the
viol are named at the end of the seventeenth century :—
Viola d'amor, with six wire strings ; viola de bardone, a
large viol, reaching to as many as forty-four strings, and
a strange instrument therefore ; viola basso, viola bas-
tardo, viola da braccio, or bratz, viola da gamba ; viola
1ma, haute-contre de violon ; viola 2da, taille de violon ;
viola 3tia, quinte de violon ; viola 4ta, alto viola, or
haute-contre ; tenore viola, or taille ; violetta, diminutive
of viola, violono, violoncello, properly the quinte de
violon, or petite basse de violon, with five or six strings ;
violone, the basse de violon, or double-bass.

Michel Todini, an ingenious person and a skilful
player on the musette, born at Saluzzo about 1625,
invented several curious instruments, and amongst them
was a viol da gamba which comprised all the four gradations of the viol.   He is also said—but we should
think this doubtful—to have been the inventor of the
double-bass, to which he gave four strings.   In Bonanni's

"Gabinetto Armonico," 1722, there is a representation of a curious instrument of the organ class invented by him, which had four distinct sets of keys, so placed that if required they could be played on by four different players at the same time, or one alone could manage the instrument. It was stated to be at the palace of Signor Verospi at Rome.

Mr. Lidel on the 22nd Nov. 1849, exhibited at a meeting of the Society of Antiquaries a viol-shaped instrument made by Tielke, 1687, which he called a barytone. It had six gut strings passing over a bridge, and fastened to an ebony tail-piece, that were played on with the bow; and eleven steel strings, which went under the bridge and were fastened to an ebony bar placed there obliquely. The steel wires vibrated from sympathy with the gut strings when the latter were struck with the bow, and the round and mellow tones of the one set of strings mingled with the crisp and metallic sound of the other, and produced a peculiarly pleasing effect, well adapted to soft music, as notturnos, &c. This instrument was exhibited as a viol d'amour at the conversazione of the Musical Society of London, July 2, 1862, and Mr. Lidel informed us that it had been given by the then Bishop of Salzburg to his grandfather, who was the composer of Lidel's "Duetts for Violin and Tenor," and other music where the viola is brought prominently forward.

CHAPTER X.

THERE are constant allusions to the violin and viol, and even to the name of crowd as previously mentioned, as well as to other instruments, in the English writers, dramatic and otherwise, in the seventeenth century; and the violin begins to obtain the favour over its older kin. In Ben Jonson's "Bartholomew Fair," Lanthorn Leatherhead, the hobby-horse man, offers amongst other toys, "What do you lack? what is't you buy? what do you lack? rattles, drums, halberts, horses, babies o' the best, fiddles of the finest." Afterwards he offers for the son of one of his customers a fiddle to make him a reveller. In the same author's "Sad Shepherd," Robin Hood says—

> "The woodman met the damsels and the swaines,
> The neatherds, plowmen, and the pipers loud,
> And each did dance, some to the kit or crowd,
> Some to the bagpipe, some the tabret mor'd."

Here we have the kit and crowd, and also the bagpipe, probably one like the musette, as instruments to dance to; and in Drayton's "Fairy Wedding" crowds and bagpipes are both introduced, the commencing word violins being probably addressed to the performers.

> "Violins, strike up aloud,
> Ply the gittern, scour the crowd!

Let the nimble hand belabour
The whistling pipe, and drumbling tabor ;
To the full the bagpipe rack,
Till the swelling leather crack."

In his "Polyolbion," in the description of a musical contest between the English and Britons, he names many instruments then in common use, of which the following are connected with our subject :—

" The trembling lute some touch, some straine the violl beat,
In sets which there were scene, the musick wondrous choice :
Some likewise there affect the gamba with the voice,
To show that England could varietie afford,
Some that delight to touch the sterner wyerie chord ;
The cythron, the pandore, and the theorbo strike :
The gittern and the kit, the wandring fidlerd like."

Earle, in his " Microcosmography," 1728, says of a poor fiddler, he " is a man and a fiddle out of case, and he in worse case than his fiddle." " A country wedding and Whitsun-ale are the two main places he domineers in, where he goes for a musician, and overlooks the bagpipe." Stephens, in his " Essays and Characters," 1615, gives the following account : " A fiddler is, when he plays well, a delight only for them who have their hearing ; but is, when he plays ill, a delight only for those who have not their hearing." Many will agree with this opinion now.

A company or party of fiddlers was frequently called a noise. One of the characters in " The Dutch Courtezan," by Marston, with the unpoetic name of Mulligrubbe, says, " O, wife ! O, wife ! O, Jacke ! how does thy mother ? Is there any fidlers in the house ? " *Mrs. Mul.* " Yes, Mr. Creakes noyse." *Mul.* " Did 'em play, laugh, make merry." They not only frequented houses of resort, but different sets seem to have attended particular houses, and they were frequently

treated with very little ceremony. An illustration of
this will be found in " Westward Hoe," by Webster and
Dekker, in the beginning of this century. A character
called Monopoly says, " Where's this noise? what a
lousy town's this! Has Brainford no music in it? "
Chamberlain (of the Sun). " They are but rosining,
sir, and they'll scrape themselves into your company
presently." *Mon.* " Plague a' their cat's-guts and their
scraping: dost not see women here, and can we, thinkst
thou, be without a noise then? " Soon afterwards the
fiddlers appear on the stage, and Sir Gosling Glowworm,
a spendthrift, says to them in the style of the gallants of
those days, " What set of villains are you, you perpetual
ragamuffins? " to which they quietly answer, as if used
to such manners, " The town consort, sir." He takes
them out with him and says, " — the chamberlain shall
put a crown for you into his bill of items." The rosining
or tuning referred to was probably a subject of complaint
in those times, just as at present in a band not sufficiently
well regulated, as Massinger says in " The Guardian "—

> " Wire-string and cat-gut men, and strong-breath'd hoboys,
> For the credit of your calling have not your instruments
> To tune when you should strike up."

In former times, as occasionally in the present, usurers
or money-lenders used to require the borrower to take
as part of the loan, certain articles of which the value
was appraised by the benevolent lender, such as choice
pictures, fine wines, and sometimes much more homely
articles. In " The Miser," by Shadwell, the character
who gives the name to the play, treats his borrower
harmoniously, including in his advance, " a Bolonia lute,
a Roman arch-lute, two gittars, a Cremonia violin, 1 lyra
viol, 1 viol de gambo, and a trump marin." Middleton,
in his play of " The Witch," in one of the scenes of

conjuring or enchantment introduces a cat playing on the fiddle; but the well-known nursery rhyme is older than this, and the fact of equal authenticity in both. We have a curious old French print, where there is a cat playing on the fiddle, and a dog with a fool's-cap, dancing; a pantaloon is also playing on the guitar; there are the figures of two fools in the engraving, one with a fool's-cap looking in through a sort of window, the other is having his head washed by a female figure called La Folie; in a chimney corner is a fat unwieldy figure with Mardy Gras as his legend, whilst an old woman is preparing cakes. Pussy's fiddle is of the viol character, with four strings and no frets. The print is called "Le Diuertissement de Mardy Gras." It has twelve lines at the bottom, of which the following four are connected with our subject :—

> " La grotesque rejouissance
> Du chat jouant du violon,
> et du chien qui dance en cadence
> de la guitarre a pantalon."

Many allusions are made to females playing on the viol da gamba, but we will only refer here to a ballad of the time of Charles I. in Mr. Chappell's book, called " Keep a good tongue in your head," where a wife is described as having numerous good qualities.

> " She sings and she plays
> And she knows all the keys
> of the viol de gambo, or lute,"

but,

> " She cannot rule her tongue."

Now, we are told that " The tongue is a little member, and boasteth great things;" " But the tongue can no man tame." As an old carol says—

> " off al the enmys that I can fynd,
> The tong is most enmy to mankynd."

Remember, however, that the tongue masculine is also here comprised; for who is there that cannot appreciate and has not rejoiced at the gentle voice of woman?—the first that enlivens us in the opening morning of life, and frequently the last that soothes us in the hour of death. In the hours of sickness, the hours of sadness, the hours of deep trial and affliction—which have or will come to all—the hours when the mind dwells impatiently on lost opportunities, and long practised errors, and futile sacrifices to the glare and vanities of the world, how often does the soft, kind voice of woman cheer the oppressed mind, and restore its lost power and vigour.

The directions given for music in the different dramas and masques of the age, the latter of which were frequent at court, will show how the viols and violins were used indiscriminately; the juxtaposition of some of the instruments will appear strange to our modern arrangements. In Marston's "Sophonisba," about 1606, the music of the fourth act is composed of organs, viols, and voices; and towards the end of the act "a treble viall, &c. a base lute, play softly within the canopy," and just previously there is "infernall music playing softly." At the opening of the fifth act the music is confined to "a base lute and a treble violl." In Campion's masque at Lord Hay's marriage, of the same date, on one side are mentioned ten musicians with bass and mean lutes, a bandora, a double sack-bote, and an harpsichord, with two treble violins; and on the other side, nine violins and three lutes. In the masque of "Silenus," 1613, Silenus has for his music, a tabor and pipe, a base violin, a treble violin, a sackbut, and a mandora; while Kawasha has a bobtail, a blind harper and his boy, a base violin, a tenor cornet, and a sackbut. We find in some of the accounts the payments made to the violins and others connected with these masques, and otherwise engaged by the court, and the names of the leading persons. As in 1610, at a masque given by Queen Anne, Thomas Lupo, who was a distinguished performer on the instrument, had 5*l.* for setting the dances to the violins; the ten violins that continually practised to the queen, 20*l.*, and four more that were added at the masque, 4*l.* In the Prince's Masque and Barriers, 1611, the same Thomas Lupo again had 5*l.* for setting the dances; the company of violins, 32*l.*, and Thomas Lupo the elder, Alexander Chisan, and Rowland Rubidge, violins, 10*l.* In a court masque in 1613, where the celebrated Inigo Jones had 50*l.* for superintending, the same Thomas Lupo had 10*l.* and John Coperary, who we may assume was the skilful John Coperario, or Cooper, was paid 20*l.*; and ten of the king's violins received 10*l.* On the 23rd Nov. 1607, there is a warrant to pay Daniel Farrant, one of the king's musicians, for the violins, 46*l.* per annum. On the 22nd March, 1608, Alex. Chesham (the same, no doubt, as Alexander Chisan) was appointed one of his Majesty's musicians for the violins; and on the 6th February, 1612, Horatio Lupo had a grant of the place of the musician on the violin for life. Charles Guerolt and Thomas Giles appear at different times as instructors in music of Prince Henry, with annuities of 100 marks each. This prince, it is known, died young; but whether in consequence of a cold taken at the time of the visit of the Count Palatine to marry his sister Elizabeth, or from other causes hinted at, it is foreign to our purpose to inquire into.

Charles I. was not only a great patron of music, but also a fine player on the bass-viol or viol da gamba himself, especially in " those incomparable phantasios of Mr. Coperario to the organ," which had an accompaniment for one violin and a bass-viol. Charles was a pupil of Coperario, who himself excelled as a performer on the viol da gamba. Charles's band in 1625 consisted of eight players on the hautboys and sackbuts, and among them Richard Blagrave; six players on the flute; six players on recorders; eleven players on violins, including Thomas Lupo, who is termed composer; six players on lutes, and among them Nicholas Lanier; four players on viols, including Alphonso Ferrabosco; one player on the harp; one keeper of the organs, and fifteen musicians for the lutes and voices, including Coperario, besides trumpeters, drummers, and fifers. On December 22, 1625, there is a discharge to his Majesty's musicians from payment of the two subsidies granted by parliament; but it does not appear whether this was from inability to pay, or in reward; but as all are included we may consider it to have been the latter. On the 20th July, 1628, there was a similar discharge from five subsidies. By warrant, dated July 11, 1626, the following payments were directed to be made :—To Nicholas Lanier, Master of the King's Music, 200l. per annum; Thomas Foord, 120l.; Robert Johnson, 60l.; Thomas Day, 64l.; and to Alfonso Ferrabosco, Thomas Lupo, and ten others, 40l.; and to two others, 20l. each. On the 7th of the same month Ferrabosco was appointed composer of music in ordinary for life, with a yearly fee of 40l., in the place of John Coperario, deceased. Many similar examples might be cited, and liveries were also given, as for instance, Oct. 22, 1628: Warrant to the wardrobe for liveries to Alfonso Ferrabosco, musician for the viols, and Henry Ferrabosco, musician for the voices and wind instruments; and Nov. 22 in the same year, a warrant to the Treasurer of the Chamber, to pay Nicholas Picart, one of his Majesty's musicians of the violins, for his wages, 30*l.* per annum, and 16*l.* 2*s.* 6*d.* per annum for his entertainment, apparel, and livery, for life.

The name of Blagrave or Blagrove was connected with the court entertainments, and distinguished in music, at a very early period, as it is at the present time. Thomas Blagrove was Master of the Revels in the time of Queen Elizabeth, and William Blagrove was Master of the Children of the Revels in the reign of Charles I. Richard Blagrove and Thomas Blagrove were successively in the same king's band of musicians for wind instruments, the latter having been appointed in 1642, in the room of his father, deceased. He had 20*d.* per diem as salary, and 16*l.* 2*s.* 6*d.* for livery, being the same as his father, and money being worth nearly five times what it is now. There was a Thomas Blagrove of a Berkshire family, who was a gentleman of the chapel of Charles II, and a player on the cornet there; he was probably the Thomas Blagrove of Charles I.'s band. He, with a Robert Blagrove, were members of Charles II.'s celebrated private band, the first with a salary of 40*l.* 9*s.* 2*d.*, and the last with 58*l.* 4*s.* 2*d.*

In the accounts of James I. there is a charge of 40*l.* for a set (probably a chest) of viols for the king, and 32*l.* for another set, and a base-vyoll for the prince; a high price, considering the value of money before referred to. Alphonso Ferrabosco had a warrant on Nov. 27, 1604, for 20*l.* to buy two viols with cases, and one box of strings, for the use and service of the prince. About 1610, two great viols for him are charged 40*l.* while a lute and viol and other necessaries for a singing-boy are only 5*l.* 18*s.* 4*d.*

James I. incorporated the musicians of London, when

they had for arms, Azure, a swan argent within a tressure
counter-flure, or ; in a chief, gules, a rose between lions,
or ; for crest, the celestial sign Lyra, called by astro-
nomers, the Orphean Lyre.   Charles I. in his eleventh
year (confirmed in his fourteenth) granted a charter to
Nicholas Laniere and others, incorporating them by the
style of " Marshall Wardens and Cominalty of the Arte
and Science of Musick in Westminster, in the county of
Middlesex," and gave them many privileges. They seem
to have been in abeyance during the civil commotions
and the rule of the Puritans, but were revived in 1661.
Their rules from October 22, 1661, to July 20, 1679,
are preserved in Harleian MS. 1911.   They claimed
considerable control over musicians ; for instance, on
January 20, 1662, " It is ordered that Edward Sadler
for his insufficiency be silenced and disabled from the
exercise of any kind in publique houses or meetings." In
the following month, perhaps to prevent their exceeding
their powers, Mr. Richard Graham was " entertained
their solicitor at law."

Braithwaite, in his " Rules for the Government of the
House of an Earl," in the time of James I, says he
should keep five musicians, who should play on the bass-
viol, the virginals, the lute, and the bandora or cittern.
At the time of any great feast, the service was to be
accompanied by sackbuts, cornets, shawms, and other
instruments, while during the repast, viols and violins
were to be played.   There is a representation given by
Strutt (" Manners and Customs," vol. iii. plate 11) of
a music party of about this date, consisting of six male
figures at a table, playing from music books ; three have
instruments of the guitar kind, one the flute, one a
violin, held low against his breast, having four strings,
S S sound-holes, a bridge, tail-piece, and finger-board ;

no frets. The remaining performer plays on a viol da gamba laid across his thighs, having five strings but seven pegs, S S sound-holes, and finger-board; but there is no appearance of frets, bridge, or tail-piece, which, as to the two latter, may be a mere omission in the original picture. The instrument itself is thick and short.

The quaint writer Tom Coryat, who is said to have introduced the use of forks into this country, for which reason he was called Furcifer, gives an amusing account of music at Venice on August 5, 1608, "especially that of a treble violl, which was so excellent that I thinke no man could surpasse it." On the following day he was still more fortunate. "I was for the time euen rapt vp with St. Paul into the third heauen. Sometimes there sung sixteene or twenty men together, bauing their master or moderator to keepe them in order, and when they sung, the instrumentall musitians played also. Sometimes sixteene played together upon their instruments—ten sagbuts, foure cornets, and two violde-gamboes of an extraordinary greatnesse; sometimes tenne, sixe sagbuts and foure cornets; sometimes two, a cornet and a treble violl. Of those treble viols I heard three seuerall there, whereof each was so good, especially one that I obserued aboue the rest, that I neuer heard the like before." He says the players on the treble viols sung and played together, and that there were two fine players on the theorbo, who also sung. The eccentric writer John Taylor, the Water Poet, seems to have been equally in raptures during his travels abroad in 1610. He describes at a town he calls Buckaburgh, not far from Minden, belonging to the Graff of Shomburgh, "a faire set of organs, with a braue sweete quire of queristers; so that when they sing, the lutes, viols, bandores, organs, recorders, sagbuts, and other musicall instruments all

strike vp together, with such a glorious delicious harmony,
as if the angelicall musicke of the sphcares were descended into that earthly tabernacle."

There were numerous publicatious in the first half of
this century (to those in the second half we shall refer
hereafter) adapted for violins and viols, and again the
strange fellowship of instruments will amuse. A few
examples must suffice, but all that are connected with
madrigals and songs of this period will be found in
" Bibliotheca Madrigaliana," by Dr. Rimbault, whose
accurate research and extensive knowledge of the literature and music of this age are well known.

Among the earliest publications in the century are
those by Thomas Weelkes, of "Madrigals of five and
six Parts, apt for Viols and Voices;" by Dowland, the
celebrated lutenist, of " Songs or Ayres, with Tablature
for the Lute or Orpherion, with the Violl de Gamba,"
and by Morley, " Aires, or Little Short Songes to sing
and play to the Lute with the Bass-viol," all in 1600.
In 1603 Thomas Robinson published "The School of
Musicke; the perfect Method of true fingering the
Lute, Pandora, Orpharion, and Viol da Gamba."
Tobias Hume, called also Captain Hume, who was himself an excellent performer on the viol da gamba, published in 1605 a work with the following curious title,
to attract amateurs; a practice not lost sight of in the
present age, when occasionally the best part of a work
is contained in a promising advertisement, or an important but fallacious title-page:—" The First Part of
Ayres, French, Pollish, and others together, some in
Tabliture, and some in Pricke-song. With Pavines,
Galliards, and Almaines for the Viole de Gambo alone,
and other Musicall Conceites for Two Base-viols, expressing Five Partes, with pleasant Reportes one from the

other, and for Two Leero Viols, and also for the Leero
Viole with Two Treble Viols, or Two with One Treble.
Lastly, for the Leero Viole to play alone, and some
Songes to be sung to the Viole, with the Lute, or better,
with the Viole alone.   Also an Invention for Two to
play upon One Viole."   We have ourselves heard two
performers play a duett on one violin.   Captain Hume
in 1607 published "Poeticall Musicke," where the bass-
viol is varied with other instruments in eight different
ways. In 1609 Rosseter published "Lessons for Consort,
for Six severall Instruments—Treble-Lute, Treble-Violl,
Base-Violl, Bandora, Citterne, and the Flute."   A short
time before this, John Dowland published, "Lacrimœ,
or Seaven Teares figured in Seaven passionate Pavans,
with divers other Pavans, Galiards, and Almands, set
forth for the Lute, Viols, or Violons, in Five Parts."
Here we observe viols and violins are both mentioned
together. About 1611 the celebrated Orlando Gibbons
brought out "Fantasies of Three Parts for Viols."

The pavans, galliards, almaines, and corantos named
in many of these publications, to which Morley adds the
passamezzo, the jig, the hornpipe, the Scottish jig, and
others, were tunes adapted to dances of the same name.

The pavans, almaines, corantos, and passamezzos,
were slow, solemn dances ; the pavans being so called
from pavo, a peacock, the ladies wearing gowns with
long trains, the gentlemen having a cap and sword ;
those of the long robe in their gowns, and princes and
peers in their mantles; the movements resembling the
spread of the peacock's tail. A great contrast to the
sliding shuffle or hop of the present day, which by
courtesy is considered to be dancing ; though even this
is graceful in the fair sex, especially when two dance
together.   Sir Christopher Hatton we know was a great

dancer, and in the " Critic " is made to turn out his toes
by way of identity : as Gray says—

> " Full oft within the spacious walls,
>   When he had fifty winters o'er him,
>   My grave lord-keeper led the brawls ;
>   The seal and maces danc'd before him."

Sir W. Leighton, in " Teares, or Lamentations of a
Sorrowful Soule," 1613, has introduced in one of the
pieces, which may be considered as a paraphrase of the
150th Psalm, the names of numerous musical instruments,
but the description is too long to be inserted here. Two
verses will suffice to show his style—

> " 3. Praise him with simballs, loud simballs,
>   with instruments were va'd by Iewes :
>   With syrons crowdes and virginalls,
>   to sing his praise do not refuse.
>   4. Praise him upon the claricoales,
>   the lute and sinfonie,
>   With dulscmers and the regalls,
>   sweet sithrons melody."

The gittron, bandore, theorba, and vialls are also
mentioned.

We may conclude this chapter by stating that Edward
Alleyn, the benevolent founder of Dulwich College, was
himself a performer on the lute, and at the time of his
death, Nov. 25, 1626, had a " lute, a pandora, a cythern,
and six vyols."

CHAPTER XI.

IT would seem from some accounts that Cromwell was not insensible to the charms of music, when he could unbend, or was in his own private domestic circle, although publicly he yielded to the Puritan feeling of his age. Theatrical representations were restrained, and music checked, although still practised in private; and in 1656-7 an act was passed against vagrants, forbidding any fiddlers or minstrels to go about to inns, ale-houses, or taverns, &c.

On the restoration of Charles II, music and festive meetings again flourished, and the revels and gaieties of the court spread in different degrees through society in general. The superiority of the violin over the viol was gradually established, as it was found to be more capable of producing power, and better adapted for execution than the latter instrument, of which the tone was frequently sweet, but at the same time of a nasal quality, and deficient in vigour. The violin proper, as we have shown, was known in England at least a century before this time, and we may have received some suggestions tending towards the modification of the viol to the form and details of the violin from the Low Countries in the time of Elizabeth, when the intercourse between the countries was not unfrequent. The first violin-makers,

L

however, of any great repute, established themselves in
Italy, where the wood probably was particularly suitable.

Charles II, in imitation of the French court, introduced his celebrated band of twenty-four violins, or, as
Durfey says,—

> "Four and twenty fiddlers all of a row,
> And there was fiddle, fiddle,
> And twice fiddle, fiddle,
> 'Cause 'twas my lady's birth-day,
> Therefore we kept holiday,
> And all went to be merry."

This band consisted of six violins, six counter-tenors,
six tenors, and six basses, with salaries varying from
40l. to 100l. per annum. The celebrated Baltzar, the
"incomparable Lubicer," who had come over to England
a few years before, was at the head of it. The anthems
and services in the Chapel Royal were sung to these
instruments instead of the ancient wind instruments,
and Evelyn complains of their French fantastical light
way of playing there. The organ was also in use.

At the commencement of Dryden's "Tempest," about
1667, the front of the stage was opened, and the band
of twenty-four violins, with the "harpsicals" and theor-
bos, which accompanied the voices, were placed between
the pit and the stage. The band was therefore placed
just as in the present time, and this seems the first notice
of their having any regular position. These twenty-
four violins were either the celebrated four-and-twenty
fiddlers, or a rival company in imitation of them. Durney
says that the different expressions of crescendo, diminu-
endo, and lentando, were first used by Matthew Lock,
in the music to the "Tempest." In Lock's own piece
of "Psyche," about 1675, no instruments are mentioned
for the ritornels but violins.

Music parties were now frequent. Anthony Wood,

who was himself a self-taught performer on the violin, which he tuned in fourths until better instructed by one Charles Griffith, gives an account of these meetings; some being before the Restoration, but in a quiet way. Gentlemen who attended them "play'd three, four, and five parts with viols, as treble-viol, tenor, counter-tenor, and bass, with an organ, virginal, or harpsicon. They esteemed a violin to be an instrument only belonging to a common fidler, and could not endure that it should come among them, for feare of making their meetings to be vaine and fidling. But before the restoration of King Charles II, and especially after, viols began to be out of fashion, and only violins used as treble-violin, tenor, and bass-violin; and the king, according to the French mode, would have twenty-four violins playing before him while he was at meales, as being more airie and brisk than viols."

He mentions among his friends, Ralph Sheldon, admired for his smooth and admirable way in playing on the viol; Thomas Jackson, a bass-violist; William Ellis, counter-tenor viol; Gervace Littleton, a violist; Will Glexney play'd well on the bass-viol; Joh. Haselwood, an apothecary, a conceited player on the bass-viol, sometimes on the counter-tenor, with little skill— being ever ready to take up a viol before his betters, was called Handlewood; Proctor (a pupil of the celebrated John Jenkyns), skilled on the lyra-viol, division-viol, treble-viol, and treble-violin; Nathan Crew, afterwards Bishop of Durham, violinist and violist, but always out of tune; Richard Rhodes, a confident Westmonasterian, a violinist, to hold between his knees; Matthew Hutton, excellent violist; and several other violists. He tells an amusing anecdote of himself and some of his companions. Himself and Will. Bull on the violins, Edm. Gregorie,

B.A. and Gent. Com. of Mert. Coll., who played on the bass-viol, Joh. Nap, of Trinity, on the citerne; and George Mason of the said Coll. on another wyer instrument, but could do nothing. They disguised themselves in poor habits, like country fiddlers, and went about to the country places, receiving drink and money for their performances. On one occasion they were met by some soldiers, who made them play in the open field, and then left them without giving them a penny. Other players named were Charles Perot, Christopher Harrison, John Vincent, Sylvanus Taylor, Henry Langley, Samuel Woodford, and Francis Parry, violists; and Kenelm Digby, violinist. Mr. Sherard, an apothecary, was a fine player on the violin, and Capt⁰ Marcellus Laroon on the violoncello. Lord Keeper North and Sir Roger L'Estrange were both fine players on the viol. Much interesting information relating to music will be found in Dr. Rimbault's edition of "North's Memoirs of Musick."

The lyra-viol, on which Proctor excelled, and which is frequently mentioned among the instruments of this time (the leero-viole in Hume's work lately referred to), and on which Pepys says his brother played so as to show that he had "a love to musique and a spirit for it," was a viol da gamba tuned differently from the common six-stringed bass, and the notation for it was written in tablature, like that of the lute. Playford says, this way of playing the viol was of recent invention, and an imitation of the old English lute or bandora. John Jenkyns, the master of Proctor, was the best performer on it then known. There would appear, however, to be some allusion to such an instrument or mode of playing, quite in the beginning of the century, as in "Lingua," by Anthony Brewer, about the end of Elizabeth, Tactus says, "But, Auditus, when shall we hear a new set of singing-books? or the viols? or the concert of instruments?" and afterwards, "Come, come, Auditus, shall we hear thee play the lyre-way or the lute-way, shall we?" Daniel Farrant, towards the beginning of the century, was one of the first who set lessons for the viol lyra-way.

That amusing writer Pepys was in the habit of frequenting musical parties as well as the theatres, where his flirtations with Mrs. Knipps and others, render it not surprising that he was occasionally obliged to keep his wife in good humour by the present of some piece of finery. He was also himself a practised musician on the lute, violin, viol, and flageolet, besides being able to sing at sight. He seems to have had a tolerable estimate of his own skill (a habit of thinking not yet obsolete). On 21st Nov. 1660, he says, "At night to my viallin (the first time that I have played on it since come to this house), in my dining roome, and afterwards to my lute there, and I took much pleasure to have the neighbours come forth into the yard to hear me." Dec. 3rd. "Rose by candle, and spent my morning in fiddling till time to go to the office." He occasionally favoured his wife with his music, to solace her domestic labours, which, according to the Diary, frequently consisted of those little artistic re-arrangements of dress so well known to ladies. 12th April, 1669, "Home, and after sitting a while, thrumming upon my viall, and singing, I to bed, and left my wife to do something to a waistcoat and petticoat she is to wear to-morrow."

He was not, however, satisfied with being a mere practical musician, but aspired to improving the theory, for on the 20th of March, 1668, he was "All the evening pricking down some things, and trying some

conclusions upon my viall, in order to the inventing a
better theory of musick than hath yet been abroad; and
I think, verily, I shall do it." However, we do not find
that he did do it, but in this he only failed with other
great men.

It might be considered presumptuous in us to suggest
even, whether the rules of harmony might not be somewhat simplified; but in such case, what would become
of the learning of those who know the nomenclature,
are acquainted with the tools, but know little of the
working, yet still keep you at bay with hard terms,
unless you are able to meet them with their own weapons.
However, all professions, whether musical, medical, legal,
or carpentering, must have their technicalities, though
the genius of the age is tending gradually to remove or
lessen them. Even, however, with the use of them we
cannot fix on the pitch in music. We find a certain
natural note has thirty-two vibrations, and *therefore* fix
upon a certain number of vibrations, the figures denoting
which form no multiple of 32, as the recognised pitch
of a note of the same name four octaves higher. We
are not agreed upon the division of the minor scale—
scarcely, indeed, of the major—and as to the variation
in the different keys, involving however, probably, some
troublesome calculations, we can give little if any explanation. Harrison, the celebrated chronometer-maker,
as mentioned in Smith's " Harmonics," took the interval
of a major third to that of the octave, as the diameter of
a circle to its circumference, and adjusted the frets on
his viol accordingly; so that, as the circumference of a
circle is a little more than three diameters (that is, about
3¼), so is a perfect octave a little more than three major
thirds. However, under all circumstances, it is not
surprising that Pepys did not do it.

He refers to different companies of musicians. The Dolphin Tavern had " an excellent company of fiddlers," and on the 27th March, 1661, he goes there " to a dinner of Mr. Harris's, where a great deal of mirth, and there staid till eleven o'clock at night; and in our mirth I sang and sometimes fiddled (there being a noise of fiddlers there), and at last we fell to dancing, the first time that ever I did in my life, which I did wonder to see myself to do." That habit of doing something to be wondered at, towards the conclusion of a tavern dinner, we are told still exists occasionally in this country. He mentions the Duke of Buckingham's musicians, to whom on one occasion he gave 3l. for a dance at his own house, as the best in town; they consisted of two violins, a buss-violin, and a theorbo. The witty Killigrew said that no ordinary fiddlers of any country were so well paid as our own. Heylin, in his " Voyage of France," 1679, says it was the custom at Tours for each man at table to pay the fiddlers a sou; they expected no more, and would not take less. Pepys was probably considered as an authority in his own circle for musical arrangements. On 7th May, 1660, Admiral Sir Edward Montagu, afterwards Earl of Sandwich, whom he calls " my Lord," gave him directions " to write for silk flags and scarlet waistcloathes; for a rich barge, for a noise of trumpets, and a set of fiddlers." On 10th April, 1661, he gives an account of a duet, not complimentary to the performers. " Here (Rochester) we had for my sake two fiddles, the one a base-viall, on which he that played, played well some lyra lessons, but both together made the worst musique that ever I heard." On the Coronation Day, 23rd April, 1661, he took a great deal of pleasure " to go up and down, and look upon the ladies, and to hear the musique of all sorts; but above all, the

twenty-four violins." On 8th May following he refers to
a circumstance which sometimes occurs in the present
day, of a country fiddler having been a person who had
seen better days. His uncle had written him to beg an
old fiddle for Perkin the miller, whose mill the wind had
broken down, and he had nothing to live by but fiddling;
he wanted it by Whitsuntide to play to the country girls.
Pepys adds that he intended to send him one on the
morrow. On the 5th Oct. 1664, he describes an instrument called the arched viall, tuned with lute strings,
and played on with keys like an organ, a piece of parchment being always kept moving; the strings being
pressed down by the keys, were thus scraped as by a
bow; and it was intended to represent several viols
played on with one bow, "but so basely and harshly
that it will never do." After three hours' stay it could
not be fixed in tune. Several instruments on this prin-
ciple have from time to time been invented, but have
not been brought into use.

In July, 1666, he heard one of Lord Lauderdale's
servants play some Scotch tunes on the violin, which he
did not appreciate, or the selection was bad, or our best
Scotch tunes are of more recent date, as no doubt many
are. The performer played "several and the best of
their country, as they seem to esteem them. by their
praising and admiring them: but, Lord! the strangest
ayre that ever I heard in my life, and all of one cast."
He mentions 8th October, 1667, the death of Saunders
by the plague at Cambridge, "the only viollin in my
time."

The greatest performer of the time, however, and one
who seems to have been in advance of his age, was
Thomas Baltzar, born at Lubeck about 1630. He came
over to England in 1655, and is said to have been the

first who taught the use of the whole shift, but it had
probably been attempted before him. He appears to
have caused almost as great a sensation in the musical
world as Paganini did, when he came over and astonished us. Anthony Wood says that at a music meeting
at Oxford, Professor Wilson stooped down humorously
to see if he had not a hoof. The following is Evelyn's
account of him, 4th March, 1655-6:—"This night I
was invited by Mr. Roger L'Estrange to hear the incomparable Lubicer on the violin. His variety on a
few notes and plaine ground with that wonderful dexterity, was admirable. Tho' a young man, yet so perfect and skilful, that there was nothing, however cross
and perplext, brought to him by our artists, which he
did not play off at sight with ravishing sweetnesse and
improvements, to the astonishment of our best masters.
In sum, he plaid on y' single instrument a full concert,
so as the rest flung down their instruments acknowledg-
ing their victory. As to my own particular, I stand to
this hour amazed that God should give so greate perfection to so young a person. There were at that time
as excellent in their profession as any were thought to
be in Europ, Paul Wheeler, Mr. Mell, and others, till
this prodigie appear'd." Davis Mell was then the
greatest English performer, and in sweetness of tone is
even said to have excelled Baltzar. The Lubicer was
made the leader of King Charles's band, but died in
July, 1663, having been of dissipated habits. He was
succeeded by John Bannister, who died in 1679, whose
son John was a fine performer on the violin, and one of
King William's band, and the first violin at Drury Lane
on the introduction of operas there.

About 1672, Nicolas Matteis came over, as great a
performer even as Baltzar. North says, every stroke

of his bow was a mouthful. Evelyn also heard him,
and thus describes him, Nov. 19th, 1674:—"I heard
that stupendous violin, Sig'. Nicholao (with other rare
musitians) whom I never heard mortal man exceed on
that instrument. He had a stroak so sweete, and made
it speak like y' voice of a man, and, when he pleas'd,
like a consort of severall instruments. He did wonders
upon a note, and was an excellent composer. Here was
also that rare lutenist Dr. Wallgrave; but nothing approach'd the violin in Nicholao's hand. He plaied such
ravishing things as astonish'd us all." On the following
2nd of December, he went to his friend Mr. Slingsby's,
the Master of the Mint, and heard Signor Francisco,
esteemed one of the greatest masters in Europe on the
harpsichord; "then came Nicholas with his violin, and
struck all mute." On the 20th November, 1679, he
again is at Mr. Slingsby's, "to heare musiq, which was
exquisitely perform'd by foure of the most renown'd
masters; Du Prue, a Frenchman, on y' lute; Sig'. Bar-
tholomeo, an Italian, on the harpsichord; Nicolao on the
violin; but above all for its sweetnesse and novelty, the
viol d'amore of 5 wyre-strings plaid on with a bow,
being but an ordinary violin, play'd on lyre way by a
German."

By a warrant dated the 24th of October, 1662, we
find that Cremona violins brought a high price, as Mr.
John Bannister, one of his Majesty's musicians in ordinary, had an order for 40l. for two Cremona violins
bought by him, and also 10l. for strings for two years.

Simpson, himself an excellent performer on the viol
da gamba, in his "Division Viol" calls the viol in Latin
chelys, and gives three figures of the instrument, which
are in fact all bass-viols. The first of these, which he
says is best for sound, is much like the modern violon-

FIG. 64.

cello, but of somewhat longer form, and has six strings
with seven frets, besides a small one in the middle of
the strings for the octave. The lower string is tuned to
the lowest D in the bass, while the others are successively
G, C, E, A, D, being two octaves; the bridge is rounded
so that each string may be taken separately. The strings
are thirty inches in length from the nut to the bridge.
The two other figures have deeper inward curvatures,
and the upper part of the model slopes off towards the
neck, instead of being rounded like the modern instrument; the strings and frets are as in the first figure
(Fig. 56). The bow is stiff but not heavy, with the hair
twenty-seven inches long, and used underhanded like the
modern double-bass bow. From the examples given by
Simpson, the performers in his time must have attained
considerable facility of execution, though probably without much tone or power.

Playford, in the "Introduction to Skill in Music,"
1683, names the treble-viol in the G cliff, the tenor-viol
in the C cliff, and the bass-viol, with six strings and
seven frets, in the F cliff; usually called the viol de
gambo or consort-viol, because the musick thereon is
played from the notes of the gamut, and not as the lyra-
viol by tablature. The bass is tuned as described by
Simpson, the treble an octave higher, and the tenor a
fourth higher than the bass; he also gives a method of
tuning by tablature. He calls the treble violin a cheerful sprightly instrument, much practised of late, usually
strung with four strings and tuned in fifths; there should
be six frets, as on the viol, but this was rarely done, and
was contrary to the character of the instrument; but, he
adds, "This (tho tis not usual yet) is the best & easiest
way for a beginner who has a bad ear;" the representation he gives has no frets. The treble violin seems to

have been tuned as at present, and the tenor a fifth lower, while the bass violin was tuned in fifths; the first string being the higher G in the bass, and the fourth therefore B flat below the line, and therefore one tone lower than the violoncello.

Mace, in his quaint book, "Musick's Monument," 1675, gives an amusing direction for the care of a lute, which he would probably extend to the violin race. He recommends the lute to be put into a bed in the day-time that is constantly used, between the rug and the blanket, but never between the sheets, because they may be moist. It will save the strings from breaking, and keep the lute in good order. He adds, no person must be so inconsiderate as to tumble down on the bed whilst it is there, as he had known several spoilt with such a trick. We should think this very probable.

" Mantua, væ miserum! nimium vicina Cremonæ."

In that once very popular book by Comenius, " Orbis Sensualium Pictus," which went through very many editions, and in several languages, among the musical instruments are introduced, "Secundo, in quibus *chordæ* intenduntur & plectuntur, ut *nablium* cum *clavicordio* utráque manu." He mentions also, " *Testudo* (cbelys) (in quâ *jugum, magadium, & verticelli*, quibus *nervi* intenduntur super *ponticulam*,) & *cythara*, dexterâ tantum, *pandura, plectro, & lyra*, intus rotâ, quæ versatur. *Dimensiones* in singulis tanguntur sinistrâ."   Thus translated : "*Secondly, upon which strings are stretched and struck upon, as the psaltery, and the* virginals, *with both hands; the* lute (*in which is the neck, the belly, the* pegs, *by which the strings are stretched upon the* bridge), *the* cittern, *with the right hand only, the* vial, *with a bow, and the* harp *with a wheel within, which*

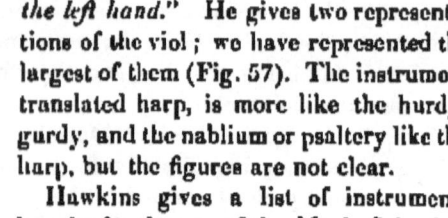

is turned about ; the stops *in every one are touched with
the left hand."* He gives two representa-
tions of the viol ; we have represented the
largest of them (Fig. 57). The instrument
translated harp, is more like the hurdy-
gurdy, and the nablium or psaltery like the
harp, but the figures are not clear.

Hawkins gives a list of instruments
bought for the use of the Music School at
Oxford, about 1667, which included " 2
violins, with their bowes and cases, bought
of Mr. Comer in the Strand ; cost 12*l.* 10*s.*

FIG. 57.

and are at 2ᵈ hand."

There were numerous publications for the varieties of
the violin and viol in the last part of this century.
Matteis had his compositions engraved on copper plates
for the use of his scholars and others, and made much
money by them.   Baltzar also composed for the violin,
viol, and " harpsicon ; " also for lyra-violin, treble-violin,
and bass.   Playford in 1655 published " Court Ayres ;
or Pavins, Almaines, Corants, and Sarabands, Treble
and Basse, for Viols or Violins ; " and in 1662, something similar ; John Jenkins, Davis Mell, and John
Bannister being among the composers.   John Jenkins,
about 1660, published twelve sonatas for two violins and
bass, with thorough bass for the organ, which are said
to have been the first of the sort known in England.
Matthew Lock and Henry Purcell both composed trios
of the same description.

There appears to have been an improvement in the
bow in this century.   It was originally made of reed or
some light and flexible wood, and in the earlier times
was much curved, somewhat similar to our double-bass
bow, and frequently of awkward make, with a strand

of coarse hair rudely stretched between the two extremities. In the sixteenth century some improvement
was made, and in the seventeenth it began to assume its
present shape, and by means of a sort of metal band
with teeth towards the handle of the bow, power was
given to alter the tension of the hair. Tourte, of Paris,
the first of this well-known family, is said to have introduced the screw and button. His son, who died in
1835, at an advanced age, made further improvements.
It is stated that he began to make them with common
wood from pipe-staffs and sugar barrels, and sold them
for twenty or thirty sous each. Afterwards he discovered
that Brazil wood was best adapted for the purpose, and
latterly sold his best bows, ornamented with mother-of-
pearl and gold, for as much as twelve louis, and those
with ebony and silver, for three and a half louis ; whilst
his common bows, without ornament, were sold for about
thirty-six francs each. He is said to have invented the
method of keeping the hair flat by means of a clasp or
plate of metal or mother-of-pearl. His violin and tenor
bows were about thirty inches long, and that for the
violoncello about an inch shorter. Simpson, we may
remember, gives twenty-seven inches as the length of
the bow, and towards the end of this century the sonata
bow, it is said, was only twenty-four inches, while the
common bow was shorter still. The usual length now
is about twenty-nine inches from the extreme point of the
head to the end of the bow, without the screw ; leaving
from twenty-five and a half to twenty-five and three
quarter inches for the useable portion of the bow. Tartini caused an improvement in this as well as other
things connected with the instrument. We need scarcely
remind our readers that we have English makers of the

bow, as Dodd, Panormo, and Tubbs, with others, who are surpassed by none.

The first of the Dodd family distinguished as a maker of bows was Edward Dodd, who was born at Sheffield, and died in Salisbury Court, Fleet Street, in 1810, at the great age, as it is stated, of 105 years. He left four sons, of whom three, John, James, and Thomas, were makers of bows; the fourth having been brought up to the medical profession. Of these, John, the eldest, is considered one of our best English makers, and his bows are much sought for. Most of them are rather short, but can easily be lengthened. He died at Richmond, where, and at Kew, he had resided for many years.

James Dodd, the eldest son of the above-named James Dodd, is now living, and supports the reputation of the family as a maker of good bows, and is also a musical-string coverer.

Louis Panormo was the son of Vincent Panormo, the instrument maker, and was himself a maker of guitars and violins. His bows were esteemed, but a lighter class is now generally preferred.

Of the family of Tubbs there are two generations still living, all excellent workmen. Thomas Tubbs, the elder of the family, died very recently, and might have vied with any workman living, especially if he could have obtained Brazil wood of fine quality for musical purposes.

CHAPTER XII.

IN 1717, the Corporation of Musicians in France had their privileges renewed under Louis XV. Lutes, violins, viols, and all wind or stringed instruments could only be made or played on by members of the Corporation, under penalty of 300 livres and forfeiture of the instruments. They were poor, however, as a body, and declared to the king that their poverty prevented them from paying the usual tribute at the time of the coronation.

Gerbert, in his valuable work " De Cantu," &c., says that stringed instruments were introduced into churches about the end of the seventeenth century, and that Campra was the first who brought them into use at Notre Dame, Paris; and they then only required two or three bass-viols or bass-violins for the continued basses, and as many violins for the preludes and ritornelles. Before this time the music in the chapel royal was confined to wind instruments. Laborde says the first masses in Italy with violins and basses, were about 1650. Tarquin Merula, master of the chapel at Bergamo, is named as one of the first musicians who introduced viols and violins into the church service in Italy, in aid of choral singing. There was great objection to their use at first, in the fear that it would tend to make the

M

sacred music too much like the secular; but Cornelius
Agrippa does not give a very flattering account of church
singing previous to their admission: " Non humanis vo-
cibus, sed belluinis strepitibus cantillent; dum hinniunt
discantum pueri, mugiunt alii tenorem, alii latrant con-
trapunctum, alii frendent altum, alii boant bassum, et
faciunt ut sonorum quidem plurimum audiatur, verbo-
rum et orationis intelligatur nihil."

Towards the middle of the eighteenth century, the
order of church music would appear to be somewhat reversed, as about 1749, Benedict XIV. refers to the use
of " violoni, violoncelli, fagotti, viole, et violini," in the
sacred services, whilst "i timpani, i corni da caccia, le
trombe, gli oboe, i flauti, i flautini, i salteri moderni,
i mandolini, & simili stromenti," were excluded. Fey-
joo, the Grand Master of the Benedictines in Spain, objected to violini, but allowed the violone called the basso,
arpa, cembalo, &c. At St. Paul's Cathedral, London,
about the time mentioned by Gerbert, there were only
four or eight voices, without any other musical instruments than the organ and the barbiton, *e.g.* fidiculare,
violoncello, theorba.

Laborde gives the composition of the orchestra of the
French opera in 1713, and also the salaries in livres, it
was the following:—

Un batteur de mesure	.	.	.	1000
Petit chœur de dix	.	.	.	6000
Douze violons	.	.	.	4800
Huit basses	.	.	.	3200
Deux quintes	.	.	.	800
Deux tailles	.	.	.	800
Trois hautes-contres	.	.	.	1200
Un tymbalier	.	.	.	150

In the year 1778, the proportions were changed, and

wind instruments introduced ; the salaries are not particularised, but the total is 69,482 livres. Un directeur, un adjoint, 24 violons, 7 flutes & hautbois, 2 clarinettes, 2 cors, 2 trompettes, 5 bassons, 6 alto, 10 basses, 4 contrebasses. The tymbales, trombones, tambourins, hautbois de foret, &c., were filled by some of the above.

The eloquent preacher, Bourdelot, was a performer on the violin, and there is an interesting anecdote of him in that capacity related by Spence. He was appointed to preach on Good-Friday, and the proper officer to attend him to church having arrived at his house, was directed to go to the study for him. As he approached he heard the sound of a violin, and the door being open a little way, saw Bourdelot stripped to his cassock playing a brisk tune on the instrument, and dancing about the room. He was much surprised, and knocked at the door, when the distinguished divine laid down his instrument, and putting on his gown, told the officer with his usual composed look that he was ready to attend him. On their way, his companion expressed to Bourdelot his surprise at what he had seen, who replied that he might be, unless made acquainted with his practice on these occasions. On thinking over the intended subject of his discourse, he found he was too depressed to treat it as he ought, and thus had recourse to his usual method—some music, with a little bodily exercise—and thus put himself into a proper frame of mind to enable him to go with pleasure to what would otherwise have been a work of pain and labour to him. It would be presumptuous in us even to hint at the adoption of such a course by any of our own spiritual pastors.

In the beginning of this century, Pere Tardieu de Tarascon is said to have introduced the violoncello as an accompaniment in the place of the viol da gamba, or

perhaps, more correctly confirmed it in the higher position of the two instruments, by means of his superior skill,
as the violoncello appears to have been used as an accompaniment before this time, and the viol da gamba did not
fall into disuse until afterwards. He used five strings at
first, four of them tuned in fifths, and the first string a
fourth higher than the present; but in 1730 this was
suppressed, the instrument then remaining as the modern
violoncello. John Sebastian Bach introduced an instrument he called the viola pomposa, in consequence, it is
said, of the heavy style of violoncello performers in his
time; a fifth string, E, was added, with the intention of
giving greater facility for the execution of the higher
passages; this instrument, however, does not appear to
have been much used. About the same time, Risch of
Weimar invented a keyed instrument, to imitate the
bass-viol, or viol da gamba; it had gut strings, played
on by small wheels properly resined, which were put in
motion by a larger wheel. De Knonow, of Haute-Lu-
sace, also made a kind of harpsichord, to be played on
with a bow; both these instruments followed the usual
fate of these inventions. A gentleman near Leeds has
invented an instrument played on by keys, the notes
being produced from gut strings by friction. At a moderate distance the sound is very good and quite orchestral,
but on nearer approach it becomes rather harsh. It is,
however, capable of being subdued in tone, and the sound
can be increased or lessened by pressure, or management
of the keys.

In the Letters of Baron de Pollnitz, he mentions, in
1739, at Mersebourg, the residence of an enthusiastic
amateur, a Duke of Saxony, a large saloon filled with
bass-viols; in the middle was one which reached to the
ceiling, and had a set of steps to mount to it, the most

powerful bass ever made. The duke himself executed some airs on a bass he called his favourite. The baron was told by one of the Court that the duke had quite a passion for these instruments, and that any one wanting a favour, made him a present of one. The giant bass was given to him by one who wished to be made a privy-councillor, and succeeded accordingly. It must have surpassed by far the great bass, of which we have formerly given an account, where a page was concealed in the body; but appears to have been rivalled afterwards by a huge double-bass, mentioned by Gardiner in his gossiping book of Music and Friends: one made for a person called Martin, who kept a public-house. It was so large that it was necessary to cut a hole in the ceiling to let the neck through, so that in fact it was tuned in the room above the player; the bow was in proportion. Boyce, a fine performer on the instrument, and a tall powerful man, went to see and try it, and with one stroke of his bow made it roar and vibrate so, as to shake the house.

In an unfinished treatise commenced by Louis Carré, who died in 1711, he mentions among the several instruments, the bass-viol, dessus de viole, archiviole, violin, poche, rebec, vielle (probably the hurdy-gurdy), and trumpet marine. Bonanni's curious "Gabinetto Armonico," 1722, abounds with representations of musical instruments, some rather fanciful, but still useful, to show the character of the instruments then in use. What he calls the viola, is like a very large violoncello, resting on the ground, with a very thick clumsy neck; the performer is sitting down; it has four strings, and no frets; the bow much like that of the double-bass. The violone is like a large double-bass, with considerable inward curvatures; there are but four strings in the representation,

although there are six screws, and Bonanni says there
are six strings ; it has also numerous frets. He mentions
another instrument of the same class, invented by the
Earl of Somerset, as referred to by Kircher, which had
eight strings.   The Latins, he says, called these instruments vitula, or vidula, or violla, whence the performers
were called vitularii. The accordo (called by Mersennus
lira moderna), to which we have before referred, was a
still larger instrument, having twelve or fifteen strings,
of which necessarily two or three were struck together ;
it also had frets. The lintercolo, or sordino, was a small

instrument of the fiddle kind,
with four strings and no frets;
it is of guitar shape, the neck
appearing to be of one piece
with the body, and with a
detached finger-board. (Fig.
58.) One of his figures is
a peasant riding on an ass,
playing on a sort of guitar,
like a banjoo with two
strings ; the performer is
evidently singing, and the
ass joining with open
mouth, forming an admira-
ble trio. The monocordo

FIG. 58.

is something like a clumsy trumpet marine, having, in
addition to the usual single string, one much shorter,
extending about half the length of the instrument, but
not nearly meeting the bridge. The tromba marina
given by him, is contracted for the space of about a third
of the length from the nut, so as to form a sort of finger-
board, though of one piece with the rest of the front ; it
has one thick string the whole length, and a small bridge

very near the bottom of the instrument; the bow is short
and like that of the double-bass. Bonanni says, that by
moving the thumb of the left hand in various places, tones
are produced like those of a trumpet (probably harmonic
notes) and that it was frequently used at sea to prevent
the trouble of blowing, and hence was called the tromba
marina. The violino represented by him is like a large
clumsy tenor; he says the Latins called it cheles, or
viola, and the Italians, viola, violino, or violone, &c.,
according to the size. The viola, or violino d'amore,
is much of the same make and style, but larger. The
violino Turchesco, used by the Turks, has a very long
neck with frets, and only two strings; the body is nearly
round and hollowed, and covered with parchment, it has
neither bridge or sound-holes, but a long foot to support
it on the ground. The Persians had a similar instrument they called Kamaantsich, in the Arab tongue
Chemena. The violino Persiano is mentioned by
Kempfer; it has four strings but no sound-holes, bridge,
finger-board, or tail-piece. The violino de' Cafri has a
small round body with a long neck, and only one string;
without bridge, finger-board, or sound-holes, and played
on with a short curved bow. An instrument of the same
sort is found among the negroes and Indians, but not
usually confined to one string. The representations of
musical instruments in this work bear a very liberal in-
terpretation, as he includes the whistle, the brass pan for
bees, the rattle, the comb, and even the postilion's whip,
with others equally simple.

Laborde, whose "Essai sur la Musique" was published
in 1780, is very fanciful in many of his representations,
introducing most poetical illustrations of some of the instruments in the hands of full-dressed ladies and gentlemen; but this is of far less consequence than the play of

imagination he has allowed in the adjuncts of several of
the ancient instruments.   He includes many that are in
Bonanni's work.   The contre-basse, he says, is much
larger than the violoncello, and is of three sorts.   One
with three strings, tuned according to his directions, G,
D, A, beginning from the lower string; one with four
strings, F, G, D, A, or G, D, G, C; and one with five
strings, E flat, A, D, G, C, or F, A, D, F sharp, A.
The quinte, or taille, or haute-contre de violon, was like
our modern tenor, having four strings, and tuned a fifth
below the violin.   The viole d'amour was a viol with
seven strings, larger than the violin, and of a softer tone.
The par-dessus de viole was of the same sort, with five
strings, and had frets, and was played on the knee.
Several other sorts of violes are mentioned, but then out
of use for a hundred years and more; as the viole de
Bordone, with forty-four strings (there was the sambuca
Lyncea, invented by Colonne, a Neapolitan, in the sixteenth century, which, it is said, had five hundred strings),
viole batarde, viole d'amour with metal strings, and viole
di braccio (from whence the German name bratsche, for
the tenor); also five sorts of violes, or violettes, differing
only in size; and the basso de viole, and le par-dessus,
then still in use.   He mentions the violon d'amour, then
obsolete, as he says, which had four metal strings placed
below the regular gut strings, and so tuned as to render
the harmonics, but produced confusion.   Also the viola
alto, or quinte, which seems to have been like the quinte
before named; it was sometimes called the violette, and
Stamitz, the son of the distinguished musician of that
name, was a fine performer on it.   The description and
fingering of the violoncello in his work were written by
Nochet, a fine performer on the instrument at that time,
and a pupil of Cervetto.   Laborde also gives a figure of
the poche, or sourdine, or kit.

There were several fine performers during this century, but with some few remarkable exceptions, this must be taken with reference to the state of practical music at the time ; as probably many members of an accomplished orchestra of the present day could have successfully competed with the greatest names on record of these times. In the present chapter we shall confine ourselves to a few Continental celebrities, and in referring to them we may mention some anecdotes known to many of our readers, but we thought our subject would be made more complete by venturing to introduce them, and we will refer to Mr. Dubourg's interesting work on the violin for many others. With respect to the extent of the usual practical skill of the early part of the century, we may state that John Lenton, in 1702, published an instructor for the violin, wherein there are no directions given for the shift ; though, as he gives the scale up to C on the second leger line, it must have been occasionally in use. He objects to the instrument being held under the chin, or so low as the girdle, in imitation of the Italians ; it is to be presumed, therefore, that he intended it should be placed upon the breast.

We may claim the great Pergolesi as a violin player, that having been his principal instrument, but one of the best known names, probably, is Tartini, who was born in 1692, and was skilled in the theory as well as the practice of music, and his method, as it is called, is still esteemed : the story of the Devil's Sonata is too well known to be repeated here. Amongst his best pupils were Pagin, Lahoussaye, and Nardini, whom Burney, in his "Musical Tour," names as the completest player on the violin in all Italy. Gavinies, who was born in 1726, had great execution, and was particularly skilful in accompanying the voice ; he is considered the founder of the French school of the violin.. Ferrari, another pupil

of Tartini, is stated to have been the first who introduced
the harmonics, and passages in octaves. Locatelli, born
in 1693, a pupil of Corelli, had more caprice of hand
and fancy than any of his time, and is said to have made
use of some of the effects afterwards reproduced by
Paganini. Guignon, the last "roi des violons," who
taught the Dauphin, the father of Louis XV, was also a
distinguished performer in this age. Pugnani, born in
1727, another pupil of Tartini, and who was teacher of
Viotti, was an absent and eccentric man: once, when
playing a cadence before a large audience, he quite
forgot himself, and walked about in the middle of the
room till he had finished it, quite unconscious that he
was not alone. On another occasion, being somewhat
at a loss in a cadence, he said to a friend near him,
" Pray that I may get safely back." Olivieri, a pupil
of his, born at Turin in 1757, was a fine performer, but
obliged to leave the theatre there in consequence of the
following sforzando passage. He was in the habit of
attending the concerts of a gentleman attached to the
Court, but arriving one day rather late, the courtier
abused him so that at length Olivieri, who was tuning
his violin, lost his temper, and broke his instrument on
the head of his astonished patron. Veracini, a Floren-
tine, born about 1685, was a fine player, but excessively
vain. A trick was once played on him by Pisendel, the
leader of the orchestra at Dresden, for the purpose of
mortifying him. He taught an inferior player in the
chapel a concerto for the instrument till he became perfect in it ; he then showed it to Veracini, who played it,
but was immediately surpassed in it by the subordinate
player. He was so vexed that it is said he threw himself out of window three days afterwards, but fortunately
escaped with only a broken leg. On his recovery he

went to Prague, and afterwards, in 1714, to London.
He had two fine Jacob Steiner violins, which he called
St. Peter and St. Paul, and affirmed that they surpassed
all the best instruments of Italy. He was shipwrecked
on his way to France, and thus lost these treasures.
Harnnc, born at Paris 1738, was a great player; it is
said that he began the instrument at the age of three,
and at six could play the most difficult music at sight.
Benda, born in Bohemia 1709, is considered the founder
of a violin school in Germany. A violin player called
Bohdanswicz, is mentioned in the latter part of this
century, who had eight children all musical, and he
seems to have endeavoured to attract audiences by numerous strange contrivances; for instance, at Vienna
he advertised for a concert a sonata for one violin, to
be performed by three persons with twelve fingers and
three bows; and an andantino, to be played by his four
daughters on one pianoforte, with eight hands and forty
fingers. Scheller, about the same time, first produced
the performance on the four strings together, unscrewing
the bow for the purpose. Rolla, born at Paris in 1757,
and who died at Milan as recently as 1837, was a distinguished player and a fine composer for the instrument;
he was also one of the finest tenor players in the world,
but it is said that his performance so affected the nerves
of females that he was forbidden to play this instrument
in public: this seems a strange restriction. A performer
called Leprince certainly turned his talents to better
account, for on his passage from Holland to Petersburgh,
having been taken prisoner by an English privateer, he
played so cheerfully to the sailors that they gave him his
liberty, and restored all his property. Diana, born at
Cremona about 1770, was a great player, and applied to
Rolla to give him instructions, which he declined, say-

ing he required none. Diana was angry at this, and
resolved to be revenged, and as Rolla was preparing a
concerto for some approaching ceremony, he watched
him closely when he was practising, and thus learned
his best passages.   Three days before the intended performance, Diana gave notice that he was going to play
in the church, as was then the custom in Italy.   Professors and amateurs flocked to hear him, and among
them Rolla; when, what was his surprise and annoyance, to hear all the best subjects and passages he had
been so carefully studying, played off by Diana as his
own.

Jarnovick, or Giornovick, born at Palermo in 1745,
was another fine performer, though it is said somewhat
deficient in tone.   There was, however, no deficiency in
his self-estimation.   "My dear Viotti," says he on one
occasion, "it must be admitted that only we two know
how to play on the violin."   He was of dissipated habits,
and irritable temper; on one occasion he quarrelled with
St. George, the celebrated fencer, who was also a fine
violinist, and struck him, when St. George with great
moderation told him he admired his talent too much to
fight with him.   He once advertised a concert at Lyons,
with six francs for admission, but nobody came.   He
was irritated, and adjourned it till the next day, reducing
the price to three francs, and a crowd of people consequently came.   After waiting for some time it was
found he had left the place, no doubt taking the money
with him.   Another anecdote is told of his breaking a
pane of glass in the shop of Bailleux, the music-seller,
for which he was required to pay thirty sous; he offered
three francs, but Bailleux having no change, Jarnovick
said, Never mind, and breaking another pane, added, We
are quits now.   Kreutzer, born at Versailles 1766, was

distinguished as a performer and composer for the instrument.

Many performers towards the end of this century belonged equally to the former part of our present century, and will be mentioned in a future chapter; but we may name Baillot, who was born near Paris in 1771, and is known not only as one of the finest French players on the violin, but as the author of one of the best set of instructions for the instrument. Bonazzi, a clever player, who died in 1802, may be noticed from his having left a collection of not less than one thousand concertos, quintetts, and quartetts, by different composers, together with forty-two violins, by Stradiuarius, Guarnerius, Amati, and other great masters, of the estimated value of 6500 ducats.

In the early part of the century, Forqueray, born at Paris in 1700, was the most skilful performer on the bass-viol of his time, as his father had been previously. Hawkins mentions Francheville as a fine performer on the viol da gamba at the Castle concerts; while at a later date Charles Franz, born 1738, and Antoine Lidl, are named as distinguished players on the baritone, or violoncelle d'amour. Franceschelli, in the early part of the century, was an excellent performer not only on the bass-viol, but on the violoncello, and was particularly admired for the manner in which he played the violoncello parts of Scarlatti's cantatas, which were so good that none but superior players could do them justice. Marc Antoine Bononcini, about the same time, was a fine performer, and is said to have been one of the first to show the capabilities of the instrument, and to make it sing, if we may use the expression. Giovanni Bononcini, the opponent of Handel, was also a good performer. The fine performance of two brothers called Saint-Sevin,

known also by the name of Labbé, about 1730, contributed much to the establishment of the violoncello, and
the disuse of the viol da gamba. Bigati was celebrated
for his style of accompaniment, and his improvising.
Playing once at the church of Avignon, and accompanying Dubrieul, they sought to outdo each other, in consequence of Boccherini being present. One of the assistants in the church was a purblind canon, whose little
dog had followed him in, but had twice been turned out
by his master. On returning after the second expulsion
of the animal, the canon saw something in the shade,
moving backwards and forwards, which he took for
granted was the tail of his intractable dog, instead of
being in any way connected with the tail-piece of a violoncello ; so he gave a heedless but vigorous kick, and
struck not the poor beast, but Digati's instrument, which,
with the unlucky canon, Bigati, and Dubrieul, all came
down together, to the great dismay of the attentive but
now astonished congregation.

Bertaud, who died in 1756, by his skill added much
to the reputation of the violoncello, and may be considered the founder of the French school. Amongst
other pupils he had the two Duports, both excellent
players, with fine tone and execution, of whom the eldest,
Jean Pierre, born at Paris in 1741, was one of the most
skilful performers of his age; he died in 1818; and his
brother, Jean Louis, born in 1749, in 1819; he has left
a valuable work on the fingering of the instrument. The
two Jansons were fine players about the same time. One
of the Jansons was in London in 1772, and is mentioned
as a pupil of Duport in one of the publications of the
day (the "Theatrical Review"), "his taste and execution is very astonishing, we cannot give him the preference of his master." On two nights one of the Duports

also played solos, "this gentleman's execution is truly
masterly, his tone very brilliant, and his taste pleasingly
delicate and chaste."   Burney, in his "Tour," mentions
the famous old Antonio Vandini, and observes that the
Continental violoncello is still played with the bow underhanded.   Louis Boccherini, who was born in 1740, excelled not only as a performer, but also in his numerous
compositions, where the instrument takes a leading or
prominent part, many of which remained popular until
a recent period, although now seldom heard ; he died in
Spain, 1806, with, it is to be feared, very reduced means
of subsistence.   Baudiot, a skilful performer, wrote instructions for the instrument ; Tricklir, born at Dijon
1750, was a fine performer ; and Levasseur is said to
have nearly equalled the Duports in tone.   Bernard
Romberg, born about 1770, was an excellent performer,
and composed some good music for the instrument ; he
also wrote an elementary book for the instrument of
considerable size, which scarcely realised the expecta-
tions raised by the work of so accomplished a musician.
His brother Andrew was a good performer, and well
known as a pleasing composer.   Max Bohrer was also a
distinguished performer, and had a brother a fine player
on the violin.   Fetis says that Duport and Lindley are
the only persons that France and England can oppose to
the two German players on the violoncello just named.

We have omitted several names of fine performers of
Continental birth, such as Geminiani, Giardini, and
others, because so great a part of their lives was spent
in England, that it seems more convenient to join them
with the English names, but without the least wish to
claim for ourselves merit that may in strictness belong
to other countries.

CHAPTER XIII.

THE bass-viol was still occasionally practised by ladies in England in the eighteenth century (indeed we have known lady performers on the violoncello at the present time). In Vanbrugh's "Relapse," it is said of one, "the parson of the parish teaches her to play on the bass-viol, the clerk to sing, her nurse to dress, and her father to dance." In "The Levellers," a dialogue between two young ladies concerning matrimony, 1703, Politica, a tradesman's daughter, describing her education at a boarding school, says she "learned to sing, to play on the bass-viol, virginals, spinnet, and guitar."

The first opera on the English stage was "Arsinoe," set to music by Thomas Clayton, and performed at Drury Lane in 1707. William Corbet was the leader, but we do not know of what instruments the orchestra was composed. Corbet, who was a fine player, advertised for sale, "Stainers' Cremona violins and bases, with the four celebrated violins of Corelli, Gobbo, Torelli, and Nic. Cosimi;" he left his best instruments to Gresham College, and 10l. a-year for the care of them.

Concerts now became frequent, gradually increasing in merit, until the establishment of the professional concerts in the latter part of the century, the Ancient Concerts, the Philharmonic, now of half a century standing, and so down to the Musical Society of London, which, if it carries out the regulations on which it is founded, promises to advance the science, to the improvement and advantage of the amateur and the professor ; and nothing can be more finished than the performance of the accomplished orchestra under its very skilful conductor Mr. Alfred Mellon.   At one of the earlier concerts in 1722, the celebrated Carbonelli played no less than two concertos, and one solo; while a concerto on the bass-violin was played by a performer called Pippo.

The component parts of an orchestra, even towards the end of the last century, were very different from those at present; several instruments, indeed, now in use, were then unknown.   For instance, in 1789, the orchestra at the Academy of Ancient Music, consisted of 1 organ, 14 violins, Barthelemon being the first; 4 violas, 3 hautboys, 2 trumpets, 2 horns, 1 drum, 4 violoncellos, 2 double-basses, and 3 bassoons.   Let us put in contrast the orchestra of the Musical Society of London on 28th January, 1863; for although the numbers are double, the proportions of the instruments can be readily seen.   Mr. Alfred Mellon conductor ; 16 first violins, Blagrove and Sainton principals ; 16 second violins, William Watson principal ; 10 violas, R. Blagrove and Webb principals ; 10 violoncellos, Paque principal ; 9 double-basses, Howell principal ; 2 flutes, 1 piccolo, 2 oboes, 2 clarionets, 2 bassoons, 4 horns, 2 trumpets, 3 trombones, 1 ophicleide, 2 cornets, 1 drum, 1 bass-drum and cymbals, 1 side-drum, 1 triangle, 2 harps.   The band of the Royal Italian Opera, Covent Garden, for 1862, which is not to be surpassed, consisted of Signor Costa conductor ; 16 first violins, Sainton principal ; 16 second violins, Willey principal ; 10 violas, Doyle principal ; 11 violoncellos, Lucas principal ; 11 double-basses, Howell principal ;

N

2 harps, 2 flutes, 2 oboes, 2 clarionets, 2 bassoons, 4 horns, 2 trumpets, 3 trombones, 1 ophicleide, 1 drum, 1 triangle, and 1 bass-drum.

In the celebrated Musical Festival in Westminster Abbey, in 1786, there were 1 organ, 106 violins, the elder Cramer being the leader, 32 violas, 28 oboes, 6 flutes, 19 violoncellos, Crosdill and Cervetto being the principals, 34 bassoons, 1 double-bassoon, 13 double-basses, 14 trumpets, 12 horns, 6 trombones, 1 drum, and 2 double drums.

The Handel Festival at the Crystal Palace in 1862, according to the announcement, comprised in the orchestra no less than 194 violins, 75 violas, 75 violoncellos, and 75 double-basses, with 86 wind and other instruments. The chorus consisted of the extraordinary number of 3120 singers, the whole under the control of that distinguished conductor Signor Costa.

The band for Handel's "Water Music," 1715, was composed, according to the valuable life of him by Mr. Schœlcher, of 4 violins, 1 viol, 1 violoncello, 1 counterbass, 2 hautboys, 2 bassoons, 2 French horns, 2 flageolets, 1 flute, and 1 trumpet. In "Julius Cæsar," 1723, he used in the orchestra, flutes, hautboys, bassoons, trumpets, a harp, a viola da gamba, a theorbo, kettle-drums, and four horns, besides what is called the quatuor of stringed instruments, the first and second violins, the viola or tenor, the violoncello, and double-bass. In his hautbois concertos, opera 3rd, 1734, there are compositions for 2 violins, 2 hautboys, 2 flutes, 2 viols, 2 bassoons, 2 violoncellos, and a thorough-bass. Many of his airs have a simple accompaniment for the violoncello with harpsichord. In some of his accompaniments the violette is mentioned, a name we have already noticed as a variety of the viol, but an air in "Orlando," 1732, is accompanied

by " 2 violette marine con violoncelli pizzicati." This
violetta marina is said to have been introduced in the
same year by Castrucci; Burney calls it a kind of viol
d'amour with sympathetic strings, and the air in "Orlando"
is the only one written for it, so it is to be presumed there
were some objections to its use.

Corbet was succeeded as leader of the opera orchestra
by Castrucci, born at Rome about 1690, a pupil of
Corelli; who is said to have been the original of Hogarth's
enraged musician, though Trusler names another. He
was difficult to manage, and was superseded by John
Clegg, a very fine player, who became insane from over-
study, and it was the fashion to go to Bedlam to hear him
play. Clegg was born in 1714, and played concertos in
public at the age of nine. Castrucci died in 1769, in reduced circumstances. Many instances have occurred in
all professions, of the mind giving way from the effect of
over-study or undue excitement, but Passenans, in " La
Russie et l'Esclavage," gives a melancholy example of
the pressure of arbitrary tyranny on over-wrought and
sensitive nerves, inducing a fit of passion and resistance,
which may be considered as a case of temporary insanity.
A Russian noble, having a serf who showed great musical
talent, sent him to Italy to study; he much distinguished
himself there, and in due time was ordered home by his
master. He was one day summoned to play before a
numerous assembly, and when any new person of rank
arrived, he had to recommence a brilliant concerto of
Viotti. Worn out at length by three hours of this work,
he asked to be allowed a little rest, when his brutal proprietor replied, " No, play on, and if you are capricious,
mind that you are my slave, and that I can have you
bastinadoed." The unfortunate young man ran down to
the kitchen in despair, and cut off the first finger of his

left hand with a hatchet, saying, " Cursed be the talent
that will not place me beyond the treatment of a slave."

The reputation of Geminiani, born at Lucca about
1680, though some give an earlier date, a pupil of Lunati
(Il Gobbo), is well established, not only for his skill as a
player, but for his arrangement of Corelli's music, and
his own concertos; he came over to England in 1714,
and died in Dublin in 1762, in the house of his friend
and pupil, Matthew Dubourg.   Dubourg, who was born
in 1703, was a fine player; and when a child played
solos at Britton's concerts.   It is of him the story is told
of playing a cadence once before Handel, when he seemed
rather undecided towards the close, but having safely
finished, Handel exclaimed, " You are welcome home,
Monsieur Dubourg."   Mrs. Delaney speaks in high terms
of him : after hearing the music in honour of St. Cecilia
at the Crown Tavern, she writes in a letter dated the
11th of Nov. 1727, " Dubourg was the first fiddle, and
every body says he exceeds all the Italians, even his
master Geminiani."   Carbonelli, a pupil of Corelli, who
came over to England in 1720, was leader of the opera
band for a time, but is probably best known as the founder
of the celebrated wine establishment bearing his name ;
he died in 1772.

Felix Giardini, born at Turin, 1716, was a pupil of
Somis, a fine player, Corelli's best pupil, and one of the
great masters of his time.   He came to England about
1749, and remained 35 years, leading at the opera during
part of the time.   He was celebrated as a solo player, and
particularly excelled in an adagio, and was remarkable
also for the volume of tone he produced.   He had amassed
a fortune, but unfortunately lost it, as many others have
done, by undertaking the management of the opera, in
which he was joined by Mingotti.   He afterwards went

to Russia, and died at Moscow, in very reduced circumstances, in 1796. Michael Christian Festing, a German, resided in London about the middle of the century; he was a fine performer, but may be more particularly mentioned with honour as one of the founders of the Royal Society of Musicians. Richard Charke, a dissipated fellow, who married Charlotte, the daughter of Colley Cibber, is said to be the first who composed medley overtures. He treated his wife ill, like a beast, or rather worse, for the animal creation does not indulge, generally, in these abominable practices, except, perhaps, the gigantic salamander, and the spider, and a few others; indeed, as to the spider, it is the lady who is in fault, but at the same time she makes her spouse useful, for when any domestic disturbances arise, she occasionally eats him. Poor Mrs. Charke lived at one time in a state of great penury, and there is an account of her life extant. Barthelemon, born at Bordeaux in 1741, was the leader of the opera band for several years, and was employed by Garrick. He is said to have excelled in the performance of Corelli's solos; he died in London in 1808.

The celebrated Viotti will be still remembered by some of our readers, for the vigour of his style and the purity of his tone, and his music is still highly esteemed. He was born in Piedmont about the middle of the century, and was the pupil of Pugnani. He came to London about 1792, and succeeded W. Cramer as leader at the opera. Viotti possessed considerable talent independent of his profession, but was also of a somewhat violent and decided disposition, and in 1798, when republican principles were rife, was sent out of the country for some real or supposed political offence, but was allowed to return in 1801; and died in London in 1824. There were several first-rate performers amongst his pupils, most of whom more properly belong to the present century, as Rode, who was also a good writer, Labarre, Libon, Mori, whose brilliant execution is familiar to many, and Pinto, who was an extraordinary performer, but died from the effects of dissipation in 1808, in his 21st year. William Cramer, just mentioned, was born at Manheim in 1745, and besides having been for some time leader of the opera band, was the leader, as before mentioned, at the Handel Commemoration in 1787. He was the father of J. B. Cramer, one of the first pianists of his time, and F. Cramer, the well known violin player, and leader at the Ancient Concerts, and others.

As we have before intimated, some names now omitted, will be mentioned as of the present century, although they belong in fact to both ; but as the well known Jean Pierre Salomon was born at Bonn as far back as 1745, we will introduce him here. He came to England in 1781, and in 1791 was first violin at the Academy of Ancient Music, and played concertos ; and at the same time we find Master Bridgetower, distinguished afterwards as a good player, playing a concerto on the violin. Salomon was not only celebrated as a performer on the violin, particularly as a quartett player, but also had considerable general knowledge and ability, and to him we are indebted for the introduction to the musical world of the celebrated twelve grand symphonies of Haydn, all of which were written expressly for his concerts. He continued for many years the leader of various concerts at the Hanover Square Rooms, and was also the leader, with a host of first-rate talent assisting him, on the opening night of the Philharmonic Concerts, fifty years since. His instrument had been formerly Corelli's.

The finest performer on the viol da gamba in England, about the middle of the century, was Charles Frederick

Abel, a German, born in 1719, who came over in 1759. He was one of the greatest performers on the instrument ever known, particularly in the performance of slow movements, which seem best to suit the character of the instrument. On the formation of Queen Charlotte's band, he was made chamber-musician, with a salary of 200*l.* per annum. He died in 1787. Dahmen about this time was a fine performer on the same instrument, as well as on the violoncello.

The elder Cervetto, whose Christian name it appears from the registry of his burial was Jacob, was born in Italy in 1682, came to London in 1728, and passed the remainder of his long life in England, his death not taking place until the year 1783. He brought the violoncello into favour by his great skill and taste, but his tone is said to have been hard. He is the musician who roused Garrick's wrath by yawning aloud in the middle of one of that great actor's pathetic speeches, which he had probably heard twenty times before; but adroitly excused himself, by saying he always yawned when he was pleased. Caporale was a rival of Cervetto, but does not appear to have equalled him. He was permanently attached to Handel's orchestra, as were Clegg and Dubourg; and he, with the elder Cervetto, Ravenscroft, and Festing, as before mentioned, were among the first subscribers to the Musical Fund, afterwards the Royal Society of Musicians. The younger Cervetto, who was called James, was born about 1747, and excelled his father -both in style and tone, which was particularly sweet, and his expression very fine. He, like his father, lived to a great age, and died in February, 1837; he had, however, retired from the profession some time previously. John Crosdill, born in London in 1755, went to Paris from 1775 to 1780. He was the first performer on the violon-

cello of his time, his tone especially was remarkably fine
and powerful, and Mr. Parke, in his " Musical Memoirs,"
mentions having heard him play the favourite minuet in
" Ariadne," in three parts, as distinctly and perfectly as if
they had been performed by three of the most distinguished
players.   He retired in 1794, having ample means.
John George Christopher Schetky, born near Frankfort-
on-the-Maine, about the year 1740, of good family, was
originally intended for the law, and was sent to the University of Jena, but did not prosecute the study, and in
the course of the Seven Years' War, under Frederick the
Great, from 1756 to 1763 served as a volunteer, and the
celebrated Blucher was the captain of his company.
Being passionately fond of music, he followed the bent of
his inclination, and studied both theoretically and practically under Emanuel Bach, and also under Schrœder
for the pianoforte.   The violoncello being his favourite
instrument, he took some lessons from Abel (the celebrated
performer on the viol da gamba), under whom he soon
became a proficient.   After travelling for several years
in Germany and France, he determined to visit England,
wishing to be present at the coronation of George the
Third, but was prevented by illness.   However, he arrived
soon afterwards in London, and not intending to settle
there, was about to return to Germany, when he obtained
an engagement as first violoncellist for the Edinburgh
Saint Cecilia Concerts, which were then of great repute.
They were very aristocratic, many amateurs of rank and
station being members, including several of the nobility,
and men eminent in the learned professions.   The leading professors were also of first-rate talent.   These concerts flourished until the Peace of Amiens, when the fa-
cilities given for travelling on the Continent induced many
people of station to go abroad, and they were thus broken

up. In the mean time Mr. Schetky had married, and remained at Edinburgh following his profession, where his talent, polished manners, and generous character caused him to associate with the best society, and he was on intimate terms with many of the distinguished literary characters of his time, and he died there at an advanced age in the year 1824. He was particularly admired for his fine adagio playing, and the delicate expression of the cantabile ; his own compositions are pleasing, particularly some of his pathetic passages, and one of the last pieces that Lindley played with a friend, after his retirement, was one of Schetky's duetts. John Christian Schetky, Esq., the present well known and accomplished marine painter to the Queen, is his son, and possesses a genuine taste and feeling for music.

In 1783 Joseph Kœmpfer came over here. He was an extraordinary performer on the double-bass, playing difficult violin passages on it, and particularly excelled in the use of the harmonics. He also invented a most useful variety of the instrument, which could be taken to pieces for the convenience of travelling. He was eclipsed, as all others were, by that giant in power and talent, Dragonetti, whom we shall mention in the ensuing chapter.

CHAPTER XIV.

IN the present century, the instruments of the violin class have been perfectly established, the viol class being now obsolete, except as matters of curiosity. But with all our advances in practical skill, we have been unable to improve on the models known three hundred years since, unless it may be in some of the minor details. Some experiments were made in France for the purpose, as was considered, of improving the shape and tone of the violin. Chanot, an officer in the French army, and the son, it is said, of the violin-maker Chagniot, proposed to make the violin of a flatter model, with the sides less curved inwards, the sound-holes straighter, and the bar in the centre of the upper vibrating plate; in fact, something in shape like the old viol, or modern guitar. It was submitted to a committee of the French Academy in 1817, who, after three trials, decided in its favour, considering the tone to be of superior quality, and not inferior, indeed, to the Italian instruments. It was not, however, brought into use, and it was found, after a time, that the tone did not last. Baud, a maker at Versailles, submitted to the Institute in 1810 a violin without bars, which he fancied interfered with the vibrations; however, the report of the Institute was not favourable. In 1819 Felix Savart, M.D., published "Mémoire sur la Construction des Instrumens

à Cordes et à Archet," in which he describes a new form
of violin, invented by him, on strictly scientific principles,
explaining his reasons at length. The shape was a tra-
pezium, not raised or arched, the sound-holes straight,
with some other peculiarities in the details. A favourable
report of it was made by a select committee, to the
Académies des Sciences and des Beaux-Arts, but the instrument did not get into use.

The nineteenth century has produced many performers of first-rate talent and celebrity. In some cases,
perhaps, the execution of mere mechanical difficulties has
been too much relied on, but in many others, exquisite
taste and expression have been joined to the most finished
execution ; and solo and quartett playing, with orchestral
music of the highest class, may now be heard, not only at
select concerts, such as the Musical Society of London,
the two Philharmonic Societies, and the Musical Union,
with its choice chamber-music, but at those more acces-
sible to the general body of society, who by its extensive
patronage shows how truly it appreciates the excellent
music presented to it. Progress in music has fully
kept pace with the progress in society. As we have before observed, several of the performers now about to be
named were also known in the last century, but the
greater part of their career was in the present. Among
them are Yaniewicz, a Pole, distinguished for his pure
tone; and Vaccari, born at Modena in 1773, whose
tone was particularly sweet, with great expression.
Kiesewetter, born in 1777, had great power with taste
and expression; he died, unfortunately, soon after attending the Leicester Festival in 1824. He was so ill during
the performance as to require to be supported to his chair;
and afterwards went on to Norwich, but was too ill to
play there, and died soon after his return. The committee

very properly paid him his stipulated sum, and a subscription was made for him at Leicester. Lafont, born in Paris 1781, had a good tone, and fine taste ; he commenced playing in public at the age of fourteen. Habeneck, born at Mézières in the same year, led the opera at Paris for a considerable time. Louis Sphor, born at Saesen in Brunswick, about 1784, and only recently dead, was celebrated not only as a fine performer, with finished execution and expression, but also as a great composer, with a perfect knowledge of the theory of music ; his compositions are, of course, well known to and admired by our readers. At the same time was born at Gênes the greatest performer on the violin that ever lived, Nicholas Paganini. So much has been said of him, and so much is known, that a slight notice here will suffice. Those who were fortunate enough to see and hear him will never forget the impression produced by his strange, almost unearthly figure, when, advancing to the front of the orchestra, he seized his violin as if it were a cherished living creature, and then, with his marvellous bow, and wonderful fingers, produced such an extraordinary effect from his beautiful tone, double stops, pizzicatos, and harmonics, on which long and rapid passages were played, that his auditors became breathless with astonishment. No doubt his extraordinary style of play has tended to advance the character and power of the instrument, and as professors of talent studied the passages introduced by him, a higher scale of eminence was established, and the great powers of execution of some of our accomplished modern performers may originate from the time of Paganini. He began the instrument at the age of six, and after a time was placed under the tuition of Giacomo Costa, the director of the opera at Gênes ; he was then placed under the excellent player Alexander Rolla. In 1805 he was director of the orchestra of the Princess Eliza, sister of Napoleon, and afterwards Grand Duchess of Tuscany. While with her he played one evening a solo on the third and fourth strings of his fiddle, and in 1810 played variations on the fourth string alone, which he performed in public for the first time at Parma, on the 16th of August, 1811. He is said to have written his first sonata at the age of eight, and many of his compositions contained such difficulties, that for some time they were considered insuperable. He died at Nice in 1840. Mayseder, born at Vienna in 1789, is known as a good writer, as well as a fine performer, and Festa is another good writer for the instrument. Joseph Reicha, born in Prague 1746, was a good player, and Artot, a Belgian, a most finished performer, died at the early age of 30, in 1845. There are so many excellent performers now constantly before the public, that it would be presumptuous in us to give any opinion on their relative merits, which would be out of our province; and therefore we will follow the example of the account given of the brave Gyges, and the brave Cloanthus, and their companions, by Virgil, and name De Beriot, born in 1802, skilled equally as a writer and a performer, and with taste and volume of tone excelled by none ; Ole Bull, the distinguished Norwegian, Ernst, Sivori, Vieuxtemps, Lotto, and Wienawski, all of first-rate talent, to whom others are from time to time, by their skill, entitling themselves to be added ; but we must particularly name Herr Joachim, whose tone, taste, and execution are unrivalled in every style. We shall name some other foreign players among those of England, as being, in fact, naturalized amongst us.

As finished players on the violoncello on the Continent, Arnold Schoenebeck, Muntzberger, Danzi, and Hus-Desforges, wrote and adapted many pieces of music for

the instrument, but their tone was not equal to their facility of execution. Kummer was a good writer as well
as player. Aubert, Breval, and Raoul all published instructions for the instrument. Lamare is mentioned as a
fine quartett player; Ganz has an excellent tone; and
Servais and Franchomme great execution. As a double-
bass player, Bottesini probably excels in execution any
previous performer; it is indeed marvellous, and the facility with which he plays passages on double stops and
harmonics must be heard to be fully appreciated. His
tone is clear and mellow as a trumpet, but has not the
wonderful power and vigour of Dragonetti's; and indeed
his instrument is of a smaller make than that of his great
predecessor.

Amongst the English players of this time, Richard
Cudmore, born at Chichester in 1787, was a fine performer
not only on the violin, but on the violoncello and pianoforte; at one concert he played a concerto on the violin
by Rode, one by Cervetto on the violoncello, and one by
Kalkbrenner on the pianoforte. Thomas Cooke had
great musical talent, both vocal and instrumental, and
played in concert at the early age of five. He was occasionally first violin at the Philharmonic Concerts, and
was for a time the principal singer at one of the theatres;
he also composed several popular glees. At a benefit
about 1823, he played solos on nine different instruments.
One of the writers can speak of him as a kind friend of
many years' standing. Charles Weichsel, for many years
the distinguished leader at the opera, played in public
also at the age of seven. Spagnoletti will also be remembered at the opera, and Venua, who for a time led the
ballet, was very skilful as a quartett player. Many others
of first-rate talent might be mentioned, and Blagrove,
with his finished execution and perfect intonation, stands

unrivalled as an English performer; while Cerrodus has
recently established his claim to stand in the first rank in
the profession, and Sainton is now so domesticated with
us, that we have placed him here instead of among the
foreign players, and his skill and taste, not to be excelled
in quartett or solo playing, are fully appreciated and admired by all lovers of music. Molique also may be considered as naturalized, distinguished alike for his the-
oretical as well as his practical talents. Moralt and Hill
will be remembered as most skilful players on the tenor.
Powell, Charles Ashley, and Crouch, together with
Reinagle of Oxford, were among the leading performers
on the violoncello, in the beginning of this century, and
to the time of their respective deaths; but the unrivalled
performer Robert Lindley stands alone as the master of
this difficult instrument, whether from the grandeur and
power of his tone, or the brilliancy of his execution;
playing on strings of such size that can alone produce
such body of sound, but which now unluckily are generally
discarded in consequence of the greater facility afforded
to the player by those of smaller size. He was born at
Rotherham in Yorkshire, on the 4th of March, 1775, and
showed his genius for music at a very early age, and, indeed, at the age of nine years played the violoncello in
the Brighton and Lewes theatres; his brothers John and
Charles being also in the orchestra. When he was of
the age of twelve, he and his brothers, as violin and tenor,
were frequently sent for when at Brighton, to play before
the Prince of Wales, and at that time he could play all
the usual solos or concertos for the violoncello. At the age
of fifteen he commenced writing music for himself, and was
anxious to get engaged at some of the professional concerts,
but could not succeed until the following year, when on
the morning of the second concert, the professor who was

to have performed a solo on the violoncello was suddenly
taken ill, and the directors in this emergency sent to
Lindley's father, to say that his son might play in the
evening as a favour. He eagerly embraced the opportunity, and played a concerto in such an admirable style,
that he was rapturously encored.   On the following
morning, two of the directors called, requesting him as a
favour to play at the next concert, when he was again encored ; and he played concertos at the nine subsequent
concerts, and was encored on every occasion, thus reaching the top of his profession at the age of sixteen, and
there remained unrivalled for the next sixty years, universally respected for his talent and integrity. At the
time of his joining the professional concerts he was a
pupil of the younger Cervetto, with whose approbation,
at the age of eighteen, he took the place of first violoncello
at the King's Theatre on the retirement of Sperate, where,
and at the Italian Opera, which he joined on its opening,
he remained for fifty-eight years, thus exceeding the time of
Theobaldo Gatti, who died in 1727, and was for fifty-two
years principal bass-viol in the French theatre.   Soon
after Lindley joined the opera orchestra, Bernard
Romberg came over to England, and Crosdill invited
him to a music party at Mr. Thompson's, where he lived,
and which was usually given after the rehearsals of the
Ancient Concerts, on Mondays during the season. Lindley
and a large party of professors and amateurs were also
present, and Romberg played many of his difficult compositions for the instrument in fine style, and with much
execution.   When the party broke up, Crosdill said to
Lindley, who he knew was going to play a concerto that
evening at a concert where Salomon, a friend of Romberg,
was to lead, " They have heard Romberg ; now, Lindley,
let them hear what an Englishman can do."   In the

evening Lindley played one of his most difficult concertos, containing passages with double stops, octaves, and even tenths, which his large and powerful hand enabled him to play readily; the applause, when he had finished, was very great. At the end of the first act, Salomon asked Romberg, who had been standing opposite to Lindley during his performance, what he thought of it. Romberg replied, " He is the devil!" With reference to his power of reading at first sight, it may be related that when he was a young man he was at a music party at Clement's Inn, when copies of Romberg's first four concertos for the violoncello were produced, which had only arrived the same morning from the Continent. Lindley played the whole of these without the slightest hesitation or difficulty.

The beauty of his tone, and extraordinary power of execution, his skill in accompanying, especially in the few but effective notes in a recitative, will be in the recollection of a great part of our readers. A friendship of very many years' standing down to the day of his death, will, we hope, prove our excuse for dwelling a little on the subject; indeed, one of the writers was the last with whom he ever played: stopping then, in the middle of a duett, like Haydn in his unfinished quartett, and saying, "I can no more," and he never again played on the instrument.

He would sometimes in private take the first violin part of a quartett, not only on the violoncello, but when with a few friends would do so on the violin, imitating, good-humouredly, some of the leading performers of the time. His son William, born in 1802, at one time gave promise of equalling his father in tone and execution, until ill-health unfortunately compelled him to leave town. They would play the violin and tenor parts of

o

Beethoven's trios on two violoncellos, a friend taking the regular violoncello part. His brother, Charles Lindley, was a fine performer, especially on the tenor, though he usually played the violoncello in public; and but for his retiring habits might have taken a high position. Lindley died on the 13th of June, 1855, after a gradual decay of some duration. One of his daughters is married to John Barnett, the eminent composer. He had some good pupils, as may be expected, and among them the accomplished musician, Lucas, the Principal of the Royal Academy of Music, may be considered the chief. He succeeded Lindley as principal violoncello at the Italian Opera, and has but very recently retired, having been succeeded by that excellent performer, Mr. Collins. There are other very good English performers, but for finished execution, taste, and expression, especially in solo and quartett playing, Signor Piatti is not surpassed.

Anfossi was known as a good player on the double-bass some thirty years since; but all former players on this instrument were surpassed by that extraordinary performer, Dominique Dragonetti, born at Venice in 1766. He came over to England in 1795; and for the greater part of their lives he and Lindley were associated together, and their performance of Corelli's music will never be forgotten by those who were fortunate enough to hear it. When young, Dragonetti practised much with a fine violin player, Mestrino, whom Dragonetti often said he considered one of the most accomplished masters of the instrument he had known. At the age of thirteen he was appointed first bass to the Opera Buffa, at Venice. The richness and power of his tone were marvellous; and his execution such that he would play the violoncello or violin part of a quartett on his unwieldy instrument, or even join in a violin duett.

We may add Mr. Chorley's truthful remarks as to the long musical union of Lindley and Dragonetti. "Nothing has been since heard to compare with the intimacy of their mutual musical sympathy; nor is a pair of figures so truly characteristic now to be seen in any orchestra. Those two are among the sights of London that have vanished for ever." *

At present Howell may be considered our principal orchestral player, with whom there are other excellent performers.

We will now proceed to give some account of the various makers to the best of our power; but the difficulties of arranging these have been great in some cases from the deficiency of genuine information—from the vagueness and contradictory nature of the results of our inquiries and researches in others, so that a degree of uncertainty pervades the history even of some of the best known names. There seems, for instance, to be a difference of opinion as to the number of makers of the name of Amati. We hope, however, to be able to supply the names of all the makers of any note, and rather than be deficient in this respect shall include many that will be but little known to the generality of our readers; we have used every means in our power to make our account as correct as possible, but we must claim indulgence for the deficiencies which we fear may be found, in consequence of the scanty, imperfect, and conflicting materials with which in numerous cases we have had to deal.

* "Thirty Years' Musical Recollections," i. 80.

CHAPTER XV.

E have already referred to the old makers, Ott, Frey, and Kerlin, and shall commence our account with the sixteenth century, wherein several foreign names occur, including the Amatis, but very few English. And the same remark will necessarily apply to makers as to performers, that in many cases they must belong to parts of two centuries. We may observe also, that we shall reserve a more detailed account of the English makers for an after part of the work.

In that curious collection of persons, occupying about ninety lines, who resort to "Cocke Lorelles Boke," printed by Wynkyn de Worde in the early part of the reign of Henry VIII., there appear "orgyn makers," and "harpe makers," but no viol makers. Are we to assume that this omission arose from the paucity of their numbers, or from their being more select in the choice of their companions.

There are many continental names handed down from this period; but, as we have before observed, the difficulty in some cases of ascertaining the dates, and even, though more rarely, the identity of the individual, is great; and we suspect that occasionally one maker may appear under two different names. The late Dr. Forster, in his "Epistolarium" and "Travels," gives the names of many makers ; but his books are very inaccurately printed, and his dates, and even frequently his names, are very confused and not to be depended on.

Pietro Dardelli, of Mantua, about 1500, made good rebeca, violas, and viols da gamba, some of which, Fetis states, still to exist in the cabinets of the curious ; and Morglato Morella, perhaps his pupil, of the same place, about 1550, made the same class of instruments. There were also Venturi Linelli or Linarolli, at Venice, 1520 ; and Peregrino Zanetto, at Brescia, 1540 ; with Lauxmin Possen, about the same time in Bavaria, who was maker for the chapel at Munich.   Jean Kohl was " luthier" to the Court at Munich in the latter half of the century ; and Fetis states that, from some old accounts, he was paid two florins for a lute.   Jean Meusiedler and Jean Gerle are mentioned as celebrated makers at Nuremberg, about 1540.   These makers were probably more particularly confined to the manufacture of violas and lutes, &c., than of violins ; but the term " luthier," as is well known, applies to makers of violins and violas, as well as lutes.

There was, however, a celebrated maker of violins as well as of viols, Gaspard Duiffoprugcar, born in the Italian Tyrol in the latter end of the fifteenth century, who flourished in the former part of the sixteenth.   He was established at Bologna in 1510, but went to Paris in 1515, by invitation from Francis I. ; the climate, however, not agreeing with him he moved to Lyons, where he is said to have died about 1530.   He made several instruments for the Chapel and Chamber of Francis, some of which are still to be found in the possession of amateurs.   They are said to have had a powerful and penetrating tone.   Choron states (1817) that Mons. Roquefort, at Paris, well known as a literary man, (and,

who had himself written a work on the Poetry, Music
and Instruments of the French, as mentioned in his
Glossary (2—33), but which was never published,) possessed three basses of this maker, having necks curiously
carved. The first had seven strings tuned thus :—

On the back was a representation of Paris in the sixteenth century, executed in different coloured wood, and
on the front was St. Luke, after Raphael.   The second
had this inscription within, "Gaspard Duiffoprugcar a
la Coste Sainct Sebastien, à Lyons."   On the back was
a representation of the Moses of Michael Angelo; a
salamander, the device of Francis I. was carved on the
neck.   The third had the figure of St. John, after Raphael, on the back, and on the finger-board the following
lines, which were frequently used by this maker :—

> " Viva fui in sylvis, sum dura occisa accuri,
>   Dum vixi, tacui ; mortua dulcè cano,"

This couplet is said to have been on the violin of Palestrina, which was probably therefore one by this maker.
The late celebrated tenor player, Hill, left some manuscript collections towards the history of the violin; he
does not in general give any authorities, and his dates
and names are in several cases doubtful; but his anecdotes and particular descriptions may probably be depended on.   He says that Mons. Cartier had a beautiful
bass-viol and an alto-viol of this maker ; but the most
interesting instrument made by him was a violin of large
pattern, the only one known, having his name and the
date 1539; this date, however, must be wrong.   The
tone was powerful and penetrating ; the head of a fool

with cap and frill was carved on the scroll. It belonged
to Mons. Merts, first violin solo of the Grand Theatre at
Brussels. Mons. Raoul had a bass-viol of this maker,
distinguished for its beauty and tone, which Fetis states
to be then in the possession of Mons. Vuillaume, and
that the back had a representation of Paris in the fifteenth
century; it was probably therefore the same as the instrument of Mons. Roquefort before mentioned, notwithstanding the difference of date stated in the picture of
Paris. There is a portrait of him in medallion, quarto
size, dated 1562. He is represented with a long beard
and surrounded with instruments, having a pair of com-
passes in one hand and the neck of an instrument in the
other.

In "Luthomonographie," it is stated, but we know
not on what authority, that Testator (il Vecchio), a
maker at Milan, in the early part of this century, appears
to have been the first who diminished the size of the
viol, and gave the name of violino to the new-fashioned
instrument. His instruments were like those of Gaspar
di Salo, but the model rather more raised, and are now
very rarely met with.

The earliest violins of any considerable repute, except
of course the early ones of the Amatis, are those by
Gaspar di Salo, who worked at Brescia from about 1560
to 1610, or a little later, if we could rely on Dr. Forster,
who states he had one with this ticket, "Gaspar di Salo,
Brescia, 1613." He describes it as rather long, and
high built, with a beautiful varnish, and perhaps the
prettiest sides ever seen, but it had a new head and
neck; the tone of the first and second strings was lively,
bright, and piercing, a dry golden sound, as Dr. Forster
calls it; the third string sweetly soft and musical, and
the fourth round and very fine. Other writers have

stated that the workmanship of Di Salo's instruments is
not highly finished, but the tone full of vigour; the S S
holes straight, large, and well cut, and parallel, forming
one distinctive mark of the school of Brescia, which was
the cradle of the Italian school.   He employed strong
wood, and used a deep brown varnish; his instruments
are scarce, and produce a good price.   Dragonetti's
instrument was by this maker, and after his death was
returned to the convent from which it originally came.
In "Luthomonographie" there is a copy of a ticket with
the date 1652, which we conclude should be 1562.   At
the Conversazione of the Musical Society of London on
the 29th January, 1862, at St. James's Hall, the celebrated performer, Ole Bull, exhibited a violin of this
maker with the following description:—

"The celebrated 'Treasury Violin' of Inspruck, by
Gaspar di Salo, with Caryatides by Benvenuto Cellini,
sculptured by special command of Cardinal Aldobran-
dini, and by him presented to the Museum of Inspruck,
in the Tyrol.   After the assault upon the said city by
the French in 1809, the museum was plundered, and the
violin carried to Vienna, where the Councillor Rhe-
hazek placed this unique gem in his celebrated collection
of ancient musical instruments, refusing to sell it at any
price.   He left it by will to Ole Bull, in 1842.   Up to
that period it had never been played upon; had no bar,
only a bridge of boxwood, sculptured and painted, and
a very short and inlaid finger-board."

As the instrument was exhibited under glass no accurate opinion can be given of it; it is smaller than any
other instrument which has been seen of this maker, and
the varnish less brown in hue than usual, being of a dull
yellow colour, and meagre.   Only the upper vibrating
plate or belly could be viewed, with the carved head,

which appeared wanting in the usual energy and expression of the great master whose work it is stated to be. This maker was particularly famous for his instruments of the viol class, and is stated by some writers to have been the master of the elder Amati, with whom, however, he was contemporary; and Giovanni Marc, del Bussetto, who flourished at Cremona from 1540 to 1580, is said with more probability to have had that honour. The violins of the latter are of long shape, the vaulting distinct, and the varnish brown; the openings of the S S holes large. 'One with the date of 1570 is mentioned having the back in two parts, the varnish a deep yellow, the corners elongated, and the model high vaulted.

Jean Paul Magini, with others of his family, will be mentioned in the following century. There were two other makers at Brescia towards the end of this century, 1580, Javietta Budiani and Matteo Bente, also Antonio Marini or Mariani, at Pisaro, from 1570 to 1620. Bente's instruments are said to be sought for by collectors. In the Fureteriana a maker of and performer on organs, spinetts, viols, violins, &c. is named about the end of this century, called Martin Chastelain of Warwick in Flanders, who was born blind.

We have now arrived at the time of the celebrated Amati family, of whom we will treat together in this chapter, whether belonging to this century or the following. There is great difficulty notwithstanding, or perhaps in consequence of the various accounts of the several families of distinguished violin makers, in making out an authentic history of them; some uncertainty will remain as to dates, though we have paid every attention and used every means to insure as much accuracy as possible. We have had inquiries made by a friend at Cremona, and have been able to procure but little addi-

tional information beyond what has already appeared in
print; and Mons. Fetis appears to have made similar
inquiries with like want of success. The following is
the most accurate account we can give of the Amati
family, which we believe to be substantially correct. It
may be observed here, that the genuineness of tickets
cannot always be depended on, as sometimes these are
imitated, and a genuine ticket may also be found on a
spurious instrument. It would be a good speculation to
buy some of these instruments for what they are really
worth, and sell them for what their owners profess them
to be worth, like Laharpe—

> " Si vous voudrez faire bientôt,
> Une fortune immense autant que légitime,
> Il vous faut acheter Laharpe ce qu'il vaut,
> Et le vendre ce qu'il s'estime."

The first maker of this name was Andreas, born at
Cremona about 1520; he made as early as 1546, Fetis
mentioning a rebec, or violin with three strings, bearing
his name with this date. The Baron de Bagge had a
viola with his name and the date 1551. He made twenty-
four violins, twelve of large, and twelve of small pattern;
six violas, and eight basses for Charles IX. of France.
These, it is said, were kept in the Chapel Royal at Versailles, until October, 1790, when they disappeared; but
M. Cartier recovered two of them many years afterwards.
Nothing, it is said, could surpass the beauty of the workmanship, the varnish being of golden amber colour,
reflecting a reddish brown. On the backs were painted
the arms of France, and other devices, with the motto
" Pietate et Justitia," not very appropriate for Charles IX.
The heads were decorated with a sort of arabesque of
much taste. In the sale of the instruments of the late
Sir Wm. Curtis, on 3rd of May, 1827, Lot 9 was a violon-

cello by Andreas Amati, Cremonensia, faciebat 1572.
The auctioneer (Mr. Musgrave) stated in the catalogue,
" A document was given to the proprietor when he purchased this instrument, stating that it was presented by
Pope Pius V. to Charles IX., King of France, for his
chapel. It has been richly painted, the arms of France
being on the back, and the motto ' Pietate et Justitia' on
the sides. The tone of this violoncello is of extraordinary power and richness." This was evidently one of
the instruments made for Charles IX. Mr. Hollander
sold it to Sir William Curtis; it was put up at 500
guineas, and bought in at 280. Andreas Amati made
numerous instruments; his violins were generally of
small and middle pattern, the model raised towards the
centre, and of proper thickness, the varnish being a clear
brown; the tone sweet, but not powerful. The greater
number of violoncellos of this maker that we have seen
have a dark reddish brown coloured varnish, with a little
tinge of yellow, the wood of the lower plate and sides
plain, and the work not so highly finished as those of
some of the later members of the family; but it must not
be forgotten he was the first of the name, and had not
arrived at the same perfection. The colour of the varnish may have been influenced by that of the old lutes,
as Mace states that was "dark-black-reddish colour,
though I believe it contributes nothing at all to the
sound; only the best authors did use to lay on that
colour, especially Laux Maller." As he progressed in
his art, Andreas improved his varnish, and made it more
transparent, and of a reddish yellow colour, with more
body, and much more grateful to the eye. He was joined
about 1568 by his brother Nicolas, who worked till 1586,
Andreas, it is supposed, having died about 1560. They
soon become distinguished by the skill of their workman-

ship and sweetness of tone. Nicolas was celebrated for
his basses, for which he used oil varnish, and the sound-
ing-boards had a very inconsiderable swelling. The
upper vibrating plate was thickest in the centre near the
bridge, and diminished about one-third to the S S holes,
and then gradually diminished towards the sides, where
the thickness did not exceed half of that in the centre.
The lower vibrating plate also diminished from the
centre to the sides in the same proportion, but was generally rather thicker than the upper plate. The first and
second strings were brilliant and pure in tone, the third
round and mellow, with power, but the fourth frequently
dry and feeble, arising from the instrument being too
narrow and short in proportion to the thickness. It may
in general be considered as a distinction that the instruments of the Amati family have a pure and sweet tone,
but not much power; those of the Stradiuarius, a rich
and powerful tone; those of the Guarnerius family, still
more volume of tone; and those of the Steiner, a sharp
piercing tone, particularly on the first string.

The next of the Amati family were Antonius and
Hieronymus (or Jerome), both sons of Andreas, of whom
Antonius, the elder, was born about 1565. They made
at first together from 1589, but afterwards separated.
Antonius was superior to his brother, and made after his
father's pattern; his instruments were sweet, but the
fourth string defective. The upper plate was rather
thick in the centre, gradually diminishing towards the
sides. The small violins of Antonius have not been
surpassed for sweetness and mellowness, but the sound is
deficient in intensity, and he endeavoured to counter-
balance the smallness of his model and the lowness of
the ribs by the height and extension of the arches. He
is said to have worked up to 1627, and to have died

about 1635.   There were some instruments made for
Henry IV. with the names of the brothers, and Mons
Cartier had one of these, which are of the greatest rarity
and value, it was dated 1595.   The model was of the
largest size, and the purfling of tortoise-shell, the oil
varnish of rich golden amber colour, which is one of the
characteristics of the Amatis.   The back was decorated
with the arms of France and Navarre, surrounded by
the insignia of the orders of Saint Michel and the Saint
Esprit above the crown of France, with many other
devices.

The instruments made when the brothers worked together were of handsome form, and richly varnished,
but generally small.   The lower plate usually made of
finely figured maple, of a deep brownish red colour, the
alternate stripes being of a rich orange buff, the variation
of colour arising from the medullary rays crossing the
fibres of the wood.   The upper plate made of fine
grained deal, and the scroll rich and elegant.   The
quality of tone is much like that of the other instruments
of the family ; and it may be observed in respect to
these, that they often do not appear strong when the
hearer is near to them, yet are heard with great distinct-
ness and effect at some distance.   Dr. Forster says he
had a beautiful instrument with a ticket, which he gives
thus, but the letter h in Anthonius seems to be an error:
" Anthonius et Hieronymus Amati, Cremonen, Andreæ,
fil. A. 1624."   Tickets are found of many makers, with
a blank space for the last figure or two to be added when
attached to an instrument; like the following, for instance, from " Luthomonographie," " Antonius Hieronimus Amati Cremonen, Andræ filii, 16 . ." Hill mentions
the following ticket in an instrument formerly belonging
to Dragonetti : " Antonius & Hieronymus Amati, Cre-

monen, Andreas fil: F. 1592." At the sale of the instruments of Sir Wm. Curtis there were two violoncellos
and a tenor by these makers. One of the violoncellos,
Lot 10, was stated by the auctioneer, in the catalogue,
to be " undoubtedly one of the most beautiful and finely
toned instruments ever manufactured by these distinguished artists, and is, moreover, in the highest state of
brilliant preservation." We have never seen any instrument with such brilliant and *golden* varnish. It can
only be compared with a new gold coin in which an alloy
of copper has been used, and which imparts a depth of
colouring so different from the undefined colour of this
coin in which silver has been used as the alloy. It was
put up at 150 guineas, and bought in for 135. The
Rev. Sir Frederick Gore Ouseley had in his possession,
in 1859, a viola made by these makers for the noble
family of Radetti at Venice, with their arms emblazoned
on the back; it was purchased from them by General
Kyd, in 1793, and given by him subsequently to Sir
Frederick's father, so that the pedigree is undoubted. It
was altered and reduced in size for General Kyd, in 1811,
by Dodd, of St. Martin's Lane. The printed ticket is,
" Antonius et Hieronymus Fr. Amati Cremonen Andreæ
fil. F. 1620." This instrument has been reduced in size,
both at the fore and hind ends; it has also been made
narrower by cutting pieces out from the joint lines the
whole length of the upper and lower plates. The wood
of the lower plate is not cut the usual way with the
figure and grain prominent, but at right angles with the
medullary rays of the wood, which, crossing the direction
of the fibres of the wood, form what is known as the
silver grain. It is made of a species of maple (*Acer
pseudo-platanus*), and the sides are of the same wood,
and the grain is the right or usual way; the head and

neck are also made of maple wood. The varnish is of
a brownish yellow tint, with a fine yellow ground; the
vehicle must have been very thin, as there is little body
of colour, although it is rich, but age may have assisted
in this particular. It is now the property of Mr. Richard
Blagrove. Hieronymus Amati had two patterns, of
which the largest is considered the best. The sides are
strong and well finished, and then tapering from the
hind-bout to the fore-bout, where the neck is attached,
thus giving a graceful appearance. The edges are ob-
tuse, and do not overlap much; the upper plate is of fine
deal, of regular grain, and is raised gradually about an
inch from the sides to the centre; the S S holes well cut,
but somewhat narrow, with their higher points approaching. The lower plates made generally of one piece,
and, together with the sides and neck, of beautiful maple,
the figure running from right to left somewhat sloping.
The volute, or scroll, is handsome, and rounded with the
greatest care. The varnish is of yellow amber, with a
mixture of light brownish tinge. The purfling broad, as
is the case with most of the Italian instruments, giving
an appearance of the finest construction; while the
school of Cremona is known by having a particular bend
in the purfling, and that of Brescia by having a double
purfling. The tone of these instruments is fine, the
second string brilliant, the third full and round, the
fourth powerful, but the first sometimes a little thin.
This Hieronymus Amati is said to have died about 1638.
Hill states that our Queen has a fine viola of his make.
There is a Joseph Amati mentioned at Bologna in the
beginning of the seventeenth century as one of the
family, who made basses and violins possessing a silvery
tone, which are now very scarce; he used the Amati
varnish.

The most celebrated maker of this family was Nicolas
Amati, the son of Hieronymus, who was born in 1596,
and died in 1684; he was a pupil of his father, and
followed the models of his family, but was more finished
and paid greater attention to the proportions.   He had
two patterns; his instruments of the earlier form being
small, but handsome, with a sweet tone, and well calculated for quartetts and other chamber music.   His instruments most sought after, however, are those of the
large or grand pattern, which are powerful as well as
sweet in tone, and the violins equal to most of those of
Stradiuarius.   The upper plate, which is generally made
of handsome deal, is flat towards the sides, but then rises
about an inch towards the centre.   The lower plate,
which, with the sides and neck, is made of beautifully
figured maple, also rises towards the centre; the sides
are well hollowed out, and the edges rounded.   The S S
holes are not far apart, but are not so straight as those
of the other Amatis.   The varnish is usually of a golden
hue, sometimes approaching to brown; the tone brilliant,
with considerable power on the first string, and round
and full on the third and fourth strings, but sometimes a
little nasal on the second string, arising, it is supposed,
from the elevation in the centre, and the diminution of
the thickness of the wood from the centre to the sides
being too great.   His instruments are much sought
after, and valued at from 80l. to 200l. each.   Fetis
mentions a remarkably fine instrument of his make, with
the date 1668, in the collection of Count de Salabue at
Milan, and another in the possession of Allard, the
violin player, which was said to be one of his best.   Dr.
Forster, writing in 1849, states that Mr. Betts had one
of the finest Amatis, which was worth 250l., and another
of Andrew and Jerome, meaning probably Antonius

and Hieronymus, valued at nearly half that sum; they had rich reddish yellow varnish. He gives tickets dated 1655, and 1661, and also the following, "Nicolaus Amati, Cremonæ, Hieronymus et Antonius Nepos, fecit Anno 1664." Whether the eccentricity of the syntax is due to the inaccuracies in Dr. Forster's book, or is a specimen of Nicolas's Latinity we cannot say. "Lutho-monographie" describes shortly several Amati instruments, and gives the following ticket, "Nicolaus Amati Cremonen. Hieronomi filii Antonii Nepos fecit: Anno 16..;" some little inaccuracy apparently here.

In the "Day Book" of the second William Forster, and the first who gave celebrity to the name, commencing 1st January, 1790, and ending on 20th April, 1799, there is the following entry on the first fly-leaf:— "No. 1. A Violoncello by Nichlaus Amatius, 1669, with Case and Bow, 17l. 17s.," meaning the price at which it was to be sold; a very insignificant one indeed compared to the present value. On the 5th July, 1804, William Forster, the third of the name, appears to have sold an Amati violin to the Rev. Mr. Vinicombe for 31l. 10s.

At the sale of Sir William Curtis's collection, lot 3 was a violoncello by Nicolaus Amati fil. Hieronymi; it was described in the catalogue as made by Antoine and Jerome, but the mistake was corrected by the auctioneer at the time of the sale. The instrument was put up at 100 guineas, and was bought by Mr. Kramer for George IV. for 70 guineas. Lot 8, was a violin by the same maker, dated 1647; it was stated in the catalogue, "This is justly considered as one of the most beautiful and finest instruments in THE WHOLE WORLD. It was put up at 150 guineas, and bought in at 185. Nicolas had two sons, of whom the elder, Hieronymus, born in 1649,

P

followed his father's art, but was inferior and made but few instruments. "Luthomonographie" gives a ticket which appears to be of this maker—" Hieronimus Amati fecit Cremonæ, 167.;" he may be considered the last of the Amatis. The "Biografia Cremonese," as we are informed, speaks of a Nicolas Amati, and an Antoine Jerome Amati, sons of Andreas Amati, who flourished from 1640 to 1670; but we do not know the authority of this work, and there is apparently some confusion of names and dates. Fetis also mentions a descendant of the family who, as recently as 1786, engaged as a work-man with Messrs. Lupot at Orleans, and his violins were much admired; but he would not disclose the nature of his varnish, saying it was a secret of the family, and left Orleans rather than divulge it. It was not known what became of him afterwards.

CHAPTER XVI.

IN the seventeenth century we have a crowd of names of makers requiring more or less notice, including Guarnerius and Stradiuarius. Some will demand nothing more than a passing notice, and of others we know scarcely anything but the name—bo lived, worked, and died.

In the early part of the century Claud Pierret, Jacques Bocquay, Veron, Antoino Despons, and Guersan were good makers at Paris, and we shall shortly refer to some other French makers. The instruments of Despons were said to be held in esteem, and to be rare; and in Britton's sale there is a violin by "Claud Pieray of Paris as good as a Cremona." Guersan was a pupil and the successor of Bocquay; his violins were of small pattern, and finely made, but are scarce. They had fine oil varnish, and some were said even to equal those of Andreas and Antonius Amati. "Luthomonographie" describes one instrument having the lower plate in two parts, and the varnish a deep yellow; also another, a viola of middle size, with the lower plate in two parts, and the varnish brownish red. We have a ticket of a maker called Valler, at Marseilles, in 1683. Giovanni Paolo Maggini, born at Brescia, was a celebrated maker from 1590 to about 1640, and is said to have been the best pupil of Gaspar di Salo. His instruments are rare, and much esteemed.

His pattern is generally large, though he made some of
a smaller form.   The model is somewhat elevated, while
the lower plate is flattened towards the extremities, but
swelling towards the sides, which are large, with the
curves lessened towards the corners.   There is a double
purfling, terminating sometimes at the top and bottom
like a trefoil.   They have generally spirit varnish of a
fine golden colour, but sometimes of a deep brown.   The
tone is less mellow than the instruments of the Stradiuarius family, and less powerful than those of the Guarnerius, having more analogy with the tone of the viol.
His ticket was thus, " Gio: Paolo Maggini in Brescia."
De Beriot, celebrated for his fine and powerful tone, of
which the younger Corvetto told one of the writers of this
work he had not heard the like since the days of Giardini, brought the instruments of this maker into notice
in England by playing on a very fine one.   Mr. George
A. Osborne, the eminent pianist and composer, and, from
his finished musical taste and skill, a most competent
judge, who has written, also, many pieces in conjunction
with De Beriot, says that the tone of this particular
instrument was equal to any he had ever heard.   Maggini left a son called Pietro Santo Maggini, who worked
from 1630 to 1680, imitating his father's models, and
was particularly noted for his double-basses.   There
were several makers of the family of Ruggeri, but it is
difficult to state their order of succession, or even their
numbers accurately.   The eldest appears to have been
Francesco, who worked at Cremona from 1640 to 1684,
or later ; there being tickets mentioned of the latter date.
He was a pupil of Antonius Amati, and followed his
principles of construction.   He made some good instruments ; his model was large, the wood thick, the purfling
broad, with deep brown varnish.   He was known by the

name of Il per, as in the following ticket, for instance,
from "Luthomonographie," "Francesco Ruger, detto il
per in Cremona dell anno 1645." This "detto il per,"
probably only means "commonly known as the father."
He had a son called Giacinto Giovanni Batista Ruggeri,
who apparently worked in the latter part of this century at
Brescia, but there is difficulty in ascertaining his dates;
he was called Il buono. His ticket is "Giacinto filio di
Francesco Ruggero detto il Per 1696." There was a
Pietro Giacomo Ruggeri, who worked at Brescia from
1700 to 1720, and might have been his son. The accomplished performer Piatti has a fine violoncello of his
make, with the following label, "Petrus Jacobus Rug-
gerius de Nicolaij Amati Cremonensis fecit Brixiæ 1717."
A Vincent Ruggeri at Cremona from 1700 to 1730 is
mentioned, but little is known of him.

Of the Grancino family, the first were Giovanni and
Paolo, who worked at Milan during great part of the
seventeenth century; Paolo, it is said, had two sons,
Giovanni and Giovanni Baptista, who worked till the
early part of the eighteenth century at the same place;
the former made good instruments after the plan of
Gaspar di Salo, but the shape was not very good, and
the wood not handsome; he left a son named Francesco,
who worked up to the middle of the eighteenth century.
A very fine instrument of one of the Giovannis was
brought over from Italy, about eighty years since, by Mr.
Waterhouse, page to the Duke of Cumberland, brother
to George III; it afterwards became the property of
Mr. Lindley, who played on it at the Italian Opera, and
its fine telling tone induced Mr. Farsyde to purchase it.
In 1837 he sold it to Mr. Thomas Masterman, of Essex.
The tone was very fine and powerful; the varnish of a
light yellow colour, mellowed by time to a slight reddish

brown. The wood of the lower vibrating plate, sides,
and head, remarkably plain; but the wood of the upper
vibrating plate exceedingly fine.

The only Albani of much reputation is Mathias, who
was born at Botzen, or Bulsani in the Tyrol, about 1621;
Fetis calls him a pupil of Steiner, while in " Luthomonographie" it is stated that he was a pupil of Nicolas
Amati, and the first instructor of Steiner; but from the
precocious talent of Steiner the probability is that he
was the teacher, if either, or they may both have worked
together under the Amatis, though their violins do not
partake of the outline or model of that family. Mathias
made some fine instruments of rather high model, the
varnish being of reddish brown; the first string generally rather brilliant but dry, the second powerful, and
the third and fourth nasal. " Luthomonographie " describes one, having the lower plate in two parts, made of
fine wood, with reddish varnish, and ornamented with
ivory and ebony; the date given is 1712, but this may
have been one of his son's, of the same name, who was
a good maker, and may have been the maker also of two
violins that belonged to Francesco Albinoni, of Milan,
with the respective dates of 1702 and 1709. Gerbert
mentions an instrument of Mathias with the date of
1654; Hill gives a ticket with the same date, which
appears to be the same as that given by Hawkins; we
have the following ticket—"Mathias Albani Fecit Bulsani
Tyrol 1651." Dr. Forster mentions a violin of Signor
Albani at Palermo, 1659; this may be the same as Paul
Albani, named by "Luthomonographie," of Cremona,
in 1650, a pupil and imitator of the Amatis, but inferior.
We have before referred to a son of Mathias, and a
Michel Albani is mentioned at Greece of a later date,
whose instruments are of no repute.

In "Luthomonographie" a ticket is given of Carlo Giuseppo Testore, showing that he worked at Cremona, "Carlo Testore me fecit Cremona del Anno 16 . ." He made good violins, after the Amati pattern, and the small double-bass played on by Bottesini, with such extraordinary execution, is of his make; Dr. Forster mentions three makers of the name, calling them the founders of the Milanese school.

Giaochino, or Giofreda Cappa, a pupil of the Amatis, was born at Cremona 1590, established himself in Piedmont 1640, and founded the school at Saluzzo. His violoncellos were his best instruments; he had two pupils, Acevo and Sapino, whose instruments were formerly esteemed. There was also a Giuseppe Cappa at Saluzzo, at the end of the century. Jean Paul Castagnery was a maker at Paris from about 1639 to 1662; his violins were esteemed for their silvery tone, but had not much power. About the same time St. Paul and Salomou, a pupil of Bocquay, were good makers at Paris; the latter made his instruments after the pattern of Guersan, and his bass-viols are said to have been good. Medard, who is supposed to have been a pupil of the Amatis, was afterwards, it is said, at Paris, and subsequently at Nancy, became the founder of the school of Lorraine in the early part of this century; he took the small pattern of the Amatis for his model, and his instruments, which were silvery and mellow, though not powerful, were sometimes mistaken for theirs. A ticket that we have seen in a violoncello belonging to Lord Stafford, is "Henry Medart a Nancy 1627." Lagetto was another Parisian maker, a little later; his instruments were also after the Amati pattern, with spirit varnish. Sympertus Niggel is another name mentioned. Joachim Tielke was a celebrated maker at Hamburg, in the latter part

of this century, and the beginning of the next, and his
instruments are still esteemed in Germany; he was the
maker of the barytone of the date of 1687, exhibited to
the Society of Antiquaries, as before mentioned, and as
a viol d'amour at one of the Conversaziones of the
Musical Society of London. Martin Hoffman was a
good German maker about the same time, and his instruments are still in request; but from their size, the
form of the sound holes, the sharp corners, and weak
edges, have an ungraceful appearance. He died at
Leipsic in 1725, leaving two sons, of whom the eldest,
Jean Chretién, was more distinguished for his lutes, and
the younger for his violins and bass viols. Other good
German makers of this century were Hans Fichtold,
about 1612, whose instruments are praised by Baron, in
his "Treatise on the Lute." Philip Mohr, at Hamburg,
about 1650; Johan Schorn, at Inspruck, about 1688;
Cornelis Weynman, Amsterdam, about 1692; Johan
Andreas Kambl, about 1635; Christian Roth, Augsburg,
1675; Nicolaus Diehl, at Darmstadt; Wolfgang Vogel,
at Nuremberg, and Martin Schott, at Prague, whose
best instruments were his lutes and theorbas. Dr. Forster
mentions a violin in his possession that came from Gotha,
of which, in the present pogonoferous age, it might be
useful to get the model; it had an appendage that could
be attached to it for the purpose of receiving the beard
of the performer.

Antonio Maria Lausa was an imitator of the school
of Brescia, in the latter part of the century; his instruments were not easily distinguished from the models he
followed, but the tone was inferior. Other makers at
Cremona were Paul Gorans, about 1614; Trunco, 1660;
and Giuliani, 1660, a pupil of Nicolas Amati, and distinguished principally for his good copies. At Milan,

Antonio Maria Lacasso, and Sanza Santino ; but there is
some doubt whether this Lacasso is not the same as
Lausa just mentioned. At Verona were Jean Baptiste
Sanoni, and Bartolomeo Obue. At Trevisa, Pietro Antonio della Caesto, said to have been a clever imitator of
Stradiuarius, and Alexandre Mezzadi, and Dominiscelli at
Ferrara, in the latter part of the century. There were
at Rome Francesco Juliano, Jerome Teoditi, and David
Techler, a German, a pupil of Steiner, and a maker of
considerable merit. He was first established at Salzburg,
and went afterwards to Venice, where he caused so much
jealousy among the other makers that at length they
threatened him with assassination unless he left the place
immediately. He very prudently took this strong hint,
and went to Rome, where, whether because the skill of
his fellow-workmen was greater, and therefore not so
much injured by him, or their jealousy less, he was
allowed to remain in peace, and ended his days there.
The following is given as a ticket: "David Techler
Liutaro Fecit Romæ Anno 1706." His violoncellos were
very large, and of powerful tone. A fine one was purchased by Capt. Robins, R.N., after the peace of 1815,
for 5l., which he afterwards sold to Mr. Lindley, who
was much pleased with it, and used to play on it after it
had been somewhat reduced for modern play. It is now
in the possession of Henry Mann, Esq., of Cleckheaton,
Yorkshire. At Modena, Antonio Cassino was a maker.
At Bologna, Florinus Florentus, and Michael Angelo
Garana, whose instruments had a sweet tone, but were
uncertain. François Gobetti, Pietro Vimercati, and
Paul Farinato, were at Venice, and it may be presumed,
therefore, among the principal persecutors of Techler ;
Vimercati is said to have made instruments after the
style of the school of Brescia, but without the tone of

Gaspar di Salo, or Maggini. Laux Maller is mentioned by Mace as the most esteemed maker of lutes, and is supposed to have been of Venice. Mace says he has seen two of his lutes ("pittifull old, Batter'd, crack'd Things") valued at 100*l.* a piece. He probably, also, made violins, and other instruments of that class. At Marseilles there was Valler, 1683, and at Mantua Racceris, 1670, said to have been in partnership with one of the Gaglianos. Egidius seems to have been the best maker of the Klotz family, working in the latter part of the century, from 1675, and generally putting his own name to his instruments; he was particular in using good wood, and his instruments are well made, and have a finer and fuller tone than any other of the Tyrolese make; they have amber varnish. He was a pupil of Jacob Steiner, and imitated him. After Steiner's reason became affected, Egidius Klotz, or his sons (for this seems a little doubtful) and Tochler, worked in his shop, and placed Steiner's tickets in the instruments then made. George, Sebastian, and Joseph, are named as his sons, and Joseph's instruments are considered superior to his father's. We have the following ticket of George: " Georg Klotz in Mittenwald an der Iser 1761 ;" also one of Joseph, but, from the date, he would seem to be more probably a grandson than a son of the original Klotz, " Joseph Klotz in Mittenwald an der Iser. An. 1774." There was also a Michael Klotz, whose ticket we have, dated 1771. Parke, in his " Musical Memoirs," says that Mr. Hay, formerly an excellent leader of the King's band, had a celebrated Klotz instrument, with a sweet and powerful tone, for which a noble lord offered him 300*l.* and an annuity of 100*l.* (the price seems incredible). Hay, having an independence, declined the offer, and on the sale of his effects after his death the instrument was sold for 40*l.* only.

A manufactory of spurious instruments seems to have been established in the Black Forest, where instruments of all the great masters were provided, just as choice pictures of the most renowned ancient painters can now, it is said, be provided to order; and, as it is whispered also, that instruments of any of the old makers may yet be found by the curious in these matters, who have sufficient confidence, and believe somewhat in the lines of Hudibras—

> " Doubtless the pleasure is as great,
> Of being cheated as to cheat."

In the eighteenth century these imitations were numerous, and were generally called Midwalders. They were sometimes oddly shaped, and had a dark brown and ugly varnish, occasionally it was too red and bright to be taken for old varnish. The genuine violins of the great masters may be readily distinguished by any person of tolerable experience, by their superior workmanship and form, and by their mellow and sweet tones. Some instruments have been improved in consequence of an accidental fracture, when after the repair, if skilfully done, the tone of a dull or stiff instrument has been benefitted. Dr. Forster mentions one that was trod upon and crushed by Signora Columba, and was so improved after the accident that it bore the motto, "a vulnere pulchrior." We cannot, however, recommend the experiment, for in one instance certainly of decided fracture that has come before our notice, the improvement was very problematical.

The celebrated Jacob Steiner was born at Absom, a village of the Tyrol near Inspruck, about 1620. He was intended for the church, but would not apply to the necessary studies, his mind being set on the manufacture of violins; and while yet almost a child he made some

of a rude form, after the model of an old instrument of
Kerlin he found in the house. His parents at last
yielded to his wishes, and he ultimately went to study
under the Amatis at Cremona, where, after some years
practice, he acquired skill nearly equal to his distinguished masters, or in beautiful finish perhaps excelled
them, and began to work on his own account. The instruments made at this period of his life are some of his
best, and also the rarest to be met with. They have a
written ticket, dated from Cremona, and signed by himself. The model is higher than that of the Amatis, the
sound holes rather smaller, and the scroll less prolonged,
and wider in the forepart: the wood broad veined, and
the varnish like that of his teachers. The finest instruments of this period are about 1644. He now married
the daughter of Antonius Amati, and established himself
at Absom ; when, being compelled to work to maintain
his family, he attended more to expeditious workmanship
in order to provide for their immediate wants, than to
working for fame, and his instruments of this period are
inferior to those of his first period ; he rarely got more
than six florins for his violins, and had to carry them
out himself. His varnish of this time was of a dark
reddish colour and opaque. After a time the merits of
his instruments became known, and as he could then get
better prices, he again made them with care, and engaged
pupils and assistants, and among them his brother Marcus, the brothers Klotz and Albani, and founded a school.
Some of his instruments of this period, made for persons
of rank, have the scrolls ornamented with heads of lions
and tigers, and other animals, adopted frequently from
the arms or crests of his patrons. The instruments of
this second period are generally dated from 1650 to
1667 at Absom, but Hawkins gives a ticket of three

years' earlier date, "Jacobus Steiner in Absom, prope
Œnipontum 1047." The wood used by him at this
time is generally of a fine grain; he took the best deal
of Switzerland for the upper, and the finest maple for
the lower plate, sides, and neck; his varnish was of
mahogany colour now embrowned by time. Mons. Alard,
at Paris, is said to have had a violin of this period of the
greatest beauty; and the excellent player Sivori also
had a very fine instrument. Mozart used to play on an
instrument of his make; and at the Salzburg Mozart
Festival, in September 1856, this with the name and date,
Jacobus Steiner, Absom, 1659, and another small one
by Andrea Ferdinand Maier, Salzburg, 1746, on which
Mozart first learned to play, were produced for sale,
having at his death come into the possession of his
sister. In "Luthomonographie" there is the following
ticket of this period, "Jacobus Steiner in Absom prope
Œnipontum, 1663." After the death of his wife, he
retired to a convent of Benedictines, where, according to
Fetis, he passed the remainder of his life; but "Luthomonographie" states that towards the end of it he lost
his reason, either from a violent attachment formed for
Clara Vimercati, (he being then approaching the age of
threescore years and ten,) or from mortification in consequence of having sold his instruments at too low a
price—two very different reasons; but at that age we
might match Plutus against Cupid. There is no doubt,
however, that he did retire to a convent, and then
wishing to distinguish himself, obtained, through the
influence of the superior, some wood of rare quality, of
a close and regular figure, from which he made sixteen
violins of a perfect model. He sent one to each of the
twelve Electors, and the remaining four to the Emperor;
and these are known as Steiner Electors. The tone is

pure and silvery, the form elegant, and the details most
highly finished; the purfling a little removed from the
edge and finely inlaid; the varnish of a transparent
golden amber colour. Fetis says that only three instruments of this third period of Steiner are known to exist;
namely, one given by the Empress Maria Theresa to
the violinist Kennis, at Liege; another bought in 1771,
for 3500 florins, by the Duke of Orleans, the grandfather
of King Louis-Philippe, who, when he gave up playing
himself, presented it to Navoigille the younger; and, in
1817, the instrument passed into the hands of Mons.
Cartier; the third was in the cabinet of Frederic William II. of Prussia.   A curious history has been told us
of a Steiner violin, for which many years ago the father
of General Morgan Neville, of Cincinnati, (the General
himself having told our informant, Mr. James Forster,
and the father having been aide-de-camp to General
Lafayette in the revolutionary war,) gave 1500 acres
of land, worth at that time a dollar per acre—a pretty
large price even at that rate, though a much higher one
than this has been given for a Stradiuarius violin.   But
what as to the value of these "dirty acres" now, when
we understand that a large part of the city of Pittsburgh
has been built on them! No marvellous reward given to
a Roman professor on the flute, or to a marvel on the
tight-rope, or flying trapeze will equal this. Sir F.
M'Clintock, in his "Voyage of the Fox," relates an
anecdote of an Esquimaux who gave a large quantity of
whalebone for a fiddle to which he had taken a fancy;
the fortunate seller afterwards disposed of this whalebone for upwards of a hundred pounds. Otto, in his
work " On the Construction of the Violin," makes observations to the following effect, respecting the Steiner
instruments. The upper plate is modelled higher than

the lower one; the highest part of the model under the
bridge extends exactly one-half of the instrument towards
the lower broad part, and then diminishes towards the
end edge, and it decreases in like manner at the upper
broad part towards the neck.   The breadth of this model
is uniformly the same as that of the bridge, from which
it diminishes towards the side edge.   The edges are very
strong and round; the purfling somewhat nearer to the
edges than in the Cremonese instruments, and also narrower.   The S S holes are beautifully cut, and somewhat shorter than the Cremonese, with the upper and
under turns perfectly circular.   The neck is particularly
handsome, and the scroll as round and smooth as if it
had been turned.   In some the screw-box is varnished
dark brown, and the upper plate deep yellow.   These
instruments are rarely to be found with any labels inside,
and they are simply written.   In the Tyrolese imitations
of Steiner they are printed, and in the genuine Cremonese instruments they are also printed.   The general
character of the Steiner instruments is free, somewhat
piercing, and sparkling, especially on the first string,
having a flute-like quality.   Some instruments of Klotz
have occasionally been confounded with those of Steiner;
but the varnish of Klotz is of a dark basis, with a tinge
of yellow, while that of Steiner is of a red mahogany
colour embrowned by time, besides the superiority of
tone.   The date of Steiner's death is unknown.

Marcus Steiner, who worked at Inspruck, is called by
"Luthomonographie" the son of Jacob; but we have seen
that he had a brother of that name who worked with
him.   His instruments were good, but inferior to those
of his namesake.

CHAPTER XVII.

E now arrive at the time of Antonius Stradiuarius, who is generally considered the
greatest maker that ever lived; and wish
we could introduce him to the sweet music
of one of his own quartett of instruments, such as we at
no distant period heard when in the charge of one of the
writers of this work.

Antoine Stradiuarius was descended from an old
family at Cremona, and was born there about the year
1644, as there is an instrument of his in existence having
a ticket written by him with the date 1736, stating his
age, ninety-two. He was a pupil of Nicolas Amati, and
made after his model, until about the year 1690; from
the year 1670, however, he placed his own name in his
instruments, having for the three previous years placed
that of his master. "Luthomonographie" describes an
instrument of the date of 1681, of a long form, with the
back in two parts, made of fine wood, and the varnish
brown, bordering on red. In the year 1690 he altered
his style, and the proportions of his instruments; his
model was larger, and the form of his arching somewhat
flatter, the gradation of the thickness of the vibrating
plates more strictly regulated, and the choice of wood
carefully attended to; but he still retained some similarity to the workmanship of his master. His best

instruments were made from about 1700 to 1725, and
then approached nearest to perfection. The wood united
beauty with great capability for conducting sound, and
his model was designed with tasto and skill that have
never been exceeded. The thickness was greatest towards the centre, in order more fully to support the
pressure of the bridge under the tension of the strings,
and gradually decreased towards the sides, to give all
the necessary vibration. The S S holes were formed
with great taste, and the scroll finely carved; the
varnish of a beautiful warm reddish or yellowish colour,
of which the secret appears to be lost. The lower plate,
sides, and neck, were made of beautifully figured maple,
the corners not too salient, and the purfling well inlaid.
The four strings are generally of equal beauty of tone
which cannot be surpassed. The details of the interior
of the instrument are equally attended to with those of
the exterior, all being the result of study and scientific
calculation, and in harmonious proportion.

After 1725 his instruments are said to have rather
fallen off in workmanship, he was now an aged man;
the arching became a little more raised, and the varnish
of a browner hue, the tone also less brilliant. Probably
he worked less himself, but gave directions to his assistants, among whom were his sons Homobono and
Francesco, who were inferior to him, and Charles Ber-
gonzo is also said to have worked with him. Several
unfinished instruments were left at the time of his death
which were completed by his sons, who placed his ticket
in them, thus causing some doubt as to the entire authenticity of the instruments towards the close of his life.
He died at Cremona in December 1737, having attained
the great age of ninety-three. He had three sons and
one daughter, Catherine, who died at the age of seventy,

Q

in 1748. Two of the sons, as before-mentioned, worked
with their father, of whom Homobono died in June 1742,
and Francesco in May 1743. The unusual duration of
his life will account for the great number of instruments
reported to have been made by him; but though there
are many that bear his tickets, genuine specimens are
scarce, and it is to be feared that instruments are sometimes put forward with great pretence, of which the
authenticity may well be doubted, the proprietors not
having the prudence of La Monnoye, in his epitaph on
" Louis Barbier Abbé de la Riviere," who, in 1670, left
100 crowns for one—

> " Ci-git un tres-grand personnage,
> Qui fut d'un illustre lignage,
> Qui poseda mille vertus,
> Qui ne trompa jamais, qui fut toujours fort sage,
> Je n'en dirai pas davantage ;
> C'est trop mentir pour cent ecus."

Antoine Stradiuarius is described as having been tall
and thin, and he was in easy circumstances, his usual
price for a violin having been four louis d'or, for which
now probably from 100*l.* to 200*l.* would be given, while
violoncellos would much exceed this price; we shall
refer to some particular instruments directly. The following ticket is given in " Luthomonographie "—" Antonius
Straduarius Cremona faciebat anno 16.. ." In the
same work there is an account of a violin dated 1702,
purchased of the family of Stradiuarius in 1790 by Giov.
Gagliano; it had never been varnished, but was acknowledged by Paganini in 1820 as a genuine instrument.
Prince Youssoupow bought it in 1854, and added it to
the celebrated collection of instruments in his palace at
St. Petersburgh. It is probably this instrument that is
described in the same work as of grand pattern, with the
back in two parts, the body, sides, and neck, of wood

much veined, with reddish varnish approaching to
yellow. A violoncello is also mentioned of middling
size, with the back in two parts, the wood fine, and the
varnish red, verging on brown; the violoncello of Count
Wielieborsky is said to be known to all the musical
world. Mons. Servais, the celebrated performer at
Brussels, had a violoncello of large pattern of extraordinary power, with a silvery mellowness of tone. We
may here observe, that in stating certain celebrated instruments to be in the possession of particular persons,
changes may occasionally have taken place since our
notes respecting the ownership were originally made, so
that our remarks may be considered to apply to the
present or comparatively recent ownership. Mons.
Franchomme, the skilful violoncellist, had an instrument
of the smaller pattern that formerly belonged to Duport,
and of the greatest value, 500l., it is said, having been
asked for it. A very fine violoncello was brought over
by the Earl of Pembroke in the last century, and by him
given to Sperati, then one of the principal performers of
the day; it became afterwards the property of Mr.
Morse, and at the sale of his musical property, in June
1816, was purchased by the third William Forster for
Mr. Cervetto, jun., at the price of 105l. After his death
it was purchased by the distinguished musician, Mr.
Lucas for 200l. and ultimately became the property of
Mr. Charles Finch of Staines. A curious circumstance
may here be mentioned, which was related by the
younger Cervetto himself to one of the writers of this
work. The elder Cervetto, before he entered the musical
profession, had been an Italian merchant, and had dealt
with Stradiuarius himself in musical instruments, and
brought some of his make over to England; but as he
could not obtain as much as *five* pounds for a violoncello,

they were taken back as a bad speculation. At the sale
of Sir Wm. Curtis's instruments, lot 7, was a violoncello
of the date 1684, said to have been made by Stradiuarius for a Corfiote nobleman, and deposited by him in a
chest with cotton, and there left for at least a century ;
it was put up at 200 guineas and bought in for 235.
Mara, the husband of the gifted Madame Mara, was a
good player, but a drunken fellow, and behaved ill to
his wife.   He brought over a fine instrument of this
maker, the tone of which was everything that could be
desired, especially that of the first string, it was musical
and rich, with much power ; the figure or mottle of the
wood was extremely beautiful.   It is believed that Mr.
Crossdill purchased this instrument from Mara, and that
he sold it in the beginning of the present century to
General Bosville, afterwards Lord Macdonald.   His son
disposed of it to Mr. Lucas, who played on it for some
time at the Italian Opera, where he succeeded Lindley
as principal violoncellist, and subsequently parted with
it to Mr. John Whitmore Isaac, of Worcester.   Before
parting with Mara we will relate a couple of anecdotes
of the effects of his temper and pride, for though he
frequently ill-used his wife, yet he was proud of her
talent, and would at times become enthusiastic in this
respect.   We will begin with the result of a drunken
bout.   When the Maras were at Berlin, Frederic the
Great heard that Madame Mara had been unable to
sing before him, in consequence of a severe beating her
husband had given her, amongst other effects of which
was a discoloured, or what schoolboys would call a
black eye.   The enraged monarch sent for the culprit,
and after giving him a severe reprimand, told him as he
was so fond of beating he should be indulged in his
propensity, and accordingly sent him away to act as

drummer in one of his regiments for a month ; a different version, however, says that this punishment was for attempting to leave Prussia without permission. The other story refers to one of his fits of enthusiasm ; being once on a visit to the Earl of Exeter, at Burleigh, the capricious lady complained to her husband, that she did not like his lordship's claret, on which Mara sent to Stamford for a chaise and four, and proceeded to London, returning the following day with a case of claret from their own cellar. It is not stated how long their visit was afterwards allowed to continue. To return to the instruments, the late Mr. Frederick Perkins had a fine instrument of this maker, possessing a pure tone of first-rate quality ; it had formerly belonged to Boccherini, and is now the property of Mr. Robert Garnett, of Sutton Coldfield.

A tenor of Stradiuarius was in the sale of Sir Wm. Curtis, lot 6, which the auctioneer stated to be one of the most valuable specimens of the maker, and not to be surpassed ; it was put up at 150 guineas, but no offer was made for it. Gardiner says that Mr. Wm. Champion gave 300 guineas for a violin and tenor of this make in one case, of a beautiful yellow colour, inclining to orange. The violins of Stradiuarius have been valued and sold for most extravagant prices, from 200 guineas upwards ; the late Mr. Betts had one for which it is stated the sum of 500l. was refused. Fetis mentions one in the possession of Mons. Vuillaume possessing united power and sweetness, a model of exterior beauty and perfection of tone, made in 1716, but rarely played on. A remarkably fine one is said to be in the collection of the Grand Duke of Tuscany, and two magnificent specimens in the possession of Count San Grado, at Venice. The highest price ever given for a violin, was for one by this maker, unless we choose to take the present value of the land given as before mentioned for a Steiner instrument. The violin to which we refer was sold in 1856, for literally more than its weight in gold, as on weighing the violin it appeared that the price given was at the rate of nearly 40*l.* an ounce. At the sale of Mr. Goding's instruments, in February 1857, Mons. Vuillaume gave 212*l.* for a tenor by this maker, for which it is said Mr. Goding had given 400*l.* to Mr. Hart; it was one of a quartett of Stradiuarius instruments, formerly belonging to Lord Macdonald. Dragonetti had a celebrated Stradiuarius double-bass, for which it is said that a well-known amateur offered 800 guineas, but 1000 were required. Stradiuarius also made viols and quintons, guitars, lutes, and mandoras.

It really would almost appear that the possession of one of these splendid instruments would make a person, in spite of nature and of the stars, to fiddle and discourse sweet music. Let it be remembered, however, that great mechanical skill is not the only requisite for fine playing; indeed, such skill may exist with scarcely any real musical feeling. Hear some of our most distinguished performers, observe the delicacy of taste and expression, joined to the most finished execution, where the sense of difficulty is overcome by the impression of the beauty of the performance. Not so with mere digital dexterity, where a considerable degree of facility has been obtained by hard practice, perhaps, and so far praiseworthy, but where no feeling of the poetry of music exists. This sort of performance reminds one of a story of a young priest, in one of the numerous French gossiping memoirs, who was a popular preacher, but one day, when in the pulpit, suddenly lost the thread of his discourse; he did not, however, lose his presence of mind, but proceeded with much gesticulation, considerable inflection of voice, and great emphasis, but, in fact, without pronouncing any sentences intelligibly; the only words striking the ear being such as, car—enfin—mais—si—donc—Messieurs, &c. When he had finished, the congregation was delighted: such energy, such learning, such eloquence. To be sure they all agreed that they could not hear very well, or connect the parts of the discourse, but attributed this to having been badly placed: either too near, or too far off, or in an awkward corner, and determined to choose better places next time, in order not to lose the advantage of such a talented preacher.

We have now arrived at another great name—Guarnerius—of which family there were several; the first being Pietro Andreas, or, as he is generally called, Andreas. He was born at Cremona in 1630, and is considered to have been a pupil of Hieronymus Amati, after whose model, with some little distinction, his instruments were made, and principally of large pattern. The tone is good, but, in general, not strong; and they frequently have a fine shape and good varnish. In Sir William Curtis's sale there were a violoncello and a tenor by this maker, each put up at 100 guineas, and bought in for seventy-nine. Andreas worked from about 1650 to 1680, or, perhaps, later. The following is a copy of a ticket in our possession, or, more correctly, in the possession of one of us, which is the case with all the tickets or labels so referred to:—"Andreas Guarnerius Fecit Cremonæ sub titulo Sanctæ Teresiæ 1675." He had two sons, Giuseppe and Pietro, of whom Giuseppe was the best, and rather followed the model and imitated the varnish of Stradiuarius, and afterwards that of his celebrated cousin and namesake. His instruments are esteemed, though the fourth string is sometimes dry and

hard, and are generally of small pattern, with a brilliant
reddish varnish.   The instruments of Pietro have a full
tone, but want brilliancy, and the form is not elegant;
the varnish of a brownish hue.   The two brothers worked
from about 1690 to 1720 ; and in the latter part of his
life Pietro removed to Mantua.   There was a very fine
violoncello by this maker in Sir William Curtis's sale,
bought in for 125 guineas.   A son of Giuseppo's is
mentioned, called Pietro, who worked at Cremona from
1725 to 1740, and followed his father's models, but with
less finish.   ·

The great artist of this family was Giuseppo, or Giuseppe Antonius Guarnerius, commonly known as Joseph,
the nephew of Andreas, often called del Jesu, in consequence of many of his tickets having I. II. S. marked on
them, and frequently a cross.   His father, Giovanni
Baptista Guarnerius, the brother of Andreas, was not a
maker himself.   Joseph was born at Cremona on the
8th of June, 1683, and became a pupil of Stradiuarius ;
but be was not a mere imitator, and was guided by
positive principles.   He worked at Cremona until the
year of his death, 1745 ; but, unfortunately, in his latter
years, he became careless and dissipated, and addicted
to drink ; his instruments became inferior in make, and
the wood and varnish also deteriorated.

It is stated that he was confined in prison for a considerable time ; and Fetis relates that while he was there
the gaoler's daughter procured some inferior tools and
wood, and assisted him in his work, and then took the
instruments out for sale in order to obtain some com-
forts for him in his reduced circumstances.   She bought
the varnish, as required, from different makers, which
accounts for the variety of tints on his later instruments.
At the commencement of his career his instruments

showed no particular marks of skill, and there was even
an appearance of negligence in his work ; but after a few
years he paid great attention to it, and was very particular in the choice of his wood. The model was carefully worked out, generally of the smaller pattern, and
the arching not much raised, gradually decreasing
towards the sides in a gentle curve, and the S S holes
finely cut: the thickness, perhaps, towards the centre of
the lower plate sometimes too strong, so as to interfere
with the vibration and power. His varnish remarkably
fine, and of a brownish red,- or sometimes of a deep
yellowish tint. He occasionally made some admirable
instruments of a larger pattern. "Luthomonographie"
describes one of these, dated 1723, having the lower
plate in two parts, the wood veined, and the varnish
brownish red. The tone of his instruments is brilliant,
and some of them are scarcely inferior to those of Stradiuarius, bearing a high price. The extraordinary performer, Paganini, played on one. At the sale of Mr.
Crossdill's instruments, in May 1826, a very fine violoncello, by this maker, was bought by Mr. Kramer for
George IV. for 125 guineas, Mr. Cervetto, jun., having
offered as much as 110l. for it. Hill mentions a
tenor of his make, of beautiful workmanship, formerly
the property of Dragonetti, and afterwards in the possession of the lamented Prince Consort. Mr. Willett L.
Adye, of Merly House, Dorsetshire, a well-known amateur, has a remarkably fine violin by this maker, of
which the history is somewhat interesting :—It belonged
to Mr. Mawkes, formerly distinguished as an excellent
performer, who left the profession to enter the Church,
and was ordained many years since. He bought it in
1831, at Spohr's recommendation, from Professor Hoffmann, of Frankfort, when he was studying under the

former celebrated musician at Hesse Cassel. Hoffmann
bought it at the time Rode was at Frankfort, it having
been a *facsimile* of an instrument by the same maker,
played on by him. Spohr told Mr. Mawkes, if he could
purchase it, he would have one of the finest instruments
in the world; and he would have given his famous Stradiuarius in exchange for it. Mr. Mawkes refused several
offers for it, and, having been the possessor of it for
about thirty years, disposed of it to Mr. Adye. The late
Mr. Mori had a fine instrument by this maker. The
following are some of our tickets of this maker:—

> " Joseph Guarnerius
> Cremonensis Faciebat 1724."

> " Joseph Guarnerius fecit
> Cremone anno 1738.   **IHS**"

Dr. Forster gives copies of two tickets by Antonius
Guarnerius, 1722; but his book cannot be depended
on. It may be observed that Joseph does not appear
to have made use of his name Antonius. A Catherine
Guarnerius is named, who was probably the daughter of
Andreas, and worked with her brothers.

CHAPTER XVIII.

HERE are numerous makers in the eighteenth century, many of whom will be known to most of our readers, while of others perhaps even the names will not have reached them. The same difficulties occasionally exist as to the identity of some of the least known persons named, and in some instances the makers will equally belong to the preceding or succeeding century.

Among the Italian makers, the family of Gagliano, at Naples, is well-known. The founder of this, as makers of instruments, is said to have been Alessandro, the son of a Marquis of the name, who was obliged to leave Naples about the beginning of the century, in consequence of some crime committed in a fit of jealousy. He retired to reside in a deep wood, and there amused himself with making violins, and finding that he succeeded, returned in a few years to his native place, where, his offence having been forgotten, he founded a manufactory for instruments. He took Stradiuarius for his model, and made good violins with a lively quality of tone, but not very powerful. He left two sons, Januarius and Nicolaus, of whom we have the following tickets: "Januarius Gagliano Filius Alexandri fecit Neap. 1741," and "Nicolaus Gagliano Filius Alexandri fecit Neap. 1785"; they followed their father's model. There are

four other makers of the name mentioned, Ferdinando
and Giuseppe, the sons of Nicolaus, who made as late as
from 1780 to 1790, or later, there being a ticket of
Giuseppe dated 1789, and Giovanni and Antonio, of
whom Giovanni is reputed the best. Giovanni, it is
said, had two sons, Rafael and Antonio, but it is by no
means improbable that this and the former Antonio are
the same person ; these sons after a few years abandoned
the manufacture of instruments, and established a factory
for strings, which became one of the best in Italy, and
they are stated in " Luthomonographie" to be still living.
The essential importance of good strings is recognized
by every performer. Angelo Angelucci, of Naples, who
died in 1665, had more than one hundred workmen in
his employ, and discovered that the best strings were
made from mountain bred sheep of seven or eight months
old.

The Bergonzis were good makers at Cremona ; a
Francisco Bergonzi is named as early as 1687, who
might have been the father of Carlo. Carlo Bergonzi,
or Baganzi worked from about 1712 to 1750, and
made some excellent instruments, which are held in considerable estimation ; they generally possess beauty and
brilliancy with a fine tone. He worked at one time with
Straduarius, but according to some of his tickets calls
himself a pupil of Nicolas Amati, as for instance, " Carlo
Baganzi allicue di Nicola Amati fecit Cremonæ anno
1729." He had a son called Nicolas living at Cremona
in 1739, whose instruments are sometimes sold for his
father's, but are inferior. A Michele Angelo Bergonzi
is mentioned of about the same date as Carlo. Lorenzo
Guadagnini, was born at Placentia towards the end of the
seventeenth century, and was living in 1742. He was a
pupil of Antonius Stradiuarius, whose models he followed,

generally of the small pattern. He finished with care, using good oil varnish, his S S holes are elegant, and his purfling neat; the first and second strings brilliant, but the third occasionally dull. After working for some time at Placentia he removed to Milan. Giovanni Baptista Guadagnini is generally called his son, but if a ticket we have seen with this name and the date 1731, is genuine, it would appear probable that he was his brother, as stated in "Luthomonographie;" he worked at the same places, and made instruments very similar to those of Lorenzo, and of about the same value; he calls himself in some of his tickets a pupil of Antonius Stradiuarius. A Giuseppe Guadagnini is mentioned at Turin in 1751, and another of the same name at Parma in 1793; and some of the family were at Naples a very few years since.

Francesco Milani, of Milan, worked on the model of Guadagnini about the middle of the century; and Guiseppe Carlo, of the same place, 1769; and Thomas Palestieri, a pupil of Stradiuarius; and Spiritus Sursano, at Coni, about the same time, if there be not some mistake in the name; Alessandro Zanti, at Mantua, about 1770; Camilus de Camile, of the same place, a good pupil of Stradiuarius; and Tommasso Circapa, and Giovanni Santi at Naples, about 1730. At Cremona, Gregorio Montade, a pupil of Stradiuarius, whose instruments were in repute in the early part of the century; Pietro Palestieri, Alberto Giordano, 1735; Davide Camillio, 1755; Nicolao Guletto, 1790; Johann Christian Ficker, 1722; Johann Gottlob Ficker, 1788, and Johann Gottlob Pfretzschner, of whom there is a ticket dated at Cremona 1794; but the three last names are evidently of German origin; and there was a musical firm of the last name at Neukirch, of which we have seen several

tickets; a Carl Frederick Pfretzschner is also mentioned
at Cremona. Lorenzo Storioni, who was living there in
1782, was the last maker of any great repute of that
celebrated place. His violoncellos especially are esteemed
for their powerful tone. His violins resemble those of
Joseph Guarnerius, and Dr. Forster speaks in high terms
of them, particularly of one then in his possession of a
singular shape, and of a dark reddish or nut brown
colour, with a metallic or golden sound as he terms it.
The celebrated performer Vieuxtemps, we are informed,
used one in 1861 for his solo instrument, which was
much admired. There were several makers called To-
nini, at Bologna, in the early part of the century; Felice,
Antonio, Carlo, and Guido; the instruments of the latter
are said to have been esteemed, and sometimes to have
been taken for those of Nicolas Amati. At Brescia,
about the same time were Gaetano Pasta, and Domenico
Pasta, and Nella Raphael of the same school, whose
instruments have good volume of tone, but are not equal,
and may be known by having the scroll sculptured, with
inscriptions on the sides. Rome was deficient in good
makers, the first who commenced making there on the
principles of the school of Cremona, was Gaspard Assa-
lone; we have already mentioned Techler, who was the
best. Antonio Pollusha, 1751, and Antonio Pansani,
1785, were also two of the principal makers there.
Florence did not abound in good makers, only three are
mentioned of any repute, Giovanni Baptista Gabrielli,
Bartolomeo Christofori, and Carlo Ferdinand Landolfi,
who is also stated to have been of Milan, and there are
tickets with his name as of this place, one called Qui-
dantus, is also named, but is probably the same as Giovanni Florenus Guidantus, whose ticket is of Bologna.
There were several makers at Venice of different degrees

of merit; they generally attended to the elegance of
form, and excellence of the varnish, but their instruments were inferior in tone to those of Cremona. One
of their most distinguished makers was Dominico Montagnana. His instruments, especially his violoncellos,
are of large size, and his varnish exceedingly brilliant.
The work altogether is excellent, and the figure or mottle
of the wood large and beautiful. The late Mr. Frederick
Perkins had a fine violoncello by this maker, which was
originally sold as a Joseph Guarnerius; it had been reduced in size, but not judiciously. It was purchased by
Mr. Alfred Guest, the professor, a pupil of Lindley, who
fully appreciates and does justice to its excellent qualities. Montagnana worked at Venice in 1725, and there
are tickets of that date; but in later years he appears to
have moved to the Tyrol, as we have the following
ticket, " Dominicus Montagnana sub signo in Ab prope
Oenipontum, fecit, Anno 1730." Santo Seraphino, of
the same period, was an excellent workman; his instruments are generally good and prized, the wood beautiful,
and of small mottle or figure, and the varnish a good
yellow with a brown tinge, which may have been caused
by age. Two brothers, Matteo and Francisco Gofriller,
in the early part of the century, made strong and good
instruments after the Cremona model, but were inferior
to the two last-named makers. Pietro Valentino Novello, and Marco Antonio Novello, have acquired a well
merited reputation, the violins of the latter especially
are good and rare. Other Venetian makers are the
brothers Carlo and Giovanni Tononi, Pietro Anselmo,
Bellosio, and Bodio. At Padua was Pietro Bagatella,
about 1766, of no great merit; but Antonio Bagatella, a
few years later, was not only a good maker, but published,
in 1782, a valuable work on the construction of instru-

ments from which Maugin, in his " Manuel du Luthier,"
took his method of tracing a fine model of a violin with only
a rule and compass, which may also be seen, somewhat
shortened at the end of Bishop's translation of Otto on
the violin.

Other Italian makers of this period are Paulo Aletsio,
at Monaco, about 1726, skilful in making bass instruments; Antonio Gragnarius, Tomasso Eberti, Giacomo
Horil, Rovelli, Gattananni, Speiler, and Guiseppe Odo-
ardi, who, although a peasant, and self-taught, made
several excellent instruments, but died at the early
age of 28; Carlo Droschi, of Parma, 1744; and J.
Andreas Borelli, 1741. Joseph Contreras is mentioned
as a good maker at Madrid about 1746, making fine
copies of Stradiuarius, which were often sold for genuine
instruments. Galerzena, a Piedmontese, is named, 1790;
Nicholas of Geneva, 1790; and Joseph Wagner of
Constance, 1773.

There are several good and well-known makers at
Paris during this century. One of the earliest was
Augustine Chappuy, about 1711, whose instruments
were much esteemed in France; another of the same
name is mentioned in 1794; Pichol, Amelingue, who,
however, principally made clarionets; Pique and Andrea
Castagneri are other names. Saunier, who was born in
Lorraine about 1740, and established in Paris about 1770,
was a favourite maker, and was the master of Noel Pieto,
born about 1760, who was esteemed as a maker of violins
and basses. Saunier was the pupil of Lambert of Nancy,
nicknamed the Lute carpenter, who made a vast number
of instruments, but not of high merit. Finth, or
Fendt, a German maker, lived in Paris from 1765 to
1780, and took Stradiuarius for his model; his instruments were good and well finished, and said to have been

sometimes taken for those he imitated; he used oil varnish; his nephew came over to England, and established himself there. François Nicolas Fourrier, generally called Nicolas, was born at Mirecourt, in 1758, but went to Paris, where he died in 1816. His instruments are frequently good; he imitated the Cremona school, was correct in his proportions, and particular in his choice of wood. Koliker also was a maker of repute at Paris towards the end of the century; and other names there are—Chevrier, Bernadel, Benoist Fleury, Gavinies, Leclerc, Simon, and Remy; also Nicolas Viard of Versailles, and Cherotte at Mirecourt. In naming this last place, we must mention Jean Vuillaume, who made good instruments there from 1700 to 1740, and had worked with Stradiuarius; Chanot was also a maker of merit there. Nicholas Lupot was born at Stuttgard, in 1758, and was the son of François Lupot, a maker at that place. Nicholas became a celebrated maker, following the models of Stradiuarius. He first worked at Orleans, where a firm of Lupot and Son existed in 1786. In 1794 he established himself in Paris, where he died in 1824. He published a work, to which we have referred occasionally, called "La Chelonomie, ou le parfait Luthier;" but it was written by the Abbé Sibire, from materials supplied by Lupot. His instruments sometimes reach a high price; and he was very skilful in repairing and restoring old instruments. Namy, also about the same time, was noted as a skilful restorer and repairer of old instruments. Ambroise Decombre, of Tournay, made some good instruments, particularly basses, from 1700 to 1735, and had worked with Antoine Stradiuarius; Jean Raut, of Bretagne, who worked at Rennes down to 1790, made good instruments on the model of the Guarnerius school.

R

There were several makers in Germany in this century, of whom some have obtained high repute. Many of them imitated the Steiner and the Cremona schools with great success. One of the best was Charles Louis Bachmann, who was born at Berlin, in 1716, and was himself a skilful performer on the viola, and chamber musician to the King of Prussia. His violins and violas were much esteemed in Germany, and rank next to those of Cremona; they were made after the model of Stradiuarius, with amber varnish, but under his own name; he lived till the year 1800. Schmidt, of Cassel, who more correctly may be called of the present century, being mentioned by Otto, in 1817, as then working, made some fine violins after the model of Stradiuarius; but the edges are larger, and the purfling inclines more towards the centre. There were several makers of the name of Rauch, towards the middle of the century, who made good instruments; as Jacques Rauch, at Manheim, from 1730 to 1740, whose violins approached those of Steiner in tone; Sebastian Rauch, in Bohemia, from 1742 to 1763; Rauch of Breslau, who made some good instruments; and Rauch of Wurtzburg. Johann Gottfried Reichel, of Absam, is named, who made after the model of Steiner; and Johann Conrad Reichel, of Neukirch, in 1779. At Prague, there were two, named Edlinger, father and son, who were more particularly in repute for their lutes; those of the father, Thomas, who was a pupil of Steiner, being equal to those of Gaspar di Salo; he was living at Prague in 1715. His son, Joseph Joachim, lived for many years in Italy, visiting Cremona, Rome, Naples, Bologna, Ferrara, and Venice; he died at Prague in 1748, and his instruments, especially his lutes, were much esteemed. The lutes of Jacobi, at Meissen, about the same time, were also in

repute. Zacharie Fischer, born at Wurtzburg in 1730,
and who was living there in 1808, announced, in 1780,
that he had a plan by which his instruments should equal
those of Steiner and Stradiuarius. This was by drying
the wood in an oven. Other makers also have tried this
plan; but it did not succeed, as it dried the wood too
rapidly, and weakened it, thus injuring the effect of the
vibrations. Johann George Vogler was also of Wurtzburg, about 1749. " Luthomonographie" mentions
Bauch, of Breslau, as one of the best makers of his time,
giving a peculiar form to his instruments; but he may
be the same as Rauch. Leopold Widhalm, at Nuren-
burg, from 1765 to 1788, was a skilful maker, his instruments closely resembling those of Steiner, and scarcely
to be distinguished from them; his harps were also in
repute at one time. Leonhard Mansiell was of the same
place, about 1724. Jaug, or Jauch, of Dresden, made
some good instruments on the Cremona model, with
amber varnish, and made of fine wood, but the tone is
occasionally weak and shrill; he was living in 1774. He
was the master of Christophe Frederic Hunger, born at
Dresden in 1718, who established himself in Leipsic,
where he died in 1787, and was esteemed for his violas
and violoncellos, which were made after the Italian
model, with amber varnish. Samuel Fritzche, of Leipsic,
his pupil, also imitated the Cremona models; and a Bar-
thold Fritz of the same place, in 1757, is named.

Jean Ulric Eberle, living at Prague in 1749, was an
excellent maker, and one of the best of the German
school, some of his instruments being scarcely inferior
to those of Cremona, for which they have been mistaken; but the tone is not so round and full. Charles
Helmer, born in Prague, 1740, was a good pupil of his;
but his fourth string frequently of an inferior quality.

Gaspard Strnad, born in 1750, was settled at Prague from 1781 to 1793 ; he made some good violins and violoncellos, and his guitars were much esteemed.   There appear to have been two Stadelmanns, or Stadlmanns, of Vienna, as we have a ticket of Daniel, 1744, and of Johann Joseph, 1764 ; these instruments successfully imitated those of Steiner, with deep yellow-coloured amber varnish.   There was an Andreas Nicolas Parth of the same place; and about 1700, an Antoine Lidl, who made improvements in the barytone ; Buchstadter, of Ratisbon, was another imitator of the Cremona model, though his make was rather flat, and he used inferior wood, with dark brown varnish ; his instruments are rather harsh, and not much esteemed.   Hassert, of Rudolstadt, made his instruments with much care, of high model, and the upper plate formed of excellent wood, but the tone rather harsh or hollow.   His brother, of Eisenach, surpassed him, and carefully imitated the Italian models, with amber varnish, and used beautiful wood for the upper plate.   Reiss, of Bamberg, also successfully imitated Steiner.   Durfel, of Altenburg, particularly excelled in his double basses.   Artmann and Binternagel, of Gotha, were imitators of the Cremona school.   A. Grobliz, established at Warsaw about 1750, made some good violins on the Steiner model. · At Erfurth, Francis Ruppert adopted rather a flat pattern ; his instruments had a powerful tone, and were well proportioned, but were slightly constructed, the sides not being lined, and the corner blocks omitted ; they were not purfled, and had a dark brown amber varnish.   Francis Schonger, of the same place, made some handsome looking instruments, but the tone dull, and they are considered inferior to those of Ruppert.   His son, George, made some good instruments in the Italian style, and had

much skill as a repairer of old ones. At Munich were
Joseph Paul Christa, about 1730, and Mathias Johann
Kolditz, or Koldjz, 1750. A Jacques Kolditz is mentioned
at Ruhmbourg, in Bohemia, who made some good violins
and violas, and died there in 1796. At Salzbourg, were
Simon in 1722; Andrew Ferdinand Mayrhof, 1740;
Jacob Weiss and Gregor Ferdinand Wenger about 1761;
and Johann Schorn. "Luthomonographie" names seven
makers at Fissen, in Bavaria, from 1756 to 1798,
including Thomas Edlinger beforementioned at Prague.
The others are Gugemmos, though there would appear
to be some mistake about this name, Johann Antony
Gedler, Johann Benedict Gedler, Franz Stoss, Iluf, and
Maldonner. Philip Knitting worked at Mittenwald, as
did Joseph Kriner and Joseph Knitl, 1791, of whom we
have a ticket, marked 2090; probably he thought a
cypher meant nothing. Straube, at Berlin, about 1770,
made some good violins after the Cremona model, with
amber varnish, and was skilful in repairing old instruments; and Johann Henry Lambert was there about
1760; Theodore Lotz, at Presburg, and François
Plack, at Schœnback, in Bohemia, about 1738, made
good violins; and there was Augustine Huller, at Schœ-
neck, 1776. At Amsterdam were Gysbert Vibrecht,
1707; Jan Bremeister, Peter Rimbouls, and Jacoba, of
whom the latter made some good instruments after the
Amati school, but could not attain their tone. François
Antoine Ernst, born in Bohemia, 1745, was an excellent violin player, and became Concert Director at
Gotha. He was a good maker also, many of his
instruments being scarcely inferior to the Cremona
model that he followed. Spohr used to play on one
of them, which is a proof of their merit. He wrote a
short memoir on the construction of the violin, which

was published in the "Musical Gazette" of Leipzic.
Jacob Augustus Otto was born at Gotha in 1762, and
died in 1830; he was established at Halle, in Saxony,
and was a good and careful maker, though for many
years of his life he seems to have been employed almost
exclusively in the manufacture of guitars; he was also
very skilful in the repair of old instruments. He had
no less than five sons who were makers; some at Halle
and some at Jena. His work on the violin is well known,
and we beg to acknowledge our obligations to it for many
particulars of the German makers. Simon Joseph
Truska, born in Bohemia, in 1734, made pianofortes as
well as violins, altos, viols d'amour, and bass-viols; he
was also a performer on the violin and violoncello; his
death took place in the Convent of Strahow, in 1809.
Matthias Frederic Scheinlein, born in 1710, lived at
Langenfeld, in Franconia, where he died in 1771; he
began as a violinist and a harpist. His son, Jean
Michael Scheinlein, born in the same place, in 1751,
was a better maker than his father, and the tone of his
instruments was full and agreeable; but both those of his
father and himself were weak in construction, and apt to
give way in repairing. They were much used in the
chapels. Michel Christophe Hildebrant, of Hamburg,
towards the end of the century, was a good maker, and a
skilful repairer. J. G. G. Heubsch wrote a work on
the manufacture of musical instruments about 1764, and
Charles Greiner, born at Wetzlar, 1753, invented an
instrument to be played on with keys, which, by moving
small cylindrical bows, put gut-strings into vibration;
another of many experiments of this sort which never
seem to have produced any permanent result. A Sweno
Deckman is named at Stockholm in 1706, and Sawes
Kiapoasse at Petersburg, 1748.

We have several other German names in our list, which it does not seem necessary to mention, nor do we propose to give a list of the Continental makers in the present century, it would be long and moreover imperfect, from the difficulty of obtaining accurate details, although we have compiled a tolerably extensive list; but our work would decidedly be defective did we not name Mons. Jean Baptiste Vuillaume of Paris, but of Continental celebrity, well known for his enterprise and intelligence, and not surpassed by any living maker. He is also equally skilled as a successful repairer and imitator of the old instruments. We have seen it stated that Paganini once broke his favourite Guarnerius violin, which Vuillaume not only thoroughly repaired, but at the same time made another so like it in every respect, that even that great master himself was puzzled to distinguish which was the real Guarnerius. Vuillaume has always some instruments of the finest make and quality in his collection; the following is one of his labels:—

"J. B. VUILLAUME,
A Paris,
3, Rue Demours aux Ternes,
Ci-devant rue Croix des Petits Champs 42."

Gand is also a maker of first-rate skill, and is the son-in-law of Lupot, to whose business he succeeded.

CHAPTER XIX.

THE supporters of the theory of the eastern origin of the bow, may perhaps suggest that there is still some uncertainty in our history of its introduction; but we submit that we have given sufficient evidence to claim it for our country. In what way the violin, as known at the present time, was first perfected in England cannot now be authenticated; but the model and outline of the violins of the earliest English makers are different from the Cremona instruments. They partake more of the high swollen model of the earlier violins, made at Brescia and in the Tyrol, but more of the former pattern than the latter, particularly in the outline of the body and the voluto or scroll of the head. We have before mentioned as the oldest makers, Joann Kerlin, 1449, of Brescia or Brittany, and Gaspard Duiffoprugcar, born in the Tyrol: neither of these names are Italian, and some may ask whether the violin-proper might have come from Brescia or the Tyrol, and passed through Germany to the Netherlands? The intercourse of the English people with the Low Countries being greater in the reign of Elizabeth than with the Italian nation, it may be suggested as the probable route by which we obtained the Continental instrument of this class, and may have somewhat modified ours accordingly. Indeed there were makers at Brescia and in Germany prior to and contemporary with those in Cremona. It must be observed, however, that the lute and viol makers of England, in olden times, were considered of high repute, and were competent themselves to introduce improvements in their instruments, and fiddles, as before-mentioned, were in use in our country in the time of Queen Elizabeth. The English makers are alluded to by Vincentio Galilei, the father of the great Galileo, in his work " Dialogo della Musica," where, according to Sir J. Hawkins' " History of Music," (Novello's edition, p. 404), he remarks, that in his time (1583) the best lutes were made in England. Yet it does not appear that they have kept to " Schools " connected with the chief makers in the art to the same extent as in Italy; consequently there is some difficulty in tracing the style from Jacob Rayman (1641), Thomas Urquhart (1650), and Edward Pamphilon (1685), the earliest makers of violins-proper known in England, to the time of Norris (1818), and Barnes and old John Betts (1823), which may be considered to terminate the chain; however, an endeavour will be made to accomplish this desired end, by comparing the style and character of the work of each maker, assisted by the dates at which they lived. In the perusal of the following pages it will be seen that many of the persons who are there taken notice of, have been prompted to try their skill as violin makers by the love of, or from being connected with music, and have been thus induced both to repair and make instruments.

The earliest authenticated name that comes down to us as a maker of viols in our country is Richard Hume, or Home, 1535; and it is stated in " Dauney's Ancient Scotch Melodies " that he was the great viol maker in Edinburgh, although an Englishman, and then had a

grant of 20*l.* to buy stuff for the same. There can be
but little doubt that many other makers of lutes and
viols were in existence at the same time and previously,
but no record of their names has been preserved. The
maker's name of the instrument of the violin kind formerly mentioned, and considered to have been made by
command of Queen Elizabeth, and given to Robert
Dudley, Earl of Leicester, is not known ; but an
engraving on the tail-pin, J$^{A}_{1G}$P, is supposed to signify the
year it was made in, and the initials of his name. Whoever he was, whether English or foreign, he must have
seen the true violin, as the improved form of sound-hole
is used, and only four strings are applied. Between the
years 1562 and 1598 there would be living several
instrument makers held in much esteem ; and Thomas
Mace, in his curious and eccentric book, " Musick's Monument," published in 1676, mentions some of them ;
however, it had better be told in his own style :—" Your
best provision, (and most compleat) will be a Good Chest
of Viols ; Six, in number ; viz. 2 Basses, 2 Tenors, and
2 Trebles : All truly, and Proportionally suited.—Of
such, there are no better in the world, than those of
Aldred, Jay, Smith, (yet the Highest in Esteem are)
Bolles, and Ross, (one Bass of Bolles's, I have known
valued at 100*l.*) These were Old ; but we have now,
very excellent good Workmen, who (no doubt) can work
as well as those, if they be so well paid for their work, as
they were ; yet we chiefly value Old Instruments, before
new ; for by experience, they are found to be far the
best."

We do not learn of any line of succession from Aldred
or Bolles ; they seem to be the last of their race as
musical instrument makers. With regard to the other
names, a little more detail can be given ; and those of

Jay and Smith will be met with in the seventeenth and eighteenth centuries.

John Ross, or Rose, the elder, who was dwelling at Bridewell in the 4th of Elizabeth (1562), and was the inventor of the bandora, an instrument of the guitar sort, with wire strings ; also made viols and instruments of that class ; but Stow says he was excelled by his son in making bandoras, " royal de gamboes," and other instruments.

In a collection of airs, called " Tripla Concordia," published in 1667, a chest of viols is advertised, containing two trebles, three tenors, and one bass, made by Mr. John Ross, the son, in 1598.

Henry Smith lived over against Hatton House, in Holborn, about 1629, and in the work just alluded to there is also an advertisement of a chest of viols, consisting of two trebles, two tenors, and two basses, made by him in 1633.

The other name (Jay), which Thomas Mace mentions, is supposed to be Thomas Jay, who, no doubt, was dead at the time he wrote the " Musick's Monument," as he alludes to the instruments of the several makers being old.   There were other viol makers, whose labels have been seen (Hill's MSS.), which will continue the link :—" John Shaw att the Goulden harp and Hoboy nere the May pole in the Strand 1656. '   Also " Christopher Wise, in Half Moon Alley, without Bishops-gate, London, 1656 ;" and " William Addison in Long Alley over against Moorfields 1670."   This brings us to Barak Norman, 1690, whom Sir J. Hawkins states (p. 793, Novello's edit.) " was one of the last of the celebrated makers of viols in England ; he lived in Bishopsgate, and afterwards in St. Paul's Church Yard."

This maker will again be alluded to in connection
with his partner, Nathaniel Cross.

The violin-proper was known in England some years
before it became the favourite in "*good society;*" and
although we find it in the band of Queen Elizabeth, yet it
was generally associated with wakes, revels, and other noisy
merry-makings; but on Charles II. introducing his band
of twenty-four violins, the instrument rose in estimation,
much to the annoyance and great grief of the author of
"Musick's Monument," that the noble and brave lute,
also the majestic theorbo, should be "over top'd with
squaling-scoulding fiddles" (p. 204). Again, in alluding
to "those choice consorts" of his period (p. 236), and
the great pleasure those performances gave both to the
listeners and performers, which he states made "the
musick lovely and contentive," he then makes further
remarks: "But now the modes and fashions have cry'd
these things down, and set up a great idol in their
room; observe with what a wonderful swiftness they now
run over their brave new ayres; and with what high
priz'd noise, viz. 10, or 20 violins, &c. as I said before,
to some single soul'd ayre; it may be of 2 or 3 parts, or
some coronto, seraband, or brawle, (as the new fashion'd
word is) and such like stuff, seldom any other; which is
rather fit to make a man's ears glow, and fill his brains
full of frisks, &c. than to season, and sober his mind, or
elevate his affections to goodness. Now I say, let these
new fashion'd musicks, and performances, be compar'd
with those old ones, which I have before made mention
of; and then let it be judg'd, whether they have not left
a better fashion, for a worse. But who shall be the
judges? If themselves; then all's right."

Yet he cannot withstand recommending the intruder,

with certain qualifications, to complete the collection of instruments requisite for the various performances (p. 246): "After all this, you may add to your press, a pair of violins, to be in readiness for any extraordinary jolly, or jocund consort occasion; but never use them, but with this proviso, viz. Be sure you make an equal provision for them, by the addition, and strength of basses; so that they may not out-cry the rest of the musick (the basses especially), to which end, it will be requisite, you store your press with a pair of lusty full-sized theorboes, always to strike in with your consorts, or vocal musick; to which that instrument is most naturally proper."

The first maker of violins in England to whom we have any guide, is Jacob Rayman, about 1641; but no record is known to indicate of whom he learned the art. It has been asserted by some persons that he made violins of a large size, but those which have been seen are small, and not of an elegant outline or model; the fore-bout being wide, the short-bout long, and out of all proportion with the lower part of the instrument. However, he was a maker of talent and ability: the tone was clear, penetrating and silvery; not possessing the reedy quality of the Cremona violins, but partaking more of the Brescia character; and his instruments were highly prized. In the extracts from the catalogue of musical instruments for sale, the property of Thomas Britton, "the small-coal man," who died in 1714, lot θ, a violin is stated as "an extraordinary Rayman;" and in a note Sir J. Hawkins remarks, "The tenor violins made by him" (Rayman) "are greatly valued." Notwithstanding the purfling is done indifferently, yet the work, generally, was neat and good, the fluting at the edge where the purfle is inlaid is deep and acute. The sound hole is rather small, like that

used at times by Steiner; the varnish very good, and of
a yellowish brown colour with a little tinge of red, and
the vehicle used appears to be oil.   Labels in genuine
violins as used by the maker are,

> " Jacob Rayman dwelling in Blackman
> Street Long—Southwark
> 1641."

> " JACOB RAYMAN at y" Bell
> Yard in SOVTHWARKE
> LONDON 1648,"

and Hawkins states he dwelt in Bell Yard, Southwark,
about the year 1650.

The three makers whose names follow, two of whom
still retain a character for excellence, are Thomas Urquhart, 1650 ; Edward Pamphilon, 1685 ; and —— Pemberton, supposed to be about 16—, 1680, but these dates
are doubtful.   Tradition has brought down to us, that
these three persons were partners, and their place of
business was on London Bridge ; but there is no evidence
such was the case, although it may be very probable, as
that locality at the date would be the best for trade.
Urquhart, it is believed, came from Scotland, and was a
maker of unusual merit for the period in which he lived ;
the violins are of the full size, with an oil varnish of a
dark amber colour inclining to brown, yet it is bright
and grateful to the eye, and much resembles the Italian
varnish.   The tone is clear, pure, and silvery ; and appreciated even at this period.   The violins and violas
are very scarce, and no violoncello has been seen of this
maker.

It has been stated that Urquhart came to England at
the time the two countries happily became united, but

this is doubtful when the dates are compared. James the Sixth of Scotland ascended England's throne 24 March, 1603, and entered London 7 May, 1603; yet nothing is known of this maker's instruments until about the date previously given.

Who instructed Edward Pamphilon in the art of violin making, or from whence he came, cannot now be ascertained. It is generally considered that Thomas Urquhart was his master, and the style of work, the colour and description of varnish favour this opinion; however he was not so successful with his violins as the elder maker. The outline is not graceful, the short-bouts are too long and out of proportion with the upper and lower parts of the instrument, the model high and swollen, and the sound-holes rather small. The varnish is either oil or turpentine of a red colour and brown tinge with a yellow ground, and now looks rich and beautiful, which age no doubt has greatly assisted. The violins—and no other instruments have been seen—are strong in wood, the tone clear, pure, and penetrating. The professors of this period greatly approve of them for orchestral uses. The following is a copy of a genuine written ticket or label, and the maker seems rather precise, as the day of the month is also added :—

> " Edward Pamphilon
> April the 3rd 1685."

Little can be related of —— Pemberton, the Christian name is not known, and some doubt exists whether he was the younger or the elder of the firm; if the latter, the supposed date of 1680 may be wrong, and he may be the J—— P——, 1578, the maker of the violin, presented to the Earl of Leicester by Queen Elizabeth; should this be so, he would be the first of the English makers that manufactured the violin as known at the present day: not that the gift above noticed is such an instrument; nevertheless, whoever made it must have seen one of more graceful form and of greater elegance; without all the elaborate and useless ornamental carving, most detrimental to tone and practical utility.

A maker named Thomas Cole was living about the same time as the three just noticed; but no instrument has been preserved to this time to support his title as a workman. The label was as follows:—

" Thomas Cole, near Fetter Lane
in Holborn. 1672."

Daniel Parker, of London, 1714-15. This maker evidently was a pupil of one of the previous persons who lived in the latter half of the seventeenth century, and by the scroll or volute of the head it would probably be Urquhart or Pamphilon; however he has shown himself a person not inclined to adhere to old instructions, but to progress in the art, and he made a first step towards improvement both in the outline and model.

Violins are the only instruments known of this maker, neither viola or violoncello has been seen, and the general character of the body of the instrument approached to the shape and form of the Amati school, however not quite so elegant. The varnish may be alcoholic, of an unpleasant brick-dust red colour, thickly laid on the instrument and not agreeable to the eye. The figure of the wood is generally handsome, the tone very good, clear, and powerful. About 1793 the violins of this maker were valued at five guineas, and in the beginning of the first half of the present century they have realized twelve and fifteen guineas, but now are again reduced in amount, from the desire of performers to possess

none but Italian instruments, and other causes which
depress the manufacture of such articles. Daniel Parker
may be considered to terminate the first school of English
violin makers. A new era now opens with the violin
makers of England, in which the style of work is greatly
improved; the model, with most of them, partaking of
that used by Jacob Stainer, or Steiner, for it is spelt
both ways, the beautiful and exquisite finish of this once
favourite maker is closely imitated, and it has influenced
all the workmen in the commencement of the eighteenth
century; indeed all through this century the Steiner
claimed preeminence; some of the violins having realized
100*l*., and on one occasion a much larger sum; whilst
the instruments of the Amati family, and other Cremonese
makers, would scarcely reach an amount remunerativo
to the vendor, which, compared with the amounts since
realized for the instruments of these deservedly great
makers, seems perfectly absurd and ridiculous; however,
in the latter part of the century the instruments of Cremona began to be sought for and appreciated.

The catalogue of musical instruments of Thomas Britton, previously alluded to, contains some names of violin
makers which may form the link between the seventeenth
and eighteenth centuries; but it is not known by whom
they were instructed. "Lot 5, a good violin by Ditton;"
this name only lives by the notice which Sir J. Hawkins
has given him. It is different with that of "Daker of Oxford," for he deserves much commendation as a violin
maker; two or three instruments of this class have been
seen, and it is a pleasing recollection to allude to them:
"Lot 20, a fine viol by Mr. Daker of Oxford." The
work, in every respect, of the modern instruments was
very good, indeed of excellent finish, the varnish of a
light yellow colour, and probably oil or turpentine was

s

the vehicle used. The tone was very pure and clear in quality, but not great in quantity.

Thomas Jay, supposed to be a descendant of the celebrated viol maker named in "Musicks Monument," who also made similar instruments, is stated to be living about 1690 to 17—, and the style of work in the few violins which have been seen, may be considered as an advancement towards superior workmanship. The instruments of Baker of Oxford and the maker under present notice are about equal in excellence. "Lot 22, another (viol) said to be the neatest that Jay ever made." This may be the maker just mentioned, or the elder one of the same name. It will be seen, about fifty years after that the work of another of this family name commanded a good price even for an inferior description of instrument. Edward Lewis was a maker of London, and stands preeminent for his good workmanship; his style was excellent, and the few violins which have been seen were varnished of a light yellow colour, however others assert that he also used a red colour with a golden ground. Be this as it may, there can be but one opinion that his violins, which are scarce, have much beauty, and are remarkable for their fine varnish. "Lot 19, another ditto (tenor) by Mr. Lewis; also Lot 24, another (bass violin) rare good one by Mr. Lewis." Some persons say that Jay and Lewis were partners, but there is no evidence known to decide this point.

Barak Norman has been mentioned as a maker of viols, and it is believed he was in business from 1690 to 1740. There is evidence of violoncellos being made in 1718, but no violin has been seen of his work. The violas and violoncellos of this maker are generally of full size, although one of the latter is known unusually small, of which mention will be made directly.

It will be seen by the varnish that he adheres to early recollections of colour, similar to the lutes and viols of old, by using a dark brown with a blackish hue, as if produced by nitric acid and accelerated in drying by heat, which heightens the colour, after which a coat or two of oil varnish to enrich the whole and help to preserve the instrument. This tint or colour may be considered the one generally used by him. The monogram will be seen inlaid either in the centre of the back, or in the upper vibrating plate just under the wide part of the fingerboard of his violoncellos; however the same device was used in the similar instruments made by Cross when they were partners. The tone, both of the violas and violoncellos, is very good and deservedly held in esteem. A tenor by this maker has been associated with the principal performers on this instrument for sixty or seventy years. Frederick Ware, celebrated for the great quantity of tone he produced, possessed it either before or at the commencement of the present century; and some time after his decease, it became the property of another professor of eminence, who delighted the frequenters of the Royal Italian Opera House in the romance or recitativo " Quale Spettacol," and aria, " Ah! Piu Bianco," in Meyerbeer's opera, " Les Huguenots," which was exquisitely sung by Mario, and the viola obligato was played by Henry Hill, which drew forth merited applause. Soon after his death the instrument passed into the ownership of Mr. Doyle, another principal viola performer of the same opera establishment. The small-sized violoncello, previously named, was seen by William Shield, the composer, at a humble shop or general dealer in the Borough; it was suspended by the head outside the house, and blowing about in the wind; although very dirty, the appearance of the instrument

attracted his notice, and an arrangement was made not
to sell the same until a friend of his had seen it. On
his return home the circumstance was mentioned to
James Crossdill, who ultimately bought the violoncello at
a very small cost; and on its being cleaned and put in
order, it was acknowledged a genuine Barak Norman,
of superior quality of tone, having much power, although
so small in size; the varnish was of a brown colour, but
not so dark as that in general use. This instrument
became a special favourite with the owner, who frequently
used the same in his professional duties, and being the
instructor to the Prince of Wales, afterwards George IV.
it was taken to Carlton House on some occasion, when
the tone much pleased the Prince, who expressed a
desire to possess it; however the professor withstood
several liberal offers. At a subsequent period a page
was sent for this instrument, as the Prince wished to use
the same that evening. The result was that the violoncello was never returned; and His Royal Highness stated
that Crossdill might keep an Amati violoncello which
had cost seventy guineas in lieu of it. About this time
also a sinecure place of one hundred pounds per annum
became vacant, which was given to Crossdill as the *amende
honorable* to sooth the disappointment and loss, which
sinecure he retained until his decease.

A violoncello made by Barak Norman in 1718 was,
in the year 1790, considered of the value of fifteen
guineas, since that time they have realized much larger
sums. Nathaniel Crosse, or Cross: it is not known by
whom this maker was instructed; his style greatly resembles that of Steiner, the fluting round the edge where
the purfle is inlaid is very acute, and his instruments are
beautifully worked in all particulars. The printed label
used by him previous to becoming a partner with Barak

Norman, may be supposed to infer that he was a pupil of Steiner (but this borders on the impossible), or that he adopted the characteristic style of that excellent foreign workman; however it bears a fabulous number, as if the instruments he had made reached to so large a figure, the last figure being added in ink:—

" Nathanaeli Crosso Stainero
fecit. No. 2417."

He lived in Aldermanbury, London, and the instruments which have been seen, chiefly violoncellos, were very similar to those he made during his partnership with the previous maker; they are small in size and squat, and are varnished of a light yellow colour, the vehicle or body varnish is considered to be made of one of the soft gums, mastic or sandarac dissolved in alcohol, which renders them of easy blemish and disfigurement by any slight scratch, similar to the defect observed in the ornamental wood-work of Tonbridge Wells. The tone is clear and rather penetrating in quality. His violoncellos are generally sold as Barak Norman's, but the style of work of the two makers, in every particular, is very different. Cross is supposed to have been living in 1751. It has been previously noticed that the monogram of the elder partner is generally, if not always, inlaid either in the upper or lower vibrating plates of the younger workman.

It cannot be stated when these two makers became partners, but there is evidence that they were so about 1720, as the following copy of a printed label used by them will prove; the Maltese cross is at the top, and only three figures are in print, leaving the pen to complete the date:—

✠
" Barak Norman
and
Nathaniel Cross
at the Bass viol in St.
Paul's Church Yard.
London.   Fecit 172—."

John Barrett certainly is of the same school as Nathaniel Cross, whoever may claim to be the originator;
but he could not have been a pupil, as some persons suppose, for it will be seen they were contemporaries; he in
1722 carrying on business in Piccadilly, and the other in
St. Paul's Church Yard in 172—.   The genuine violins
that have been seen are of a long and high model,
approximating to the Amati pattern, with the Steiner
blended in the same.   There is a characteristic mark in
this maker's violins (for no other description of instruments have been seen), they all have ink lines instead of
purfle, and the fluting where the ink lines are and purfle
should be is very acute, similar to the work of N. Cross,
forming almost the inner half of a circle.   A perfect instrument of this maker is in the possession of Mr. C. Ward,
of Chapel Street, West, May Fair; the tone of which
is very pure and of superior quality, but not powerful.
The varnish on this violin when first used must have
been a pale yellow colour, but age has mellowed and
produced a brown tint.   The same defect exists with the
body varnish as that used by the maker previously noticed.
Copies of printed labels or tickets used by him in the
violins are as under:—

" John Barrett, at the Harp and Crown
in Pickadilly, 1722."

In 1731 the following was in use; a lyre with the crown
on the top of it, printed on the left corner before the
name, and in the date only two figures were printed,
leaving space for the other two, to be added by a
pen:—

> "Made by John Barrett, at y* Harp
> & Crown in Pickadilly, London, 1731."

The value of this maker's violins, in 1802, was considered
to be six guineas; since then they have produced eight
and ten guineas; but now a cloud o'er-shadows them as
well as all other English makers.

The name of Joseph Hare is little known as a violin
maker, nor can it be stated of whom he learned the art;
however, he deserves especial notice as being, it is considered, the first person in England who used the flat
model in his instruments. The varnish was a rich red
colour, very good, and transparent. From the improvement in the principles or mode of work, and a varnish
of different colour and brilliancy than previously used
by the makers, it may be inferred that he was self-taught,
and the first of a new school, but having no imitators until
more modern times, when the Stradiuarius pattern became paramount. The following is a copy of the printed
label used:—

> "Joseph Hare at y* Viol & Flute
> near the Royal Exchange
> in Cornhill London
> 1720"

Peter Wamsley was a maker that once stood high in
repute, his violoncellos more especially realizing great
prices; the work was good and neat, with a bias towards
the outline and model of John Barrett, but modified.
Most of his violins, violas, and violoncellos, have only

ink lines instead of purfle, although there are exceptions, and but few instruments are known that have this
ornamental and useful inlaying. The varnish is generally of a red colour, with a brown tinge; but there are
some instruments that have a brownish yellow colour,
rather opaque. This maker fell into a great error by
endeavouring to anticipate age, and worked the instruments so thin, the violoncellos in particular, that many
years since they were liable to compress for want of sufficient thicknesses to withstand the tension of the strings;
and in hot rooms they gave way in tone for want of
greater stamina. Professors said "they played them
out," and were far from satisfying either in quality or
endurance. From this defect the tone is mostly hollow
in sound, and wolfy, if the musical term may be allowed,
which may be expressed by stating that many faulty
or hard notes are created by this imperfect mode of
gauging the instruments. However, there are a few
violoncellos known of this maker in which more wood
has been left, and the tone of them is good. The
external appliances to remedy the defect alluded to will
be a low bridge of rather hard wood, and strings of
small size, with a sound-post full long and tight. Peter
Wamsley made but few double basses, which are now
very scarce. Those which have been seen were very
good in tone, and stronger gauging; the varnish was of
the red colour similar to that used in his other instruments.
The following are copies of printed labels used by this
maker :—

> " Made by Peter Wamsley
>   at ye Golden Harp in Pickadilly
>   London
>   1727."

The two last figures added with a pen. The two labels

following are printed on a narrow slip, and the last figures on each are also added with a pen :—

> "made by Peter Wamsley at the
> Harp and Hautboy in Pickadilly 1735."

Also—

> " made by Peter Wamsley at the Harp and
> Hautboy in Pickadilly London. 1737."

The next printed label is very small, with plain black lines as a border to it :—

> " Peter Wamsley
> Maker at the Harp
> & Hautboy in Picaddilly
> 17 London 51."

There can be but little doubt that Henry Jay was a descendant of the one previously named in the latter part of the seventeenth and beginning of the eighteenth centuries, but there is no proof that it be so, although the style of work almost justifies the assertion. He was a good and neat workman, and was celebrated for the kits he made for the use of dancing-masters, each one realizing five or six pounds. The varnish was of red colour, with a brownish hue. The labels he used were chiefly written, but some are printed :—

> " Made by Henry Jay
> in Long Acre. London. 1746."

Where it appears he resided for twenty-two years ; then the following printed label was adopted, the two last figures put in with a pen :—

> " Made by Henry Jay in
> Wind-Mill Street, near
> Piccadilly. London. 1768."

If the surmises regarding this family of Jay be correct, they will have held a prominent place as makers of lutes,

viols, and violins, for more than one hundred years
and passed through the transition state from the more
antiquated instrument to that of more perfect character,
Henry Jay being the last of the family as a maker.

There were several violin and violoncello makers
residing in the City, in the latter half of this century,
who appear to have adopted small sized violoncellos, not
exactly of the squat pattern used by Nathaniel Cross,
but something of that character, and still adhering to
the high model. It is not known who instructed them ;
but neither their work or goodness of tone has added any
lustre to their names, although the instruments have
been made more than one hundred years. Unless the
various thicknesses are properly blended, age will not do
much to improve them. The instrument must be good
from its first manufacture to derive the essential qualities
which age certainly imparts, although it cannot be denied
that age and much use may improve these instruments.
These makers form a portion of the links in the chain
we are endeavouring to elucidate. The first of this
class is,

> " Robert Thompson att the Bass Violin
> In pauls Ally St. pauls church yard
> London   1749,"

who appears to have taught his sons, or some other relatives, as there are others of the same surname.

> " Made by
> Thompson & Son
> at the Violin &c
> the West end of
> St. Pauls Church Yard
> London
> 1764."

Probably this is the firm mentioned in the Musical Directory of 1794 :—

> " Samuel and Peter Thompson
> Instrument Makers and Music Sellers
> No. 75. St. Pauls Church Yard."

In 1775 and 1785 printed labels from instruments exist as—

> " Made and Sold by
> Cha'. and Sam'. Thompson
> in St. Paul's Church Yard ;"

but it is not known if they were relatives of those previously mentioned ; the dates and locality create a probability that they were so.

There was also another maker of this class who used a written label without date :—

> " Sold by John Johnson
> Cheap Side. London."

And others printed were used in 1753 and 1759, the last figure put in with a pen :—

> " Made & Sold by John Johnson
> at the Harp & Crown in Cheapside
> 17 London 53."

And the same for the later year.

Thomas Smith was a pupil of Peter Wamsley ; the model and outline of his instruments were similar to his master's, but fortunately thicker in wood. As a maker, he held a good position in his day ; but at the present time the violoncellos are considered deficient in quality of tone. The first concerto that the late eminent Professor Robert Lindley played in public was upon a violoncello of this maker, and the instrument is still in possession of his second son, Mr. John H. Lindley. The varnish on the instruments is meagre and poor, of a

brownish yellow colour, and not even approaching that
used by his instructor. From 1756 to 1766 the following
narrow printed labels were in use, so much like that formerly adopted by his master, that the conclusion may be
drawn he had succeeded Wamsley in the business, and
merely altered the name in the plate :—

> " made by Tho'. Smith at the Harp and
> Hautboy in Pickadilly. London. 1756."

The violoncellos of this maker, in 1799, were sold for
a price varying from five guineas to eight pounds, and it
is questionable if he made either violins or tenors.

John Norris and —— Barnes were instructed in violin
making by the foregoing Thomas Smith, and they were
fellow-apprentices. On the completion of the allotted
time they had to serve, they became partners ; and as
there is evidence of their dwelling in Windmill Street
on the 10th February, 1785, it may approximate to the
time at which they commenced business on their own
account. The Musical Directory previously alluded to,
for 1794, shows at that time they had removed to No. 34,
Coventry Street, Haymarket. No instrument of any
description has been seen as made by either of these
persons, and it is generally considered they became
dealers in and repairers of violins, &c. A violoncello is
known stamped with their names on the back, at the
top, near the neck, but it is certainly the work of Edmund Aireton. The partnership was not one of conge-
nial nature, and as soon as the expiration of the deed
of partnership would allow it they separated. It is stated
that Barnes retired from business and kept a farm at
Hayes, near Uxbridge, and that he died there ; however,
the church books have been examined, and there is no
evidence of his death. It is more probable that he opened
a house of business in the old locality, as the Directory

for 1794 has "Robert Barnes, violin maker, Windmill Street, Haymarket"; therefore, as the firm is also mentioned in the same book as existing, perhaps 1794 was the year of separation. The following is a copy of the label used by them :—

> " Made by Norris and Barnes
> Violin Violincello and Bow Makers
> To Their Majesties
> Coventry Street. London."

John Norris continued to carry on business at the usual residence; but statements differ regarding his retiring in favour of his shopman, Richard Davis. Some assert he died at Coventry Street, others say it was at a relative's house in Walham Green; but it is certain he is interred in the burial-ground of Fulham Church. The spot is marked by a stone, on which is engraved—

> " John Norris
> Died 10 March 1818,
> Aged 79 years."

Richard Duke attained to great celebrity as a maker, and was quite the fashion at the period in which he lived; but there is no positive evidence of whom he learned the art of making violins, tenors, and violoncellos, all of which instruments have more of the Steiner pattern in them "than is consistent with a fine reedy tone," which in the violins is clear and silvery. The pattern rather long, and a yellow varnish. Some of the tenors are small in size, about the length of a violin, and the endeavour has been made to obtain a larger and deeper tone by making them very broad; the tone is good, but more power is wished for on the two lower strings. The varnish of some of these instruments is very poor; the colour seems to have been obtained by a weak solution of walnut-stain, and a thin coat of varnish put on afterwards. The few violoncellos which have been seen are of a long pattern, with high model, and a yellow varnish; the tone very good. At one period he lived in Red Lion Street, Holborn. The following are copies of some of the labels used in the various instruments, and they mostly were written with pen and ink:

" Rich⁴ Duke
Londini fecit   1767."

Also, a similar one in 1769; but eight years afterwards he had changed his abode, and the label used was

"Richard Duke
Maker
Holborn. London. Anno 1777."

Probably about this time a printed one was adopted; but there is no date upon it:—

" Richard Duke maker
near opposite
Great Turn-Stile
Holbourn. London."

There was a son of the foregoing, whose name is also believed to be Richard Duke; and by the style of work he evidently was instructed by his father. However, the world did not smile on him, and in the early part of the present century he solicited purchasers of his violins and tenors, from house to house, of those in the trade. Both father and son generally stamped their names on the back of the instruments, at the top, near the button. At times the surname only, and at others with London underneath the name.

John Edward, or better known as old John Betts, and his nephew, Edward, commonly named Ned Betts, were both pupils of the elder Richard Duke; they came from

Stamford, Lincolnshire, or its vicinity. John Betts was born in the year 1755, and in due time was sent to London to learn violin-making, but whether he proved a first-rate workman cannot be certified; report speaks to the contrary. As a dealer, great knowledge of the Italian makers is assigned to him. The instruments which bear his name often show an altered style, occasioned by the various workmen employed by him at different periods; namely, John Carter, Ned Betts, Panormo, Bernhard Fendt, and his sons, and others could also be mentioned. Much of their work, particularly of the nephew and the Fendts, being imitations of the Italian and old English makers, some of which are excellent copies. Dr. Forster, in his "Epistolarium," vol. ii., page 140, states: "Some of the best modern imitations of the Cremona violins are those of John Betts, of London, who for many years sold them, together with others of his own excellent form, in his house, under the Royal Exchange, in London." John Betts died March, 1823, and is buried at Cripplegate Church. Copy of a label used in 1782:—

"J⁰. Betts N⁰. 2
Near Northgate the
Royal Exchange
London 1782."

The nephew had ability as a maker of violins, and was employed by his uncle; his own style is admired, the tone being good, bold, and masculine; but he became more proficient as an imitator of the old makers, both of Italy and England. It paid better, as Hʳ. Hill observes, than adhering to modern workmanship. The time of his death is not accurately known; probably between 1815 and 1820. It is certain he died before his uncle.

Here may be considered to terminate the succession
and second portion of violin-makers, from Jacob Rayman to John Betts, notwithstanding the last name, as a
house of business, still exists. However, as the successors
have not studied the art of violin-making, they can only
be considered as dealers. Mr. Arthur Betts, who succeeded to the business of his brother, old John Betts,
was a teacher and professor of the violin, and held an
honourable position as a performer. At his death, the
business became the property, or perhaps was under the
guidance of the elder son, the present Arthur Betts, who
had been a clerk in a large banking establishment in
Lombard Street, consequently not a person using the
various tools to develop a violin or violoncello.   There
was another nephew, named —— Vernon, who acted as
shopman in the latter years of his uncle, old John Betts,
and soon after the death of the latter, in 1823, opened a
house of business in Cornhill, or near that locality ; but
in a very few years death terminated his career. He
could not make a violin, and was only the dealer.
Although but few allusions have been made to the
Cremona instruments in this portion of the book, yet
they were gradually arriving in England during the
period just noticed, and their superiority of tone created
a want which the supply, unfortunately, could not satisfy ;
it therefore led to the debasement of genuine instruments
to gratify the love of gain.   Two instruments were made
out of one, by taking portions—say the head and upper
vibrating plate or belly—then adding the sides and
lower vibrating plate or back, also *vice versâ*, or any
other mode of separation ; then perfecting the whole as
a violin, or whatever instrument it might be. Of late
years these instruments have been brought before the
public for sale, and it is greatly to be deplored that a

truly genuine one is rarely to be seen. A new handle or neck is of no importance; but to divide a perfect article creates a disgust for the perpetrators, whoever they may have been.

It is a triumph of skill to be able to make a violin that shall be considered by the connoisseur and all others as a genuine Cremona; but then comes the test of true honesty: will you stoop and degrade yourself by selling it as a genuine article?

There are still several names in the eighteenth century to be noticed, which occasionally causes an encroachment on the present century, many of whom were indifferent workmen, and employed by the music publishers; they may be called fiddle-makers, not artists in making a violin; however, when a more favourable statement can be made of their skill it shall be mentioned. The names are arranged alphabetically.

CHAPTER XX.

STLEY, No. 9, Fleet Lane, 1785.
BAINES, pupil of Matthew Furber.
BARTON, GEORGE, Elliot Court, Old
Bailey.   Died about 1810.

CARTER, JOHN, worked for John Betts, and respected
by him.   It is said his employer paid the expense of his
funeral.   Label used :—

"J. Carter. Violin—Tennor
& Bass Maker, Wych Street, Drury Lane
London.   1787."

CLARK, Turnmill Street, Clerkenwell, pupil of Matthew Furber.

COLLIER, SAMUEL, musical instrument-maker, at Corelli's Head, on London Bridge, 1755.

COLLINGWOOD, JOSEPH, at the Golden Spectacles, on
London Bridge, 17—.

CONWAY, WILLIAM, 1745.

CROWTHER, JOHN, Haughton Street, Clare Market,
about 1755.   Worked occasionally for John Kennedy,
as well as the music-houses.   Died about 1810.

DICKSON, JOHN, Cambridge, 1779.

DICKINSON, EDWARD, 1754 and 1790.   Printed label
used :—

" Edward Dickinson
maker at the Harp &
Crown in the Strand
near Exeter Change
London 1754 "

EVANS, RICHARD. This name was in the Crwth
mentioned in the former part of this work, which looked
much older than the date in the following label, with its
peculiar spelling:—

" Maid in the Paris of
Lanirhengel by Richard
Evans Instrument maker
in the year 1742."

FRANKLAND, Robin Hood Court, Shoe Lane, 1785,
occasionally employed as an outdoor workman by William Forster, numbers two and three.

FURBER, DAVID, was the first of this name that made
instruments. The times of his birth and death are not
known; but the grandson, John Furber, said he was
buried at Clerkenwell Church. He no doubt showed
ability, as John Johnson, a violin-maker, living in Cheap-
side, in 1759, gave him further instruction.

FURBER, MATTHEW, was the son of the previous
named David Furber, and was taught by his father.
Died about 1790, and buried at Clerkenwell Church.

The second and third sons of the foregoing Matthew,
named Matthew and John, were taught by their father;
but whether the eldest son James was a fiddle-maker is
not known. Matthew, the second son, died about 1830-1,
and was buried at Clerkenwell Church. John Furber,
in 1841, was living in Cow Cross, Smithfield, and has
instructed his son, Henry John; both father and son, it

is believed, are living at this time. Copy of a written label used by the elder John :—

> "John Furber maker
> 13 John's Row top of Brick Lane
> Old S'. Saint Luke.　1813."

HARBUR, or HARBOUR, ——, in 1785, lived in Duke Street, Lincoln's-inn Fields, and moved to Southampton Buildings, Holborn, in 1786.

HARRISS, CHARLES, lived at Cannon Street Road, Ratcliffe Highway, and was a Custom House officer, tide-waiter, as well as a fiddle-maker, and was chiefly employed in making instruments for shipping orders and the trade, but it is not known of whom he learned to work. Samuel Gilkes, who will be noticed elsewhere, was an apprentice of this person (*vide* the third William Forster).

HARRISS, CHARLES, was the eldest son of the above, and fellow-apprentice with Gilkes. However, little is known regarding him; he became possessed of some property in Northamptonshire from a branch of the family, and was called Squire Harriss; but some adverse circumstances compelled him to seek employment amongst the trade about the middle of the present century.

HEESOM, EDWARD, Londoni. Fecit 1749.

HOLLOWAY, J., 31, Gerard Street, Soho, 1794.

MARSHALL, JOHN, was a tolerably good workman, and the violins which have been seen are made of the Steiner pattern. Some of the labels used by him were as follows :—

> " Johannes Marshall
> Londini.　Fecit 1750."

The above was printed on a narrow slip of paper, with

plain line border. The label which follows is taken from Hill's MSS. :—

"Johannes Marshall (in vico novo juxta Covensam hortum) Londini. fecit 1757."

And this is a written label in our own collection :—

"Marshall. London 1759."

On this last he makes known—

"Good Beef 1ᵈ A pound
But trades all very Bad."

MARTIN, ——, was living at Hermitage Bridge, Wapping, in the years 1790 and 1794.

MERLIN, JOSEPH, appears to have possessed a mental development for invention, with mechanical skill, which powers were exerted to produce many articles, both musical and otherwise, and were exhibited at his museum in Princes Street, Hanover Square. In Madame D'Arblay's "Diary and Letters," vol. ii., p. 432, she states—"He invented many ingenious objects, some of which were of real utility, but most were mere playthings, or objects of curiosity. He was at one period of his career quite 'the rage' in London, where everything à la Merlin—Merlin chairs, Merlin pianos, Merlin swings, &c.;" also, it may be added, Merlin fiddles, and Merlin's mechanical pegs for violins and violoncellos. Frequent mention is made of him in the second volume of this Diary, with statements of sayings and actions, which shows she considered him a vain, conceited person. The violins he made were of the high model, similar to Steiner; the work was good, but the tone was of the usual quality of high-built instruments. The printed label he used was an oval to enclose the name and his ambition, with the direction written underneath. Here is another instance of the uncertainty of the number of instruments made by the figures on the labels. A copy of a label, with the date 1778, has the number of 100 upon it; and an original one, in 1779, has No. 104; therefore we must leave our readers to guess where he begun. The word "Improved" has been written with a pen on both labels :—

> " Josephus Merlin
> Cremonæ Emulus
> N° 104   Londini   1779
> Improved
> Queen Ann   N° 66   Street East
> Portland   Chapel "

Dubourg, in his work on the violin, p. 244, gives an amusing tale of a "Skating Fiddler," and alludes to a circumstance of which Merlin was the cause, and which occurred at Carlisle House, Carlisle Street, Soho Square; but no doubt much deplored by the lady who gave the entertainment.

Mier, of London, in 1786; but nothing is known of his instruments at this period.

Miller. The original printed announcement of this person is much injured and mutilated, and it is questionable whether it be not that of the widow, as the last three letters appear to be " lez "; or it may be the termination of Eliza. Some interest may be created in the statement made, therefore a copy of the label is given:—

> " Sold by . . . . lez Miller at the Signe of the
> Citern London Bridge all Sorts of Musical
> Instruments and Strings fitt for them
> & old Instruments mended & also there
> you may have all Sorts of New Tunes &c
> Musick Books & Songs ruled Books
> and ruled Paper at Reasonable rate."

The houses on London Bridge were all cleared away between the years 1757-1759 ("Chronicles of London Bridge," second edition, p. 378, *et seq.*); but this label seems much older.

MORRISON, JOHN, it is believed, was born about 1760, and it is not known who taught him the fiddle trade. He had a small shop in Princes Street, Soho, the beginning of this century, but quitted it in 1819, and, after residing in Shadwell for a time, ultimately located in Little Turnstile, Holborn, where he died between the years 1820-30. His work was very common, and he was mostly employed in making instruments for the music houses.

NAYLOR, ISAAC, was a pupil of Richard Duke, and lived at Headingley, near Leeds, Yorkshire, 1778-1792.

NEWTON, ISAAC, was a maker of average goodness, and occasionally employed to repair and make violins and violoncellos for Betts; the new instruments being varnished at the house of the latter, as the varnish of his own was a dingy yellow, somewhat like that used by Smith. He died about 1825, and his age is supposed to be between seventy and eighty years.

PEARCE, JAMES AND THOMAS, were brothers, and very common workmen, living in Peter Street, Saffron Hill, one of the Rookeries of London, the latter part of the last century or the beginning of the present one.

PRESTON, JOHN. It is not known if this person be related to John Preston the music publisher, who formerly resided at 97, Strand, London, and also called himself a musical instrument maker; but the latter only dealt in them as a music house. Labels used by the former of this name—

" Preston Pavement York 1789 ;
and

" John Preston, York.
1791.   Fecit."

POWELL, ROYAL AND THOMAS, were brothers, and both
neat workmen of average goodness; and were employed
about 1785-6 or 1787, as outdoor workmen by William
Forster, numbers two and three. The label used by one
of them—

" Made by thomas
Powell Nº 18 Clemens
Lane Clare Market
1793."

There were two sons of the above Thomas, also named
Royal and Thomas. In 1800 they were living in St.
John's Square, St. Lukes, and it is said they were between
twenty and thirty years of age at that time, but nothing
is known of their work; however one of them went to
sea, and being able to repair violins, met with favour
from his lieutenant, who was an amateur on the instrument.

SATCHELL AND FORSCHLE. In the Musical Directory
for 1794, p. 57, we find the name of this firm as, " Instrument Makers, No. 21, Mark Lane;" but whether or no
they made violins we are unable to assert. None have
been seen. It may be probable they were military instrument makers. The first name is also met with in
the " Memoirs of Harriot Duchess of St. Albans," by
Mrs. Cornwall Baron Wilson, vol. i. p. 208 :—" The
latter apartments Mrs. Entwistle considered might be let
for a shop, so as nearly to pay the whole rent; but Miss
Mellon received an application from a tenant, connected
with her own loved profession, which she favoured beyond any other more advantageous one ; and she let the
ground-floor at a rate which was quite a matter of charity.

Her tenant was Mrs. Benson, the sister of Mrs. Stephen Kemble, both daughters of Satchell, the musical instrument maker to the Prince of Wales."

SIMPSON, JOHN. Although instruments have been seen possessing printed labels similar to that given at the conclusion of this article, yet it is doubtful if he was a maker of the violin class. Those fiddles which have been seen were not of good workmanship or tone, and looked like the style of those usually sold at the music houses. There can be little doubt but this John Simpson was the father of the following James Simpson, therefore prior to the date ascertained of the latter, the label being so much alike and in the same locality :—

> " John Simpson,
> Musical Instrument Maker,
> At the Bass Viol and Flute,
> in Sweeting's Alley,
> Opposite the East door of yᵉ Royal Exchange
> London."

The Musical Directory for 1794, p. 60, gives the name of a firm : "James Simpson and Son, Instrument Makers, No. 15, Sweeting's Alley, Cornhill." The label used was—

> " J. & J. Simpson,
> Musical Instrument Makers,
> At the Bass Viol & Flute,
> in Sweeting's Alley,
> Opposite the East Door of the Royal Exchange,
> London."

SMITH, WILLIAM. There were two makers of this name, or it may be the same person moved to another place, and it is believed he or they were not related to

the Thomas Smith of former years.   One of the labels
used was " W= Smith, Real Maker, London, 1771."
The other—

> " William Smith,
> Violin Maker,
> Hedon, 1786."

TAYLOR.   About 1820 this person was living in
Princes Street, Drury Lane ; but at that time an elderly
man, perhaps near seventy years of age.   It is said he was
regularly initiated into the business of fiddle-making, but
it cannot be learned from whom he gained the knowledge.
In the latter period of his life, double-bass-making and
repairing became the favourite instruments to work upon ;
and he must have arrived at some excellence, as Signor
Dragonetti occasionally employed him.

THOROWGOOD, HENRY.   The work of this maker is not
known, but the following is a copy of the printed label
used by him ; the two first figures only of the date were
upon it :—

> " Made and Sold by
> Henry Thorowgood
> at the Violin & Guitar under the
> North Piazza of the Royal Exchange
> 17   London."

TORING, or TORRING, kept a shop in Shug Lane,
Haymarket, now better known as Tichborne Street, about
the spot at which the opening is made, and the County
Fire Office is the corner.   He was a player on the fiddle
as well as a maker and repairer of it, and attended
balls ; however report says he did not reach much excellence in any department.   The late Mr. Hendric, the
perfumer, of Tichborne Street, who died in April 1862,
at the age of eighty-four years, had a lively recollection
of dancing to Torring's fiddling, and the inquiries of him

regarding this person seemed to recall all the pleasures of youth. It may be interesting to state that Shug Lane is an abbreviation of Sugar House Lane, taking its name from a sugar baker's establishment having been built there in Charles the Second's reign. It was then the high road from the village of Charing to Tyburn.

WEAVER, SAMUEL. No instruments have been seen of this person's make; but the copy of a printed label is as follows:—

"All Sorts of
Musical Instruments
made & Sold by
Sam¹ Weaver
on London Bridge."

WIGHTMAN, GEORGE. Nothing is known of this workman or his instruments, but he used a written label thus:—

"George Wightman
Wood Street London 1761."

WRIGHT, DANIEL. The same remarks as the preceding may be applied to this maker; the date being about 1745:—

"Made by Daniel Wright
in Holborn, London."

WORNUM. The Musical Directory for 1794, p. 71, gives this name as a violin and violoncello maker, No. 42, Wigmore Street. No instruments have been seen.

YOUNG, JOHN, lived at the west corner of London-house Yard, in St. Paul's Church-yard, at the sign of the Dolphin and Crown, about the year 1724, and is styled a maker of violins and other instruments by Sir John Hawkins (Novello's edition, p. 807): "He lives not by his works!" Nevertheless concerts of instrumental music were advanced by him and his son, Talbot Young.

CHAPTER XXI.

LTHOUGH many of the persons in the list just ended were very common workmen, yet there were others, during the same period, who by their talent and industry were gaining a position and becoming some of England's best artists in violin, viola, and violoncello making; not only creating a style of finish in their work by which they are known, but also producing a quality and character of tone to which professors will allude and draw comparison. With those names of violin-makers it is intended to commence with the oldest date and carry each school through to the present time, enumerating, as far as our knowledge will enable us, all those persons who have been pupils, and others who have followed a similar style, that the character and style of each artist may be kept separate.

Dr. Thomas Forster, in the preface to his "Epistolarium," vol. ii. p. 4, states the Forster family to be very ancient, and believed to have come from Normandy with William the Conqueror; also, that distinguished services were rendered at the battle of Crecy and also at Agincourt by one of this name, for which the king conferred the coat-of-arms and created General Sir Ferdinand Forster, knight banneret.

It is not known from what branch of the family Dr.

Forster reckons; however, it is in Scotland and the northern counties of England we must search for the Forster family, to which our inquiries are directed. In the "Border History of England and Scotland," by the Rev. George Ridpath, there is frequent mention of the name, and a statement that one Adam Forster, or Forrester, was sometimes serving as a royal commissioner, and at other times as an ambassador from Robert III. of Scotland to Richard II. and Henry IV. of England; also acting as conservator, with others, to various truces and peace arrangements regarding the Border district, from 1397 to 1402, and that about the last date he had been made Sir Adam, and was taken prisoner at the battle of Homeldon, and with other captives was " committed to the care of the steward of the household, to wait the king's pleasure." Whether he died a natural death, is not known; but to trust to the clemency of the Bolingbroke, who had been opposed, makes the result very doubtful. In 1424 we find John Forster acting as conservator to a truce between England and Scotland, and in 1429 he appears to become Sir John Forrester, Baron of Liberton, serving as a Scotch commissioner, with other persons named, for "mutual redress of injuries, and the speedy and effectual execution of justice in all matters under debate between the subjects of the two kingdoms;" and in the same year he is named John Forster of Corstorsyn. From the last date above stated until 1553, there is no mention of this name; we then find Sir John Forster, knight, was acting as the arbitrator for England; and in 1557, "about Martinmas, the Earl of Northumberland sent his brother, Sir Henry Percy, accompanied with Sir John Forster and others, chiefly those of the Middle March, to make an inroad into Scotland; they were met by Sir Andrew Ker and

a great body of the men of Tiviotdale, in the neighbourhood of Cheviot, almost on the boundary between the
kingdoms. A sharp engagement ensued, in the beginning
of which the English were beaten back ; but recovering
themselves, they gained a considerable advantage over
the Scots, taking prisoner their leader, with several of
his followers. Sir John Forster fought bravery (bravely)
in this skirmish, wherein he was sore wounded, and had
his horse killed under him ; and to his prowess was
chiefly ascribed the victory gained by his countrymen."

In 1561 Sir John Forster was warden of the Middle
Marches, and retained that appointment for many years.
When James VI. of Scotland passed through Northumberland, in 1603, to ascend the English throne, he was
met by Sir Nicholas Forrester, the sheriff of that county,
by order of the Council of England.   There is frequent
mention of the name in the " Border Minstrelsy," and Sir
Walter Scott, in the edition of 1848, has occasionally
added notes which enter into particulars of much interest
connected with our subject of inquiry.   The song of
" Jamie Telfer of the Fair Dodhead," the second stanza,
vol. ii. p. 13, has—

> " There was a wild gallant among us a',
> His name was Watty wi' the Wudspurs ;
> Cried—' On for his house in Stanogerthside,'
> If one man will ride with us ! ' "

Note 3, a house belonging to the Foresters, situated
on the English side of the Liddel.

Again, at p. 21, in the song, " The Raid of the Reids-
wire," second stanza—

> " We looked down the other side
> And saw come breasting ower the brae,
> Wi' Sir John Forster for their guyde,
> Full fifteen hundred men and mae."

Note 4, " Sir John Forster, or, more properly, Forrester, of Balmborough Abbey, warden of the Middle Marches in 1561, was deputy-governor of Berwick, and governor of Balmborough Castle. He made a great figure on the Borders, and is said, on his monument at Balmborough Church, to have possessed the office of Warden of the Middle Marches for thirty-seven years. This family ended in the unfortunate Thomas Forster, one of the generals of the Northumbrian insurgents in 1715; and the estate, being forfeited, was purchased by his uncle, Lord Crewe, and devised for the support of his magnificent charity."

There is also a note to the song, "Dick o' the Cow," p. 72. "A challenge had been given by an Englishman, named Forster, to any Scottish Borderer, to fight him at a place called Kershopefoot, exactly upon the Borders. The Laird's Jock's only son accepted the defiance, and was armed by his father with his own two-handed sword. The old champion himself, though bedridden, insisted upon being present at the battle. He was borne to the place appointed, wrapped, it is said, in blankets, and placed upon a very high stone to witness the conflict. In the duel his son fell—treacherously slain, as the Scottish tradition affirms. The old man gave a loud yell of terror and despair when he saw his son slain, and his noble weapon won by an Englishman, and died as they bore him home. . . . The stone on which the Laird's Jock sat to behold the duel, was in existence till wantonly destroyed a year or two since. It was always called the Laird's Jock's Stone. 1802. [The reader will find Sir Walter Scott recurring to the fate of the Laird's Jock in 1828. See Waverley Novels, vol. xli. p. 377.]" There is also an official tract in the British Museum worthy of notice regarding this name,

and the portion connected with our subject is now extracted from the "Archæologia," vol. xxii. p. 161. It is
thus headed: "Copy of a Manuscript Tract addressed
to Lord Burghley, illustrative of the Border Topography
of Scotland, A. D. 1590; with a Platt or Map of the
Borders, taken in the same year, both Preserved in one
of the Royal MSS. in the British Museum. Communi-
cated by Henry Ellis, Esq. F.R.S., Secretary, in a Letter
addressed to the Right Honourable the Earl of Aberdeen,
K.T, President.

"*Read, 31st May, 1827.*

"My Lord,   British Museum, May 29, 1827.
"Among the Royal Manuscripts in the British Museum
is a volume of Saxton's Maps (Bibl. Reg. 18, D 111),
published in 1579, upon the margins of which the names
of the justices of the peace in England at that time, or
soon after, are written, with occasional miscellaneous
remarks. Several manuscript maps and draughts of
sea-ports, towns, &c. are added in different places of the
volume, likewise accompanied by memoranda in the
handwriting of Lord Burghley, to whom the volume at
one time belonged.
"Among these latter articles is a manuscript map with
the date of December, 1590, entitled, ' A Platt of the
Opposite Borders of Scotland to the West Marches of
England.' Upon this the different castles and houses of
strength, with the names of many of the owners, are
minutely specified, and I cannot but think that a copy
of it would be valuable for the ' Archæologia ' of the
Society of Antiquaries. At the bottom of this map or
platt is written, ' The moste of these places on the
Scottish syde are tower and stone houses, with some

fewe plenashed Townes, as Dumfreis, Annand, Lough-
mahen, and such like; for the rest not put downe, they
are but onsetts or stragling houses, th' inhabitants
followers of some of these above described. For those
on the English Coaste, they are referred to the tract
lately sent to your L. of the Description of them in
particular.' The tract here alluded to, follows a page or
two after, and if my judgment does not deceive me, is a
curious abstract of the state of Border topography towards the close of the reign of Queen Elizabeth. I
have had it transcribed, and here present it to your
Lordship and the Society.

        " I am, my Lord,
           " Your Lordship's faithful Servant,
                        " HENRY ELLIS.
" To the Right Hon. The Earl of
    Aberdeen, K.T., President of
    the Society of Antiquaries."

Then follows " The Division of the severall Charge
of the West Borders of England and Scotland." At
p. 166, " LEVEN or KIRKLYNTON. Next it towardes the
Borders runneth the river Leven. Upon which river
dwelleth Grames, Etheringtons, and Forsters, and others;
under the governance of a bayliffe for a gentleman, one
Mr. Musgrave of Haton, lord of that mannor called Kirklynton. But the castle where he should lye is Scaleby.
Now in these tenauntes, who are able border men, if they
were well governed, is a great quietnes for staunching of
theft, for they are the onely men that ride both into
England and Scotland, who cannot be letted without
their masters residence, or careful watch of the country
within them."
    Page 168. " The severall surnames of the English

Borderers and their dwellings. Eske. Upon both sides
of the river dwell the Grames, which is the greatest
surname at this daie upon the West Border. For the
Grames of Eske and Leven are able to make V C ser-
viceable men.

" Leven. Upon this river also dwelleth many Grames,
and above Kirklynton in Sompert dwelleth a great surname of Fosters, and about Hethersgill is a surname of
Hetheringtons. Bewcastle. There dwelleth Fosters,
Crosers, and Nixsons, but sore decayed."

By reference to the platt or map in the work from
which the foregoing has been copied, it will be seen that
the strong houses of the Forsters's were opposite to that
portion of the country held by the Armstrongs on the
Liddle, therefore hard knocks no doubt had been inter-
changed. Stancgirthside has been previously mentioned ;
more to the eastward, on the banks of the same river,
was another castle held by Robert Forster; and more
easterly still is Kirksopfoote, where the duel took place
between the Laird's Jock and a Forster, before alluded
to, therefore we may infer this castle also to have belonged to the latter name.

We have thus endeavoured to trace the name of Forster
to the locality in which those connected with our inquiries
were known to have resided, but we are not prepared,
at present, to prove they were related to the statesmen
and warriors previously named, although there are some
circumstances which makes this more than probable ;
but as the Scotch say, " it is not proven," therefore no
further comment will be made on the subject. The first
of this family who made violins was John, but whether
the name was spelled Forester, Forster, or Foster, is now
difficult to determine ; the general belief is, that the first
mode was the original, and the probable cause of the

variations may be the careless manner, in early times, of writing names which may be seen in the church register, also in the engraving upon the tombstones of this family. At this distant period of time there is much difficulty in obtaining correct information of the town or village in which he was born, but in the researches made ten or twelve years since amongst the aged inhabitants of Brampton, in Cumberland, they named several places in that part of the country from whence he probably came; but none could assert what pursuit or vocation he followed in early years; almost the whole of them said he came from " Ayont the Wood," but others named Kirklington, Bewcastle, Longtown in the Netherby quarter; but the town which had more advocates than any other was Kirkandrews, on the Esk, which, from the many kind inquiries made on this matter by Mr. Samuel Irving, of Stanwix, Carlisle, may be considered to be proved almost to a certainty; but it should be "Ayont the Wood, in Nichol Forest, in the parish of Kirkandrews, on the Esk." From this place the aged people said, he moved to little Easby, two or three miles from Brampton, in the parish of this last name, and left there for the town of Brampton, at which place they all agreed he died about 1790, at the great age of one hundred and two or three years, and was buried at the old parish church, a mile, or little more, from the " Town Foot."

The family, however, state that he left Longtown for Brampton. On searching the church book of burials we find a John Foster buried 7 Oct. 1781, aged ninety-three years; but there is no statement to identify that it is the desired one; however, as this date so nearly coincides with the information gained, and will agree with the birth of his son William, supposing that he married at twenty-four or twenty-five years of age, it is assumed that this must be the record of his death; consequently he would have been born in or about 1688.

Only vague accounts could be learned of the vocation he followed, but it was generally asserted that, latterly, he made spinning-wheels, or was a wheelwright, and at one period of his life he was a gun-maker, and considered by all of them to be "a very ingenious man, and occasionally made fiddles." A violin was seen in 1850, said to be his make, and with some degree of truth could be traced back. The work was rude and unfinished, the model very high, resembling the Steiner, but the outline approached nearer to the pattern of the Amati. It was much decayed and worm-eaten, and if strings had been to the instrument, it is doubtful if it would have borne tuning to try the tone. This violin was possessed by Joseph Rook, a violin maker and performer, who lived in Rickergate, Carlisle. He had been intimate with Joseph Forster, grandson (if we are correct with the identity) of this said John, from the first year of the present century.

Not only were many of the facts just enumerated known to the family, but it can be added that John Forster was of stature more than six feet, also of athletic frame of body, with great muscular development.

Presuming the identity of John Foster or Forster is established, then William Forster was the son of the previous named John; but as there are four in this family of the same Christian name connected with violin making, a number will be attached to each for the advantage of any required reference. It cannot be positively asserted whether William Forster (1) was born in Brampton; it is believed to be so, but there is no proof; however he must soon have located there. He was born about 1713-14, and by the books of the old church of that town he married in 1736; his first wife, who died in the prime of life, being only forty-four years of age; but she had borne him a son who added lustre to the name in after years. This William Forster (1) was a spinning-wheel maker by trade; also repaired and made violins. In the former vocation he gained some celebrity, as the following extract from a letter of Joseph Rook, written in Nov. 1850, when he was in his seventy-seventh year, shows:—" I can give no more of the history of your ancestors at Brampton than I have already given you, only your great grandfather William was a noted maker of spinning-wheels as well as violin maker, and his son Joseph, my old acquaintance, practised making wheels so long as they were in use in the country, but it is many years since they were put out of use by the invention of machinery."

Whether in or about 1775-7 he was pressed in pecuniary circumstances, or whether the love of the drama tempted him to accept, as inmates or lodgers, a family connected with the theatrical company then performing at Brampton, yet it was in his house that Miss Harriot Mellon was born! This information is obtained, or rather, it should be stated, corroborated by one that became employed in the sequel of events (the fact being known to the family); therefore it had better be given in his own language, written December 1850, although there are some trifling inaccuracies which, at his age, may be overlooked:—" * * * * I must endeavour to exert myself and will give an account of a remarkable circumstance that happened in your G. Grandfather's House at Brampton. Upon a time a Company of Itinerant Comedians were at Brampton, and one of them of the name of Melon and his Wife had an apartment in your G. Grandfather's House during their stay at Brampton.

Mrs. Melon was brought to bed of a Daughter, the Child was Baptized at Brampton; they left and nothing was heard of them afterwards. About Oct'. 19, 1824, a Lady with a Splendid Equipage containing a number of Carriages and Servants of every description arrived at the Howard Arms in search of her Register, and the Lady in question was M⁰. Coutts; that some time after that became Dutchess of S⁰. Albans. She inquired if your G. Grandfather was living, [and] she gave such a description as the people soon knew it was Will⁰. Forster; a certain proof that her Father and Mother had talked about your G. Grandfather repeatedly; she went to see the place where she first drew breath in, and saw Jo; and had some conversation with him. She no doubt would ask him many things and understanding that he played the Violin she desired him to raise her a Band of a few Violins and Violoncells and go to Carlisle where she gave a splendid Breakfast to all the Genteel people in Carlisle and the neighbourhood. We were verry handsomley rewarded for our trouble: a Guinea a piece for us in Carlisle and something handsom for Joseph for coming from Brampton. The Splendid doo, was on the 21 of Oct'. 1824, at the Bush Inn, Carlisle. About mid-day she set off for London with all her retinue. I consider this something marvelous but an absolute truth as good a subject for a Novel as ever Sir W. Scott had.

" Your &c

"S. A. Forster."   " JOSEPH ROOK.

A violin of this maker is possessed by one of the writers of this book, and it has a label inside thus:—

" William Forster
Violin Maker
in Brampton."

The work is not of a high class; the tone deserves commendation, although more quality could be desired. The varnish is alcoholic, and not very transparent, nor is the instrument purfled; but on the whole it is an evident improvement on the fiddle seen of his father's make. The following is a copy of the inscription engraved on the tomb-stone, in the burial-ground of the old parish church of Brampton, about a mile, or little more, from the Town Foot :—

"In memory of W^a. Forster
Violin Maker of Brampton
who died March 4th. 1801
aged 87 years."

Being recorded on this grave-stone as a violin-maker, and the spinning-wheel trade not being mentioned, may probably have arisen from the celebrity his son, William, had achieved in London as a maker of musical instruments of the violin genus.

CHAPTER XXII.

ILLIAM FORSTER, the second of this name, but the first who gave renown to it as a maker of violins, violas, violoncellos, and double basses, became one of England's greatest artists, and received the patronage of royalty and many of the nobility. He was also greatly appreciated by the professors of these instruments; and is better known in the musical world, and amongst the trade, as "Old Forster."

From a memorandum written by his son, William Forster (3), in one of his old account-books, stating that "my father died on the 14 Dec'. 1808, aged 68, on the 4th of May last," it is considered, in the absence of more positive information, that this date may be correct, but no corroborative proof could be found in the book of the register of births belonging to the old church of Brampton, Cumberland. However, there is a baptismal register at the Presbyterian Chapel of that town, "1739, May 5th, William, lawful Son to William Foster, Brampton," which no doubt relates to this person; therefore he would be rather older than stated by the son.

William Forster (2) was instructed by his father in making spinning-wheels and violins, both of which trades he followed during the earlier years of his life, and further obtained employment by playing the violin at the various merry-makings and other festivities of the locality. Report says he excelled in the performance of reels; and the elder branches of the surviving family know that in after years, when trying violins which had either been made or repaired, the owners would frequently request to have one of them played. He also composed several Scotch reels, some of which were published by himself, when it was the custom of each music establishment at Christmas time to bring out a book of dance-tunes for the new year.

Whether it was ambition that first occasioned him to come to London in the hope of bettering his fortunes, or whether, as some persons say, it was an aversion of his parent to the female whom he loved, and who ultimately became his wife, that induced him to leave his native place, we are unable to say; the most probable cause may be the disrespect shown to the memory of his mother by the other parent marrying a second wife only four months after the death of the first. The time of his leaving Brampton is not known; but if the above suppositions be correct, then it would be about 1739, ho being between twenty and twenty-one years of age; whatever the irritating cause may have been, it must have been felt most acutely, as he left with little or no pecuniary resources, and engaged himself to a drover to assist in bringing cattle to the south.

The neighbourhood of the Commercial Road and Prescott Street, Goodman's Fields, is said to be the first locality he resided in; and, not being able to get employment in either business which he had learned, he at length obtained work as a gun-stock maker, occasionally making violins and selling them to the music shops. The privations and sufferings endured during this period of his life he was always of opinion caused

the aggravated dyspepsia and other constitutional evils
which were never eradicated; indeed, it is questionable if
some of the present generation are not sufferers from the
internal debility then created, which has descended to
them, although their own struggles in life have been
sufficient to cause it.   Ultimately he gained permanent
employment at a music-shop on Tower Hill, kept by a
person named Beck; and the violins made by him being
much approved of, with a quick sale of them, he solicited
for greater remuneration; the employer refusing to ac-
cede, he left him and came westward to a house on the
right-hand side, and about the middle of Duke's Court,
St. Martin's Lane, Charing Cross.   The houses are all
now pulled down, and the National Picture Gallery
erected partly on the site; he pitched his tent here for a
time, and afterwards resided in St. Martin's Lane, near
to and on the same side as May's Buildings.   The following is a copy of the label used at that period :—

> " William Forster,
>   Violin Maker
> in S'. Martin's Lane.   London
>   1762."

While residing here, a Colonel West, of the Grenadier
Guards, who was the father of the late Temple West, of
Malvern Lodge, Worcestershire, Esquire, gave him an
order for a new violin, to be made similar to a pattern
then shown, which he completed so successfully that the
colonel became a kind, generous, and sincere patron.
He also, being an amateur desirous of improving the
violin, had numerous experiments tried in the manufacture of such instruments, which this artisan executed for
him.   The advantages thus gained were always grate-
fully acknowledged by William Forster (2) as being of

essential assistance and advancement to him in the art. He always felt pleasure in stating that his first real success in life was through Colonel West.

Between the years 1762 and 1782 his skill and exertions had been rewarded, and he had become a music-seller and publisher; he had also changed his residence. Sometime during the above period a different label had been used in the instruments, particularly the violon-cellos, and it bears evidence of being part of a title-page of some work published by him, which probably had not been successful; he therefore used the name as a label, which is in a written character, with some ornamental engraving cut through, that is neither useful, nor, in this particular, any embellishment. In those instruments where this label is used, it will generally be found that the name William Forster, in the Roman letter, is placed also on the inside of the short bouts, just above the lining which is attached to the sides and the back. It is the same printing taken off the label used in 1762, as will be readily seen by the ornamental flourishes corresponding and now cut through. At what time he first was honoured by working for royalty we are unable to state, as the account-books before the 14th November, 1773, have either been destroyed or lost; and those books which still exist were kept imperfectly. However, there is proof of his living in St. Martin's Lane in 1781, and he may have moved to 348, Strand, in 1784-5. The following copy of a label or card will show he had this high patronage before changing his residence to the more public thoroughfare; and it also shows that the varnish he used had become celebrated and specially referred to:

" William Forster
Violin, Voloncello, Tenor & Bow-maker

Also Music Seller,
To their Royal Highnesses the
Prince of Wales and Duke of Cumberland
Opposite the Church S^t. Martin's Lane. London.

N.B.

The above Instruments are made in the best manner
and finished with the original varnish
and a Copy of every Capital Instrument in England
may be had."

The house was the corner of Duke's Court, and believed
to be that one nearest to Charing Cross. The Duke
of Cumberland here mentioned was the brother of
George III., who died in September 1790. He was a
great patron of musical art, and performed on the violin.
An incident occurred at the house above stated with this
Prince, who had called to try a violin that had been
repaired. Whilst amusing himself in playing various
pieces to test the quality of tone, a noisy peel struck up
from " the bells of Saint Martin's," which sadly interfered with his power of resolving any improvement or
not ; he therefore said, hastily, " confound those bells ; I
cannot hear a note for them ;" and immediately opened
the door at the end of the shop, leading to the sitting-
room, on the table of which had been placed the family
dinner, which was one of humble quality, but yet gave
forth savoury exhalations. With all promptness and
courtly ease he exclaimed, " Forster, what a nice dinner
you have, I'll have some with you," and drew a chair to
the table, and, perhaps for the first time in his life, par-
took of—shall it be named ? Yes ; black puddings !

In 1781 negotiations were commenced, through the
kind assistance of General Jerningham, with that genius
and improver of modern instrumental music, Guiseppe,

or, as he has always signed his letters, Joseph Haydn. Agreements and other documents were drawn up and signed for the supply of certain pieces of music, as sonatas, trios, quartets, and sinfonias. These transactions, no doubt, will be of interest to the lovers of music, therefore they are now made public, together with some original letters connected with the works of this intelligent composer. The opening of commercial transactions between Guiseppe Haydn and William Forstor (2) is copied from the account of the solicitor, named James Mainstone; the first entry bears date 17th August, 1781.

" Attending Mr. Forster in conference on a contract, intended to be entered into by Mr. Forster with Mr. Haydn, for Mr. Forster's purchasing of him and printing his compositions, and advising thereon."

" Taking Instructions for drawing Agreem* between Mr. Haydn and him, for the sale and purchase of Mr. Haydn's Musical Compositions by Mr. Forster."

" Drawing same, fo. 15."

" Attending to read over and settle same."

" Engrossing same for Execution."

" Attending and advising Mr. Forster as to the mode of execution of same by Mr. Haydn, and which he was to communicate to Gen.' Jerningham, who had undertaken to get it signed by Mr. Haydn at Vienna."

The document alluded to in the above, no doubt, was sent to General Jerningham, as the following answer is elicited by it :—

" Sir,—I received your favour 21 ins', & send you here enclosed a letter for Mr. Guiseppe Hayden, to whom I have wrote very circumstantially, and inclosed to him a procuration which he is to get drawn up either in French, German, or Lattin, and authenticated by two witnesses, and a publick notary, which gives it full force in all Countries; you may depend on it that what I have sent to Mr. Hayden is to the full as strong as the letter of Attorney you sent me in which there's nothing but a repetition of words.

" If you receive from Hayden a letter for me, send it to Lady Jerningham's in Grovener square, she will take care I gett it; when Hayden has sent you his procuration to print his musick, lett me know it, and am,

" Sir,

" Your most obed.ᵗ humble Serv.ᵗ

" CHARLES JERNINGHAM.

" Cawsey, *August* 24th, 1781."

This letter is addressed to Mr. William Forster, Musical Instrument Maker, Duke's Court, St. Martin's Lane, London; and has also written upon it—

" A Monsieur.

" Monsieur Juiseppe Hayden
de Chappelle de S : A' Le Prince
Esterhazy de Galantha   •
en Autriche.   A Vienne."

THE AGREEMENT.

" Je reconnois d'avoir reçu de Monsieur Guillaume Forster, Marchand et Imprimeur de Musique; demeurant dans le Strand à Londres la Somme de Soixante et dix livres Sterling, pour les Simphonies, Sonates, et autre pieces de ma composition ci-dessous mentionées, et qui comencent de cette façon Savoir.   No. 1 une Simphonie à plaisieurs Instruments qui comence ainsi :—

"Trios à 2 Flutes traversieres et Violoncello qui comencent de cette manier :—

" Premier Recueil de trois Sonates, pour le Clavecin,
avec l'accompag d'un Violon :—

" Second Recueil de 3 autres Sonates, pour le Clavecin, avec l'accompag d'un Violon.

" Et je certifie, et déclare à tout lo monde qui j'ai
vendu au dit Monsieur Guillaum Forster les dites Simphonies, Sonatas et autres pièces, et que je lui ai envoie
les manuscripts aux dates suivantes, savoir :—

" Les six Sonatos pour deux flûtes traversières et
violoncello, le 31 de May 1784.

" Le Simphonies marquées ci-dessus No. 1 et 2 par
Monsieur le General de Jerningham, lo 19 de Juin
1784.

" Les Simphonies No. 4, 5, et 6, avec le dit premier
Recueil de 3 Sonatas, pour le clavecin, le 25 d'Octobre
1784.

" Les Simphonies marquées ci-dessus No. 7, 8, et 9,
le 8 de Novembre 1784.

" Et le dit Second Recueil de 3 Sonatas pour le clavecin le 28 d'Octobre 1785.

" Je certifie aussi, et déclare, qu'il m'en paya le prix
convenu, entro lui moi ; et qui montoit en tout à la ditte
some de soixante et dix livres Sterlins, par des lettres
d'Echange sur Vienne ; qu'il m'a remis pour cet effet
(à l'ecception du prix de deux Simphonies No. 1 et 2,

x

le prix des quelles il paya pour mon compte à Monsieur
le General de Jerningham, alors à Londres). Et je
certifie et déclare de plus, que le dit Guillaum Forster
est le seul Propriétaire des dites pièces; que je lui ai
ainsi vendu, et que je lui ai cedé et transporté tous mes
droits et toutes mes pretensions là-dessus. En fois de
quoi j'ai souscrit mon nom à cet Ecrit a Esterhaz ce.
1786.   " GUISEPPE HAYDN,
                    " Maestro di Capella di S. Alt. S.
                       il principe Esterhazy." L.S.

The following exhibit is also written on the same
document :—

    " D.   Forster ag'. Longman & an'.
    " This paper writing was shewn to Jos. Haydn at the
time of his exam*. in this Court before   JA. EYRE."

There is next a letter from Haydn in German relating
to the sale of some symphonics, and pianoforte sonatas,
together with the composition, known as " The Last
Words." The following is a translation of it :—

" SIR,   " Estoraz, the 8th April, 1787.
    " After a long silence I must at length inquire after
your health, and at the same time inform you of the
following new musical works which are to be had of me:
namely, six grand symphonics, a grand concerto for
pianoforte, three short divertimentos for pianoforte for
beginners, with violin and bass ; one sonata for pianoforte alone.
    " An entire new work, consisting of purely instrumental
music, divided into seven sonatas, of which each sonata
lasts from seven to eight minutes, together with an
introduction, and at the end a terremoto or earthquake.
These sonatas are composed in accordance with the

words which our Saviour Christ spoke upon the cross; these seven words are—

1st words, Pater, dimitte illis, quia nesciunt quid faciunt.

2nd words, Hodie mecum eris in Paradiso.

3rd words, Mulier, ecce filius tuus.

4th words, Deus meus, Deus meus, ut dereliquisti me?

5th words, Sitio.

6th words, Consummatum est.

7th words, In manus tuas commendo spiritum meum.

"Immediately after follows the conclusion; namely, the Earthquake.

"Each sonata, or each subject, is produced simply by instrumental music, in such a manner as to leave the deepest impression on the mind of the most unmusical. The whole work lasts somewhat more than an hour, but there is after each sonata some pause, that one may be able to think on the next following subject. All the sonatas together contain somewhat more than four of my symphonies. The whole will be contained in thirty-seven pages.

"Also, I have three more pretty notturnos, quite new, with violin obligato, not at all difficult, with a flute, violoncello, two violins ripieno, two French horns, viola, and contre-bass.

"If you should wish to have some of these musical pieces, you will have the kindness to let me know, and at the same time also the price which you are willing to give me for them, as soon as possible. The seven sonatas are already nearly copied out fair upon soft paper, and waiting an early answer. I am, with much esteem,

"Your most obedient Servant,

"JOSEPH HAYDN.

" I beg you will answer me in the French language.

" I hope to visit you at the end of this year, but as I have not yet received an answer from Mr. Bremner, I shall go for this winter to Wegel Argagiers; meanwhile I thank you for the accommodation you have offered me."

Then are the three following letters in rench :—

" MONSIEUR,

" Je vous envoie la musique composée d'après les sept dernières paroles que Jesus Crist prononces sur la croi pour les quelles je laisse à votre disposition de m'envoyer ce que vous jugerez que j'ai mérite.

" J'espére que j'aurai peut-être le satisfaction de vous voir cet hiver en attendant. Je suis très parfaitement,

" Monsieur,

" Votre très-humble et

obeiss². Serviteur,

" JOSEPH HAYDN.

" Estors, le 28 Junii, 787."

" MONSIEUR,

" J'espére que vous avez reçu ma lettre, & la musique de sept paroles ; je vous fair à savoir, que je composé Six quartets et six sinfonie, qui ne sont pas encore sorti de ma main. Si vuos vuole les achté vous même, aye la bonté de me le faire savoir par la premier occasion, je vous donne toutes les douze pièces pour vint-cinq guinés. Je suis avec tout l'estime possible

" Votre très-humble Servit.

" JOSEPH HADYN.

" Estors, le 8th Août, 787."

This is addressed

" To Mr. Forster, Musical Instrument Macker To the Prince of Wales, No. 346 in the Strand, London."

"Monsieur,

"J'ai reçu votre lettre avec un grand plaisir. Je vous fais savoir, que j'ai reçu do Mons. le Général Jerningham ciuq guiné ; mais vous verrez vous même, que pour une tel musique comme les Septs Paroles j'ai plus mérite ; vous pourrez bien encore me donner au moins cinq guiné. Je vous envoies en attendant six quattuors pour lesquels vous aurez la bonté en égard au contrat de m'envoier vingt guiné sitôt qu'il sera possible. Je no manquerai pas do vous envoier les Six Sinfonies par la primièr occasiono. J'attend bientôt une réponse do vous, et je suis avec touto l'estimo possible,

"Monsieur,

"Votre très-humblo obéiss'.

"Serviteur,

"Joseph Haydn.

"Estoras, le 20 7ᵇʳᵉ. 787."

The next is a letter in German, dated the 28th of February, 1788, of which the following is a translation :

"Estoras, Jan. 28th, 788.

"My dear Mr. Forster,

"Are you not annoyed with me, that on my account you have had trouble with Mr. Longman. I will satisfy you another time on that point. It is not my fault, but that usurer, Mr. Artaria. So much I promise you, that as long as I live neither Artaria nor Longman shall receive anything from or through me. I am too honourable and upright to annoy or injure you. So much, however, you will of yourself plainly perceive, that whoever will have six new pieces from me must give more than 20 guineas. I have, in fact, some time ago concluded a contract with somebody who pays me for every 6 pieces

100 and more guineas. Another time I will write you more. Meanwhile I am with all respect,

"Your obedient servant,

"JOSEPH HAYDN.

" To Mr. Forster, Musical Instrument Maker
    to the Prince of Wales, No. 348, in the
        Strand, London."

On the fly-leaf of one of the old account-books for 1786 is written, " The dates of the years when Haydn's works came," which are as follows:—

Aug'.	22,	1781	. . . .	Haydns Ov'. N° 1
June	20,	1782	. . . .	D° D° „ 2
Feb'.	14,	1784	. . . .	D° D° „ 4
„	24,	1784	. . . .	D° D° „ 5
May	6,	1784	. . . .	D° D° „ 6
July	6,	1784	. . . .	D° Trios, op. 38
Nov'.	22,	1784	. . . .	D° Ov'. N° 7
„	26,	1784	. . . .	D° D° „ 8
Dec'.	6,	1784	. . . .	D° D° „ 9
Jan'.	3,	1785	. . . .	D° Sonatas, op. 40
Dec'.	26,	1785	. . . .	D° „ op. 42

The above are alluded to in the agreement, and the terms for which they were composed there specified.

The following compositions arrived as under :—

" July 16, 1787. Rccd. of Haydn M.S.S. of the Cruci-fixion published with the title of ' Passione.' Ten guineas was paid for this instrumental piece; and the Postage cost fifteen shillings.

" 5 Oct'. 1787. Received the M.S.S of Haydn's quar-tets, op. 44. Twenty guineas was paid for these; and the Postage cost twenty shillings."

On the 3rd December, 1787, there is an entry of

" Paid Postage of six Overtures from Haydn £2. 5. 0."
It is supposed these are the sinfonias Nos. 10 to 15.

Perhaps some extenuating reasons should be offered
why the classical composition of the "Passione" should
have received so small a remuneration as ten guineas;
small, indeed, does this amount appear, compared with
the sums given for trifling songs, when we hear of as
much as fifty pounds being paid to a fashionable and
favoured composer for a mere ballad. However, let it
be remembered that the name of Haydn was little known
at that period except by those who cultivated the science;
also, that instrumental music was not much appreciated.
Perhaps it is not yet sufficiently admired by the British
public, although greatly advanced—first, through the
exertions of a Committee of English Musical Professors
who gave promenade concerts, à la Musard, at the
Lyceum Theatre, about the year 1836-7, and introduced
a sinfonia and overtures during the evening's performance, interspersed with waltzes, quadrilles, and other
light pieces.   The first season or two was remunerative
to the common wealth; but soon after they ceased to be
so, or were given up from other causes. Soon after, a
professor, named Eliason, a violin-player, made a similar
venture, but success did not attend his rule, he bringing
Julien to this country to conduct them. At length concerts of this class were carried on under the management
of Julien, who ultimately introduced vocal music, omitting some of the classical instrumental pieces, which
gave a new and greater delight to the audience ; consequently they were very successful.   But now the rising
taste is fully shown by "the rush" for a place at the
"Monday Night Popular Concerts," where the music that
is performed consists only of the most classical compositions, performed by a few professors of the highest

standing in the art. But to return from this digression; the "Passione" is a large, or, as the trade would say, "heavy work," from the number of plates required, and all other expenses attendant on bringing it before the public; the probable cost in 1766-7 would be as here enumerated:—

	£	s.	d.
65 Pewter plates, at 1s. 6d. per plate .	4	17	6
Engraving the same, at 4s. 6d.　do. .	14	12	6
Copper title and engraving	1	11	6
66 quires of perfect paper for 75 copies, at 1s.	3	6	0
Printing 75 copies, at 1s. 2d. . . .	4	7	6
	28	15	0
Cost of the manuscript	10	10	0
Making in the aggregate	£39	5	0

Fifty copies was the first number which was printed; and about the year 1817-18 another twenty-five were struck off, making a total of seventy-five copies; the full price of each copy was fifteen shillings; but many of those first printed were sold to subscribers for 10s. 6d. each, and it is questionable if any of the remaining copies realized more than the trade price of twelve shillings, therefore averaging them at the last sum a total of forty-five pounds would be the result. However it is known that several copies of those last printed were disposed of as waste paper, therefore no very profitable trade speculation. Publishing orchestral and other instrumental music in England was not, nor is it at this time, a successful adventure; but William Forster (2) appreciated the merit of Haydn's music and hazarded the result; being the first in this country to introduce the works of this talented composer to public notice. It may be interesting to give a condensed list of the numerous works of Joseph Haydn, published by him and his son William Forster (3), the plates being all destroyed.

Sinfonias known by letters from A to W . . 23
Do.   numbered 1 to 15 15
Do.   „   1 to 12, with a star . . 12
Do.   Op. 10, Three; Op. 12, Four; Op.
         15, Six; Op. 29, Three; Op. 31,
         Six; and Op. 35, Six 28
Do.   The London, or the celebrated in the
         key of D 1
Do.   La Chasse, the Concertante and the
         Toy 3
Do.   The Passione 1

Some of which sinfonias were also known by other designations, as " The Candle one," letter B, in which each performer extinguishes the light at his desk and retires from the orchestra. In letter F, the fourth string is lowered in one of the movements. Letter L, the minuet and trio for the second parts of each have the same notes reversed or played backwards. Letter Q, it is said, was the exercise given in to the College at Oxford when the Doctor's degree was presented. No. 14, La Reine de France. No. 4 with star, The Roxalana. The Toy, in which children's toys are used with the other instruments.

Quartets—Op. 33, Six; Op. 44, Six; Op. 65,
       Six; Op. 72, Three; Op. 74, Three . . 24
Violin Solos, Six; Duet—Violin and Violon-
       cello, One; Trios—Flute, Violin and Vio-
       loncello, Six; Sonatas, with accompaniments
       for Violin and Violoncello—Op. 40, Three;
       Op. 42, Three; Op. 43, Three 22

Being one hundred and twenty-nine pieces besides a few others of lesser importance.

The Steiner pattern was the one adopted by William Forster (2) to work by, in 1762; and for several years later it was more or less used; however, about ten years afterwards the Amati outline was employed, but the model was high and swollen, and very deficient in the elegant *ensemble* of those instruments constructed through the remaining years of his life.

The violins of the first period were coloured of a brown tint, as if produced with dilute walnut stain and then varnished. The violoncellos are of a dark red with a blackish tinge, and much stronger of gum than that used for the treble instruments. The exact period is not known when such fine varnish was used by this maker; but a violoncello was made in 1772 for the chemist who had assisted him in the knowledge of the method to dissolve the gum amber; therefore the improvement, probably may date from that year; although the varnish on this particular instrument is not to be compared for beauty or richness of colour with those of later times. A further notice will be taken of this violoncello when relating its history.

The violas and violoncellos of this maker were the most esteemed, he was not as successful with the violins, although many of them are very good; and the reasons may be that sufficient attention was not paid to the various thicknesses of the gauging connected with the height of the model used; however it is certain the violins had not such fine tone as the other instruments. Many violas could be enumerated of known excellence, as the one made for Dr. Walcot, *alias* Peter Pindar; also, for Bartolozzi, the celebrated engraver; and another made for Mr. Henry Leffler, a professor, formerly of the Italian

Opera, and husband to the celebrated singer of that name. This viola is now possessed by Gordon Gairdner, Esq. of Hamilton Terrace, St. John's Wood ; and others could also be named. Many violoncellos could have attention drawn to them for their special excellencies, but a few only will be noticed; and a reference to the list of the instruments made, which will soon be specified, will more fully develope the names of eminent persons and professors of high repute that had them. Robert Lindley used one at the Italian Opera for nearly forty years ; he named it "The Eclipse." This violoncello is now in the possession of Mr. Charles Lucas, the principal of the Royal Academy of Music. James Crossdill had a famous one. Cervetto the younger had one that was burned when the Italian Opera House, Haymarket, was destroyed by fire on the 17th June, 1789. The regret felt at the loss of this instrument was so acute, that he retired from the profession, being sure he never could have another violoncello that would suit his purposes so well. The fact may be explained thus :—When a young man he procured the instrument, and with the professional practise it ripened in tone as he ripened in years, therefore was greatly admired and appreciated. But it would tire to fill up space with the many fine violoncellos that could be brought to notice. There were only four double basses made by William Forster (2), three of which were made by the command of his Majesty George III. ; and some interest was excited regarding one of them, which will be seen by the two following letters from professors in the king's private band. Mr. H. Niebour was the person who had to play upon it when completed.

"Sir,—You will probably receive a letter from Mr. Niebour concerning a double-bass upon a much larger

scale than the one we already have. I hope you will
have no objection to attempt the making it. His Majesty, from the specimen you have given, has a very high
opinion of what you could produce on an enlarged scale.

> " I am, Sir,
>
> " Your sincere friend,
>
> " And humble servant,
>
> " H. Compton.

" Gariboldi has, I understand, one coming from Italy ;
do not let us bo outdone. I shall not be in town till
Tuesday next, I wish to see you on the above subject,
and will call on you on Wednesday. Get my tenor
finished and sent home by that time. Don't forget Nico-
lay's tenor."

No date was to the above letter, but it may have been
received about the time the following one was written.

> " Windsor, *July 4th*, 87 (1787).

" Sir,—By his *Majesty's* order you are to form a
plan for a new double-bass ; it is to be at least four
inches wider, if not more, than that which you made, and
the depth according. You are to make it as well as
possible—so as not to let aney exceed it in England—
as Garriboldic has sent to Itally for an uncommon large
one, so you are desired to exert your utmost skill, and
exceed both in goodness and size by the performance at
the Abby next year. I shall be glad of my violincello
as soon as possible.

> " Am with respect,
>
> " Sir, your hum[k]. ser[t].
>
> " H. Niebour."

The body of a fifth double-bass was made, but from
some cause was laid aside ; however it was completed in

October, 1822, for Mr. Samuel Deacon, of Leicester, who, it is believed, still retains it. All the double-basses were made of the same shape as the violoncello; not tapered off and bevelled at the fore end of the sides, and the back for greater convenience to the performer, but at the same time a probable injury to the tone.

Previous to giving the list of instruments made by William Forster (2), assisted by his son and workmen, it will be proper to mention that it can only approximate to correctness from the deficiency in the account-books before referred to. It is with some difficulty that the list in its present state has been accomplished; but, as far as enumerated, it may be relied on. The numbers on the instruments do not assist to arrive at satisfactory conclusions, as they are occasionally marked for those made in each year, at other times altogether omitted, and sometimes marked in succession from year to year.

Three distinct classes of work were adopted; but the style, to a certain extent, was retained through all of them; therefore known as from this maker. The commonest instruments were not purfled, and they had oil varnish of an inferior quality; and in later times, when the name became famous, few of this class were made in consequence of the deceit and fraud practised by persons getting them purfled, and selling them as "genuine Forster's," for a larger sum than they were really worth.

The next class was much better finished; they were all purfled, and a superior varnish used; therefore formed an intermediate instrument to the next or highest style of workmanship, in which everything was embodied to conduce to excellence, to beautiful appearance, and to the finest tone.

The earliest or first entry that is met with in the old

account-books now in existence is on the 14th November,
1773:—

1773. *Violin*—Mr. Cole.   *Tenor*—Mr. Mainstone.

1774. *Violins*—Mr. Crosdill; Mr. Hay; Mr. Stone.
Tenor—Mr. Stone, of Okehampton.   *Violoncellos*—
Mr. Ritchards; Col'. Hamilton.

1775. *Violins*—Mr. Minehouse, Clare Hall, Cambridge; Mr. Hawkes, Steiner copy.   *Tenor*—The Rev.
Mr. Waller.

1770. *Violin* — Mr. Hackwood.   *Violoncello*—Mr.
Skardon.

1777. *Tenor*—The Rev^d. Mr. North.

1778. *Double Bass*—The Rev^d. Mr. Hodgson.

1779. *The account-books are lost or destroyed.*

1780. *Tenor*—G. M. Molineux, Esq^m.   *Violoncello*
—The Rev^d. Mr. Hodgson.

1781. *Tenor*—Mr. Hawkes.

1782. *Kits*—Mr. Bishop (three).   *Violins*—Mr. G.
Burchell, Musician, Manchester ; Mr. Mainstone, At-
torney, Essex S'. Strand; Mr. Edmund Lee, Dublin
(three) ; Mr. A. Foster, Whitehaven, Cumberland (four);
Tenor—Mr. Edmund Lee, Dublin.   *Violoncellos*—His
Royal Highness the Prince of Wales (two).

1783. *Violins*—Mr. Jones (two) ; Colonel Edgerton ;
Mr. Sykes ; D'. Pollock ; Mr. Wilson, Kensington.
Tenors—Mr. Cheere ; Mr. Borghi.   *Violoncellos*—Mr.
Ashley ; Mr. Gray, Marsham Street, Westminster ;
Rev^d. J. G. Honnington, Eaton; Mr. Hole, Jesus Col-
lege, Cambridge ; Mr. Cervetto; Mr. G. Lewis, Moss
Hills, Leominster, Herefordshire.

1784. *Kits*—Mr. Bishop.   *Violins*—Mr. Ware ; Mr.
Cousins (two); Mr. Johnston ; Mrs. Gibbs ; Mr. Emly,
at Mr. Gilbert's, Bodmin, Cornwall.   *Tenors*—Captain
Armstrong ; Rev^d. Mr. Rokeby ; Mr. Ayres, Woolwich.

Violoncellos—Mr. Webb, Temple ; Mr. Dixon, Felstead, Essex ; Rev⁴. Mr. Savery ; Mr. Yatman ; Shaw, Esqr., North Street, opposite Whitfield's Tabernacle ; Mr. Johnston.

1785. *Violins*—Mr. Warler; Mr. Compton (two); Mr. Cole ; Sir John Palmer ; Rev⁴. Mr. North ; Mr. Ware (three); Mr. Smith, Grange Court ; one sold in the shop; Mr. Marsh, Attorney at Law, Canterbury ; Mr. Dale. *Tenors*—Mr. Compton (two); Longman ; Mr. Abbot; Sir John Palmer; Lord Rivers ; Mr. Holcroft, 46, Upper Mary-le-bone Street, near Tichfield S⁴., Oxford Road ; Mr. Jeremiah Clark, Organist, Birmingham; Mr. Panton. *Violoncellos*—Mr. Dorrien ; Mr. Broadwood ; one sold in the shop; Mr. Compton ; Mr. Tucker; Sir John Palmer; Rev⁴. Mr. Savery, Plymouth ; Mr. Bradstreet, S^t. John's College, Cambridge ; Robert Williams, Esqr., Trinity College, Cambridge, by order of D^r. Bostock ; Mr. Gricsbach.

1786. *Violins*—Rev⁴. Mr. Savery (two) ; Mr. Barrett, Organist, Northampton (two); Mr. W. Dale; Mr. E⁴. Clay, King Street, Covent Garden ; Honble. Mr. Champion Dymocke, N°. 120, New Bond Street ; Mr. Holcroft, Upper Mary-le-bone S⁴., Tichfield Street, Oxford Road, (two) ; Lord Malden ; Mr. Wood, Devonshire Street ; Brimner; Mr. Smith, Grange Court. *Tenors* —Captain Lucas; Mr. Nathaniel Dance ; Mr. Dymoke ; Mr. Clarke, Organist, Birmingham ; Lord Malden ; General Jerningham ; Mr. Jackson, Clerkenwell Close ; Mr. Mitchell ; Mr. Compton. *Violoncellos*—Mr. Smith, Grange Court; Mr. Claget; Mr. Bartolozzi ; Mr. Compton ; Colonel Edgerton, G^t. George Street, Hanover Square ; Mr. Vinicombe; Mr. Borghi ; Rev⁴. Mr. Townley ; Mr. Dance; Mr. Tucker ; Mr. Roper, Hertford S⁴., May Fair.

1787. *Violins*—Mr. Smith, Grange Court; Mr. Eley,
for Lady Nudegate; Rev⁴. Mr. Savery (two); Mr.
Blake. *Tenors*—Mr. Stephenson (two); Mr. Baum-
garten, sent to the Ox Inn, for him at Liverpool. This
Viola was paid for by the M.S.S. of his five celebrated
Fugues for the Organ; Mr. S'. Ledger. *Violoncellos*—
Mr. Hare; Mr. Gordon, Nᵒ. 3 Bass; Mr. Cervetto for
Mr. Randel, Southampton Street, Bloomsbury; Dʳ. Cha'.
Bostock, Weverley Abbey, near Farnham, Surrey; Mr.
Johnstone; Mr. Oliphant, Sloane Square; Mr. Corfe,
Salisbury; His Grace the Duke of Richmond; Mr.
Holcroft; Mr. Hunter, Kings Arm Yard, Nᵒ. 4 Bass;
Mr. Morse. *Double Bass*—His Majesty King George
the third.

1788. *Violins*—Mr. Kellner for Mr. Grandler; Rich⁴.
Dupuis, Esqʳ. Queen's Dragoon Guards; The Rev⁴. Dʳ.
Cha'. Bostock; Mr. Emley. *Tenors*—George Dorrien,
Esqʳ. Nᵒ. 19, Somerset Street, Portman Square; Cap'.
Cooper, 75, Lambs Conduit Street; Mr. Lanzoni; Dʳ.
Cha'. Bostock; Mr. Pennington; Captain Lucas; Mr.
John Skynner, Birmingham. *Violoncellos*—Mr. Ben-
son, sent to Salisbury; Rev⁴. Mr. Savery; Mr. John
Skynner, Birmingham; Mr. Pickering; Mr. Clark,
Birmingham; Mr. Buckley, Manchester, Nᵒ. 5 Bass;
Sheldon, Esqʳ., Sunning, near Reading, Berks; Mr.
Shaw; Mr. Iscard.

1789. *Violins*—Mr. Fuller, 5, Dover Street; Captain
Cooper, Lamb's Conduit Street; Mr. Blake for Mr.
Rogers, Stamford; Mr. Wᵐ. Griesbach; Mr. Webb;
Mr. Stephenson; Rev⁴. Dean Palmer, Great Torrington,
Devon; Prado, Esq'., Twickenham. *Tenors*—Rev⁴.
Mr. Savery; Mr. Fuller, 5, Dover Street. *Violoncellos*
—Mr. Tho'. Smith, Emanuel College; Mr. Stewart,
Hill Street, Berkeley Square; Mr. H. A. Hole, Exeter;

Lord Delewar; the Rev⁴. Mr. Lewin, Bushey Mill, Watford; Mr. Corfe, Salisbury; Mr. Cervetto, a new Steiner copied Bass, Nº. 1; Miss Abrams; Rev⁴. Dean Palmer, Great Torrington, Devon; Major Price, Tiverton, Devon; Rev⁴. Mr. Morres, Windsor. *Double Bass*—His Majesty King George the third, a large Double Bass.

1790. *Violins*—Mr. Smith for Mr. Cater; Mr. Smith; Rev⁴. Mr. Wright; Miss Abrams; Mr. Newbery, Surgeon of His Majesty's Ship *Assistance*, Portsmouth; Mr. J. B. Pierson. *Tenors*—Mr. Hunter, Kings Arm Yard, Coleman Street; Mr. Smith for Mr. Cater; Mr. Thoˢ. Shaw, Drury Lane Theatre; Miss Abrams; Mr. Papendick. *Violoncellos*—Earl of Uxbridge; Mr. Aldersey; Mr. Cervetto (two), Nˢ. 2 and 3 made in 1789, Steiner copies; Peter Shaw, Esqʳ.; Mr. Hole, Nº. 2, 1790; Mr. J. B. Pierson; R. Sheldon, Esqʳ., Skitty Hall, near Swansea.

1791. *Violins*—Mr. Schooner, 11, Upper John Street, Tottenham Court Road; Charles Shaw Lefevere, Esq. Bedford Square; Captain Henry, Tenterden, Kent (two); Mr. Blake for Mr. Rogers, Lincoln (two); Mr. Holcroft, Steiner copy; Mr. Yalman.

1791. *Tenor*—Lord Balgonie. *Violoncellos*—Mr. Twining, Junʳ. Strand; Mr. Otley; Mr. Fuller; Peter Shaw, Esqʳ.; Lord Archibald Hamilton; Mr. Yatman.

1792. *Violins*—Mr. Barrett, Organist, Northampton; Lord Archibald Hamilton; Mr. French.

1792. *Tenors*—Captain Henry, Tenterden, Kent; Mr. Yatman, Percy Street. *Violoncellos*—Mr. Eley (two); Captain Henry, Tenterden, Kent; Dr. Eden, Red Lion Street, Clerkenwell; Mr. Cervetto.

1793. *Violins*—Mr. Yatman; Rev⁴. Mr. Lewin; Mr. H. Potter, 39, Margaret Street, Cavendish Square; also another for Mr. G. Nicholls. *Tenor*—Mr. Morse.

Y

1793. *Violoncellos*—Mr. Armstrong, Apothecary, Portman Square; Mr. Scola; Mr. Eley; Mr. Cervetto.

1794. *Violins*—Mr. Cole, Carlton House; Rev⁴. Mr.
Clark, Bedale, Yorkshire; Mr. French; Mr. Smith,
Bromley.

1794. *Tenors*—Although no tenors appear to have
been sold in this year, yet there is an entry worthy of
remark. "*Dr. Haydn. Putting in order and stringing a tenor.*" *Violoncellos*—Mr. Lindley; Mr. Attwood.

1795. *Violins*—Mr. Blake for —— Dare, Esqʳ. Nottingham Place; Captain Boden; Captain Chalmers;
Mr. Nicks.

1795. *Tenor*—Captain Chalmers. *Violoncellos*—His
Majesty George the Third; William Franks, Esqʳ. Beech
Hill; Mr. Ware, Senʳ.; Dr. Brown, Artillery Lane;
Mr. Attwood; Wᵐ. Sheldon, Esqʳ.; Mr. Eley; Captain
Chalmers.

1796. *Violins*—Mr. French; Colonel St. Clare, 25,
Regᵗ.

1796. *Violoncellos*—Mr. Brant, Highbury Terrace,
Islington; Rev⁴. H. A. Hole, Exeter.

1797. *Tenors*—Mr. Bright, Stradiuarius copy, large;
Dr. Walcot.

1797. *Violoncellos*—Mr. Yatman (two); Wᵐ. Sheldon, Esq.

1798. *Violins*—Rev⁴. Mr, Vinicombe, a mute violin;
Mr. Osbaldiston, Twickenham; Mr. G. Ashley, Stradiuarius copy; Mr. Bauch.

1798. *Tenor*—Mr. Corson. *Violoncello*—Mr. Linley.

1799. *Violins*—Rev⁴. Mr. Chudleigh; Mr. Blake, 7,
Nottingham Street, Marylebone, for Mrs. Farhill, 43,
Mortimer Street, Cavendish Sqʳ.; Mr. Blake, for Mr.
Deane, 21, Nottingham Place, Marylebone; Mr. Yat-
man, a mute violin. *Violoncellos*—Rev⁴. Mr. Poole, at

Mr. Ruscombi Poole's, attorney at law, Bridgewater, Somersetshire.

1800. *Violins*—Mr. T. Blake, 55, Hans Place, Sloane Street (two).

1800. *Tenor*—Mr. Yatman.

1801. *Violins*—Mr. French, for the Grotto Concert; Mr. Yatman.

1801. *Tenor*—Mr. French, for the Grotto Concert.

1802. *Violin*—Mr. B. Blake, 55, Hans Place, Knightsbridge.

1803. *Tenor*—Mr. Corson, Brentford. *Violoncello*—Rev[d]. H. A. Hole.

1804. *Tenor*—Rev[d]. D'. Nicholas.

1805. *Violoncello*—Mr. Yatman; *Double Bass*—His Majesty George the Third.

1806. *Violoncello*—Rev[d]. H. A. Hole.

A statement has been made public and believed to be correct, although no entry appears in the account books to prove it, that the last violoncello, and probably the last instrument made by William Forster (2), was manufactured by express wish for Mr. Crossdill; and it was one of the violoncellos offered at the sale of his musical property, on the 9th May, 1826. " Lot 6. A violoncello—of the long Stradiuarius pattern—by Forster, Sen., the very last instrument manufactured by that justly celebrated maker, and most highly valued by Mr. Crossdill, with bow, in a most excellent dove-tail case, covered with leather, brass nails, lock and key."

It was bought for forty-six guineas by Thos. Dodd, the dealer in musical instruments, for Edward Prior, Esq. late of York Terrace, Regent's Park. Henry Hill, in his manuscripts alluding to this William Forster, writes that he was " a highly and justly esteemed maker of violoncellos, &c. &c.; it is said he was not originally

bred to the occupation, but came to it by chance or
accidental preference; if so, he must have possessed a
rare talent, for his instruments are second in merit to
none, but the best Europe has ever known; especially
his *amber coloured violoncellos*, they are renowned for
mellowness, a volume and power of tone, equalled by
few, surpassed by none. His dark red coloured are not so
much admired, though the difference in merit is scarcely
discernible. He was not so successful with his violins
and altos; he does not appear to have given the same
care and judgment to their production; he followed the
grand Amati in his forms and model without being a
mere copyist, and had a rare excellence in the facture of
the violoncello peculiarly his own. The expression—*a
true Forster tone*—is not a *jeux d'esprit.*"

William Forster (2) died at the residence of his son,
No. 22, York Street, Westminster, on the 14th Dec.
1808, and was buried, on the 21st of the same month,
in the family grave at the Church of St. Martin's in the
Fields, Charing Cross, on the north side, near to the
steps, and opposite to his former residence, the corner
of Duke's Court. A black marble slab once marked
the spot, but it has been taken away, and probably the
ashes of the dead were desecrated and blown hither and
thither at the time the alterations of that locality took
place, and the neighbourhood altered to its present appearance.

HISTORY OF A VIOLONCELLO MADE BY WILLIAM FOSTER (2).

This violoncello was made in or about the year 1772,
and is well known in the musical circle under two names
or designations—"The Rev⁴. Mr. Hole's or Crossdill's
violoncello." It is of the Amati outline, with a very

high and unusual model, and was originally manufactured for Mr. Charles Alexander, a chemist, who had
greatly assisted the maker in the method of dissolving
the gums amber and copal for varnishes. At the time
the order was given, it was promised that if a better
instrument could be supplied than any hitherto made, it
should now be produced for the essential services rendered. How or when this violoncello became the property of Mr. Hugh Reinagle, of Oxford, is not known,
but we arrive at positive information regarding it by an
article in an old newspaper—" *The General Advertiser*
for Tuesday, 6 November, 1787"—which has been preserved by the family as being identified with this instrument, and as the paragraph is amusing, it is given verbatim. " The rage for music was never more conspicuous
than now. A few days ago, a violoncello, made by
Forster, was sold for the sum of one hundred guineas
and an Amati bass, worth at least fifty guineas, in exchange. The purchaser was Mr. Kole (Hole), an amateur, in whose praise much has been, though too much
cannot be said. This valuable instrument was formerly
the property of Mr. Hugh Reinagle, the celebrated bass
player, whose death has been universally lamented by
the *musical cognoscenti*. At his demise it was bought
by Mr. Gunn, who has now sold it. To such a nicety
is the manufacture and sale of musical instruments now
brought, that a fiddle, like a race-horse, must have a
pedigree, and his whole *get* announced, before any attention will be given to it." The Rev. H. A. Hole was
one of the best amateur performers on the violoncello of
the day, and it is remarkable he should have been so, as
the two first joints of the forefinger on the left hand had
been amputated, in consequence of mortification having
set in, therefore he was compelled to use the thumb from

the first position; he must also have possessed great
courage, for after the operation of taking off the first joint
by the surgeons in attendance, he, from symptoms experienced, wished them to operate on the second joint,
which they deemed useless; when on their retiring to
partake of some refreshment, he excused himself, and
went to his dressing-room and cut off the injured part,
with his penknife, at the second joint, and then returned
to the surgeons to have the wound properly dressed.   On
medical examination of the joint he had operated on,
they acknowledged that disease had taken place, and
that at some future time it must have been amputated.
So choice was he of this violoncello that, when he travelled with it, he endeavoured, if possible, to secure an
inside place in the mail or stage coach; but there were
times when it was otherwise conveyed, and on one of
these the instrument received the fracture in the back,
with other injuries not of such serious nature; however
when it was repaired, William Forster (2), and other
persons did not consider the tone at all affected, although
detrimental to its appearance.   The following letter will
explain Mr. Hole's feelings regarding the injuries :—

" By this time you have received my old and *once famous*
violoncello.   It is a melancholy accident, and as you did
not as usual enter it at 500*l.* value, I cannot recover any
compensation from the carrier.   He has made this pro-
position, that he will pay all expenses of repairing; and
you will please to state to me the real damage done to
the value of the instrument, if it were to be sold, that I
may attempt to recover it, or have some allowance.   You
will please to repair it as soon as possible, & not send to
me, as I shall be in London in March.

" Yours very truly,

" *January* 13, 1798.   " H. A. HOLE.

" P.S.—Lest it should come to a law suit, you should also take Lindley's evidence, adding the loss sustained by the accident, or any other person else you think right."

From the date of the above letter, the link of interest in this violoncello is now lost, until 1814, when Mrs. Hole sends a letter to William Forster (3), dated from the " Vicarage House, Okehampton, Devon, May 29th, 1814," a portion of which is as follows :—

" I wish to ask your advice in regard to my late husband's violoncello—I mean the *fine instrument* made by your father which Mr. Hole bought of Mr. Reinagle, and which he so highly valued. Mr. Hole was offered for it, some years ago, 500*l.* If I could get a very large sum for it, I might be induced to sell it ; but, as I am perfectly aware of the very great value of it, I will not part with it otherwise.　•　•　•　•　•

" I remain, Mr. Forster,

" Y' ob' hu' Ser'

" S. HOLE."

It will be observed, that the widow states the violoncello was " bought of Mr. Reinagle." The previous extract from the old newspaper says Mr. Gunn. It is not in our power to prove which Professor it really was that sold the instrument to the Rev. H. A. Hole ; indeed, it little matters, as both were eminent men of the period. Perhaps the newspaper claims the greatest reliance, being printed at or about the time when the violoncello changed ownership ; and Mrs. Hole's remark is made in 1814.

We now arrive at the commencement of a correspondence between Mrs. Hole and Mr. James Crossdill relative to the disposal of the violoncello ; there is also a letter to William Forster (3) which corroborates the sale. The three letters are as follows:—

" Mrs. Hole,
" Mrs. Horne's,
" Uxbridge Common.

" Sir,

" I take the liberty of troubling you with a letter in consequence of a conversation which I had with Mr. James before you left Denham, when Mrs. J—— informed me of your most kind and friendly offer of taking Mr. Hole's violoncello under your care, and of disposing of it to the best advantage. I beg to assure you that I feel the kindness of this offer, which I shall be happy to accept. Mr. Robert Hole (Mr. Hole's brother) has made several inquiries amongst his professional friends as to the value of the violoncello. They all agree in saying, that for so *very* fine an instrument we should scarcely be justified in parting with it for less than two hundred guineas. Mr. Hole, I know, refused a much larger sum for it some years ago. As I am afraid of sending the violoncello to London by a public carriage, and my daughter goes to London in my mother's carriage on Monday next, the 23rd, will you permit me to send it on that day in the carriage, and it shall be deposited safely at Mr. Thompson's between twelve and one o'clock ? I shall esteem it a favour if you will have the goodness to inform me, before the 23rd, if I may take this liberty.

" I remain, sir,
" Y' ob' hu' ser'
" S. Hole.

" Jan. 16, 1815."

The above letter is addressed to

"— Crosdale, Esq.
" at — Thompson's, Esq.
" Grosvenor Square,
" London."

The next letter is dated,

" May 22nd, 1815,
" Sir, " Uxbridge Common.

" I beg to return you my most sincere thanks for your *very* kind and friendly exertions, and for the great trouble which you have taken about the violoncello. Believe me, it affords me great pleasure that the instrument is in *your* hands. It was highly valued by my dear and much lamented Mr. Hole, and I am certain that there is no person he would so much have wished to have it as yourself. I called this morning at Messrs. Hall and Co. Uxbridge, that I might be able to acknowledge to you the receipt of the 70*l.* for the violoncello, but the clerks informed me that no intimation had been received from Messrs. Masterman and Co. of the 70*l.* lodged in their hands, the reason of which is, that they receive communications from them *only* on a Thursday, and on that day, therefore, I shall receive the money. Wishing you a long continuance of health to use the violoncello, which will, I dare say, sometimes remind you of your departed friend,

" I remain, sir,
" Y^r much obliged and
" Faithful hu' ser'
" May 22." " S. Hole.

Addressed to

" James Crosdill, Esq.
" — Thompson's, Esq.
" Grosvenor Square,
" London."

The following letter written to William Forster (3) and dated 21 May, 1815 :—

> " Mrs. Hole,
> " Mrs. Horne's,
> " Near Uxbridge,
> " Middlesex.

" MR. FORSTER,

" I have a very beautiful violoncello here of the late Rev. H. A. Hole's of your father's making. As I keep two for my son, I wish to dispose of this. I have sold the *fine* instrument, about which I wrote to you, to Mr. Crosdale. Will you take this, or dispose of it for me? I will not part with it under 25*l.* Mr. Monzani has offered to dispose of it for me, but as you are an old acquaintance of the late Mr. Hole's, and it is your father's instrument, I prefer making you the first offer of it. Let me know immediately whether you will take it, or dispose of it for me, and I will send it up to you safely by the coach. I am not certain, but I think Mr. Hole called the instrument a Steiner.

> " I am, Mr. Forster,
> " Yours, &c.
> " S. HOLE."

Mr. James Crossdill had retired from the musical profession several years before the purchase of this famous instrument, and after his death all his remaining violoncellos, seven in number, were sold by auction on the 9th May, 1826, at which time Robert Lindley, the celebrated violoncellist of the day, bought it for fifty guineas. Two or three gentlemen had attended the auction with the intention of buying this well-known violoncello; but on Lindley naming the first price for it, fifty guineas, no person then present would compete; and, on the auctioneer announcing the purchaser's name, great approbation was

shown, and the room resounded with plaudits. Fortunately for Mr. Robert Lindley the person sent, by command of George IV., to buy this and two other violoncellos, was absent in the ante-room, talking with some
acquaintance, when Lot 2 was put up; therefore the
opportunity of buying was lost.   He (Mr. Kramer,
Master of the King's Private Wind Instrument Band),
learning that his chance was gone, offered Mr. Lindley
100l. for his bargain, but it was not accepted.   After
delighting the musical public with his performances and
extraordinary quality of tone on this instrument for nine
or ten years, with the fine and glorious sweeping chords
when accompanying the Recitatives, of which style he
claims to be the original, and with the leading notes
for the singer, which notes sung with the vocalist,
always merited a portion of the applause.   No doubt
many persons remember, with feelings of exquisite pleasure, his accompaniments to Handel's air, " O Liberty ! "
also Haydn's " In native worth ;" and Mozart's " Batti,
Batti ; " but above all that unrivalled performance of
the violoncello obligato to Dr. Pepush's cantata " Alexis,"
which, in the original composition, is only a simple semiquaver movement ; but, with his new reading, it became
a performance of wonder and excellence.   Many other
parts, in orchestral pieces in which the violoncello was
made prominent could also be enumerated, which caused
Bernard Romberg, a contemporary and rival, to acknowledge " he was great in the orchestra, great as an
accompanyist, and great as a soloist." About 1835-6,
Mr. Lindley sold this violoncello to Captain West, of
the 1st Regiment of Royal Life Guards, for 200l. in
money, a violoncello valued at 30l., and a picture considered worth 100l.   During this ownership, Monsieur
Servais played on the violoncello at Paris, and delighted

—indeed, if report speaks true, astonished—the Parisians with the fulness of tone produced, being so different from that thin and hard quality of tone which they had been accustomed to hear. Captain West stated that Onslow and other celebrated musical composers had endeavoured to persuade him to sell the instrument to Servais. Be this as it may, the violoncello again came into the English market, and was purchased by the late Frederick Perkins, Esq., of Chipstead Place, Seven Oaks, Kent, about the year 1839; but this date cannot be positively asserted, although believed not to be much in error. This fine violoncello is now the property of Lieutenant-General Sir Hope Grant, G.C.B.

CHAPTER XXIII.

ILLIAM FORSTER, the third of this name as a violin-maker, was the son of the previous William Forster (2), and was born on the 7th January, 1764, in Prescott Street, Goodman's Fields; it is believed the house was No. 12. He must have evinced an early talent as a workman, for the first violin in the list of the best instruments he made is entered in the year 1779; but precocious talent, in general, seldom advances; at first it bursts forth like the bright rays of the sun from behind a dense cloud; the praises then bestowed, and the flattery given, make it conclude it is perfection, and produce a self-confidence and sufficiency that often lead to idleness, and consequently it ceases to exert mental energies, and the probability is its possessor becomes of lymphatic temperament, and moves not onwards to keep pace with the world's advancement. However, there may be a cause in this instance why he became averse to the confinement and toil of the work-room. He was fond of the drama, and associated with private theatricals. It has been told to one of the family, by the late Mr. Charles Wodarch, a cousin of the Kembles, and formerly the leader of the orchestra of Covent Garden Theatre, that he had talent for acting, and that he had seen him perform the characters of Scrub, in "The Beaux's Stratagem;" and Fribble, in the farce of "Miss in her Teens;" and that in the former character he considered him better than the public's great favourite, Mr. Keeley.

It would appear, by a statement in Mr. James Mainstone's bill of costs, that the father and son had been partners at one period; but the nature of the compact is so strange that it can scarcely be believed; and the only thing which entitles it to credence is an old catalogue which is supposed to have been printed before 1787, as Haydn's quartets, op. 44, are not inserted. There is no proof of this partnership by books of accounts, or by knowledge of the elder branches of the present family; but there is full evidence of the son having all the music portion of the business, with liberty to obtain work in his own behalf, by the books which commence 17th July, 1786, being the day after his marriage, the father having his own account-books and customers through all the years that had previously passed, and continued until his death.

The following extract made from the account of the lawyer:—

"1783. Oct'. 1ᵐ. Attending and taking Instructions for drawing agreement between Mr. Forster Sen'. and Mr. Forster Jun'. for the former serving the latter during three years under a special Contract."

"Drawing Articles of Agreement accordingly fo 18."

"7ᵗʰ. Attending the Party to read over and settle same."

"Nov'. 1. Engrossing same two parts. Stamps.
　　　　　Attending Execution."

Should this contract have been acted on, which is very doubtful, it shows how much a parent will yield to the wishes of a son, who was the only surviving offspring.

The work of William Forster (3) was of high finish
and neatness, but he did not take an interest in his vocation, though there are some of the instruments made by
him exceedingly good in tone. He was generally deno-
minated "Young Forster," and the labels put into the
instruments were signed William Forster, Jun'., the Jun'.
being added with a pen, as also the year in which the
instrument was made, and the number of it. These
particulars were also written inside the instrument, on
both vibrating plates, and at the tail-pin, under the varnish. Some persons have often obliterated the Jun'. at
this place, no doubt for dishonest purposes, as the instruments of this maker do not command so large a price as
those of his father.

The following is a copy of an original label, the Royal
Arms at one corner, and the Prince of Wales's Feathers
on the opposite corner:—

"William Forster Jun'.
Violin, Violoncello, Tenor & Bow-maker
1810   Also Music Seller   N°. 43
To their Royal Highnesses the
Prince of Wales and the Duke of Cumberland."

The label used in later years had the Feathers of the
Prince of Wales on one corner, and the Lion upon the
Crown, surrounded by the Garter, on the other side,
the paper of the label being much narrower than the
former label; the number of instrument, the year, and
the Jun'. to be added with a pen:—

"William Forster
Violin, Violoncello, Tenor & Bow-maker
to their Royal Highnesses the Prince of Wales
& Duke of Cumberland. London."

After pioneering through the account-books of this
violin-maker from 1786 to 1816 it is found that a list of
the instruments manufactured cannot be produced even
approaching tolerable accuracy, therefore it is abandoned. Four different classes of instruments were made
by William Forster (3), assisted by his son and workmen; and about the year 1786-7 the German fiddles, of
cheap and common workmanship, were introduced into
England, it is believed, by Astor, of Wych Street, Strand,
of whom tales could be told connected with German clocks
and German musical wind instruments; and entries are
seen in the books for fiddles as low as nine shillings,
which were mostly sold to dealers; but others have par-
ticipated in the low prices. Moreover, there are many
exchanges and re-purchases of instruments, so that it is
very probable the same instrument may have been disposed of more than once.

All these circumstances baffle the endeavour to produce a similar list to that previously given of the instruments made by his father. There is a book, however,
in the writing of William Forster (3), still preserved,
which has some account of the instruments made by him.
It is imperfect as regards the numbers, particularly of
the second-class violins and tenors, and there is no mention of the violoncellos of inferior workmanship. The
following are the entries, with slight alteration in the
arrangement:—

" Number of best Violins made by W⁻. Forster Jun'.

		Put down to the year
Forster, Jun'. N⁻. 1, 2, 3, and 4	. . . . .	1779
„	„ 5, 6, 7, and 8	1780
„	„ 9 and 10	1782
„	„ 11, 12, 13, and 14	1783

Put down to the year

Forster, Jun'. N™. 15, 16, 17, 18, and 19 . . .	1784
,, ,, 20, 21, and 22, this last of small size	1785
,, ,, 23	1789
,, ,, 24, 25. and 26	1793
,, ,, 27, 28, 29, 30, 31, 32, 33, 34, 35, 36, 37, 38, 39, and 40 . .	1813
,, ,, 41, 42, and 43, all three of small size	1814

In another part of the book is inserted, "Violins at
.£3 3s. 0d."

Put down to the year

Forster, Jun'. N°. 1	1782
,, ,, 2 and 3	1783
,, ,, 4	1789

Many more of this class violin have been seen entered
in the account-books as disposed of, so far as they were
examined.

The best tenors were made as follows :—

Put down to the year

Forster, Jun'. N™. 1, 2, and 3	1783
,, ,, 4, 5, 6, 7, 8, 9, and 10 . .	1784
,, ,, 11 and 12	1785
,, ,, 13 and 14	1786
,, ,, 15	1787
,, ,, 16, 17, 18, 19, and 20 . . .	1789
,, ,, 21	1793
,, ,, 22	1794
,, ,, 23	1795
,, ,, 24 and 25	1798

Then follow " Tenors at £3 3s. 0d."
Forster, jun. Nos. 1 and 2, made in the year 1783,

z

and No. 3 in the year 1789. The same remark as made on the violins of this class, can be applied to the tenors.

With the list of violoncellos made of the first class there has been taken a little more care; but it is far from perfect; and no account whatever of instruments of five guineas value and less has been kept, although numerous entries in the account-books prove that such were made and sold.

" Best violoncellos made by Wm. Forster, jun."

No.   Put down to the year
1, for Mr. Clay   1787
2, Sold to Mr. Hook—3, for Mr. Tillard   .   1788
4, Sold to Mr. Cartwright   1789
5, ...   1791
6, Mr. Crouch—7 and 8, ...   1792
9, 10, 11, and 12   1795
13, Crouch—14, Col'. Hawker   1797
15, Lindley—16, Yatman   1797
17, Day   1798
18, Major Bothwell—19, James Leffler   . .   1801
20, Rev. Mr. Landon—and 21, Lieut. Heaviside   1801
22, Crosdill—23, Henry Bedford, Esq.   . .   1804
24, Sold to Oxford—and 25, Lord Aylesford .   1804
26, Col'. Bothwell—27, Crosdill   1805
28, Lord Aylesford   1806
29, ...   1807

About this time the eldest son, William Forster (4), was becoming perfected in the art; and there is a remark written on the margin, " The first violoncello made by my son was made for Charles Ashley." This instrument, it is believed, was the violoncello known in the musical circle as the " Blood Red Knight."

The following No. 30 shows that the son either assisted

in or made the whole, as it has " Bill No. 2 " attached
to it, and a similar remark continues to several other
instruments:—

No.	Put down to the year
30, Bill No. 2—31, Bill No. 3, Lord Lewisham	1807
32, Bill No. 4, Gladstanes—33, Bill No. 5, Hole	1807
34, Bill No. 6—35, Bill No. 7, Blake, Bath	1807
36, Bill No. 8—37, Bill No. 9, Cervetto	1809
38, B and G No. 10—39, B and G No. 11, Captain Deacon	1810
40, B and G No. 12—41, B and G No. 13 —42, B and G No. 14	1810
43, G, and 44, Bill No. 15	1810
45, 46, 47, Lindley—48, 49, 50, 51, 52, Mr. Bedford, Steiner pattern—53, Lindley, Steiner pattern, and 54	1811
55, 56, 57, the two last had by Mr. Lindley, and of the Steiner pattern—58, Lord Aylesford—59, Steiner pattern — 60, 61, 62, and 63, these four last were of the Stradiuarius pattern	1812
64, 65, 66, and 67, the two last had by Lindley, and of the Steiner pattern	1813
68, 69, 70, 71, these four were the Stradiuarius pattern	1814
72, Bill (No. 16) for Iscard—73, Bill (17) Stradiuarius pattern	1815
74, Bill and Andrew, Steiner pattern	1823

Five or six double-basses, of second-class workmanship,
were made chiefly for letting out on hire; and there
was one of the best work finished for a person named
M'Calla, which instrument was destroyed either when
the Royalty Theatre, at the east part of London, was

burned down in 1826, or crushed to pieces when the roof of the Brunswick Theatre unfortunately fell in, killing several of the performers whilst at rehearsal, on the 28th Feb. 1828. The latter is believed to be the cause of its destruction. These double-basses were all made of the same shape as violoncellos. Some interest may be attached to the violoncello marked No. 26, 1805. It was made of the long Stradiuarius pattern, similar to Mara's celebrated violoncello of that Italian maker, and was first sold to Colonel Bothwell. Ultimately Robert Lindley bought it of Messrs. Withers and Co., and the tone is so grand and fine that it became the favourite violoncello. It is the instrument on which he performed when he made his last public appearance, and played the celebrated trio of Corelli with Charles Lucas and James Howell, at the Philharmonic Concert in the season of 1850. From the commanding tone of this violoncello, and its being made in the year 1805, Lindley named this instrument " Nelson," being the year in which this great Admiral fell at the battle of Trafalgar.

This violoncello is now the property of A. Allan Webbe, Esq. of Hereford Street, Park Lane, who purchased it of the younger son of Robert Lindley, soon after the decease of his talented parent.

William Forster (3) was a person fond of speculating in houses, for which he had not judgment or ability, and much too amiable and kind, although of hasty temper, to be the landlord of such small houses as were purchased. Better property was occasionally bought, but something unlucky was always attached to it; so that the whole of these transactions may be considered a complete failure. But the climax which brought ruin upon him was entering into a grocery business, about 1815-16, with another person of whom he had little

knowledge. The consequences may be arrived at very
easily. These misfortunes compelled the sacrifice of the
freehold and leasehold property, also what money remained in the funds, all of which descended to him from
the father, and were absorbed to liquidate large debts,
greatly to the detriment of a family of thirteen children
then living, consisting of nine daughters and four sons;
one son had died in the early part of this century by an
accident through the carelessness of the nurse. A broken
spirit and the despondency which existed in the latter
years of the life of W. Forster (3), were very painful to
witness; and at length death relieved him of mental and
bodily sufferings on the 24th July, 1824, and he was
buried a few days afterwards in the family grave, in the
churchyard of Saint Martin's in the Fields.

We have now arrived at the fourth and last of the
name of William Forster that have been makers of
violins, tenors, and violoncellos. He was the eldest son
of the previous W. Forster (3), and was born the 14th
of December, 1788, at No. 348, Strand; he possessed
good mechanical abilities, with mental endowment for
invention; but this last qualification was chiefly employed upon articles of pleasure and enjoyment, although
many branches of the business were improved and faci-
litated by him. He little cared whether it was wood or
metal he was working, all were made obedient to his
manipulation. He was an excellent workman, and the
instruments he made were beautifully finished. But the
workroom had little inducements for him; athletic and
rural sports absorbed his thoughts, and having a hasty
temper little could be accomplished with him at home.
He was instructed in violin-making partly by his grandfather and father; but his wild career could not be subdued, and at length it was deemed advisable to place him

from home, and Thomas Kennedy undertook the task,
and by humouring his foibles, gained more control over
him than perhaps any other person, except his mother.
He returned home again, but soon left it and joined the
theatrical company of the late — Trotter, Esq. of
Worthing, who had the Kent and Sussex circuit; sometimes acting on the stage, and at others playing the
violoncello in the orchestra. At Worthing, he indulged
with other persons in athletic pastimes; and in one of
these trials of strength received some internal injury,
from which, perhaps, he never thoroughly recovered.
He made very few instruments on his own account, probably twelve or fifteen. Two or three of these were
violins, and one violoncello of the best class; the latter
instrument was made for the late Mr. James Brooks, a
professor on the violoncello, the remainder being of inferior workmanship for wholesale orders. He, however,
would occasionally repair instruments; but having,
generally, an engagement as a violoncello player either
at the Sans Pareil, Sadlers' Wells, or the Surrey
Theatre, then called the Circus, he little sought for that
kind of employment. During this period of his life
fishing was the absorbing desire, and he would take
every opportunity to walk to some favoured spot at
Woodford in Essex, or to places on the river Wandle
celebrated for the sport.

It is said that he performed clown at the Sans Pareil
Theatre during the whole of one Christmas holiday-time,
under the name of Signor Paulo, who was too ill and
unable to fulfill his engagement. His wild career
weakened his constitution; and being recommended to
go out of town for change, he accepted an engagement
as violoncellist at Cheltenham. On a leisure evening,
whilst playing a game of chess or drafts, a fit of apoplexy

deprived him of life, almost instantly, on the 8th October, 1824, in the prime of manhood, being only thirty-
six years of age.

The particulars regarding Gilkes perhaps should be
inserted here; but it is deemed advisable to carry the
family name to a close, as the one next mentioned, who
yet struggles with the " battle of life," is the last of the
race that is likely to be violin, viola, and violoncello
maker.

Simon Andrew Forster is the fourth son of William
Forster (3), and was born on the 13th May, 1801, at No.
348, Strand, the house which was known as the *Courier*
Newspaper Office, and pulled down for the approaches
to Waterloo Bridge from Catherine Street. He is indebted to his father and brother William Forster (4),
particularly the latter, for the knowledge acquired in
making violins, tenors, and violoncellos, &c. Gilkes also
has a small claim, but very small, of imparting instruction. It was not to his interest to do so, therefore the
progress in early years was not very rapid. However,
at that period, perhaps the work-room may have been
neglected, as music was studied as a profession in the
choir of Westminster Abbey, which gave the right of
education in Westminster School. Notwithstanding
Gilkes did not do his duty, when it is taken into consideration how much his position in life was advanced
by the improved knowledge imparted to him in the style
of work of the family, and the receipt of wages at the
time from the parent. This deficiency was fully recti-
fied by the attentions of the father and brother, after
Gilkes had ceased to work for the house.

A list will now follow of the best instruments, and the
year in which they were made, also the name of the
person who first purchased them. The label used in

them was as follows, and the initials signed on the opposite corner to the number—

> " S. A. Forster
> Violin, Tenor & Violoncello Maker
> N°.   London."

The name and London are engraved in the old English letter, and the other part in the written character. It is also written with a pen, " S. A. Forster, London," and the number of the instrument by the tailpin, under the varnish, and on both vibrating plates inside the instrument. In most instances the dates take place from the time the body of the instrument was put together, and not always finished in sequence.

Violins of the First Class.

No.

1, Mr. George Key	1828
2, Charles Rowland, Esq'.	1830
3, Stowel Chudleigh, Esq'.—4, R. H. W. Ingram, Esq'.	1835
5, Mr. Henry Thorn—6, Mr. William Cramer	1839
7, J. W. Cochrane, Esq'.—*(this violin had the prize medal awarded at the Great Exhibition of* 1851)	1839
8, Unsold—9, Mr. Thomas Key—10, Sir James Emerson Tennant—11, Unsold— and 12, Mr. Thomas Key	1839
13, Mr. Richard Stannard—14, Rev⁴. R. G. Buckston	1844
15, James Uglow, Esq'.—and 16 to 26 are still unfinished	1844

Violas or Tenors of the First Class.

No.

1, James Reynolds, Esq'.—2, doubtful . .	1839
3, Frederick James Rawlins, Esq'. . . .	1840

No.

4, William Davis, Esqr.—5,John Beardmore,
Esqr.—6 and 7, Unsold—8, 9, and 10,
still unfinished—and 11, Captain Edward J. Ottley—(*this viola had the
prize medal awarded at the Great Exhibition of* 1851) 1843

From No. 3 to 11 are instruments all of very large
size.

Violoncellos of the First Class.

From No. 1 to 12 were marked when the instrument
was varnished, therefore shows some irregularity in the
completion of them; but from No. 13 they were numbered when the body of the instrument was put together.

No.

1, Mr. John Smith 1825
2, Robert Lindley, Esq.—and 3, Mr. John
Smith 1826
4, Dr. Boisragon 1827
5, Mr. Acraman 1828
10, Colonel John Montague 1830
8, James Forster—and 9, Mr. William Glan-
vill 1831
6, Colonel Whitby—7, Rev^d. Dr. Barrett—
and 11, Mr. Thomas Binfield, for W.
Cull, Esqr. 1832
12, Christopher Rawlins, Esqr. 1835
13, Mr. T. J. Noble—14, Honble. Major Legge,
for the Bishop of Oxford—15, Stowel
Chudleigh, Esqr.—16 and 17, E. Wool-
lett, Esqr.—18, Sir Richard Bulkely
Phillipps, Bart.—19, Henry Knight,
Esqr.—20, Honble. Major Legge (this
was a very small violoncello for the son;

No.   it has since been cut down and converted into a tenor) 1836
21, Frederick Perkins, Esqʳ.—22, Charles
Lucas, Esqʳ. 1836
23, Mr. Henry Thorn 1836
24, —— Gribble, Esq. 1837
25, R. H. W. Ingram, Esqʳ.. 1838
26, James Lintott, junʳ. Esqᵒ.—27, George J.
Eyre, Esqʳ. 1839
28, William Davis, Esqʳ.—29, Walter Pettit,
Esqʳ. 1839
30, Honᵇˡᵉ. Arthur Lascelles—31, Captain Edward J. Ottley—and 32, Captain Hunter Blair 1839
33, James Howell, Esqʳ.—34, 35, 36 and 37
are still unfinished—and 38, Joseph
Laing Oldham, Esq.—(*this violoncello
had the prize medal awarded at the
Great Exhibition of* 1851) 1841

No.   Double Basses of the First Class.
1, Mr. Boulcott. 1833
2, Mr. S. J. Noble—and 3, Frederick Perkins, Esqᵒ. 1835
4, Samuel Brook, Esqʳ. 1836
5, Unsold 18

From these large instruments being heavy and cum-
bersome to handle in the working of them, it became
imperative to have assistance, even in some essential
parts, through debility of constitution.

The second class instruments had only this writing at
the tailpin, "Forster, No.——;" and alcoholic varnishes
have been used with all of them. The memory will not
assist to state exactly how many instruments of this class

have been made; perhaps not more than twenty-four violins, four or five tenors, and about ten violoncellos. A correct account of these has not been kept, as the interest in them experienced a check by the cheap and very common instruments from Germany, France, and other countries, which sadly interfered with the welfare of the English artizan, who could not compete in price, as this class of foreign goods could be purchased for a less sum than the materials cost for making them.

The foregoing facts have taken a long time to collect and arrange, and the details from their length may be deemed to require some apology. It was considered, however, that they might be useful to the rising generation, and to a future age. At the present time we should be much gratified to know how many instruments had been made by the Amati, the Stradiuarius, and the Guarnerius families, and especially by Joseph Guarnerius, as his instruments are in great request. Many boast of possessing one, yet when examined and compared how different the style of work, and quality of the varnish, so that even the tales told about the prison and the keeper's daughter scarcely justify the dissimilarity.

George Pearce was born in Wurminster, on the 16th November, 1820, and came to London with his parents in the fourth year of his age. He entered into the service of Simon Andrew Forster, as an errand boy, in July 1834, and soon evinced a mechanical talent, and showed expertness in the use of the tools; he was, therefore, instructed in the art of violin-making, and became a very neat and first-rate workman. As years advanced, however, he selected companions of vitiated minds and debased habits, and he was consequently discharged in July, 1844, for neglect of his duties. He ultimately gained employment as a fret-cutter at Messrs. Broad-

wood's pianoforte manufactory, where he continued until
the 3rd July, 1850, on which day he died through his
own act and deed by swallowing poison, and was buried
at the Victoria Cemetry, Bethnal Green, on the 9th of
the same month. It is not known whether any instruments were made by him on his own account, but he for-
warded many of those of his employer, and in one instance only did he make a first-class instrument all
through, which was a violin; but he was fully capable
to execute work of the highest finish. He was not
related to James and Thomas Pearce before noticed.

It will now be requisite to retrace a few years to give
the particulars of Samuel Gilkes, who was born in 1787,
at a village named Morton Pinkney, near to Blisworth,
Northamptonshire, and was sent to London to learn
fiddle-making of the elder Charles Harriss alluded to in
a former part of this work, and completed his term of
apprenticeship about 1809-10. In the course of the
latter year he became journeyman to William Forster
(3), and at length, being initiated into the style of
work of his employer, we find, by the remark B and G
in his list of instruments made, that Gilkes assisted in
making the violoncello No. 38, which appears to be the
first instrument he had joined with others in making, and
continued to do so during the whole of his engagement,
which lasted for nine or ten years, sometimes alone, at
others assisting, but always under the surveillance of his
superior, who minutely examined the gauging before the
instruments were put together. It will be well to take
special notice of the year 1810, for, after he had commenced business on his own behalf, at 34, James Street,
Buckingham Gate, Westminster, a report was freely
propagated by some one that Gilkes was the pupil of
Old Forster (2), and, strange to relate, it went so far as

to state that he had imparted to him, in preference to the family, the method of making the fine varnish. The date of 1810 is sufficient to falsify these statements, as William Forster (2) died in 1808, and it is most probable that Gilkes had never seen him. Samuel Gilkes became an excellent workman, and received much patronage during his own career, both as a maker and dealer, which, however, was of short duration, for he died in November 1827, at his residence, previously given, and was buried in his native village. He made instruments of three or four different classes, and supplied many to music sellers and dealers in the country; but we are unable to state the number or quality of those manufactured. The label used was as follows:—

"Gilkes
From Forster's
Violin, and Violoncello Maker
34 James Street, Buckingham Gate
Westminster."

His son, William Gilkes, who was born in Grey Coat Street, Tothill Fields, Westminster, about 1811, was taught violin-making by the father, and succeeded him at his residence, but subsequently was in Dartmouth Street; however, he did not long continue as a maker of musical instruments, giving a preference to per. forming on the violin in quadrille bands, and occasion. ally at theatres. At length the business was given up altogether, and he accepted some appointment on board one of the ships of the Peninsular and Oriental Steam Navigation Company. No instrument has been seen made by William Gilkes, therefore an opinion cannot be offered as to his capabilities of workmanship.

John Hart was born 17th December, 1805, in Westminster, near to the Green Coat School, and was apprenticed to Samuel Gilkes, in May 1820, and his term of servitude had not long expired when his master died. From that time he could not obtain much employment in the vocation he had learned, consequently he accepted an engagement at Lang's Shooting Gallery, next door to the Haymarket Theatre, and in time the house he now resides in was opened as a depôt for guns and pistols, with a few violins interspersed. At length the Joe Manton's, the Purday's, and the guns of other makers, had to give place to violins, violas, and violoncellos, with Italian names, he having become a dealer in them, and no person in a similar business—if report can be relied on—has had greater success in their journey through life. He has sons, but whether they have been taught to make violins is not known. Dealing in this class of property being far more remunerative than making it, we may infer the former claims the preference. The label used by him :—

" John Hart
Maker
14 Princess Street, Leicester Square
London. Anno 18— "

Before concluding with the Forster school it will be requisite to give one other name, although he was not a pupil, but at first only an amateur maker, and ultimately partly obtained a living by working at the business, and adopted the style of the Forster family, probably from the half-brother of William Forster (2) being his acquaintance. His name was Joseph Rook, late of Rickergate, Carlisle, who was born 7th June, 1777, at Calbeck, Cumberland. As a youth, he sorted copper ore, and in 1795 worked as a farm-servant to a Mr. Scott, of Haltcliff, near Hesket New Market, who was also an amateur fiddle-maker, and from whom some knowledge was gained. In 1800 he went to Carlisle to reside, and was engaged at the theatre to play the violin, and became acquainted with Joseph Forster in consequence of being made one of the musicians to the corporation; both also belonged to the band at the winter assemblies. In June 1807, Joseph Rook was appointed vicar-choral at the cathedral, and held that office until 25th December, 1840, when a retiring pension was given to him, which, in November 1850, he still enjoyed, and it is believed it was continued until his death, which took place in September 1852, and his body was interred at St. Mary's Church, Carlisle.

In a letter, dated 7th December, 1850, alluding to violins, he writes—"I never made many; I have made Twelve Tennors, and Five Violoncellos; no Double Basses. I marked my name with a small stamp,

"'J. Rook
Carlisle.'

I generally wrote my name in the inside of the Bellys with a black lead pencil."

He could not supply a label, having mislaid or lost them. Only violins of this maker have been seen, the work of which was very neat, and the tone pure, but weak; the varnish of a brownish yellow colour, and transparent.

CHAPTER XXIV.

NOTHER northern name now claims attention. Alexander Kennedy was born in Scotland, but neither the date nor the locality is precisely known. However, a surviving relative states that he died about 1785-6, and was considered to be ninety years of age. His work was very good, both inside and outside, and the purfling excellent. The Steiner model was followed minutely, and spirit varnish of a brownish yellow colour was used. He only made violins. The following was written inside a violin of this maker, but portions of it had been effaced by some repairs :—

<blockquote>
"Alexander Kennedy, Musical
In   made this Jan' 3rd. 1742/3
This Violin   A. Kennedy Living in Oxford
Market. 1742/3."
</blockquote>

And a written label was used in a violin of rather later date, thus :-

<blockquote>
"Alexander Kennedy, Musical Instrument
Maker, Living in Market Street in Oxford
Road, London. 1749."
</blockquote>

The foregoing maker instructed a nephew, John Kennedy, who, in the earlier part of his life, resided in Cooper's Gardens, near Shoreditch Church ; afterwards in Houghton Street and Clement's Lane, Clare Market ;

and lastly, in Long Alley, Sun Street, Moorfields, where he died in adverse circumstances about 1816, aged eighty-six years, and was buried at Shoreditch Church. The age is doubtful, as he was considered an older person by those who had been intimate with him. Violins and tenors were the only instruments he made, and all were of the high model or Steiner pattern.

At one period he was in full employ, having two or three assistants, and chiefly made instruments for the music publishers, and written labels were used. The present Thomas Kennedy (the son) states that no violoncellos were made by his father, and it is very doubtful if any were made by his workmen.

Thomas Kennedy was born in Houghton Street, Clare Market, on the 21st January, 1784, and was the eldest son of the previous John Kennedy by the third wife. He was apprenticed to Thomas Powell, the violin-maker, 17th June, 1795; but he is more indebted to his father for the knowledge of the business, and became a neat and good workman. In making the common class instruments he was exceedingly quick and rapid in every department. At the commencement of the present century he occasionally worked for William Forster (3), but soon entered business on his own account in Princes Street, Westminster, and at length located at 364, Oxford Street, at which place he lived for thirty-three years.

In June 1849 he was enabled to give up business, and retired to Cummin's Place, Pentonville, where his active mind and good health still enable him to reap amusement from his previous vocation. He was much employed by Messrs. Goulding, D'Almaine, and Co., and other music-houses. The exact number of instruments that were made by him is not known, but he says

A A

"he must have made at least 300 violoncellos, and the other instruments in proportion; perhaps not quite so many." Although he married very early, yet he has had no family; consequently he will be the last of this race as violin-makers.

Associated with the name of Kennedy, as fiddle-makers, are James Brown, the elder and younger, both of whom, in early life, were silk-weavers, particularly the father, and lived in the locality of Shoreditch. About 1804 an intimacy arose with the Kennedy family, whereby James Brown the elder acquired some knowledge of fiddle-making; and, being made more perfect in the use of the tools by Thomas Kennedy, he at length became a repairer and maker of instruments for future support. About 1830 he slipped down the stairs of his dwelling-house, in Wheeler Street, Spitalfields, and broke one of the ancles; the fracture being most severe, the relatives were advised to take him to the hospital. Within a week of the accident, mortification set in, and he died at the age of seventy-five years, in September 1830 or 1834; the son does not remember the date accurately, but he thinks the former year; and he says they (father and son) resided in Wheeler Street for forty-six years, but not always in the same house. James Brown, the younger, was born November 1786, and learned to make fiddles of his father; but, to assist in other branches of the trade, he was mostly employed in making the various bows for the instruments. Since the death of his father, the greater attention has been given to the manufacture of violins, violoncellos, and double basses. This person died in 1860 at his residence in White Lion Street, Norton Folgate, in his seventy-fourth year. The father and son were good average workmen, but no marked style of finish. A son of this last person learned to make instruments of his father; but, when about twenty years of age, he quitted the business to play the contra-basso at theatres; and it is believed he now has some professional engagement in Australia, as success did not attend his exertions at "the Diggins."

In the early part of the eighteenth century there were three persons of the following names: Edmund Airton, or Aireton, Henry Hill, and Joseph Hill, who became violin-makers, but it is not known for certainty which of them claims the seniority, nor can it be told who instructed them; but the style of work is remarkably similar, also the colour and quality of the varnish the same on most of the instruments which have been seen; therefore it is probable all three learned of the same master. From a circumstance which occurred in removing a label, dated 1735, out of a genuine violoncello made by Peter Wamsley, on the underneath side of which was written Edmund Airton, it is probable that the father of the first of the above three names was a workman in the employ of Wamsley, although nothing is known of him, who surreptitiously wrote his name on the master's label previous to attaching it to the violoncello. The date will not allow of its being the person first named, therefore it will be considered that Edmund Airoton claims the priority from family connections. Little is known of this maker, although he was an excellent workman, and produced instruments of a high order, both for tone and neat finishing. About 1805, he was residing in Hog Lane, now better known as Crown Street, Soho; and Thomas Kennedy says, " he was about eighty years of age, and that the shop had more the appearance of a general dealer than a maker of violins, tenors, and violoncellos; " also, he further positively stated the name was spelled " Aireton."

The few instruments which have been seen show that he made inferior as well as highly-finished ones; the violins and tenors were of the Stradiuarius pattern, and of the lower class work, with a glossy varnish, evidently alcoholic, made more ductile by admixture of a soft gum, or, what is more probable, with Venice turpentine. The most perfect specimen that we know of this maker is a violoncello, formerly the property of the late Robert Lindley, who sold it to George J. Farsydo, Esq., of Fylingdales, near Whitby, Yorkshire, in whose possession it still remains, and is fully appreciated. This instrument has an oil varnish of yellow colour, with a slight tinge of red, the pattern rather long, and the model high. The head has a peculiarity which deteriorates from its gracefulness by the volute or scroll having nearly a whole turn more than is usual; they are not, however, all made in that form. It would appear that he occasionally worked for the trade, as a violoncello of this maker has been seen stamped on the back, under the button, with letters exceedingly small, and one name above the other, thus :—

" Norris
and
Barnca."

Also, a spurious label of "Banks" was placed inside.

If conclusions may be drawn from the dates which are known, then William Hill will be the elder of two brothers who settled in London, and in the year 1741 was residing in Poland Street. Henry Hill, a relative, in his MSS., gives copies of two labels that were used, thus :—

" William Hill, Maker, in Poland Street,
near Broad Street.   1741."

And   " William Hill, Maker, in Poland Street,
         near Broad Street, Carnaby Market.   177—."

The work of this maker so much resembles that of
Edmund Aireton almost in every particular, except the
voluto of the head, that many persons would be deceived.
The varnish is a beautiful transparent yellow colour ; no
doubt of oil.   The tone is not rich in quality, although
good ; and if both vibrating-plates, particularly the
upper one, were thickened in the centre, advantageous
results would be obtained ; or, first, for external appliances, may be tried a Parisian bridge of the present form
of Aubert's make, which, there is little doubt, would
prove beneficial, and make the tone more rich in quality.   These suggestions may be applied to all the violoncellos of this family-name ; but an exception has to
be made with the present William E. Hill, whose work
is not sufficiently known to offer an opinion.   Joseph
Hill was brother to the former William Hill, and the
grandson, in his MSS., states that Joseph Hill lived in
Dover Street, Piccadilly, and afterwards in the Haymarket, which dwelling was destroyed by fire, with the
loss of all the stock in trade.   After that calamity,
he resided in the locality of Lock's Fields, Newington,
Surrey, about 1792-3, and his death is believed to be in
1794.   The printed label used was as follows :—

> " Joseph Hill, Maker,
> At the Harp and Flute,
> in the Hay Market,
> 17   London   69."

The last figure put in with a pen.   There are also copies
of written labels, at the same place, in 1772.   The grandson further states that this maker " enjoyed a high reputation in his day for his instruments, which have consi-

derable merit, tho' not of the highest order ; his violoncellos and contra-bassi are deservedly held in much
esteem.   There were many of the same family violin-
makers, but none who enjoyed (or) so highly reputed as
William and Joseph ; " both of whom, on the authority
of the present William Ebsworth Hill, came from
Bromsgrove, Worcestershire.   There were two sons of
the former Joseph Hill, named Joseph and Lockey
Hill, who perhaps should have been placed in the list
of fiddle-makers for the trade and music publishers, for
such were their general employments ; but, for reasons previously stated, it has been preferred to keep each
school separate.   Joseph Hill died about 1840, and
Lockey Hill about 1845.   Mr. Henry Hill, an excellent
performer on the viola, who, for several years previous
to his death, held the highest place in the profession,
was a son of the above Lockey Hill.   The present
William Ebsworth Hill is another son of Lockey Hill,
and may be considered to be self-taught in making
violins, although related to a maker, he having been too
young to have reaped any advantage from the knowledge
of his father.

CHAPTER XXV.

ENJAMIN BANKS was born in the early part and died in the latter part of the eighteenth century. His parents' names were George and Barbary; but there is no evidence to show that his father was a musical instrument maker. As a portion of the information obtained regarding this clever workman is from a grandson, Mr. B. T. Banks, we will quote his own letter:—

"June 23ᵈ, 1841. Though I have made many inquiries both before and since my return from London, I have not been able to gain any information respecting my late grandfather and uncle, until this week, or I should certainly have written to you sooner. The enclosed I have copied from a leaf which I suppose belonged to the old family Bible about a hundred years ago. You will perceive that the first is my grandfather and the other my uncle. Should I be able to learn the exact time when the latter died I will immediately let you know."

A copy of the paper enclosed in the above letter:

"Benjamin Banks, the son of George and Barbary Banks, born July 14th, 1727. Died Feb'. 18ᵗʰ, 1795."

"Benjamin Banks, one of the sons of the above Benj'. Banks. Born Sep'. 13ᵗʰ, 1754. Died about 1818."

It is generally believed that the first-named Benjamin Banks was born in Salisbury; that he resided in Catherine Street of that city is evident from the various labels

put into the instruments made by him. His burial-place
is supposed to be the parish church of Saint Thomas,
Sarum. Although no trace can be obtained from whom
he learned the trade, it may, as in many other instances
with violin makers, be an innate love of the art which
urged him onwards, so that he ultimately became one
of England's best manufacturers. Too much cannot be
said in praise of this justly celebrated maker of violins,
violas, and violoncellos. The work of all the better class
of instruments, both inside and out, is excellent; the
tone good of all, but that of the violoncellos in particular
is full, sonorous, and much esteemed by the professors.
He mostly worked from the pattern of the Amati, both
in model and outline; the style of finishing is very
marked and decided, so that persons at all conversant
with musical instruments of this class can easily tell the
maker. Much anxiety seemed to be shown that he, as
the maker, should be known; for many of his instruments have labels in various parts of them; also they
are stamped upon in several places either with the name,
or B. B., but no fixed plan of marking them seemed
adhered to. One label used was—

" Benjamin Banks,
Fecit,
Salisbury."

Other printed labels have been used at various dates
thus—

" Made by Benjᵃ. Banks,
Catherine Street, Salisbury, 1773."

Another—

" Benjamin Banks Musical Instrument
Maker. In Catherine Street, Salisbury, 1780."

And frequently they are stamped on the back or lower

vibrating plate, under the button, " B. Banks, Sarum."
This maker was not successful with the varnish put on
the various instruments; there is a want of brilliancy in
the colouring, and a sad defect in the method of application, which destroyed the grain of the upper vibrating
plate and gave it a white appearance, or, as the trade
would pronounce, " the grain was killed." The colours
of his varnish were a deep red with a blackish tinge,
and a yellow brownish red; the latter seemed preferred
for those instruments of special make or order. One of
the writers of this book has a violoncello of this maker,
having the latter coloured varnish, and the quality of
tone is very fine : it is of the Steiner model, but rather
long, and the Steiner sound hole is used. It was a
present to him from his valued friend, that eminent performer, the late Robert Lindley. A violin by the same
maker is in possession of Mr. Charles Lucas, the varnish
on which has rather more red in it. No contra-basso
or double-bass has been seen of this maker, and it is
doubtful if he or any of the family ever made one.

There is a class of instruments, more particularly violoncellos, which were made for Longman and Broderip,
the music publishers, by this Benjamin Banks, and probably assisted by his sons or other workmen; the pattern
of which is long and more of the Steiner model; the
work much inferior, and a red varnish used having all
the appearance of the tint being produced by an aqueous
extract. The names of Longman and Broderip are
stamped on the back, under the button, but no writing
or label to indicate by whom the instruments were made;
the style, however, even in these instruments is easily
recognized. The average price of this maker's best violoncellos, between 1790 and 1794, was from ten to twelve
guineas; and in the first half of the present century some

of them have realized as much as fifty pounds. Fashion, however, has now declared against these excellent instruments of the Banks family, and all English manufacture must give place to those with foreign names.

About the year 1826 a violoncello of this maker was in possession of the Pembroke family, which was made entirely from the wood of a cedar of Lebanon which formerly grew in Wilton Park, but had been blown down, and a portion of it was used for the purpose above stated. The tone was not good, from the wood being too dense for the upper vibrating plate; but it may be considered a curiosity, and as such no doubt the earl who ordered it to be made considered it. His lordship having had a silver plate let into the under vibrating plate, or back, on which was engraved the particulars regarding the tree, also the name of the instrument maker. Although this violoncello was seen at the town residence of the Dowager Countess of Pembroke in Privy Gardens, Whitehall, there is every probability that it may be now at Wilton House, near Salisbury; and if it could not be seen with facility at the family mansion, there is much to admire and elevate the mind by viewing the fine collection of choice paintings of the old masters, and a quadrangle containing sculpture of a high order.

Benjamin Banks, the younger. There was some doubt, at one time, whether or no this Benjamin Banks, the second son of the former of that name, was a maker of musical instruments; for we learn that about the latter part of the last century he was connected with a person named Cahusac, in a boot and shoe shop, on Fish Street Hill. There appear to have been intermarriages between the families of Banks and Cahusac, and Cahusac and Banks. Ultimately he became associated either with his father-in-law, or a son of the same, in the musical establishment of Astor, in Cornhill, and one of the Cahusacs succeeded to that business. From the circumstance of his being connected with a musical business, and the violin makers generally considering there was an old and young Benjamin Banks who were manufacturers, it was inferred that he could work at the business, and these suppositions have proved correct. In September, 1857, a violoncello was seen, the property of Mr. John Harding, surveyor, living in Salisbury, which had written on the inside of the upper vibrating plate at the hind bout of the first string side, the following—

"Made by Benj". Banks,
No. 30, Sherrard Street,
Golden Square.   London.
From Salisbury."

A written label also was inside the instrument, the same as the above, but omitting "From Salisbury." It can be asserted, almost with certainty, that the elder Benjamin Banks never resided in London; therefore we conclude the above label alludes to the younger of that name, who having tried musical instrument-making in London, and not succeeding, became connected with the shoe shop. He was born on the 13th September, 1754, as previously stated. After his residence in Salisbury and London, he retired to Liverpool, where his two brothers, James and Henry, were living, probably about 1814, for in the month of March in that year he bought a grave at Saint Mary's Church, Edge Hill. He died on the 22nd January, 1820, and at the time of his death was residing in Hawk Street, Liverpool. Upon the grave-stone it is engraved that his age was sixty-eight years; in the Book of Burials it is stated as sixty-five; the latter corresponds with the time of his birth given by the nephew.

As the two brothers, James and Henry Banks, appear to have been associated together, or partners in the musical business soon, if not immediately, after the death of the father, they will not be separated in this account. James Banks was the fourth son, and Henry Banks the sixth son of the first-named Benjamin Banks, both of whom were born in Salisbury. James seemed to inherit, as an artisan, all the excellencies of his parent. He worked from the same patterns, the style of finishing being similar and the tint of varnish the same; but occasionally the red-coloured varnish had more black in it than was used by the father. Henry Banks did not work at the violin trade, but was a pianoforte tuner and repairer. There are numerous labels in instruments showing they were in trade together; and in 1802 they had also become music-sellers. The following is a copy of a label at that period :—

> " James and Henry Banks,
> Musical Instrument Makers,
> and Music Sellers,
> 18   Salisbury,   02."

The caprice of the parent, regarding the marking of instruments, descended to the sons, as we find a different label used two years afterwards :—

> " James and Henry Banks,
> Salisbury.   1804."

And, " J. & H. Banks " stamped on the blocks and other parts of the various instruments. They carried on their various departments of business in Catherine Street, Salisbury, until 1811, when they sold the same to Mr. Alexander Lucas, the father of the present Mr. Charles Lucas, the Principal of the Royal Academy of Music, and went to reside in Liverpool. They first located in

Church Street, opposite Saint Peter's Church; the site, or rather a portion of that on which Compton House now stands; afterwards they moved to Bold Street in the same town. A Welshman named William Davis, or Davies, who was living in Liverpool in the year 1849, had been in the employ of these two brothers as a porter in or about 1818, and he spoke in high commendation of their kindness, and stated, "they had a good business, were the best masters he ever had either before or since. Henry was a capital tuner of pianos, and was frequently from home for a fortnight travelling about the country, and went as far as Wales to tune instruments. He did not work at the violin making, but was connected with the pianoforte department. The hands of James, when he knew him, were much contracted, yet he was an excellent repairer of violins, &c. *O it was beautiful to see how he repaired them.* All three are buried at Saint Mary's Church, Edge Hill, and I helped to put them into the grave." A son of the above Henry Banks, whose name is also Henry, and had an office at No. 2, Mersey Chambers, Liverpool, about 1849-50, corroborates much of that asserted by Davis, and also said, "his father did not work at the violin trade, and that his uncle was the maker of violins, tenors, and violoncellos; that the contraction in the hands was caused by gout, and that his uncle was never married." He also said that " very few, if any instruments were made at Liverpool; but some may have been finished there that were previously begun." James and Henry Banks sold the goodwill of their business to two brothers named Palmer, who found in a cellar a number of unfinished instruments of the violin class, which were sold by them in that state; but it was not known to whom they were disposed. On the tombstone at the church before-named it is engraved that James Banks died 15th June, 1831, aged seventy-five years. Some error exists here, unless a period of nearly three years occurred between his birth and christening, as that ceremony took place on the 7th Sept. 1758, at St. Thomas' Church, Sarum. Henry Banks died on the 16th Oct. 1830, aged sixty years. The church Book of Burials of the date 23 Oct. 1830, states the age to be fifty-six, but the former age is nearer correctness, he being christened 2nd Jan. 1771. At the time of his decease he was residing in George Street. He was found drowned in the Princes Dock, and it is said he could not have been very long in the water, as his watch was still in action when the body was discovered. The various extracts from the books of St. Thomas' Church, Salisbury, were kindly made by the late Mr. J. T. Biddlecombe, the clerk to the church, who further stated there were no memoranda or notices taken at what period the birth of either James or Henry Banks took place. He was an intimate acquaintance of the Banks family when they lived in Salisbury.

It has been said by an elderly gentleman, now deceased, who well knew the Banks family before they went to reside at Liverpool, that the elder Benjamin Banks (the father) had an apprentice named Wheeler, who he believed came to London to obtain employment or commence business himself as a maker of violins, &c. Nothing whatever is known of him, nor has any instrument been seen to establish a name worthy of his instructor. There are many violoncellos with the label of James and Henry Banks which may be considered generally very good; and two in particular are in the possession of Mr. Charles Lucas, which have a full and powerful tone, of excellent quality, and were used by him when principal violoncellist at the Royal Italian Opera, Covent Garden.

CHAPTER XXVI.

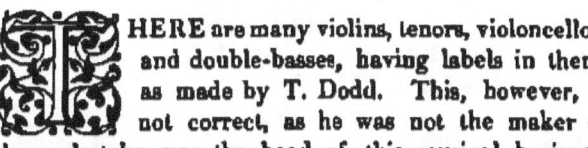 HERE are many violins, tenors, violoncellos, and double-basses, having labels in them, as made by T. Dodd. This, however, is not correct, as he was not the maker of them ; but he was the head of this musical business, therefore all the instruments had his name attached. Several of this family have been associated with violin-bow-making and covering of musical strings. The father of the above Thomas Dodd, named Edward, was born at Sheffield, but his occupation is not known. He died in 1810, at a house in Salisbury Court, Fleet Street, and was buried at St. Bride's Church, in that locality, being of the great age of 105 years. Thomas Dodd was the third son of this Edward, and appears to have been either unsettled or unsuccessful in the various businesses he adopted for support. At first he was a brewer, and from 1786 to 1789 there is evidence he was a violin bow-maker, residing in Blue Bell Alley, Mint Street, Southwark. In or about 1798, he commenced as a dealer in and maker of violins in New Street, Covent Garden, the corner of Bedford Bury, and then employed a young man named Bernhard Fendt to make the various instruments ; and in March of the same year John Frederick Lott was engaged to assist, although not educated in the art of making violins. More will be stated of these two persons presently. In 1809, T. Dodd left this abode and moved to 92, St. Martin's Lane, Charing Cross, the corner of Cecil Court ; and about

1823-4 he left this house and went to No. 3, Berner's
Street, Oxford Street, where he ventured on making
harps, which had a mechanical improvement of an index
in the metal-plate, at the head of the instrument, showing
what pedals were down. These harps were patronized
and used by Dizi, the celebrated performer of that day.
After this, pianoforte-making engaged his attention; but
it is said, with all these numerous adventures, success did
not attend his efforts. The time of his death is not accurately known. A nephew states he was buried at St.
Giles's-in-the-Fields. An oval label was used at first,
as follows :—

" T. Dodd,
Violin, Violoncello,
& Bow Maker,
New Street,
Covent Garden."

And when residing in St. Martin's Lane the label had
the representation of a violin or violoncello, with the
bow placed obliquely under two of the strings, occupying the centre, and the other particulars engraved
parallel with the instrument :—

" Dodd   Maker
92 Saint Martin's   Lane.

Note.—The only Possessor
of the Recipe for prepar-
ing the Original Cre-
mona Oil Varnish. In-
struments Imported &
Repaired."

Perfect copies of Stradiva-
rius, Amati, Stainer, &c.
&c.

From this establishment emanated numerous imitations, both of English and foreign violin-makers, as well as those with his own name.

Two sons of Thomas Dodd, named Thomas and Edward, were instructed in violin-making by Bernhard Fendt. Thomas had ability as a workman, and died in the early part of this century, whilst his father was residing in St. Martin's Lane. Edward appears to have given more attention to the manufacture of the harp and pianoforte, and was accidentally drowned on the 29th of April, 1843, in presence of one of his sons, "a youth whom he had just apprenticed to the sea, and who was going away that evening."

Perhaps, before quitting this family-name, some notice is due, and should be taken, of John Dodd, the celebrated violin-bow-maker, *the Tourte of England*. He was the eldest-son of the first-named Edward, and in early years was a gun-lock fitter, afterwards a money-scale maker, but ended in being England's best bow-maker. It is considered that at one period, 1786-9, he lived in Southwark; afterwards he went to Kew, in Surrey, and resided there several years; at length he moved to Richmond, in the same county, where he died, and was buried at the Old Church of that place.

Bernhard Fendt was born at Inspruck, in the Tyrol, about 1775-6, which place he left at the age of seven years, and went to reside in Paris with his uncle Fendt, or Fent, as the name is spelled in France, of whom he learned to make violins and violoncellos, &c. Very few facts of his early years are known by the surviving relatives, nor can they state when he first came to England; we, however, learn from other sources that he was engaged by Thomas Dodd, and entered into his employ in January 1798, and remained there for eleven years;

after that period he went to old John Betts, and continued there until the death of his master, in 1823. He then became the workman to the nephew, John Vernon, with whom he stayed until this person's decease. Bernhard Fendt was a workman of high merit, and at the commencement of his career in England the style of work was that known as of Tyrol. A quartett of instruments of this maker was purchased by Mr. Henry N. Turner, of Upper Belgrave Place, Pimlico, at Dodd's house, about 1800-1, which shows the character of the work in a decided manner. However, of late years, his great excellence consisted in the fine imitations of the Italian and other violin-makers. He may be considered to have formed a school, as there were four sons and one grandson instructed in the art, as well as the elder Lott and two of his sons; also John N. Lentz. All these persons may be considered as indebted to him, as the first cause, for their knowledge of violin-making, and, with the exception of the latter person, they were all excellent workmen. A daughter of Bernhard Fendt states that her father died in Aylesbury Street, Clerkenwell, about 1832-3, and was buried in Clerkenwell Church-yard; also that his age was considered to be fifty-seven years.

Bernhard Simon, or Simmon Fendt, was the eldest son of the foregoing Bernhard Fendt, and was born in 1800. He was taught violin-making by his father, probably in the workshop of Old John Betts, with whom he remained until the death of the latter in 1823. Soon after this he was either engaged as workman, or became a partner with —— Farn, who commenced as a dealer in violins in Lombard Street, City; but, this person dying a few years afterwards, he then joined with George Purdy, a professor of dancing and fencing, and commenced business in Finch Lane, City, in September

1832, the firm being known as Purdy and Fendt. In June 1843 they also opened a house of business in Oxendon Street, Haymarket; and about 1850 both these places were closed, and the business concentrated in 74, Dean Street, Soho. Bernhard Simmon Fendt died 6th March, 1852, at 7, Smith Street, Brompton, and it is said he was interred in the burial-ground of Pentonville Chapel on the 12th of the same month, aged fifty-two years. A doubt arises if the burial-place bo correct, although stated by a relative, as the son, who died in the same year as the parent, was buried at the Brompton Cemetry.

Martin Fendt was the second son of the elder Bernhard Fendt, and was born in July 1812. He learned to make violins under the guidance of his father, and during the whole of his short life was employed by Arthur Betts, the brother of Old John Betts. Martin Fendt died in Bell Alley, Coleman Street, City, in July 1845, aged thirty-three, and is buried in a churchyard near to that locality, the name of which is not known. Jacob Fendt was the third son of the former Bernhard Fendt, and was born about 1815. He was instructed in violinmaking by his eldest brother, and occasionally worked for W. Davis, of Coventry Street, having succeeded G. F. Lott at that establishment. He was also employed, at some other period, by Turner, the dealer in violins, whilst residing in the Poultry. Jacob Fendt died about October 1849, in Blue Anchor Court, Whitecross Street, Finsbury, and his age considered to be thirty-four or thirty-five years.

The fourth son, Francis Fendt, was also instructed in violin-making by his eldest brother, and for some time continued to work for the firm (Purdy and Fendt). In 1850, he was residing in Liverpool, obtaining a very precarious subsistence. Whether he be alive now is not known, neither can the time of his birth be ascertained.

William Fendt was the second son of Bernhard Simmon Fendt, and was born in 1833, in Finch Lane, City. He learned violin-making of his father, and became an export workman. He died in his twentieth year, at 7, Smith Street, Brompton, in 1852, and was buried in the Brompton Cemetry.

As the youngest son of John Frederick Lott states that his father died on the 13th April, 1853, aged seventy-eight, he would have been born in 1775. Previous to entering the employ of Thomas Dodd, in March, 1798, he had been a chair maker, therefore his knowledge of violin-making was acquired of Bernhard Fendt. For several years previous to his death, he carried on the musical business in King Street, Seven Dials, at which place he died, and was buried in the church-yard of Saint Giles-in-the-Fields. He was celebrated for making double-basses.

There are two sons of this person, the oldest named George Frederick Lott, born about 1800-1, and the younger of the same name as the father. Both of them, at different periods, were in the employ of W. Davis of Coventry Street; and much of the adventurous life of the younger, in after years may be read in the novel, "Cream," and "Jack of all Trades," by Charles Reade. The two sons are still living.

Johann Nicolaus Lentz was a German, from the Tyrol, and in the latter part of the last century had been servant to a gentleman in Duke Street, St. James's. Being an acquaintance of Bernhard Fendt, he had picked up some knowledge of violin and violoncello-making, and in consequence he began as a maker in the early part of this century. The varnish used by him was similar to that upon the instruments known as Dodd's and the elder Lott. The printed label, which has been seen, was as follows, the date being put in with a pen :—

"Johann Nicolaus Lentz, Fecit
near the Church, Chelsea. 1803."

The names of the two violin makers which follow, Matthew Hardio and his son Thomas Hardie, perhaps, in a strict sense, should not be placed in this section; they were, however, clever workmen, especially the older, and endeavoured by attention to the gauging to accomplish great power of tone in the violins, tenors, and violoncellos which they made. Although the work was not at all times as neat as could be desired to rank them as first-rate workmen, yet they frequently gained the object they tried for, and could execute first-class work if the mind was not under the baneful influence of whiskey. Matthew Hardie was held in much esteem as a violin maker in his locality, and was living in "The Calton," Edinburgh, in the latter half of the last and the beginning of the present century, about the point where the Waterloo Bridge now crosses that street. He died in the workhouse of St. Cuthberd's, or West Church parish, about 1825-6, and it is believed that he was interred in the burial ground of the Grey Friars Church of Edinburgh.

Thomas Hardie, the son of the former Matthew, was born in 1804, and it is believed learned violin-making of his father ; he was a clever workman, but his dissolute and intemperate habits lost him the employ he could have commanded, and of late years the utmost penury was the penalty. He died on the 19th January, 1856, aged fifty-two, and his death was caused by falling "down a stair in the lawn market;" and through the kind exer-

tions of a person who knew him, a small subscription
was raised, and he was buried in the ground of the Grey
Friars Church of Edinburgh, where the father is supposed to be interred.

The place at which the fatal accident occurred was
such " that the most sober person might have fallen
there, the door of the house from which he emerged
opening at once upon a stair without any landing-place."
Charles Reade appears to have drawn the picture of this
person in his novel of " Christie Johnstone," at p. 122,
under the name of Thomas Harvey, but too much intel-
lect has been assigned to him.

There was a violin maker connected with Matthew
Hardie, named John Blair, but nothing is known of his
ability as a workman.

Whether or no the chamber double-bass can be called
an invention, or an enlarged violoncello strung differently,
or whichever way it may be considered, the merit of the
adaptation is due to an amateur on the violoncello, named
Barraud, who held an appointment in the Treasury, and
the instrument is generally known as the Barraud bass.
These instruments were first made about 1820, and
became rather popular, but soon lost their favouritism,
partly arising from the excessive pressure required on
the strings, to produce anything like a musical sound.
It was tuned an octave below the violoncello, therefore
the strings were necessarily large and heavy. When
first introduced to the public only three covered strings
were applied, but latterly all four were covered with
wire, the fourth being double covered. These instruments were first made for the inventor by John Morrison,
then by Thomas Kennedy, and lastly by Samuel Gilkes,
who increased the dimensions of them.

A further modification of this instrument was intro-

duced in November, 1844, by Mr. Thomas William
Hancock, one of the violoncello performers at the Royal
Italian Opera, under the name of the "basso di camera,"
at a special meeting convened for that and other purposes, of the Queen Square Select Society, in the presence
of many amateurs and professors of music, who gave a
unanimous vote of approval. These instruments were
made at W. Davis's, in Coventry Street, Haymarket.

It was tuned two octaves below the violin, which
method gave the G one note lower than the present
mode of tuning the double-basses of three strings; but
this also had its difficulties to the amateur by causing
transposition, and still requiring additional physical
energies, although not so great as the one first invented.

Mr. Hancock has recently adopted another mode of
stringing which renders the instrument less difficult to
the amateur, the description of which he has kindly
supplied for our guidance :—

"The mode of tuning was originally two octaves below
the violin, and the same number of strings were used, the
two lowest, however, being covered ones ; but Mr. Hancock, finding the highest string gave a compass unnecessary for the performance of music written for the contra
basso (for which the basso di camera was introduced as a
substitute for chamber music), has reduced the number of
strings to three, consequently the higher string is now A,
the second D, and the third G, one note lower than the
double-bass ; this alteration leaves a compass sufficiently
extensive, as the octave to the first string is reached with
the same facility as on the violoncello, and with the same
smoothness. By the removal also of the first string E,
amateurs on the violoncello are at once enabled to apply
their knowledge of that instrument to the basso di camera,
which was not quite so easy in the arrangement first adopted.

Size and character of the strings now used.

First. A very large violoncello, second or small double-bass first.

Second. The usual violoncello fourth covered with wire of the smaller size.

Third. A violoncello second, or double-bass first, covered with wire of the largest size used for violoncello fourths, and the string altogether to be about ¼ of an inch thick.

Dimensions of the basso di camera.

	Inches.
Length of the body	36
Breadth of do. fore end	16½
Do. hind end	21
Do. across the sound holes . . .	11
Depth of the sides	7
Length of the neck	12¼
Length of the string from the nut to the bridge	31

Machine pegs are desirable for instruments of this class."

CHAPTER XXVII.

NAMES of violin and fiddle makers, also dealers of the nineteenth century, not previously noticed. The style or character of the work of the greater number of them is not known :—

ABSAM, THOMAS, originally a joiner by trade, then made cases for violins, and at length made fiddles for Pickard, of Leeds, 1810-1849. Label used :—

> " Made by
> Thomas Absam,
> Wakefield, Feb'. 14,
> 1833."

ASKEY, SAMUEL, of London, at first was a tinman, and John Morrison taught him to make fiddles; about 1825, he worked for George Corsby; died in or near 1840 by falling down a cellar.

BALLANTINE, of Edinburgh; but, in 1856, he was living in Glasgow.

BOOTH, WILLIAM, Sen., born 1779, and at first was a hairdresser. In 1809, he commenced as a maker and repairer of fiddles, and then lived in Leeds. It is believed he died in 1857 or 1858 :—

> " W⁰. Booth maker
> Leeds. 1828."

BOOTH, WILLIAM, Jun., son of the former, born at

Leeds in 1816. After being engaged by Henri Gugel
from 1834 to 1838, he returned to Leeds, and commenced business as an instrument maker in the latter
year. He was a clever workman, but greatly afflicted
in health. Died 1st June, 1856, aged thirty-nine years,
and buried at the Burmantofts Cemetry.

BROWN, ANTHONY, it is said, learned violin-making of
Joseph Panornio, others state of John Morrison, and became celebrated for his guitars. In 1855, he was living
in Rosomond Street, Clerkenwell; but since that period
he has been to "the diggings," and has returned with a
little of the mineral riches of that land. He is not related to the other family of similar name.

COLE, JAMES, of Manchester, learned a portion of the
business with — Tarr, afterwards with George Crask, all
of the same locality. A label was used until the year
1858, but now discontinued; and at this period the
various instruments are stamped inside " J. Cole."

CORSBY, —, of Northampton, may be living, but very
doubtful.

CORSBY, GEORGE, of Princes Street, Soho, London.
It is believed he is a brother of the first named, and both
were instructed in the musical business by the father.
Nothing is known of the parent.

CRASK, GEORGE, of Salford, Manchester.

DAVIS, RICHARD. This person has been alluded to
under the name of the firm, Norris and Barnes. He
entered their employ in a humble capacity, the latter
part of the eighteenth century, and was shopman when
Norris died, in 1818, he then succeeded to the business
more as a dealer than a manufacturer, having little
knowledge of the use of the tools. He retired from
business in favour of his cousin William Davis, and went
to Bussage, near Stroud, Gloucestershire, his native place,

and died there in April, 1836, and was interred at the parish church of Bisley.

The cousin continued the business until December, 1846, more as a dealer and repairer of violins, for he cannot be considered a maker, and brought Charles Maucotel from France to this country to work for him. At the above period he sold the business to Edward Withers, and retired to Bussage, where he still resides.

DEARLOVE, MARK, of Leeds, from 1812 to 1820, or perhaps longer; however, he was not originally taught the business. There is a son of this person named Mark William Dearlove that may still be living, who occasionally employed T. Abson, John Gough, and Charles Fryer—the latter became a partner with him, and died about 1840. Copy of label:—

" Dearlove and Fryer,
Musical Instrument
Manufacturers,
Boar Lane, Leeds,
1828."

DELANY, JOHN, of Dublin, used two kinds of labels, one of them very small, thus:—

" Made by John Delany,
No. 17, Britain Street,
Dublin. 1808."

In the other, which is much larger, he is overflowing with good-will to the human family and self-love to his own abilities, which were most doubtful if realized:—

" Made by John Delany
In order to perpetuate his memory
in future ages.   Dublin,
1808.

Liberty to all the world,
black and white."

DENNIS, JESSE, was apprenticed to John Crowther about 1805, and afterwards turned over to Matthew Furber to complete his instruction. He was living in Ewcherst Street, Walworth Common, in Feb. 1855, and was then sixty years of age.

DORANT, WILLIAM, of 63, Winfield Street, Brick Lane, Spitalfields, in the year 1814.

EGLINGTON. The copy of a label that has been seen in a fiddle of inferior workmanship, and had chequered purfle. The tone was very good :—

> " Eglington. Fecit,
> Drury Lane,
> London. 1802."

FARN, was merely the dealer, and is mentioned under the name of Bernhard Simmon Fendt.

FERGUSON AND SON, living in Edinburgh at the beginning of this century.

FIRTH, G., of Leeds, pupil of Wm. Booth, Sen. Copy of the label used :—

> " G. Firth,
> No. 110, Briggate,
> Leeds. 1836."

GIBBS, JAMES, was a maker employed by J. Morrison, G. Corsby, and S. Gilkes. Died about 1845, at No. 2, New Street, New Cut, Lambeth, and buried in the Churchyard in Waterloo Bridge Road, Lambeth.

GOUGH, WALTER, brother to — Gough, the leader of some of the minor theatres. Died about 1830.

HIGGINS, P. H., of Montreal, was an exhibitor in the Great Exhibition of 1851.

J'ANSON, EDWARD POPPLEWELL, of Manchester, pupil of William Booth, Jun.

MACGEORGE, of Edinburgh, about the period of Matthew Hardie.

MACINTOSH, of Dublin. See Perry and Wilkinson.

PERRY, THOMAS, and WILKINSON, WILLIAM, of Dublin. The violins bearing the name of this firm are very neat and well made; but it is not known if they were workmen themselves. The elder Tobin, who was an excellent workman, is said to be a pupil of the first name, and did much work for Old John Betts. Latterly he kept a shop in West Street, Soho. He died in great poverty in the poor-house of Shoreditch.

There was another pupil named Macintosh, and said to be the successor of Perry, who died between 1830 and 1840. Copy of label, the date of which is doubtful, either 1817 or 1827, used by the firm, in which the long bow appears drawn to the fullest extent, as regards the number of instruments manufactured :—

<blockquote>
" Made by
Tho'. Perry and.W^m. Wilkinson,
Musical Instrument Makers,
No. 4, Anglesea Street,
No. 4361.   Dublin. 1817 or 1827."
</blockquote>

And in a label dated 1821 the number is put in as reaching 4534.

STIRBAT, D., of Edinburgh, considered by some persons to be a good workman. Copy of label :—

<blockquote>
" D. Stirbat. Fecit,
Edinburgh. 181 .."
</blockquote>

Space left to put in the last figure of the year.

STURGE, H., has resided in several places. In 1811 he lived in Stephen Avenue, Clare Street, Bristol; and in 1853 his labels show he was living in Huddersfield, stating on one of them he was from London, and on the other from Bristol. He is considered to be only a repairer of instruments.

TARR, —, of Manchester, was formerly a cabinet maker, then a fiddle maker; and in 1855 took to photography. It is said he excelled with his double-basses.

TOBIN, RICHARD. See Perry and Wilkinson.

TURNER, JOHN ALVEY, of 19, Poultry, City, and latterly of Cornhill. He was only a dealer, and died in February, 1862.

WITHERS, EDWARD, can only be considered as the dealer, and purchased the business of William Davis in December, 1846, first employing Charles Maucotel as a workman, then Boullangier, both of whom have left him and commenced on their own account. The business is still carried on by Edward Withers, in Coventry Street, Haymarket, where in 1851-2 was introduced an American alteration in the mode of making violins, violoncellos, &c., known as Wm. B. Tilton's Patent, which consisted of bevelling the blocks at each end of the instrument that both vibrating plates should be more free, and the required support was given by letting in a bar of wood into the blocks the whole length of the instrument. Although in some few instances an improvement was perceptible, yet it may be considered a failure, and is now laid aside.

WILKINSON, WILLIAM. See Perry and Wilkinson.

NAMES OF FOREIGNERS THAT HAVE LOCATED IN ENGLAND AS VIOLIN MAKERS.

PANORMO, VINCENT, who is generally alluded to as Old Panormo, was born on the 30th November, 1734, in a village named Monreale, a few miles from Palermo, in Sicily. He was endowed with much mechanical ability, and, unassisted, from sixteen years of age took delight in making various descriptions of musical instruments. The eldest son of the above-named, Francis Panormo, who attained his seventy-fourth year in 1842, has stated that his father made many descriptions of instruments; but most excelled in violins, violoncellos, double-basses, and hautboys. Vincent Panormo became a resident in several parts of Italy, France, England, and Ireland. The first time he came to England was in 1772, the second in 1789, being driven from France by the Revolution, where it is said " he was doing well." The violins, violoncellos, and double-basses of this maker are deservedly much esteemed, and valued for their pure and Italian quality of tone and appreciated by the professors on these instruments. He died in London about 1813.

In the MSS. of Hill is given the copy of the following labels :—

" Vincenzo Panormo me fece Marsiglia, 1760, Sicily ;" and " Vincenzo Panormo, Londra. 1791."

There was another son of the above Vincent, named JOSEPH PANORMO, who was a good workman and thoroughly knew the theory of violin-making. At one period he resided in New Compton Street, afterwards in King Street, Soho. He died about twenty-five years since in the greatest destitution.

PANORMO, GEORGE LEWIS, was another son of the former Vincent, and became celebrated for his guitars, and was in the highest esteem as a bow maker ; he was then living in Oxford Street, and latterly in High Street, Saint Giles-in-the-Fields. The time of his death cannot be stated with accuracy, probably ten or twelve years since.

Some persons assert there was another son of Vincent, named Edward Panormo, who, at times, resided in Ire-

land and London. We do not know him, and it may
probably allude to a grandson of Vincent, who of late
years has been living in the latter city; the precise
locality, however, is not known, as he has changed his
abode many times within the last few years.

MAUCOTEL, CHARLES, was born at Mirecourt, 1st Nov.
1807, and learned violin-making of a relative, by marriage, of his mother, whose name was Bloise Mast. In
1834 he located in Paris, and was employed by Gand;
ultimately he was engaged by W. Davis, of 34, Coventry
Street, and came to London in Dec. 1844, and worked
at that house for two years. On the disposal of the
business to Edward Withers he remained in the employ
about eighteen months, and then left and commenced on
his own account at No. 8, Rupert Street, Haymarket.
He retired from business about August, 1860, partly
through impaired health; but it is generally believed the
real cause was that a relative had left him property.
He was a good workman, and knew well the vocation he
followed.

Copy of the label used, with space left to add the last
figure of the year :—

       " Carolus Maucotelus
       fecit Londini, 185 C†M."

CHARLES, THERESS, came from Mirecourt, and on his
card is printed " from Maucotel;" for several years past
he has been established on his own behalf as a violin
maker, and now resides in King Street, Soho.

CHANOT, whose business is now in Wardour Street,
Soho, was engaged as workman to Maucotel, and on the
latter retiring he commenced on his own account.

BOULLANGIER, at one time was in the employ of Edward Withers, but now has an establishment of his own
in Dean Street, Soho.

INDEX.

THE END.

CHISWICK PRESS:—PRINTED BY WHITTINGHAM AND WILKINS,
TOOKS COURT, CHANCERY LANE.

Library of Old Authors.

ELEGANTLY PRINTED IN FCAP. 8VO.

*The following Works are already published, each Author
sold separately.*

 HE DRAMATIC AND POETICAL WORKS OF JOHN
MARSTON. Now first collected, and edited by J. O.
HALLIWELL. 3 vols. 16s.

THE VISION AND CREED OF PIERS PLOUGHMAN. Edited
by THOMAS WRIGHT; a new edition, revised, with additions to the
Notes and Glossary. 2 vols. 10s.

INCREASE MATHER'S REMARKABLE PROVIDENCES OF
THE EARLIER DAYS OF AMERICAN COLONIZATION.
With introductory Preface by GEORGE OFFOR. Portrait. 5s.

JOHN SELDEN'S TABLE TALK. A new and improved Edition,
by S. W. SINGER. Portrait. 5s.

THE POETICAL WORKS OF WILLIAM DRUMMOND OF
HAWTHORNDEN. Edited by W. B. TURNBULL. Portrait. 5s.

FRANCIS QUARLES' ENCHIRIDION. Containing Institutions—
Divine, Contemplative, Practical, Moral, Ethical, Œconomical, and
Political. Portrait. 3s.

THE MISCELLANEOUS WORKS IN PROSE AND VERSE OF
SIR THOMAS OVERBURY. Now first collected. Edited, with
Life and Notes, by E. F. RIMBAULT. Portrait after Pass. 5s.

GEORGE WITHER'S HYMNS AND SONGS OF THE CHURCH.
Edited, with Introduction, by EDWARD FARR. Also the Musical Notes,
composed by ORLANDO GIBBONS. With Portrait after Hole. 5s.

GEORGE WITHER'S HALLELUJAH; OR, BRITAIN'S SECOND
REMEMBRANCER, in Praiseful and Penitential Hymns, Spiritual Songs,
and Moral Odes, with Introduction by EDWARD FARR. Portrait. 6s.

THE POETICAL WORKS OF THE REV. ROBERT SOUTH-
WELL. Now first completely edited by W. B. TURNBULL. 4s.

THE MISCELLANIES OF JOHN AUBREY, F.R.S. (on Omens,
Dreams, Day Fatality, Apparitions, Portents, Knockings, &c. &c.)
The fourth Edition, with some Additions, and an Index, Portrait, and
Cuts. 4s.

A CATALOGUE OF BOOKS

ON

HISTORY, BIOGRAPHY, TOPOGRAPHY, HERALDRY AND
FAMILY HISTORY, OLD POETRY, AND THE DRAMA,
PHILOLOGY, BIBLIOGRAPHY, FINE ARTS,
DIVINITY, &c., &c.,

PUBLISHED OR SOLD BY

JOHN RUSSELL SMITH,

36, SOHO SQUARE, LONDON. (W.)

THE Conquest of Britain by the Saxons. A Harmony of the History of the Britons, the Works of Gildas, the "Brut," and the Saxon Chronicle, with Reference to the Events of the Fifth and Sixth Centuries. By DANIEL HENRY HAIGH, D.D. Thick 8vo. *plates of Runic inscriptions,* *cloth,* 15s. 1861

The Anglo-Saxon Sagas. An Examination of their Value as Aids to History, serving as a Sequel to "The Conquest of Britain by the Saxons." By DANIEL HENRY HAIGH, D.D. 8vo. *cloth,* 8s. 6d. 1861

It analyses and throws new historical evidence on the origin of the Poems of Beowulf, the Lament of Deor, the Saga of Waldhere, Scyld Scefing, the Fight at Finnesham, the Story of Horn, the Lay of Hildebrand, &c., &c.

Rambles in Western Cornwall, by the Footsteps of the Giants; with Notes on the Celtic Remains of the Land's End District and the Isles of Scilly. By JAMES ORCHARD HALLIWELL, Esq., F.R.S. Fcp. 4to, *elegantly printed by Whittingham,* *cloth,* 7s. 6d. 1862

Celtic Inscriptions on Gaulish and British Coins; intended to supply Materials for the Early History of Great Britain, with a Glossary of Archaic Celtic Words, and an Atlas of Coins. By BEALE POSTE. 8vo. *many engravings, cloth,* 10s. 6d. 1862

Vindication of the "Celtic Inscriptions on Gaulish and British Coins." By BEALE POSTE. 8vo. *with vignettes and a plate,* *cloth,* 1s. 1862

History of the Nonjurors: their Controversies and Writings, with Remarks on some of the Rubrics in the Book of Common Prayer. By the Rev. THOS. LATHBURY, M.A. 8vo, *cloth,* 6s. (pub 14s.) 1845

History of the Convocation of the Church of England, from the Earliest Period to the Year 1742. By the Rev. THOMAS LATHBURY, M.A. *Second Edition, with considerable Additions,* thick 8vo, *cloth,* 5s. (pub 12s.) 1853

History of Parish Registers in England, and Registers of Scotland, Ireland, the Colonies, Episcopal Chapels in and about London, the Geneva Register of the Protestant Refugees, with Biographical Notes, &c. By J. SOUTHERDEN BURN. *Second Edition,* 8vo, *cloth,* 10s. 6d. 1862

The Footsteps of Shakespere; or, a Ramble with the Early Dramatists, containing new and interesting Information respecting Shakespere, Lyly, Marlowe, Greene, and others. Post 8vo, *cloth,* 5s. 6d. 1862

Gleanings in Graveyards: a Collection of Curious Epitaphs. Collated and compiled by H. E. NORFOLK. *Second Edition,* post 8vo, *cloth,* 2s. 6d. 1861

Tiw; or, a View of the Roots and Stems of the English as a Teutonic Tongue. By the Rev. W. BARNES, B.D., author of the "Dorset Poems," "Philological Grammar," "Anglo-Saxon Delectus," &c. Fcp. 8vo, *cloth,* 5s. 1862

"I hold that my primary roots are the roots of all the Teutonic languages; and, if my view is the true one, it must ultimately be taken up by the German and other Teutonic grammarians, and applied to their languages."— THE AUTHOR.

Retrospective Review (New Series); consisting of Criticisms upon, Analysis of, and Extracts from, curious, useful, valuable, and scarce Old Books. 8vo. Vols. , and II. (*all printed*) *cloth.* 10s. 6d. (original price £1. 11s.)

1853-54

These two volumes form a good companion to the old Series of the *Retrospective*, in 16 vols.; the articles are of the same length and character.

Master Wace, his Chronicle of the Norman Conquest, from the Roman de Rou. Translated into English Prose, with Notes and Illustrations by EDGAR TAYLOR, F.S.A. 8vo. *many engravings from the Bayeux Tapestry, Norman Architecture, Illuminations, &c. cloth,* 15s. (original price £1. 8s.)

1837

Only 150 copies printed, and very few remain unsold; the remaining copies are now in J. R. Smith's hands, and are offered at the above low price, in consequence of the death of Mr. Pickering; hitherto no copies have been sold under the published price.

Contributions to Literature, Historical, Antiquarian, and Metrical. By MARK ANTONY LOWER, M.A., F.S.A., Author of "Essays on English Surnames," "Curiosities of Heraldry," &c. Post 8vo. *woodcuts, cloth,* 7s. 6d.

1854

Contents: 1. Local Nomenclature—2. The Battle of Hastings, an Historical Essay—3. The Lord Dacre, his sorrowful end; a Ballad—4. Historical and Archæological Memoir on the Iron Works of the South of England, with numerous illustrations—5. Winchelsea's Deliverance, or the Stout Abbot of Battayle; in Three Fyttes—6. The South Downs, a Sketch; Historical, Anecdotical, and Descriptive—7. On Yew Trees in Churchyards—8. A Lyrical Garland of Sussex Worthies; a plaintant Ballade—9. A Discourse of Genealogy—10. An Antiquarian Pilgrimage in Normandy, with woodcuts—11. Miscellanea, &c. &c. &c.

Barker.—Literary Anecdotes and Contemporary Reminiscences of Professor Porson and others, from the Manuscript Papers of the late E. H. Barker, Esq., of Thetford, Norfolk, with an Original Memoir of the Author. 2 vols. 8vo. *cloth,* 12s.

1852

A singular book, full of strange stories and facts.

Anecdotes and Characters of Books and Men. Collected from the Conversation of Mr. Pope and other eminent Persons of his Time. By the Rev. JOSEPH SPENCE. With Notes,

Pope.—Additional Facts concerning the Maternal Ancestry of Pope, in a Letter to Mr. Hunter. By ROBERT DAVIES, F.S.A. Post 8vo. 2s.

1858

Life, Progresses, and Rebellion of James, Duke of Monmouth, &c. to his Capture and Execution, with a full account of the "Bloody Assize," under Judge Jefferies, and copious Biographical Notices. By GEORGE ROBERTS. 2 vols. post 8vo. *plates and cuts, cloth,* 7s. 6d. (original price £1. 4s.)

1844

Two very interesting volumes, particularly so to those connected with the West of England.

Biographia Britannica Literaria, or Biography of Literary Characters of Great Britain and Ireland. ANGLO-SAXON PERIOD. By THOMAS WRIGHT, M.A., F.S.A., &c. Membre de l'Institut de France. Thick 8vo. *cloth,* 6s. (original price 12s.)

1842

—— The Anglo-Norman Period. Thick 8vo. *cloth,* 6s. (original price 12s.)

1846

Published under the Superintendence of the Council of the Royal Society of Literature.

There is no work in the English Language which gives the reader such a comprehensive and connected History of the Literature of these periods.

Essays on the Literature, Popular Superstitions, and History of England in the Middle Ages. By THOMAS WRIGHT, M.A., F.S.A. 2 vols. post 8vo. *elegantly printed, cloth,* 16s.

1846

Contents: Essay 1. Anglo-Saxon Poetry—2. Anglo-Norman Poetry—3. Chansons de Geste, or historical romance of the Middle Ages—4. Proverbs and Popular Sayings—5. Anglo-Latin Poets of the Twelfth Century—6. Abelard and the Scholastic Philosophy—7. Dr. Grimm's German Mythology—8. National Fairy Mythology of England—9. Popular Superstitions of Modern Greece, and their connexion with the English—10. Friar Rush and the Frolicsome Elves—11. Dunlop's History of Fiction—12. History and Transmission of Popular Stories—13. Poetry of History—14. Adventures of Hereward the Saxon—15. Story of Eustace the Monk—16. History of Fulke Fitzwarine—17. Popular Cycle or Robin Hood Ballads—18. Conquest of Ireland by the Anglo-Normans—19. Old English Political Songs—20. Dunbar the Scottish Poet.

Literature of the Troubadours. Histoire de la Poésie Provençale, par M. FAURIEL,

ilton ; a Sheaf of Gleanings after his
Biographers and Annotators. By the Rev.
JOSEPH HUNTER. Post 8vo. 2s. 6d.   1850

Junius.—The Authorship of the Letters
of Junius elucidated, including a Biographical
Memoir of Lieut.-Col. Barré, M.P. By JOHN
BRITTON, F.S.A., &c. Royal 8vo. *with portraits of Lord Shelburne, John Dunning, and
Barré, from Sir Joshua Reynolds's picture, cloth,*
6s.—LARGE PAPER, in 4to. *cloth,* 9s.   1848

An exceedingly interesting book, giving many particulars of the
American War, and the state of parties during that period.

The Table Talk of JOHN SELDEN.
With a Biographical Preface and Notes by S.
W. SINGER. Fcap. 8vo. *third edition, por-
trait, cloth,* 5s.   1860

—— LARGE PAPER (*for the connoisseur
of choice Books*). Post 8vo. *cloth,* 7s. 6d. 1860

" Nothing can be more interesting than this little book, containing
a lively picture of the opinions and conversations of one of the
most eminent scholars and most distinguished patriots England has
produced. There are few volumes of its kind so pregnant with
facts, combined with the most profound learning; it is impossible
to open it without finding some important fact or discussion, something practically useful and applicable to the business of life,
Coleridge says, ' There is more weighty bullion in this book in
than I ever found in the same number of pages in any uninspired
writer.' . . . . . . Its merit had not escaped the notice of
Dr. Johnson, though his politics opposed to much of its contents, for
in reply to an observation of Boswell, in praise of the French
Ana, he said, ' A few of them are good, but we have one book of
that kind better than any of them—Selden's Table Talk.'"—*Mr.
Singer's Preface.*

The Life and Times of Daniel De Foe ;
with Remarks, Digressive and Discursive. By
WILLIAM CHADWICK. 8vo. pp. 472, *portrait, cloth,* 10s. 6d.   1859

" Daniel De Foe devoted his life and energies to the defence of free
institutions and good government. He was the Radical of his
day. He not only wrote, but suffered for truth and liberty. He
was impoverished and persecuted for his labours in this cause;
nay, he was repeatedly imprisoned for his principles, or for his
unwavering attachment to them, and for his insidious and bravely
in effecting them. He was the rigorous and indefatigable opponent of priestism, of ecclesiastical domination, and of the Popish
tendencies of his time. We might not approve of all he wrote
against the Catholics, but we should remember that he lived and
felt, as we cannot, how universally opposed to true freedom is the
Catholic system. Although we love in very different lines from
those in which De Foe lived, yet his life is full of pregnant lessons
for the liberals and friends of religious freedom of our day."—
Bradford Review.

Wayland Smith.—A Dissertation on a
Tradition of the Middle Ages, from the
French of G. B. DEPPING and FRANCISQUE
MICHEL, with Additions by S. W. SINGER,
and the amplified Legend by OEHLENSLAGER.
12mo. *cloth,* 3s. 6d.   *Pickering,* 1847

Robin Hood.—The Great Hero of the
Ancient Minstrelsy of England, " Robin
Hood," his Period, real Character, &c., in-
vestigated, and perhaps ascertained, by the
Rev. JOSEPH HUNTER. Post 8vo. 2s. 6d.
                                        1852

Notes on Ancient Britain and the Britons.
By the Rev. W. BARNES, author of the
" Philological Grammar," " Anglo-Saxon
Delectus," " Dorset Dialect," &c. Foolscap
8vo. *cloth,* 3s.   1858

" Mr. Barnes has given us the result of his Collections for a Course of
Lectures on this subject, and has produced a series of theories of
the Ancient Britons, their language, laws, and modes of life,
and of their social state as compared with that of the Saxons,
which will be read with considerable interest."—*Notes and
Queries.*

" We are very glad to meet with this pleasant and readable ' Notes '
of Mr. Barnes's. They are very unaffected essays, imparting
much warmth to the old records of British lore, and evincing
from real study. He has found out the value of the old Welsh
laws, and has made some useful comparisons between them and
those of the Saxons with much freshness & not slightest novelty."—
Guardian.

Taliesin ; or, the Bards and Druids of
Britain. A Translation of the Remains of
the earliest Welsh Bards, and an examination
of the Bardic Mysteries. By D. W. NASH,
member of the Royal Society of Literature.
8vo. *cloth,* 14s.   1857

Excerpta ex Scriptoribus Classicis de
Britannia. A Complete Collection of those
passages in the Classic Writers (104 in
number), which make mention of the British
Isles, Chronologically Arranged, from Ante-
Christi 560 to Anno Dom. 1333. By the
Rev. Dr. J. A. GILES. 8vo. *cloth,* 3s.
(original price 7s. 6d.)   1846

An Introduction to every History of Great Britain.

History of England, under the Anglo-
Saxon Kings. By Dr. J. M. LAPPENBERG.
Translated by BENJ. THORPE, with Additions
and Corrections, by the Author and Translator.
2 vols. 8vo. *cloth,* 12s. (original price £1. 1s.)
                                        1845

History of England, under the Norman
Kings, with an Epitome of the early History
of Normandy. By Dr. J. M. LAPPENBERG,
translated with Additions by BENJ. THORPE.
8vo. *cloth,* 15s.   1857

Agincourt ; a contribution towards an
authentic List of the Commanders of the
English Host in King Henry the Fifth's Ex-

Britannic Researches; or, New Facts and Rectifications of Ancient British History. By the Rev. BEALE POSTE, M.A. 8vo. (pp. 448), *with engravings, cloth,* 13s. 1853

"The author of this volume may justly claim credit for considerable learning, great industry, and, above all, strong faith in the interest and importance of his subject. . . . On various points he has given us additional information, and afforded us new views, for which we are bound to thank him. The body of the book is followed by a very complete index, so as to render reference to any part of it easy; that we the more ourselves, on account of the multifariousness of the topics treated, the variety of persons mentioned, and the many works quoted."—*Athenæum*, Oct. 8, 1853.

"The Rev. Beale Poste has long been known to antiquaries as one of the best read of all those who have elucidated the earliest annals of this country. He is a practical man, has investigated our buried monuments and manuscripts, and we have in the above-named volume the fruit of many years' patient study. The objects which will occupy the attention of the reader are—1, The political patterns of the principal British powers before the Roman conquest—under the Roman dominion, and struggling unsuccessfully against the Anglo-Saxon race; 2, The Geography of Ancient Britain; 3, An investigation of the Ancient British Historians, Gildas and Nennius, and the more obscure British chroniclers; 4, The ancient stone monuments of the Celtic period; and, lastly, some curious and interesting notices of the early British Church. Mr. Poste has not touched on subjects which have received much attention from others, save in cases where he had something new to offer, and the volume must be regarded, therefore, as an entirely new collection of discoveries and deductions tending to throw light on the darkest, as well as the earliest, portion of our national history."—*Atlas.*

Britannia Antiqua, or Ancient Britain brought within the Limits of Authentic History. By the Rev. BEALE POSTE. 8vo. pp. 386, *map, cloth,* 14s. 1857

A Sequel to the foregoing work.

Letters of the Kings of England.—Now first collected from the Originals in Royal Archives, and from other Authentic Sources, private as well as public. Edited, with Historical Introduction and Notes, by J. O. HALLIWELL. *Two handsome volumes,* post 8vo. *with portraits of Henry VIII. and Charles I., cloth,* 8s. (original price £1. 1s.) 1848

These volumes form a good companion to Ellis's Original Letters. The collection comprises, for the first time, the love-letters of Henry VIII. to Anne Boleyn in a complete form, which may be re-

Inquiry into the Particulars connected with the Death of Amy Robsart (Lady Dudley), at Cumnor Place, Berks, Sept. 8, 1560; being a refutation of the Calumnies charged against Sir Robert Dudley, Anthony Forster, and others. By J. T. PETTIGREW, 8vo., 2s. 1859

The Fawkes's of York in the 16th Century, including Notices of Guy Fawkes the Gunpowder Plot Conspirator. By ROBERT DAVIES, F.S.A. Post 8vo., 1s. 6d. 1850

Historical Sketches of the Angling Literature of all Nations. By ROBERT BLAKEY. To which is added a Bibliographical Catalogue of English Books on Angling and Ichthyology, 12mo. *cloth,* 5s. 1856

The Pilgrim Fathers.—Collections con-cerning the Church or Congregation of Protestant Separatists formed at Scrooby, in North Nottinghamshire, in the time of James I., the Founders of New Plymouth, the Parent Colony of New England. By the Rev. JOSEPH HUNTER, F.S.A., *and an Assistant Keeper of Her Majesty's Records.* 8vo. *cloth,* 8s. 1854

This work contains some very important particulars of these personages, and their researches previously to their leaving England and Holland, which were entirely unknown to former writers, and have only recently been discovered, through the indefatigable exertions of the Author. Prefixed to the volume are some beautiful Prefatory Stanzas by Richard Monckton Milnes, Esq., M.P.

Love Letters of Mrs. Piozzi (formerly Mrs. Thrale, the friend of Dr. Johnson), written when she was Eighty, to the handsome actor, William Augustus Conway, aged Twenty-seven. 8vo. *sewed,* 2s. 1843

"—— written at three, four, and five o'clock (in the morning) by an octogenary pen; a heart (as Mrs. Lee says) twenty-six years old, and an H. L. P. *facit il vit be, all your own."—Letter V.*, *ved. Feb., 1820.*

"This is one of the most extraordinary collections of love epistles we have chanced to meet with, and the well-known literary reputation of the lady—the Mrs. Thrale, of Dr. Johnson and Miss Burney Celebrity—considerably enhances their interest. The letters themselves it is not easy to characterise; nor shall we venture to decide whether they more bespeak the dwindling of

Worthies of Weſtmoreland; or, Biographies of notable Perſons born in that County ſince the Reformation. By GEORGE ATKINSON, Eſq. Serjeant at Law. 2 vols. poſt 8vo. *cloth*, 6s. (original price 16s.) **1849**

England's Worthies, under whom all the Civil and Bloody Warres, ſince Anno 1642 to Anno 1647, are related. By JOHN VICARS, Author of " England's Parliamentary Chronicle," &c. &c. Royal 12mo. *reprinted in the old ſtyle (ſimilar to Lady Willoughby's Diary), with copies of the 18 rare portraits after Hollar, &c., half-morocco*, 5s. **1845**

Liſter.—The Autobiography of JOSEPH LISTER (a Nonconformiſt), of Bradford, Yorkſhire, with a contemporary account of the Defence of Bradford and Capture of Leeds, by the Parliamentarians, in 1642. Edited by THOS. WRIGHT, F.S.A. 8vo. *cloth*, 2s. **1842**

Forman.—The Autobiography and Perſonal Diary of Dr. Simon Forman, the celebrated Aſtrologer, 1552-1602, from unpubliſhed MSS. in the Aſhmolean Muſeum, Oxford. Edited by J. O. HALLIWELL. Small 4to. *ſewed*, 5s. **1849**

Only 150 copies privately printed. It will form a companion to Dr. Dee's Diary, printed by the Camden Society, who also printed this work but afterwards ſuppreſſed it.

Life, Poetry, and Letters of Ebenezer Elliot, the Corn-Law Rhymer (of Sheffield). Edited by his Son-in-Law, JOHN WATKINS. Poſt 8vo. *cloth, (an intereſting volume)*, 3s. (original price 7s. 6d.) **1850**

Weſley.—Narrative of a Remarkable Tranſaction in the Early Life of John Weſley. Now firſt Printed, from a MS. in the Britiſh Muſeum. 8vo. *ſewed*, 2s. **1848**

A very curious love affair between J. W. and his houſekeeper; it gives a curious inſight into the early œconomy of the Methodiſts. It is entirely unknown to all Weſley's biographers.

Gounter's (Col., of Racton, Suſſex) Account of the Miraculous Eſcape of King Charles II. out of England. Now firſt printed. Poſt 8vo. 2s. **1846**

This little tract takes up the narrative where the Royal memoir breaks off. It was unknown to Mr. Hughes, the editor of the " Boſcobel Tracts."

The Connection of Wales with the Early Science of England, illuſtrated in the Memoir of Dr. Robert Recorde, the firſt

A Rot Amongſt the Biſhops; or, a Terrible Tempeſt in the Sea of Canterbury, ſet forth in lively emblems, to pleaſe the judicious Reader. By THOMAS STIRRY, 1641, 18mo. (*A Satire on Abp. Laud), four very curious woodcut emblems, cloth*, 3s.

A fac-ſimile of the very rare original edition, which ſold at Bindley's ſale for £11.

Cartwright. — Memoirs of the Life Writings, and Mechanical Inventions of Edmund Cartwright, D.D., F.R.S., *inventor of the Power Loom, &c.* Edited by E. H. STRICKLAND. Poſt 8vo. *engravings, boards*, 2s. 6d. (original price 10s. 6d.) **1843**

It contains ſome intereſting literary hiſtory, Dr. Cartwright numbering among his correſpondents, Sir W. Jones, Crabbe, Sir H. Davy, Fulton, Sir S. Raffles, Langhorne, and others; he was no mean Poet, as his Legendary tale of " Armine and Elvira" (given in the Appendix) witneſs; Sir W. Scott ſays it contains ſome excellent poetry, repriced with unuſual felicity.

Collection of Letters on Scientific Subjects, illuſtrative of the Progreſs of Science in England. Temp. Elizabeth to Charles II. Edited by J. O. HALLIWELL. 8vo. *cloth*, 5s. **1841**

Compriſing letters of Digges, Dee, Tycho Brahe, Lower, Harriot, Lydyatt, Sir W. Petry, Sir C. Cavendiſh, Brancker, Pell, &c.; alſo the autobiography of Sir Samuel Morland, from a MS. in Lambeth Palace, Nat. Torpoley's Corrector Analyticus, &c. Coſt the ſubſcribers of the Hiſtorical Society of Science £1.

Morland.—Account of the Life, Writings, and Inventions of Sir Samuel Morland, Maſter of Mechanics to Charles II. By J. O. HALLIWELL. 8vo. *ſewed*, 1s. **1838**

Autographical Miſcellany; a Collection of Autograph Letters, Intereſting Documents, &c., executed in facſimile by FRED. NETHERCLIFT, each facſimile accompanied with a page of letter-preſs by R. SIMS, of the Britiſh Muſeum. Royal 4to. A HANDSOME VOL., *extra cloth*, £1. 1s. (original price £1. 16s.) **1855**

Containing fifty examples of hitherto unpubliſhed Letters and Documents of Blake, Bothwell, Buonaparte, Burns, Calvin, Camden, Cavier, Catherine de Medicis, Charles I., Chatterton, Congreve, Cranmer, Cromwell, Danton, D'Aubigne, Dryden, Edward VI., Elizabeth, Elizabeth (Inner of Louis XVI.), Franklin, Galileo, Glover, Goethe, Goldſmith, Henry VIII., Hyde (Anne), James II., Jenſon, Kepler, Koſciuſko, Latimer, Layola, Louis XIV., Louis XVI., Luther, Malsherbes, Maria Antoinette, Marlborough, Marmontel, Mary Queen of Scots, Melancthon, Newton, Penn, Pompadour, Pole (Cardinal), Raleigh, Sidney, Robeſpierre, Rowtrim, Rubens, Sand, Schiller, Spenſer, Sterne, Taſſo, Voltaire, Walpole (Horace), Waſhington, Wolfe, Wolley, Wren, and

A Life of Shakeſpeare, including many particulars reſpecting the Poet and his Family, never before publiſhed, by J. O. HALLIWELL, F.R.S., &c. In one handſome volume, 8vo. *illuſtrated with 76 engravings as uſual, of objects, moſt of which are new, from drawings by Fairholt, cloth,* 15s. 1848

This work contains upwards of forty documents reſpecting Shakeſpeare and his family, never before publiſhed, beſides numerous others, indirectly illuſtrating the Poet's biography. All the anecdotes and traditions concerning Shakeſpeare are here, for the firſt time, collected, and much new light is thrown on his perſonal hiſtory, by papers exhibiting him as felling Malt, Stone, &c. Of the ſeventy-ſix engravings which illuſtrate the volume, more than fifty have never before been engraved. It is the only life of Shakeſpeare to be bought ſeparately from his works.

New Illuſtrations of the Life, Studies, and Writings of Shakeſpeare, by the Rev. JOSEPH HUNTER. 2 vols. 8vo. *cloth,* 7s. 6d. (original price, £1. 1s.) 1845

Supplementary to all editions of the works of the Poet.

⁕ Part 1, price 3s, and Parts 3, 4, and 5, together price 4s., may be had to complete copies.

A Critical Examination of the Text of Shakeſpeare; together with Notes on his Plays and Poems, by the late W. Sidney Walker. Edited by W. Nanſon Lettſom. 3 vols. foolſcap 8vo. *cloth,* 18s. 1860

"Very often we find ourſelves differing from Mr. Walker on readings and interpretations, but we ſeldom differ from him without reſpect for his ſcholarſhip and care. He are not the wild profils at work which neither goods nor men have fiamach to endure, but the ſuggeſtions of a trained intelligence and a chaſtened taſte. Future editors and commentators will be forced to conſult theſe volumes, and conſider their ſuggeſtions."—*Athenæum.*

"A valuable addition to our Philological Literature, the moſt valuable part being the remarks on contemporary literature, and the mode of learning by which the exact meaning and rendition of a word is ſought to be eſtabliſhed."—*Literary Gazette.*

By the ſame Author,

Shakeſpeare's Verſification, and its Apparent Irregularities explained by Examples from early and late Engliſh Writers. Foolſcap 8vo. *cloth,* 6s. 1854

"The reader of Shakeſpeare would do well to make himſelf acquainted with this excellent little book previous to entering upon the ſtudy of the poet."—*Mr. Singer, in the Preface to his New Edition of Shakſpeare.*

A Few Notes on Shakeſpeare, with Occaſional Remarks on the Emendations of the Manuſcript-Corrector in Mr. Collier's copy of the folio, 1632, by the Rev. ALEXANDER DYCE. 8vo. *cloth,* 5s. 1853

* Mr. Dyce's Notes are peculiarly delightful, from the ſtores of illuſtration with which his extenſive reading not only among our writers, but among thoſe of other countries, eſpecially of the Italian poets, has enabled him to enrich them. All that he has recorded is valuable. We read his little volume with attention.

Curſory Notes on Various Paſſages in the text of Beaumont and Fletcher, as edited by the Rev. Alexander Dyce, and on his "Few Notes on Shakeſpeare," by the Rev. JOHN MITFORD. 8vo. *ſewed,* 1s. 6d. 1856

A Few Words in reply to the Rev. A. Dyce's "Few Notes on Shakeſpeare," by the Rev. JOSEPH HUNTER. 8vo. 1s. 1853

Strictures on Mr. Collier's New Edition of Shakeſpeare, publiſhed in 1858, by the Rev. ALEXANDER DYCE. 8vo. *cloth,* 7s. 6d. 1859

The Grimaldi Shakeſpeare.—Notes and Emendations on the Plays of Shakeſpeare, from a recently diſcovered annotated copy by the late Joe. Grimaldi, Eſq. Comedian. 8vo *woodcuts,* 1s. 1853

A humorous ſquib on Collier's Shakeſpeare Emendations.

A Few Remarks on the Emendation, " Who Smothers her with Painting," in the Play of Cymbeline, diſcovered by Mr. Collier, in a Corrected Copy of the Second Edition of Shakeſpeare, by J. O. HALLIWELL, F.R.S., &c. 8vo. 1s. 1852

The Shakeſpeare Fabrications; or, the MS. Notes of the Perkins folio, ſhown to be of recent origin; with Appendix on the Authorſhip of the Ireland Forgeries, by C. MANSFIELD INGLEBY, LL.D. Foolſcap 8vo. *with a facſimile, ſhewing the pſeudo old writing and the pencilled words, cloth,* 3s. 1859

Eſſay on the Genius of Shakeſpeare, with Critical Remarks on the Characters of Romeo, Hamlet, Juliet, and Ophelia, by H. M. GRAVES. Poſt 8vo. *cloth,* 2s. 6d. (original price 5s. 6d.) 1826

Hamlet.—An Attempt to aſcertain whether the Queen were an Acceſſory, before the Fact, in the Murder of her Firſt Huſband, 8vo. *ſewed,* 1s. 1856

"This pamphlet well deſerves the peruſal of every ſtudent of Hamlet."—*News and Review.*

Remarks on the Moral Influence of Shakeſpeare's Plays, with illuſtrations from Hamlet, by the Rev. THOMAS GRINFIELD. 8vo. *cloth,* 3s. 1850

The Sonnets of Shakeſpeare, *rearranged* and divided into Four Parts, with an Introduction and Explanatory Notes. Poſt 8vo.

On the Sonnets of Shakespeare, identifying the persons to whom they are addressed, and elucidating several points in the Poet's History, by JAMES BOADEN. 8vo. ᴄ. (.
1837

Shakespeare's Autobiographical Poems, being his Sonnets clearly developed, with his Character, drawn chiefly from his Works, by C. A. BROWN. Post 8vo. *cloth*, 4s. 6d. 1838

Pericles, Prince of Tyre, a Novel, by GEO. Wilkins, printed in 1608, and founded upon Shakespeare's Play, edited by PROFESSOR MOMMSEN; with Preface and Account of some original Shakespeare editions extant in Germany and Switzerland, and Introduction by J. P. COLLIER. 8vo. *sewed*, 5s. 1857

Account of the only known Manuscript of Shakespeare's Plays, comprising some important variations and corrections in the "Merry Wives of Windsor," obtained from a Playhouse Copy of that Play recently discovered, by J. O. HALLIWELL. 8vo. 1s. 1843

"Who was 'Jack Wilson,' the Singer of Shakespeare's Stage?" An Attempt to prove the identity of this person with John Wilson, Doctor of Music in the University of Oxford, A.D. 1644, by E. F. RIMBAULT, LL.D. 8vo. 1s. 1846

Shakespeare's Will, copied from the Original in the Prerogative Court, preserving the Interlineations and Facsimiles of the three Autographs of the Poet, with a few Preliminary Observations, by J. O. HALLIWELL. 4to. 1s. 1838

Traditionary Anecdotes of Shakespeare, collected in Warwickshire in 1693. 8vo. *sewed*, 1s. 1838

Observations on an Autograph of Shakespeare, and the Orthography of his Name, by Sir FRED. MADDEN. 8vo. *sewed*, 1s. 1838

Was Lord Bacon the Author of Shakespeare's Plays? A Letter to Lord Ellesmere, by W. H. SMITH. 8vo. 6d. 1856

Bacon and Shakespeare, an Inquiry touching Players, Playhouses, and Play-writers in the Reign of Q. Elizabeth; to which is appended an Abstract of a Manuscript Autobiography of Tobie Matthews, by W. H. SMITH. Foolscap 8vo. *cloth*, 2s. 6d. 1857

A Pilgrimage to Stratford-upon-Avon, the Birthplace of Shakespeare, by C. V. GRINFIELD. 12mo. *portrait and plates, cloth*, 2s. 6d. 1850

—— with R. B. Wheler's Guide to Stratford-upon-Avon. 4 *plates*, in 1 vol. 12mo. *cloth*, 3s. 6d. 1850

Historical Account of the Monumental Bust of Shakespeare, in the Chancel of Stratford-upon-Avon Church, by ABR. WIVELL. 8vo. 2 *plates*, 1s. 6d. 1827

Wivell's Supplement to his Work on the History and Authenticity of the Shakespeare Portraits. 8vo. 12 *portraits, boards*, 6s. (original price 21s.) 1827

Criticism applied to Shakespeare, by C. BADHAM. Post 8vo. 1s. 1846

Vortigern, an Historical Play, represented at Drury Lane, April 2, 1796, as a supposed newly discovered Drama of Shakespeare, by WILLIAM HENRY IRELAND. New Edition, *with an original Preface*, 8vo. *facsimile*, 1s. 6d. (original price 3s. 6d.) 1832

The preface is both interesting and curious, from the additional information it gives respecting the Shakespeare Forgeries, containing also the substance of the author's "Confessions."

Comparative Review of the Opinions of JAS. Boaden, in 1795 and in 1796, relative to the Shakespeare MSS. 8vo. 2s. 1796

A Letter to Dr. Farmer (*in Reply to*

Brief Hand-Lift of Books, MSS., &c., illuſtrative of the Life and Writings of Shake-ſpeare, collefted between 1842 and 1859, by J. O. HALLIWELL. Poſt 8vo. *only 30 copies privately printed, cloth, 12s.* 1859

Compendious Anglo-Saxon and Engliſh Dictionary, by the Rev. J. BOSWORTH, D.D., F.R.S., &c., *Anglo-Saxon Profeſſor in the Univerſity of Oxford.* 8vo. *cloſely printed in treble columns, 12s.* 1860

"This is not a mere abridgment of the large Dictionary, but almoſt an entirely new work. In this compendium one will be found, at a very moderate price, all that is moſt practical and valuable in the former expenſive edition, with a great accesſion of new words and meaning."—*Author's Preface.*

Anglo-Saxon Delectus; ſerving as a firſt Claſſ-Book to the Language, by the Rev. W. BARNES, B.D., of St. John's College, Cambridge. 12mo. *cloth, 2s. 6d.* 1849

"To thoſe who wiſh to poſſeſs a critical knowledge of their own Native Engliſh, ſome acquaintance with Anglo-Saxon is indiſpenſable; and we have never ſeen an introduction better calculated than the preſent to ſupply the wants of a beginner in a ſhort ſpace of time. The declenſions and conjugations are well ſtated, and illuſtrated by references to Greek, the Latin, French, and other languages. A philoſophical ſpirit pervades every part. The Delectus conſiſts of ſhort pieces on various ſubjects, with excerpts from Anglo-Saxon Hiſtory and the Saxon Chronicle. There is a good Gloſſary at the end."—*Athenæum, Oct. 10, 1849.*

Introduction to Anglo-Saxon Reading; compriſing Ælfric's Homily on the Birthday of St. Gregory, with a copious Gloſſary, &c., by L. LANGLEY, F.L.S. 12mo. *cloth, 2s. 6d.* 1839

Ælfric's Homily is remarkable for beauty of compoſition, and intereſting, as ſetting forth Auguſtine's miſſion to the "Land of the Angles."

Anglo-Saxon Verſion of the Life of St. Guthlac, Hermit of Croyland. Printed, for the firſt time, from a MS. in the Cottonian Library, with a Tranſlation and Notes by CHARLES WYCLIFFE GOODWIN, M.A., Fellow of Catherine Hall, Cambridge. 12mo. *cloth, 5s.* 1848

Anglo-Saxon Verſion of the Hexameron of St. Baſil, and the Anglo-Saxon Remains of St. Baſil's Admonitio ad Filium Spiritualem. Now firſt printed from MSS. in the Bodleian Library, with a Tranſlation and Notes by the Rev. H. W. NORMAN. 8vo. *Second Edition, enlarged, ſewed, 4s.* 1849

The Holy Goſpels in Anglo-Saxon, edited from the original MS., by BENJAMIN

Guide to the Anglo-Saxon Tongue; on the Baſis of Profeſſor Raſk's Grammar; to which are added Reading Leſſons, in Verſe and Proſe, with Notes, for the uſe of Learners, by E. J. VERNON, B.A., OXON. 12mo. *cloth, 5s.* 1855

"Mr. Vernon has, we think, acted wiſely in taking Raſk for his model; but let no one ſuppoſe from the title that the book is merely a compilation from the work of that philologiſt. The accidence is abridged from Raſk, with correfted reviſion, correction, and modiſcation; but the ſyntax, a moſt important portion of the book, is original, and is compiled with great care and ſkill; and the latter half of the volume conſiſts of a well-choſen ſelection of extracts from Anglo-Saxon writers, in proſe and verſe, for the practice of the ſtudent, who will find great aſſiſtance in reading them from the grammatical notes with which they are accompanied, and from the gloſſary which follows them. This volume, well ſtudied, will enable any one to read with eaſe the generality of Anglo-Saxon verſers; and its cheapneſs places it within the reach of every claſs. It has our hearty recommendation."—*Literary Gazette.*

Anglo-Saxon Verſion of the Story of Apollonius of Tyre, upon which is founded the Play of Pericles, attributed to Shakeſpeare, from a MS., with a Tranſlation and Gloſſary by BENJAMIN THORPE. 12mo. *cloth, 4s. 6d.* (original price 6s.) 1834

Analecta Anglo-Saxonica.—A Selection, in Proſe and Verſe, from Anglo-Saxon Authors, of various ages, with a Gloſſary by BENJAMIN THORPE, F.S.A. *A New Edition, with corrections and improvements.* Poſt 8vo. *cloth, 8s.* (original price 12s.) 1841

A Philological Grammar, grounded upon Engliſh, and formed from a compariſon of more than ſixty Languages. Being an Introduction to the Science of Grammars of all Languages, eſpecially Engliſh, Latin, and Greek. By the Rev. W. BARNES, B.D., of St. John's College, Cambridge; Author of "Poems in the Dorſet Dialect," "Anglo-Saxon Delectus," &c., 8vo. (pp. 322), *cloth, 9s.* 1854

"Mr. Barnes' work is an excellent ſpecimen of the manner in which the advancing ſtudy of Philology may be brought to illuſtrate and enrich a ſcientiſic expoſition of Engliſh Grammar."—*Edinburgh Guardian.*

"Of the ſcience of Grammar, by induction from the philological facts of many languages, Mr. Barnes has, in this volume, ſupplied a conciſe and comprehenſive manual. Grammars may differ as to the regularity of the principles on which a nation have conſtructed their forms and uſages of ſpeech, but it is generally allowed that ſome conformity or ſimilarity of practice may be traced, and that an attempt may be made to expound a true ſcience of Grammar. Mr. Barnes has ſo far grounded his Grammar upon Engliſh as to make it an Engliſh Grammar, but he has conſiderably referred to comparative philology, and ſought to render his work illuſtrative of general form, in conformity with principles common, more or leſs, to the language of all mankind. More than ſixty languages have been compared in the courſe of preparing

A Fragment of Ælfric's Anglo-Saxon Grammar, Ælfric's Glossary, and a Poem on the Soul and Body of the XIIth Century, discovered among the Archives of Worcester Cathedral, by Sir Thomas Phillipps, Bart. Folio, PRIVATELY PRINTED, *sewed*, 11. 6d.
1838

Two Leaves of King Waldere, and King Gudhere, a hitherto unknown Old English Epic of the 8th Century belonging to the Saga Cycle of King Theodoric and his Men. Now first published with a modern English reading, Notes and Glossary, by George Stephens, *English Professor in the University of Copenhagen.* Royal 8vo. *with four Photographic Facsimiles of the MS. of the 9th Century, recently discovered at Copenhagen,* 15l.
—*without Facsimiles,* 7s. 6d. 1860

Popular Treatises on Science, written during the Middle Ages, in Anglo-Saxon, Anglo-Norman, and English, edited by Thomas Wright, M.A. 8vo. *cloth,* 3s.
1841

Contents.—An Anglo-Saxon Treatife on Aftronomy of the Tenth Century, now first published from a MS. in the British Museum, with a tranflation; Livre des Creatures, by Phillippe de Thaun, now first printed, with a tranflation (extremely valuable to Philologifts, as being the earlieft fpecimens of Anglo-Norman remaining, and explanatory of all the fymbolical figns in early fculpture and painting); the Bestiary of Phillippe de Thaun, with a tranflation; Fragments on Popular Science from the Early English Metrical Lives of the Saints (the earlieft piece of the kind in the English Language.)

Skelton (John, *Poet Laureate to Henry VIII.*) Poetical Works: the Bowge of Court, Colin Clout, Why come ye not to Court? (his celebrated Satire on Wolfey), Phillip Sparrow, Elinour Rumming, &c.; with Notes and Life by the Rev. A. Dyce. 3 vols. 8vo. *cloth,* 16s. (original price £1. 11s.) 1843

"The power, the ftrangenefs, the volubility of his language, the audacity of his fatire, and the perfect originality of his manner, make Skelton one of the moft extraordinary writers of any age or country."—*Southey.*

Early History of Freemasonry in England. Illuftrated by an English Poem of the XIVth Century, with Notes by J. O. Halliwell. Post 8vo. *fecond edition, with a facfimile of the original MS. in the British Mufeum, cloth,* 2s. 6d. 1844

" The marvel which the curious poem, of which this publication is chiefly compofed, has excited, is proved by the fact of its having been rendered into German, and of its having reached a fecond edition, which is not common with fuch publications. Mr. Halliwell has carefully revifed the new edition, and improved its..."

Torrent of Portugal; an English Metrical Romance. Now first published, from an unique MS. of the XVth Century, preferved in the Chetham Library at Manchefter, edited by J. O. Halliwell, &c. Post 8vo. *cloth, uniform with Ritfon, Weber, and Ellis's publications, cloth,* 5s. 1842

" This is a valuable and interefting addition to our lift of early English metrical romances, and an indifpenfable companion to the collections of Ritfon, Weber, and Ellis."—*Literary Gazette.*

The Vision and Creed of Piers Ploughman, edited by Thomas Wright; a new edition, revifed, with additions to the Notes and Glossary. 2 vols. foolfcap 8vo. *cloth,* 10s. :156

" The ' Vifion of Piers Ploughman ' is one of the moft precious and interefting monuments of the English Language and Literature, and alfo of the focial and political condition of the country during the fourteenth century. . . . Its author is not certainly known, but in clafs of compofition can, by internal evidence, be fixed at about the year 1362. On this and on all matters bearing upon the origin and object of the poem, Mr. Wright's hiftorical introduction gives ample information. . . . . In the thirteen years that have paffed fince the firft edition of the prefent text was publifhed by the late Mr. Pickering, our old literature and hiftory has been more ftudied, and we truft that a large circle of readers will be prepared to welcome this cheaper and carefully revifed reprint."—*Literary Gazette.*

Sir Amadace; a Middle-North-English Metrical Romance of the XIIIth Century, reprinted from two texts, with an Introduction by George Stephens, *Professor of Old English in the University of Copenhagen.* 8vo. *sewed,* 2s. 6d. 1860

Rara Mathematica; or, a Collection of Treatifes on the Mathematics and Subjects connected with them, from ancient inedited MSS., by J. O. Halliwell. 8vo. *fecond edition, cloth,* 3s. 1841

Contents:—Johannis de Sacro-Bosco Tractatus de Arte Numerandi; Method ufed in England in the Fifteenth Century for taking the Altitude of a Steeple; Treatife on the Numeration of Algorifm; Treatife on Clafles for Optical Purpofes, by W. Bourne; Johannis Robyns de Cometis Commentaria; Two Tables fhewing the time of High Water at London bridge, and the Duration of Moonlight, from a MS. of the Thirteenth Century; on the Menfuration of Heights and Diftances; Alexandri de Villa Dei Carmen de Algorifmo; Preface to a Calender of Almanack for 1430; Johannis Norfolk in Artem progreffionis dumunat; Notes on Early Almanacks, by the Editor, &c. &c.

Philological Proofs of the Original Unity and Recent Origin of the Human Race, derived from a Comparifon of the Languages of Europe, Afia, Africa, and America, by A. J. Johnel. 8vo. *cloth,* 6s. (original price 12s. 6d.) 1843

Nugæ Poetica; Select Pieces of Old English Popular Poetry, illustrating the Manners and Arts of the XVth Century. Edited by J. O. HALLIWELL. Post 8vo. *only 100 copies printed, cloth,* 5s. 1844

Anecdota Literaria; a Collection of Short Poems in English, Latin, and French, illustrative of the Literature and History of England in the XIIIth Century; and more especially of the Condition and Manners of the different Classes of Society. By T. WRIGHT, M.A., F.S.A., &c. 8vo. *cloth, only* 250 *copies printed,* 5s. 1844

Dictionary of Archaic and Provincial Words, Obsolete Phrases, Proverbs, and Ancient Customs, from the Reign of Edward I. By JAMES ORCHARD HALLIWELL, F.R.S., F.S.A., &c. 2 vols. 8vo. containing upwards of 1000 pages, *closely printed in double columns, cloth, a new and cheaper edition,* 15s. 1861

It contains above 50,000 words (embodying all the known scattered glossaries of the English language), forming a complete key for the reader of our old Poets, Dramatists, Theologians, and other authors, whose works abound with allusions, of which explanations are not to be found in ordinary Dictionaries and books of reference. Most of the principal Archaisms are illustrated by examples selected from early localised MSS. and rare books, and by far the greatest portion will be found to be original authorities.

A Glossary; or, Collection of Words, Phrases, Customs, Proverbs, &c., illustrating the Works of English Authors, particularly Shakespeare and his Contemporaries. By ROBERT NARES, Archdeacon of Stafford, &c. A New Edition, with considerable Additions, both of Words and Examples. By JAMES O. HALLIWELL, F.R.S., and THOMAS WRIGHT, M.A., F.S.A. 2 thick vols, 8vo. *cloth,* £1. 8s. 1859

This Glossary of Archæ-ancient Nares is by far the best and most useful work we possess for explaining and illustrating the obsolete language and the customs and manners of the sixteenth and seventeenth centuries, and it is quite indispensable for the readers of the literature of the Elizabethan period. The additional words and examples are distinguished from those in the original text by a † prefixed to each. The work contains between five and six thousand additional examples, the result of original research, not merely supplementary to Nares, but to all other compilations of the kind.

Thompson (E.) on the Archaic Mode of expressing Numbers in English, Anglo-Saxon, Friesic, &c. 8vo. (*an ingenious and learned pamphlet, interesting to the Philologist*).

Glossary of Provincial and Local Words Used in England. By F. GROSE, F.S.A.; with which is now incorporated the Supplement. By SAMUEL PEGGE, F.S.A. Post 8vo. *cloth,* 4s. 6d. 1839

Specimens of Cornish Provincial Dialect, collected and arranged by Uncle Jan Treenoodle, with some Introductory Remarks and a Glossary by an Antiquarian Friend; also a Selection of Songs and other Pieces connected with Cornwall. Post 8vo. *with a curious portrait of Dolly Pentreath, cloth,* 4s. 1846

The Cornish Thalia, being original Comic Poems, illustrative of the Cornish Dialect. By J. H. DANIEL. Post 8vo. 6d. 1861

A Glossary of the Words and Phrases of Cumberland. By WILLIAM DICKINSON, F.L.S. 12mo. *cloth,* 2s. 1859

Nathan Hogg's Letters and Poems in the Devonshire Dialect, *The fourth edition, with additions,* post 8vo. *sewed,* 1s. 1860

" These letters, which have achieved considerable popularity, evince an extensive acquaintance with the vernacular of the County and its idioms and phrases, while the courteous flow of wit and humour throughout, cannot fail to operate forcibly upon the risible faculties of the reader. In the Witch story Nathan has excelled himself, and it is to be hoped we have not seen his last effort in this branch of local English literature. The superstitions of Jan Vaggis and Jan Plant are most graphically and amusingly pourtrayed, and the various incidents whereby the influence of the 'Evil Eye,' is sought to be counteracted, are at once ludicrous and irresistible."—*Plymouth Mail.*

Poems of Rural Life, in the Dorset Dialect, with a Dissertation and Glossary. By the Rev. Wm. BARNES, B.D. *Second edition, enlarged and corrected,* royal 12mo. *cloth,* 10s. 1847

Hwomely Rhymes; a Second Collection of Poems in the Dorset Dialect. By the Rev. W. BARNES. Royal 12mo. *cloth,* 5s. 1859

" The author is a genuine poet, and it is delightful to catch the pure breath of song in verse which affect themselves only as the mould reborn of rare words and Saxon inflections. We have no intention of setting up the Dorset patois against the more extended provincialisms of Scotland, still less of comparing the Dorietshire poet with the Scotch; yet we feel here that their genius would have delighted the heart of Burns, that many of them are not unworthy of him, and that (at any rate) his best productions cannot express a more cordial sympathy with external nature, or a more loving interest in human joys and sorrows."—*Literary Gazette.*

John Noakes and Mary Styles: a Poem

A Gloffary of Words ufed in Teefdale, in the County of Durham. Poft 8vo. *with a map of the diftrict, cloth,* 2s. 6d. (original price 6s.) 1849

"Contains about two thoufand words. . . . It is believed the firft and only collection of words and phrafes peculiar to this diftrict, and we hail it therefore as a valuable contribution to the hiftory of language and literature . . . the author has evidently brought to bear an extenfive perfonal acquaintance with the common language."—*Darlington Times.*

Dialect of South Lancafhire, or TIM BOBBIN's Tummus and Meary; revifed and corrected, with his Rhymes, and an enlarged Gloffary of Words and Phrafes, chiefly ufed by the Rural Population of the Manufacturing Diftricts of South Lancafhire. By SAMUEL BAMFORD. 12mo. *fecond edition, cloth,* 3s. 6d. 1854

Leicefterfhire Words, Phrafes, and Proverbs. By A. B. EVANS, D.D., *Head Mafter of Market-Bofworth Grammar School.* 12mo. *cloth,* 5s. 1848

A Gloffary of Northamptonfhire Words and Phrafes; with examples of their colloquial ufe, with illuftrations from various Authors; to which are added, the Cuftoms of the County. By Mifs A. E. BAKER. 2 vols. poft 8vo. *cloth,* 16s. (original price £1. 4s.) 1854

"We are under great obligation to the lady, fifter to the local hiftorian of Northamptonfhire, who has occupied her time in producing this very capital Gloffary of Northamptonfhire provincialifms."—*Examiner.*

"The provincial dialects of England contain and preferve the elements and rudiments of our compound tongue. In Mifs Baker's admirable 'Northamptonfhire Gloffary,' we have rather a repertory of urbanities than vulgarities. But it is much more than a vocabulary; it preferves not only dialectical peculiarities, but bold and difappearing cuftoms; and there is hardly a page in it which does not throw light on fome obfcurity in our writers, or recal old habits and practices."—*Chriftian Remembrancer, Quarterly Review.*

A Gloffary of the Provincialifms of the County of Suffex. By W. DURRANT COOPER, F.S.A. Poft 8vo. *fecond edition, enlarged. cloth,* 5s. 1853

Weftmoreland and Cumberland.—Dialogues, Poems, Songs, and Ballads, by various Writers, in the Weftmoreland and Cumberland Dialects; now firft collected; to which is added, a copious Gloffary of Words peculiar to thofe Counties. Poft 8vo. (pp. 408), *cloth,* 9s. 1839

A Gloffary of Provincial Words and Phrafes in ufe in Wiltfhire, fhowing their Derivation in numerous inftances, from the Language of the Anglo-Saxons. By JOHN

Spring Tide; or, the Angler and his Friends. By J. Y. AKERMAN. 12mo. *plates, cloth,* 3s. 6d. 1851

Thefe Dialogues incidentally illuftrate the Dialect of the Weft of England.

The Yorkfhire Dialect, exemplified in various Dialogues, Tales, and Songs, applicable to the County; with a Gloffary. Poft 8vo. 1s. 1839

A Gloffary of Yorkfhire Words and Phrafes, collected in Whitby and its Neighbourhood; with examples of their colloquial ufe and allufions to local Cuftoms and Traditions. By an INHABITANT. 12mo. *cloth,* 3s. 6d. 1855

The Hallamfhire (*diftrict of Sheffield*) Gloffary. By the Rev. JOSEPH HUNTER, author of the Hiftory of "Hallamfhire," "South Yorkfhire," &c. Poft 8vo. *cloth,* 4s. (original price 1s.) 1829

Archæological Index to Remains of Antiquity of the Celtic, Romano-Britifh, and Anglo-Saxon Periods. By JOHN YONGE AKERMAN, Fellow and late Secretary of the Society of Antiquaries. 8vo. *illuftrated with numerous engravings, comprifing upwards of five hundred objects, cloth,* 15s. 1847

This work, though intended as an introduction and a guide to the ftudy of our early antiquities, will, it is hoped, alfo prove of fervice as a book of reference to the practifed Archæologift.

"One of the firft wants of an incipient Antiquary is the facility of comparifon; and here it is furnifhed him at one glance. The Plates, indeed, form the moft valuable part of the book, both by their number and the judicious felection of types and examples which they contain. It is a book which we can, on this account, fafely and warmly recommend to all who are interefted in the antiquities of their native land."—*Literary Gazette.*

Remains of Pagan Saxondom, principally from Tumuli in England, drawn from the originals. Defcribed and illuftrated by JOHN YONGE AKERMAN, F.S.A. One handfome volume, 4to. *illuftrated with 40 COLOURED PLATES, half-morocco, £3.* 1855

The plates are admirably executed by Mr. Bafire, and coloured under the direction of the Author. It is a work well worthy the notice of the Archæologift.

Veftiges of the Antiquities of Derbyfhire, and the Sepulchral Ufages of its Inhabitants, from the moft Remote Ages to the Reformation. By THOMAS BATEMAN, ESQ., of Youlgrave, Derbyfhire. In One handfome volume, 8vo. *with numerous woodcuts of*

Deſcriptive Catalogue of the Antiquities and Miſcellaneous Objeſts preſerved in the Muſeum of Thomas Bateman, Eſq., at Lomberdale Houſe, Youlgrave, Derbyſhire. 8vo. *plates and woodcuts, cloth, (very few printed)* 10s. 6d. 18 55

Reliquiæ Antiquæ Eboracenſis; or, Relics of Antiquity, relating to the County of York. By W. BOWMAN, of Leeds, aſſiſted by ſeveral eminent Antiquaries. 4to. 6 Parts (complete), *plates*, 15s. 1855

Reliquiæ Iſurianae ; the Remains of the Roman Iſurium, now Aldborough, near Boroughbridge, Yorkſhire, illuſtrated and deſcribed. By HENRY ECROYD SMITH. Royal 4to. with 37 *plates, cloth,* £1. 5s. 1852
The moſt highly Illuſtrated work ever publiſhed on a Roman ſtation in England.

Eboracum ; or, York under the Romans. By the Rev. C. WELLBELOVED, *of York.* Royal 8vo. *with* 19 *plates, cloth,* 6s. (original price 12s.) 1842

Roman Sepulchral Inſcriptions ; their Relation to Archæology, Language, and Religion. By the Rev. JOHN KENRICK, M.A., F.R.S. Poſt 8vo. *cloth,* 3s. 6d. 1858

Deſcription of a Roman Building, and other Remains, diſcovered at Caerleon, in Monmouthſhire. By J. E. LEE. Imperial 8vo. *cloth,* with 20 *intereſting etchings by the Author, ſewed,* 5s. 1850

Selections from an Antiquarian Sketch Book. By JOHN EDWARD LEE, *of Caerleon.* Imperial 8vo. *ſewed,* 2s. 6d. 1859
Compriſing 15 litographed from the Author's drawings of objeſts in Switzerland, Scotland, Ireland, Yorkſhire, Hereford, ſhire, and Monmouthſhire, with ſhort deſcriptions.

Ulſter Journal of Archæology ; conduſted under the ſuperintendence of a Committee of Archæologiſts at Belfaſt. Handſomely printed, in 4to. *with engravings.* Publiſhed Quarterly. Annual Subſcription, 12s. Nos. 1 to 28 *are ready.*

Deſcriptive Catalogue of the Collection of Antiquities and other Objeſts illuſtrative of Iriſh Hiſtory, exhibited in the Belfaſt Muſeum, at the Meeting of the Britiſh Aſſociation, Sept. 1852, with Antiquarian Notes. 8vo. *ſewed,* 2s. 6d. 1853

Archaeologia Cambrenſis.—A Record of the Antiquities, Hiſtorical, Genealogical, Topographical, and Architectural, of Wales and its Marches. Firſt Series, *complete,* 4 vols. 8vo. *many plates and woodcuts, cloth,* £2. 2s. 1846-49
Odd Parts may be had to complete Sets.

—— Second Series, 6 vols. 8vo. *cloth,* £3. 3s.

—— Third Series. Vol. I. *cloth,* £1. 10s ; Vol. II. ; Vol. III. - ; Vol. IV. £1. 10s. ; Vol. V. £1. 10s.
Publiſhed by the Cambrian Archæological Aſſociation.

The Cambrian Journal, illuſtrative of the Hiſtory, Topography, and Literature of Wales. 8vo. Vol. I. 12s. ; Vols. II., III., IV., V., and VI. 10s. *each. cloth* 1854-61
Publiſhed under the auſpices of the Cambrian Inſtitute.

Suggeſtions on the Ancient Britons, in 3 Parts. By G. D. BARBER, M.A. (commonly called G. D. Barber Beaumont) Thick 8vo. *cloth,* 14s. 18s.

A Manual for the Study of the Sepulchral Slabs and Croſſes of the Middle Ages. By the Rev. E. L. CUTTS. 8vo. 300 *fine woodcuts, cloth,* 6s. (original price 12s.) 1849

Notices of Sepulchral Monuments in Engliſh Churches from the Norman Conqueſt to the Nineteenth Century. By the Rev. W. HASTINGS KELKE. 8vo. *many woodcuts,* 2s. (original price 3s. 6d.) 1850

Cyclops Chriſtianus ; or, an Argument to diſprove the ſuppoſed Antiquity of the Stonehenge and other Megalithic Erections in England and Brittany. By the Hon. ALGERNON HERBERT. 8vo. *cloth,* 4s. (original price 6s.) 1849

Introduction to the Study of Ancient and Modern Coins. By J. Y. AKERMAN, F.S.A. Foolscap 8vo. *with numerous wood engravings from the original Coins (an excellent introductory book), cloth,* 6s. 6d. 1848
Contents :—SECT. 1.—Origin of Coinage.—Greek Regal Coins.— 2. Greek Civic Coins.—3. Greek Imperial Coins.—4. Origin of Roman Coinage.—Conſular Coins.—5. Roman Imperial Coins.—6. Roman Britiſh Coins.—7. Ancient Britiſh Coinage.— 8. Anglo-Saxon Coinage.—9. Engliſh Coinage from the Conqueſt.

Eſſays, Philological, Philoſophical, Ethnological, and Archæological, connected with the Prehiſtorical Records of the Civiliſed Nations of Ancient Europe, eſpecially of that Race which firſt occupied Great Britain. By JOHN WILLIAMS, A.M., OXON, Archdeacon of Cardigan. Thick 8vo. with 7 *plates, cloth,* 16s. 28s

Tradeſman's Tokens ſtruck in London and its Vicinity, from 1648 to 1672, deſcribed from the originals in the Britiſh Muſeum, &c. By J. Y. AKERMAN, F.S.A. 8vo. *with 8 plates of numerous examples, cloth,* 29s.—LARGE PAPER in 4to. *cloth,* £2. 12. 1849

This work comprises a liſt of nearly 3000 Tokens, and contains ornamental illuſtrative, topographical, and antiquarian notes on perſons, places, ſtreets, old tavern and coffee-houſes ſigns, &c. &c. &c., with an introductory account of the coins which led to the adoption of ſuch a currency.

Tokens iſſued in the Seventeenth Century in England, Wales, and Ireland, by Corporations, Merchants, Tradeſmen, &c. Deſcribed and illuſtrated by WILLIAM BOYNE, F.S.A. Thick 8vo. 42 *plates, cloth,* £2. 2s. —LARGE PAPER, in 4to. *cloth,* £3. 3. 1858

Nearly 9500 Tokens are deſcribed in this work, arranged alphabetically under Counties and Towns. To the Numiſmatiſt, the Topographer, and Genealogiſt, it will be found extremely uſeful.

Ancient Coins of Cities and Princes, Geographically Arranged and Deſcribed— Hiſpania, Gallia, Britannia. By J. Y. AKERMAN, F.S.A. 8vo. *with engravings of many hundred Coins from actual examples.* Cloth, 8s. 6d. (original price 18s.) 1846

Coins of the Romans relating to Britain. Deſcribed and Illuſtrated by J. Y. AKERMAN, F.S.A. *Second Edition,* greatly enlarged, 8vo. *with plates and woodcuts, cloth,* 10s. 6d. 1844

The "Prix de Numiſmatique" was awarded by the French Inſtitute to the author for this work.

Mr. Akerman's volume contains a notice of every known variety, with copious Illuſtrations, and is publiſhed at a very moderate price; it ſhould be conſulted, not merely for their particular coins, but alſo for facts moſt valuable to all who are intereſted in Romano-Britiſh Hiſtory."—*Archæol. Journal.*

Numiſmatic Illuſtrations of the Narrative Portions of the New Teſtament. By J. Y. AKERMAN. 8vo. *numerous woodcuts from the original Coins in various public and private Collections, cloth,* 5s. 1846

And in him (Mr. Akerman) more eſpecially, the caſe of religion can bring in ſupport of commendation for light thrown upon this...

Numiſmatic Chronicle and Journal of the Numiſmatic Society. Edited by J. Y. AKERMAN. Nos. 1 to 79. Publiſhed Quarterly, at 3s. 6d. *per Number.*

This is the only repertory of Numiſmatic Intelligence ever publiſhed in England. It contains papers on coins and medals, of all ages and countries, by the firſt Numiſmatiſts of the day, both Engliſh and Foreign.

Odd parts to complete ſets.

Liſt of Tokens iſſued by Wiltſhire Tradeſmen in the Seventeenth Century. By J. Y. AKERMAN. 8vo. *plates, ſewed,* 2s. 6d. 1846

Lectures on the Coinage of the Greeks and Romans, delivered in the Univerſity of Oxford. By EDWARD CARDWELL, D.D., Principal of St. Alban's Hall, and Profeſſor of Ancient Hiſtory. 8vo. *cloth,* 4s. (original price 8s. 6d.) 1832

A very intereſting hiſtorical volume, and written in a pleaſing and popular manner.

Hiſtory of the Coins of Cunobeline, and of the Ancient Britons. By the Rev. BEALE POSTE. 8vo. *with numerous plates and woodcuts, cloth (only 40 printed),* £1. 8s. 1854

Celtic Inſcriptions on Gauliſh and Britiſh Coins, intended to ſupply materials for the Early Hiſtory of Great Britain. By the Rev. BEALE POSTE. 8vo. *with plates and woodcuts,* 1860

Numiſmatic Atlas of the Roman Empire, exhibiting on one large ſheet a complete Series of the Heads of the Emperors, Empreſſes, Tyrants, Kings, &c., A.C. 44 to A.D. 476, copied from ſpecimens of their actual coins, with a Table of their comparative rarity. By W. WHELAN. *Mounted on cloth, folded in a caſe, and lettered,* 3s. 6d. 1860

To the collectors of Roman Coins this Chart will prove a great intereſt and value, as it gives, at one view, moſt authentic repreſentations of 216 Coins, from Cæſar to Romulus Auguſtus, and to the ſtudent of Roman hiſtory, a valuable vade-mecum in all his memory.

Cambridge.—Hiſtoria Collegii Jeſu Cantabrigienſis, à J. Shermanno, olim præs. ejuſdem Colegii. Edita J. O. HALLIWELL. 8vo. *cloth,* 2s. 1840

Some Account of the Ancient Borough Town of Plympton, Devon. With Memoirs of the Reynolds Family. By WILLIAM COTTON. Fcap. 8vo. *folding plan of Plympton Caftle, and Photograph Portrait of Sir Joshua Reynolds, cloth, 5s.* 1859

Journey to Berefford Hall, in Derbyfhire, the Seat of Charles Cotton, Efq., the celebrated Author and Angler. By W. ALEXANDER, F.S.A., F L.S., late Keeper of the Prints in the British Mufeum. Crown 4to. *printed on tinted paper, with a fpirited frontifpiece, reprefenting Walton and his adopted Son, Cotton, in the Fifhing-houfe, and vignette title-page. Cloth, 5s.* 1841

Dedicated to the Anglers of Great Britain and the various Walton and Cotton Clubs. Only 100 printed.

A Brief Account of the Deftructive Fire at Blandford Forum, in Dorfetfhire, June 4, 1731. By MALACHI BLAKE, *reprinted from the edition of 1735, with a plan and two views.* 4to. *cloth, 2s. 6d.* 1860

Helps to Hereford Hiftory, Civil and Legendary, in an Ancient Account of the Ancient-Cordwainers' Company of the City, the Mordiford Dragon, and other Subjects. By J. D. DEVLIN. 12mo. *(a curious volume), cloth, 3s. 6d.* 1848

"A feries of very clever papers."—*Spectator.*
"A little work full of Antiquarian information, profeffed in a pleafing and popular form."—*Nonconformift.*

Notes on the Churches in the Counties of Kent, Suffex, and Surrey, mentioned in Domefday Book, and thofe of more recent Date; with fome Account of the Sepulchral Memorials and other Antiquities. By the Rev. ARTHUR HUSSEY. Thick 8vo. *fine plates, cloth, 18s.* 1853

Kentifh Cuftoms.—Confuetudines Kanciæ. A Hiftory of Gavelkind, and other remarkable Cuftoms, in the County of Kent. By CHARLES SANDYS, Efq., F.S.A. *(Cantianus) illuftrated with facfimiles, a very handfome volume, cloth, 15s.* 1851

Hiftory and Antiquities of Richborough, Reculver, and Lymne, in Kent. By C. R. ROACH SMITH, Efq., F.S.A. Small 4to. *with many engravings on wood and copper, by F. W. Fairholt, cloth, £1. 1s.* 1850

"No antiquarian volume could difplay a trio of names more ruiteur, fucccfsful, and intelligent, on the fubject of Roman-Britifh remains, than the three here reprefented — Roach Smith, the

Critical Differtation on Profeffor Willis's "Architectural Hiftory of Canterbury Cathedral." By C. SANDYS, of Canterbury. 8vo. 2s. 6d. 1846

"Written in no quarrelfome or captious fpirit; the highest compliment is paid to Profeffor Willis where it is due. But the author has made out a clear cafe, in fome very important inftances, of incorrectnefs that have led the learned Profeffor into the conftruction of ferious errors throughout. It may be confidered as an indifputable companion to his volume, containing a great deal of extra information of a very curious kind."—*Athenæum.*

Hiftory of Romney Marfh, in Kent, from the time of the Romans to 1833; with a Differtation on the original Site of the Ancient Anderida. By W. HOLLOWAY, author of the "Hiftory of Rye." 8vo. *with maps and Notes, cloth, 12s.* 1849

Hiftory and Antiquities of the Town of Lancafter. Compiled from Authentic Sources. By the Rev. ROBERT SIMPSON. 8vo. *cloth, 8s.* 1852

A Defcription of Blackpool, in Lancafhire. By W. HUTTON, *of Derby.* 8vo. *Third Edition, 1s. 6d.* 1817

A Defcriptive Account of Liverpool, as it was during the laft Quarter of the Eighteenth Century, 1775—1800. By RICHARD BROOKE, F.S.A. A handfome volume. Royal 8vo. *with illuftrations, cloth, 12s. 6d.* (original price £1. 5s.) 1853

In addition to information relative to the Public Buildings, Societies and Commerce of the Town, the work contains fome curious and interefting particulars, which have never been previoufly publifhed, refpecting the purfuits, habits, and amufements of the inhabitants of Liverpool during that period, with views of its public edifices.

Hand-Book of Leicefter. By JAMES THOMPSON. 12mo. *Second Edition, woodcuts, bds., 2s.* 1846

Hiftory and Antiquities of Bofton and the Villages of Skirbeck, Fifhtoft, Friefton, Butterwick, Benington, Leverton, Leake, and Wrangle. By PISHEY THOMPSON. Royal 8vo. pp. 900, *illuftrated with 100 engravings, cloth, £1. 11s. 6d.*—Folio, LARGE PAPER, cloth, £3. 3s. 1856

Hiftory of the Difhopric of Lincoln, from its origin to and endowment at Sidnacefter until the removal of the Seat of the See to Lincoln. Thick 8vo. *(very few printed) cloth, 12s.* (original price £1. 1s.) 1855

Hiftory and Antiquities of the Parifh of Hackney, Middlefex. By WILLIAM ROBINSON, LL.D. 2 vols. in 1. 8vo. *maps Yates,*

Memorials of the Hamlet of Knightsbridge, with Notices of its Immediate Neighbourhood. By H. G. DAVIS, post 8vo. *plates, cloth, 5s.* 1859

London in the Olden Time; being a Topographical and Historical Memoir of London, Westminster, and Southwark; accompanying a Pictorial Map of the City and Suburbs, as they existed in the reign of Henry VIII., before the Dissolution of the Monasteries; compiled from Authentic Documents. By WILLIAM NEWTON, Author of a Display of Heraldry. Folio, *with the coloured map, 4 feet 6 inches by 3 feet 3 inches, mounted on linen and folded into the volume, leather back, cloth sides, £1. 1s.* (original price £1. 11s. 6d.) 1855

The Cries of London, exhibiting several of the Itinerant Traders of antient and modern times, copied from rare engravings or drawn from the Life. By JOHN THOMAS SMITH, with Memoir and Portrait of the Author. 4to. *plates, bds.*, 10s. 6d. (original price £1. 11s. 6d.) 1839

History of the Royal Foundation of Christ's Hospital, Plan of Education, Internal Economy of the Institution, and Memoirs of Eminent Blues. By the Rev. W. TROLLOPE, 4to. *plates, cloth,* 1s. 6d. (original price £3. 3s.) 1834

Analysis of Domesday Book for the County of Norfolk. By the Rev. GEORGE MUNFORD, *Vicar of East Winch.* In 1 vol. 8vo. *with pedigrees and arms, cloth,* 10s. 6d. 1857

"Many extracts have been made, at various times, for the illustration of local descriptions, from the great national (but almost unintelligible) record known as Domesday Book; but Mr. Munford has done more to the cause of his own county, for he supplies a complete epitome of that part of the survey relating to Norfolk, giving not only the topographical and statistical facts, but also a great deal that is instructive as to the manners and condition of the people, the state of the churches and other public edifices, the mode of cultivation and land tenure, together with a variety of points of interest to the archaeologist and antiquary."—*Bury Post.*

Gleanings among the Castles and Convents of Norfolk. By HENRY HARROD, F.S.A. 8vo. *many plates and woodcuts, cloth,* 17s. 6d.—LARGE PAPER, £1. 3s. 6d. 1857

"This volume is creditable to Mr. Harrod in every way, alike to his industry, his taste, and his judgment. It is the result of an

River Tyne.—Plea and Defence of the Mayor and Burgesses of Newcastle against the Malevolent accusations of Gardiner, (author of "England's Grievance on the Coal Trade,") 1653; with Appendix of Unpublished Documents respecting the River Tyne. By M. A. RICHARDSON. 8vo. *(only 150 printed),* 2s. 1849

History of the Parish and Town of Bampton, in Oxfordshire, with the District and Hamlets belonging to it. By the Rev. Dr. GILES. 8vo. *plates, Second Edition, cloth,* 7s. 6d. 1848

A Parochial History of Enstone, in the County of Oxford. By the Rev. JOHN JORDAN, Vicar. Post 8vo. *a closely printed volume of nearly 500 pages, cloth,* 7s. 1856

Roman Remains discovered in the Parishes of North Leigh and Stonesfield, Oxfordshire. By HENRY HAKEWILL. 8vo. *map and 2 plates,* 2s. 1836

Topographical Memorandums for the County of Oxford. By Sir GREGORY PAGE TURNER, Bart. 8vo. *bds.,* 2s. 1820

Survey of Staffordshire, containing the Antiquities of that County. By SAMPSON ERDESWICK, with additions and corrections by Wyrley, Chetwynd, and others. Edited by HARWOOD. Thick 8vo. *plates, bds.,* 13s. 6d. (original price £1. 5s.) 1844

The History and Antiquities of Lambeth. By JOHN TANSWELL, Esq., of the Inner Temple. 8vo. *with numerous illustrations, cloth,* 4s. 6d. (original price 7s. 6d.) 1858

History of Winchelsea, in Sussex. By W. DURRANT COOPER, F.S.A. 8vo. *fine plates and woodcuts,* 7s. 6d. 1850

Chronicle of Battel Abbey, in Sussex; originally compiled in Latin by a Monk of the Establishment, and now first translated, with Notes, and an Abstract of the Subsequent History of the Abbey. By MARK ANTONY LOWER, M.A. 8vo. *with illustrations, cloth,* 9s. 1851

This volume conveys other matters of local and general interest, unknown—New Facts relative to the Norman invasion; The Foundation of the Monastery; The Names and Rentals of the Original Townsmen of Battel; Memoirs of several Abbots, and Notices of their Disputes with the Bishops of Chichester respecting Jurisdiction; The Abbey's Possessions; A Search of Thomas à Becket.

History and Antiquities of the Ancient Port and Town of Rye, in Suffex; compiled from the Original Documents. By WILLIAM HOLLOWAY. Thick 8vo. (*only* 200 *printed*) *cloth, £1. 1s.* 1847

Defcriptive Catalogue of the Original Charters, Grants, Donations, &c., conftituting the Muniments of Battel Abbey, alfo the Papers of the Montagus, Sidneys, and Webfters, embodying many highly interefting and valuable Records of lands in Suffex, Kent, and Effex, with Preliminary Memoranda of the Abbey of Battel, and Hiftorical Particulars of the Abbots. 8vo. 234 *pages, cloth, 11s. 6d.* 1835

Hand-Book to Lewes, in Suffex, Hiftorical and Defcriptive; with Notices of the Recent Difcoveries at the Priory. By MARK ANTONY LOWER. 12mo. *many engravings,* 1s. 1846

Suffex Martyrs: their Examinations and Cruel Burnings in the time of Queen Mary; comprifing the interefting Perfonal Narrative of Richard Woodman, extracted from "Foxe's Monuments." With Notes by M. A. LOWER, M.A. 12mo. *fewed,* 1s. 1852

Memorials of the town of Seaford, Suffex. By M. A. LOWER. 8vo. *plates,* 3s. 6d. 1855

Haftings, Paft and Prefent, with Notices of the moft Remarkable Places in the Neighbourhood, with an Appendix on Natural Hiftory. 12mo. *two maps, cloth,* 3s. 6d. 1855
A very fuperior Guide Book.

Hiftorical Notices of the Parifh of Withyham, in Suffex, and of the Family of Sackville. By the Hon. and Rev. R. W. SACKVILLE WEST. 4to. *arms, views, tombs, &c., cloth, £1. 1s.* 1857

History and Antiquities of the Town of Marlborough, and more generally of the entire Hundred of Selkley in Wiltfhire. By JAMES WAYLEN, Efq. Thick 8vo. *woodcuts, cloth,* 14s. 1854
This volume defcribes a portion of Wilts not included by Sir R. C. Hoare and other topographers.

Hermes Britannicus, a Differtation on the Celtic Deity Teutates, the Mercurius of Cæfar, in further proof and corroboration of the origin and defignation of the Great Temple at Abury, in Wiltfhire. By the Rev.

History of the Parifh of Broughton Gifford, in Wiltfhire. By J. WILKINSON, M.A., Rector. 8vo. *pedigrees and arms,* 3s. 6d. 1859

Natural History of Wiltfhire, as comprehended within Ten Miles round Salifbury. By W. G. MATON, M.D. 8vo. PRIVATELY PRINTED, 2s. 1843

The Ancient British, Roman, and Saxon Antiquities and Folk-Lore of Worcefterfhire. By JABEZ ALLIES, F.S.A. 8vo. pp. 500, *with 6 plates and 40 woodcuts, Second Edition, cloth,* 7s. 6d. (original price 14s.) 1852

"The good people of Worcefterfhire are indebted to Mr. Jabez Allies for a very handfome volume illuftrative of the hiftory of their native county. His book, which treats On the Ancient Britifh, Roman, and Saxon Antiquities and Folk-lore of Worcefterfhire, has now reached a fecond edition; and as Mr. Allies has embodied in this, not only the additions made by him to the original work, but alfo feveral feparate publications on points of folk-lore and legendary intereft, few counties can boaft of a more induftrioufly or carefully compiled hiftory of what may be called its popular antiquities. The work is very handfomely illuftrated."—*Notes and Queries.*

Hiftorical Account of the Ciftercian Abbey of Salley, in Craven, Yorkfhire, its Foundation and Benefactors, Abbots, Poffeffions, Compotus, and Diffolution, and its exifting Remains. Edited by J. HARLAND. Royal 8vo. 12 *plates, cloth,* 4s. 6d. 1854

The History and Antiquities of the Diftrict of Cleveland, comprifing the Wapentake of Eaft and Weft Langbargh, North Riding, Yorkfhire. By JOHN WALKER ORD, F.G.S.L. A handfome 4to. volume, *with plates,* 42 *woodcuts, and* 43 *pedigrees, cloth,* £1. 11s. (original price, £2. 11s.) 1846
*** Copies whole bound, calf extra, marbled leaves, £1. 10s.

Hiftorical and Topographical Account of Wenfleydale, and the Valley of the Yore, in the North Riding of Yorkfhire. By W. JONES BARKER. 8vo. *illuftrated with Views, Seals, Arms, &c., cloth,* 4s. 6d. (original price, 8s. 6d.) 1854

"This modeft and unpretending compilation is a pleafant addition to our topographical literature, and gives a good general account of a beautiful part of England comparatively little known. It is handfomely printed with a number of finely executed woodcuts by Mr. Howard Dudley. . . . No guide to the diftrict exifts applicable alike to the well-filled and fcantily furnifhed purfe—a defect which the author has endeavoured to fupply by the prefent volume."

The Early Ecclefiaftical History of Dewfbury. By Rev. J. B. GREENWOOD, with Dr. WHITAKER'S History of the Parifh; reprinted, with Notes, and an

Extracts from the Municipal Records of the City of York, during the Reigns of Edward IV., Edward V., and Richard III., with Notes, illustrative and explanatory, and an Appendix, containing some Account of the Celebration of the Corpus Chrifti Festival at York, in the Fifteenth and Sixteenth Centuries. By ROBERT DAVIES, *Town Clerk.* 8vo. *new, cloth*, 4s. (original price, 10s. 6d.) 1843

The History of Dumbartonshire, with Genealogical Notices of the principal Families in the County; the whole based on authentic Records, Public and Private. By JOSEPH IRVING. Thick 4to. (pp. 636), *maps, plates, and portraits, cloth,* £4. 1860

The Popular Rhymes, Sayings, and Proverbs of Berwickshire, with Illustrative Notes. By GEO. HENDERSON. 12mo. *cloth*, 3s. 1856

History of the City of Dublin. By J. T. GILBERT. Vols. I., II., and III. (vol. IV., *completing the work, in the press*), 8vo. *cloth*, 10s. 6d. each. 1854

"From the unpublished Anglo-Irish legiſlative enactments, and from hitherto ... [small print paragraph, illegible] ... *Dublin University Magazine.*"

The History and Antiquities of St. David's, in Pembrokeshire. By W. BASIL JONES and EDW. AUGUSTUS FREEMAN. 4to. *many fine plates by Le Keux, and woodcuts (a handsome volume), cloth,* £2. 1856

Description and History of the Castles of

The History of Radnorshire. By the REV. JONATHAN WILLIAMS. 8vo. *with illustrations, bds.*, 12s. 6d. 1859

Visits to Fields of Battle in England, of the 15th. Century; with some miscellaneous Tracts and Papers, principally upon Archæological Subjects. By RICHARD BROOKE, F.S.A. Royal 8vo. *plates, cloth*, 15s. 1857
[small print descriptive paragraph, illegible]

Family Topographer, being a compendious Account of the Ancient and Present State of the Counties of England. By SAMUEL TYMMS. 7 vols. 12mo. *cloth*, 6s. 6d. (pub. at £1. 15s.) 1832-4
[small print paragraph, illegible]

The Tourist's Grammar, or rules relating to the Scenery and Antiquities incident to Travellers, including an Epitome of Gilpin's Principles of the Picturesque. By the REV. T. DUDLEY FOSBROKE. Post 8vo. *bds.*, 2s. (original price 7s.) 1826

Annals and Legends of Calais; with Sketches of Emigré Notabilities, and Memoir of Lady Hamilton. By ROBERT BELL CALTON, author of "Rambles in Sweden and Gottland," &c., &c. Post 8vo. *with frontispiece and vignette, cloth*, 5s. 1852
[small print paragraph, illegible]

Patronymica Britannica, a Dictionary of Family Names. By MARK ANTONY LOWER, M.A., F.S.A. Royal 8vo. pp. 500, *with illuſtrations, cloth, £1. 5s.* 1860

This work is the reſult of a ſtudy of Britiſh Family Names, extending over more than twenty years. The favourable reception which the Author's "Engliſh Surnames" obtained in the ſale of Three Editions, and the many hundreds of communications to which that work gave riſe, have convinced him that the ſubject is one in which conſiderable intereſt is felt. He has therefore been induced to devour a large amount of attention to the origin, meaning, and hiſtory of our family deſignations—a ſubject which, when inveſtigated in the light of ancient records and of modern philology, proves highly illuſtrative of many habits and cuſtoms of our anceſtors, and forms a very curious branch of Archæology.

The preſent work is by no means intended to ſuperſede the "Engliſh Surnames." That publication bears the ſame relation to the PATRONYMICA as the grammar of a language does to its dictionary. There the principles upon which ſurnames were aſſumed are diſcuſſed, and a conſiderable number of them are claſſified, but here many thouſands of family names are treated individually and alphabetically.

Engliſh Surnames. An Eſſay on Family Nomenclature, Hiſtorical, Etymological, and Humorous. With ſeveral illuſtrative Appendices. By MARK ANTONY LOWER, M.A. 2 vols. poſt 8vo. THIRD EDITION, ENLARGED, *woodcuts, cloth, 12s.* 1849

This new and much improved Edition, beſides a great enlargement of the Chapters, contained in the previous editions, comprises ſeveral that are entirely new, together with Notes on Scottiſh, Iriſh, and Norman ſurnames. The "Additional Prolection," beſides the articles on Rebuſes, Alluſive Arms, and the Roll of Battel Abbey, contain diſſertations on Inn Signs, and Remarks on Chriſtian Names, with a copious Inder of many thouſand Names. Theſe features render "Engliſh Surnames" rather a new work than a new edition.

Pedigrees of the Nobility and Gentry of Hertfordſhire. By WILLIAM BERRY, late, and for fifteen years, Regiſtering Clerk in the College of Arms, author of the "Encyclopædia Heraldica," &c., &c. Folio (only 125 printed). *Bds., £1. 5s. (original price £3. 10s.)* 1844

Pedigrees and Arms of Devonſhire Families, as recorded in the Herald's Viſitation of 1620, with additions from the Harleian MSS. and the Printed Collections of Weſtcote and Pole. By JOHN TUCKETT. 4to. Parts I. to VI., each 5s. 1859-60

Archer Family.—Memorials of Families of the Surname of Archer in various Counties in England, and in Scotland, Ireland, Barbados, America, &c. 4to. *but few copies printed, cloth, 11s. 6d.* 1860

Scrafe Family.—Genealogical Memoir

Druce Family.—A Genealogical Account of the Family of Druce, of Goring, in the County of Oxford, 1735. 4to. only 50 copies PRIVATELY PRINTED, *bds, 7s. 6d.* 1853

Hiſtories of Noble Britiſh Families, with their Genealogies, and Biographical Notices of the moſt diſtinguiſhed Individuals in each. By HENRY DRUMMOND, M.P., Illuſtrated with Portraits, Views, Armorial Bearings, Monuments, Seals, &c. (THE ARMS, SEALS, AND PORTRAITS MOST BEAUTIFULLY COLOURED, MANY LIKE MINIATURES). 2 vols. imperial folio, *half-bound in morocco, top edges gilt, by Hayday, £8. 8s.* 1842, &c.

—— The ſame, in Parts. *£6.* 1842, &c

The families are thoſe of Aſhburnham, Arden, Compton, Cavil, Harley, Bruce, Perceval, Dunbar, Hume, Dundas, Drummond, and Neville. No genealogical book has ever been, up to the preſent time, ſo ſumptuouſly got up in England. Publiſhed by the late Mr. Pickering at Twenty-four Guineas.

Genealogical and Heraldic Hiſtory of the Extinct and Dormant Baronetcies of England, Ireland, and Scotland. By J. BURKE, Eſq. Medium 8vo. SECOND EDITION, 638 *cloſely printed pages, in double columns, with about 1,000 arms engraved on wood, fine portrait of JAMES I., cloth, 10s. (original price £1. 8s.)* 1844

This work engaged the attention of the author for ſeveral years, comprises nearly a thouſand families, many of them among the moſt ancient and eminent in the kingdom, each revived down to its repreſentatives or repreſentatives ſtill exiſting, with elaborate and minute details of the alliances, achievements, and fortunes, generation after generation, from the earlieſt to the lateſt period.

The Blazon of Epiſcopacy. Being a complete Liſt of the Archbiſhops and Biſhops of England and Wales, and their Family Arms drawn and deſcribed, from the firſt Introduction of Heraldry to the preſent time. By the Rev. W. K. RILAND BEDFORD. 8vo. pp. 144, and 62 *pages of drawings of Arms, cloth, 15s.* 1858

This work depicts the arms of a great number of Engliſh Families not to be found in other works.

* There has been an account of induſtry beſtowed upon this curious work which is very creditable to the author, and will be found beneficial to all who care for the ſubject on which it has been employed."—*Athenæum.*

A Plea for the Antiquity of Heraldry, with an Attempt to Expound its Theory and Elucidate its Hiſtory. By W. SMITH ELLIS.

A Manual for the Genealogiſt, Topographer, Antiquary, and Legal Profeſſor, conſiſting of Deſcriptions of Public Records; Parochial and other Regiſters; Wills; County and Family Hiſtories; Heraldic Collections in Public Libraries, &c., &c. By RICHARD SIMS, *of the Britiſh Muſeum, Compiler of the "Index to the Heralds' Viſitations," the "Hand-book to the Library of the Britiſh Muſeum,"* &c. 8vo. SECOND EDITION, pp. 540, *cloth,* 15s. 1861

This work will be found indiſpenſable by thoſe engaged in the ſtudy of Family Hiſtory and Heraldry, and by the compiler of County and Local Hiſtory, the Antiquary and the Lawyer. In it the Public and other Records moſt likely to afford information to genealogical inquirers are fully deſcribed, and their places of print depoſit indicated. Such Records are—The Domeſday Books—Monaſtic Records—Cartæ Antiquæ—Liber Niger—Liber Rubeus Teſta de Nevil—Placita in variam Curia—Charter Rolls—Cloſe Rolls—Coronation Rolls—Coroners' Rolls—Eſcheat Rolls—Fine Rolls—French, Gaſcon, and Norman Rolls—Hundred Rolls—Liberate Rolls—Memorials Rolls—Obituary and other Rolls—Inquiſitions Poſt Mortem—Inquiſitions ad quod Damnum—Fines and Recoveries—Lay Manors and Signet Bills—Privy Seals—Forfeitures, Pardons, and Attainders—Patent, Muſter Records—County Palatine Records—Scotch, Iriſh, and Welſh Records—alſo Wills—Parochial and other Regiſters —Regiſters of Univerſities and Public Schools—Heraldic Collections—Records of Clergymen, Lawyers, Surgeons, Soldiers, Sailors, &c., &c.

The whole accompanied by valuable Liſts of Printed Works and Manuſcripts in various Libraries, namely :—at the Britiſh Muſeum —The Bodleian, Aſhmolean, and other Libraries at Oxford— The Public Library and that of Caius College, Cambridge—The Colleges of Arms in London and Dublin—The Libraries of Lincoln's Inn, and of the Middle and Inner Temple—at Chetham College, Mancheſter; and in other repoſitories too numerous to mention.

The more important of theſe Liſts are thoſe of Monaſtic Cartularies —Extracts from Fines and other Rolls—Eſcheats—Inquiſitions, &c.—Tenures in Capite—Rentals—Subſidies—Crown Lands —Wills—Parochial and other Regiſters—Heralds' Viſitations— Royal and Noble Genealogies—Peerages, Baronetages, Knightage—Pedigrees of Gentry—County and Family Hiſtories— Monumental Inſcriptions—Coats of Arms—American Genealogies—Liſts of Gentry—Members of Parliament—Freeholders— Officers of State—Juſtices of Peace—Mayors, Sheriffs, &c.— Collegians, Church Dignitaries—Lawyers—The Medical Profeſſion—Soldiers—Sailors, &c.

To theſe is added an "Appendix," containing an Account of the Public Record Offices and Libraries mentioned in the work, the mode of obtaining admiſſions, hours of attendance, fees for ſearching, copying, &c., Table of the Regnal Years of Engliſh Sovereigns; Tables of Dates uſed in Ancient Records, &c.

Reign of Edward I. to Queen Anne; alſo, a *Gloſſary of Dormant Engliſh, Scotch, and Iriſh Peerage Titles, with reference to preſumed exiſting Heirs.* By Sir T. C. BANKS. 2 vols. 4to. *cloth,* 15s. (pub. at £1. 3s.) 1844

—— LARGE PAPER COPY (*very few printed*). 2 vols. £1. 1s. 1844

A book of great reſearch, by the well-known author of the "Dormant and Extinct Peerage," and other heraldic and hiſtorical works. Theſe kind of genealogical particulars ought to become a copy while it is ſo cheap. It may be conſidered a ſupplement to his former works. Vol. ii. pp. 510–100, contains an hiſtorical Account of the firſt Settlement of Nova Scotia, and the foundation of the Order of Nova Scotia Baronets, diſtinguiſhing thoſe who had ſeizin of lands there.

Calendar of Knights, containing Liſts of Knights, Bachelors, Britiſh Knights of the Garter, Thiſtle, Bath, St. Patrick, the Guelphic and Ionian Orders, from 1760 to 1828. By F. TOWNSEND, *Windſor Herald.* Poſt 8vo. *cloth,* 3s. (original price, 9s.) 1828

A very uſeful volume for Genealogical and Biographical purpoſes.

On the Nobility of the Britiſh Gentry, or the Political Ranks and Dignities of the Britiſh Empire compared with thoſe on the Continent. By Sir JAMES LAWRENCE. Poſt 8vo., 2s. 6d. 1825

Uſeful for Foreigners in Great Britain, and of Britons abroad, particularly of thoſe who deſire to be preſented at foreign courts, to accept foreign military ſervice, to be inveſted with foreign titles, to be admitted into foreign orders, to purchaſe foreign property, or to intermarry with foreigners.

A Diſplay of Heraldry. By WILLIAM NEWTON. 8vo. *many hundred engravings of Shields, illuſtrating the Arms of Engliſh Families,* cloth, 14s. 1846

Curioſities of Heraldry, with Illuſtrations from Old Engliſh Writers. By MARK ANTONY LOWER, M.A., Author of "Eſſays on Engliſh Surnames." *With illuminated Title-page, and numerous engravings from deſigns by the Author.* 8vo. *cloth,* 14s. 1845

"The preſent volume is truly a worthy ſequel (to the 'SURNAMES') in the ſame curious and antiquarian line, blending with remarkable taſte and intelligence, ſuch a fund of amuſing anecdote and illuſtration, that the reader is almoſt ſurpriſed to

Playing Cards.—Facts and Speculations on the History of Playing Cards in Europe. By W. A. CHATTO, author of the "History of Wood Engraving, with Illustrations by J. Jackson." 8vo. *profusely illustrated with engravings, both plain and coloured, cloth,* £1. 1s. 1848

The inquiry into the origin and signification of the suits and their marks, and the heraldic, theological, and political emblems pictured from time to time, in their changes, opens a new field of antiquarian interest ; and the perseverance with which Mr. Chatto has explored it, leaves little to be gained by his successors. The plans with which the volume is executed add considerably to its value in this point of view. It is not to be denied that, take it altogether, it contains more matter than has ever before been collected in one view upon the same subject. In spite of its faults, it is exceedingly amusing ; and the most critical reader cannot fail to be entertained by the variety of curious matter and learning which Mr. Chatto has somehow contrived to draw into the investigation."—Atlas.

"Indeed the entire production deserves our warmest approbation."—Literary Gazette.

"A perfect fund of antiquarian research, and most interesting even to persons who never play at cards."—Tait's Magazine.

"A curious, entertaining, and really learned book."—Rambler.

Holbein's Dance of Death. With an Historical and Literary Introduction, by an Antiquary. Square post 8vo. *with 53 engravings—being the most accurate copies ever executed of these Gems of Art—and a frontispiece of an ancient bedstead at Aix-la-Chapelle, with a Dance of Death carved on it, engraved by Fairholt,* cloth, 9s. 1849

"The designs are executed with a spirit and fidelity quite extraordinary. They are indeed on A truthful."—Athenæum.

"Ces 53 planches des Schletstuber font d'une exquise perfection."—Longfels, L'Sol'sor in Dances des Morts.

"Biblia Pauperum." One of the Earliest and most Curious BLOCK-BOOKS, reproduced in facsimile from a Copy in the British Museum. By J. PH. BERJEAU. Royal 4to. *half-bound,* £2. 2s. 1859

The Biblia Pauperum, known also by the title of Historia Veteris et Novi Testamenti, is a sort of woodcuts, in which the Old and New Testament are both brought to memory by pictures, and some lines of text in Latin. This name, Biblia Pauperum, is derived from its use by Monks of the poorer orders, commonly called Pauperes Christi.

As a specimen of the earliest woodcuts and of printed block-books, destined to supersede the manuscripts anterior to the valuable invention of Gütenberg, the Biblia Pauperum is well worthy the attention of the Amateur of Fine Arts as well as of the Bibliographer. It consists of forty engravings, printed on one side only of the leaves, and disposed so as to have the figures opposite each other . . .

. . . Heimevoters, and after him by Ottley—the Introduction gives, for the first time, the vols of the Text printed on both sides in the upper compartment, as well as an English Explanation of the Subject.

ONLY 250 COPIES HAVE BEEN PRINTED, UNIFORMLY WITH MR. S. LEIGH SOTHEBY'S "Principia Typographica."

The Bayeux Tapestry Elucidated. By the Rev. Dr. JOHN COLLINGWOOD BRUCE, Author of the "Roman Wall." 4to. *a handsome volume, illustrated with 17 COLOURED plates, representing the entire Tapestry, extra bds.,* £1. 1s. 1856

Memoirs of Painting, with a Chronological History of the Importation of Pictures by the Great Masters into England since the French Revolution. By W. BUCHANAN. 2 vols. 8vo. *bds.,* 7s. 6d. (original price £1. 6s.) 1824

Catalogue of the Prints which have been Engraved after Martin Heemskerck. By T. KERRICH, *Librarian to the University of Cambridge.* 8vo. *portrait, bds.,* 3s. 6d. 1822

Titian.—Notices of the Life and Works of Titian the Painter. By Sir ABRAHAM HUME. Royal 8vo. *portrait, cloth,* 6s. 1829

Sir Joshua Reynolds' Notes and Observations on Pictures, chiefly of the Venetian School, being Extracts from his Italian Sketch Books ; also the Rev. W. Mason's Observations on Sir Joshua's Method of Coloring, with some unpublished Letters of Dr. Johnson, Malone, and others ; with an Appendix, containing a Transcript of Sir Joshua's Account Book, showing the Paintings he executed, and the prices he was paid for them. Edited by WILLIAM COTTON, Esq. 8vo. *cloth,* 5s. 1859

"The Scraps of the Critical Journal, kept by Reynolds at Rome, Florence, and Venice, will be obtained by high-class stamps."—Leader.

Catalogue of the Portraits painted by Sir Joshua Reynolds, in whose possession they are, and whether engraved, &c. Compiled from his autograph memorandum books, printed catalogues, &c. By WILLIAM COTTON. 8vo. *sewed,* 3s. 1857

Ecclesiastical Architecture of the County of Essex, from the Norman Era to the Sixteenth Century, with Plans, Elevations, Sections, Details, &c., from a Series of Measured Drawings and Architectural and Chronological Descriptions. By JAMES HADFIELD,

Hiſtoire de l'Architecture Sacree du quatrième au dixième Gècle dans les anciens évêchés de Genève, Lauſanne, et Sion. Par J. D. BLAVIGNAC, Architecte. One vol. 8vo. (pp. 450), *and* 37 *Notes*, and a 4to. Atlas *of 82 plates of Architecture, Sculpture, Frescoes, Reliquaries, &c. &c., £2. 10s.* 1853

A very remarkable Book, and worth the notice of the Architect, the Archæologist, and the Artiſt.

Hiſtory of the Origin and Eſtabliſhment of Gothic Architecture, and an Inquiry into the mode of Painting upon and Staining Glaſs, as practiſed in the Eccleſiaſtical Structures of the Middle Ages. By J. S. HAWKINS, F.S.A. Royal 8vo. 21 *plates, bds.,* 4s. (original price 18s.) 1813

Handbook to the Library of the Britiſh Muſeum; containing a brief Hiſtory of its Formation, and of the various Collections of which it is compoſed; Deſcriptions of the Catalogues in preſent uſe; Claſſed Liſts of the Manuſcripts, &c.; and a variety of information indiſpenſable for Literary Men, with ſome Account of the principal Public Libraries in London. By RICHARD SIMS, *of the Department of Manuſcripts, Compiler of the Manual for the Genealogiſt, &c.* Small 8vo. (pp. 438), *with map and plans, cloth,* 5s. 1854

It will be found a very uſeful work to every literary perſon of public inſtitutions in all parts of the world.

* A little Handbook of the Library has been publiſhed, which I think will be moſt uſeful to the public."—*Lord Seymour's Reply to the Houſe of Commons, July,* 1854.

* I am much pleaſed with your book, and find it in abundance of information which I wanted."—*Letter from Albert Way, R/t., F.S.A., Editor of the "Proſpective Proverbiorum," &c.*

* I take this opportunity of telling you how much I like your nice little 'Handbook to the Library of the Britiſh Muſeum,' which I ſincerely hope may have the ſucceſs which it deſerves."—*Letter from Thos. Wright, Eſq., F.S.A., Author of the 'Biographia Britannica Literaria,' &c.*

* Mr. Sims's 'Handbook to the Library of the Britiſh Muſeum' is a very comprehenſive and inſtructive volume. . . . I venture to predict for it a wide circulation."—*Mr. Bolton Corney, in "Notes and Queries," No. 112.*

Catalogue (*Claſſified*) of the Library of

century, including alſo Notices of Latin Plays written by Engliſh Authors during the ſame period, with particulars of their Authors, Plots, Characters, &c. By JAMES ORCHARD HALLIWELL, Eſq., F.R.S. 8vo. cl, 12s. 1860

∗ Twenty-five copies have been printed on THICK PAPER, price £1. 1s.

Catalogue of a unique Collection of 400 Ancient Engliſh Broadſide Ballads, printed entirely in the black letter, lately on ſale by J. RUSSELL SMITH. With Notes of their Tunes, and Imprints. Poſt 8vo *a handſome volume, printed by Whittingham, in the old ſtyle, half-bound, 5s.* 1856

—— A copy on THICK PAPER, *without the prices to each, and a different title-page,* ONLY 10 COPIES SO PRINTED, 10s. 6d.

Bibliotheca Cantiana.—A Bibliographical Account of what has been publiſhed on the Hiſtory, Topography, Antiquities, Cuſtoms, and Family Genealogy of the County of Kent, with Biographical Notes. By JOHN RUSSELL SMITH. In a handſome 8vo. vol. (pp. 370) *with two plates of facſimiles of Autographs of 33 eminent Kentiſh Writers,* 5s. (original price 14s.) 1837

A Bibliographical Liſt of all the Works which have been publiſhed towards Illuſtrating the Provincial Dialects of England. By JOHN RUSSELL SMITH. Poſt 8vo., 2s. 1839

* Very ſerviceable to ſuch as proſecute the ſtudy of our provincial dialects, or are collecting works on that curious ſubject. . . . We very cordially recommend it to notice."—*Metropolitan.*

A Bibliographical Catalogue of Engliſh Writers on Angling and Ichthyology. By JOHN RUSSELL SMITH. Poſt 8vo., 2s. 6d. 1856

Bibliotheca Madrigaliana. — A Bibliographical Account of the Muſical and Poetical Works publiſhed in England during the Sixteenth and Seventeenth Centuries, under the

Some Account of the Popular Tracts, formerly in the Library of Captain Cox, of Coventry, A.D. 1575. By J. O. HALLIWELL. 8vo. (*only* 50 *printed*), *sewed*, 1s. 1849

Catalogue of the Contents of the Codex Holbrookianus (a Scientific MS., by Dr. John Holbrook, Master of St. Peter's College, Cambridge, 1418-1431). By J. O. HALLIWELL. 8vo., 1s. 1840

Account of the Vernon Manuscript. A Volume of Early English Poetry, preserved in the Bodleian Library. By J. O. HALLIWELL. 8vo. (*only* 50 *printed*), 1s. 1848

Shakespeariana, a Catalogue of the Early Editions of Shakespeare's Plays, and of the Commentaries and other Publications illustrative of his Works. By J. O. HALLIWELL. 8vo. *cloth*, 3s. 1841

"Indispensable to everybody who wishes to carry on any inquiries connected with Shakespeare, or who may have a fancy for Shakspearian Bibliography."—*Spectator.*

Catalogue of the Manuscripts in the Library of Gonville and Caius Coll., Cambridge. By Rev. J. J. SMITH, Fellow and Librarian. 8vo. *cloth*, 10s. 6d. 1849

Bibliographical Miscellany. Edited by JOHN PETHERAM. 8vo. Nos. 1 to 5 (*all published*), *with general title*, 1s. 1859

CONTENTS.—Particulars of the Voyage of Sir Thomas Button for the Discovery of a North-West Passage, A.D. 1612—Mr Dudley Digges' Of the Circumference of the Earth, or a Treatise of the North-East Passage, 1611-13—Letter of Sir Thomas Button on the North-West Passage, In the Inner-Paper Office—Bibliographical Notices of Old Music Books. By Dr. Rimbault—Notices of Suppressed Books—Martin Mar-Prelate's Rhymes—The Hardwicke Collection of Manuscripts.

"The Game of the Chesse," the First Book printed in England by WILLIAM CAXTON, reproduced in facsimile, from a Copy in the British Museum, with a few Remarks on Caxton's Typographical Productions, by VINCENT FIGGINS. 4to. pp. 184, *with* 23 *curious woodcuts, half-morocco, uncut*, £1. 1s. —*or, in antique calf, with bevelled boards, and carmine edges*, £1. 8s. 1859

Frequently as we read of the Works of Caxton and the early English Printers, and of their Black-Letter Books, very few persons ever had the opportunity of seeing any of these productions, and forming a proper estimate of the ingenuity and skill of those who first practised the "Noble Art of Printing."

THE TYPE HAS BEEN CAREFULLY IMITATED, AND THE WOODCUTS FACSIMILED BY MISS BYFIELD. The Paper and Water-marks have also been made expressly, as near as possible, like the original; and the Book is accompanied by a few remarks of a practical nature, which have been suggested during the progress of the work, and the necessary fonts and comparisons.

Historical Sketches of the Angling Literature of All Nations. By ROBERT BLAKEY. To which is added a Bibliography of English Writers on Angling. Fcap. 8vo. *cloth*, 5s. 1856

Bibliotheque Asiatique et Africane, ou Catalogue des Ouvrages relatifs à l'Asie et à l'Afrique qui ont paru jusqu'en 1700. Par H. TERNAUX-COMPANS. 8vo. *avec supplément et index, sewed*, 10s. 6d. 1841

The Writings of the Christians of the Second Century, namely, Athenagoras, Tatian, Theophilus, Hermias, Papias, Aristides, Quadratus, &c., collected and first translated complete, by the Rev. Dr. GILES. 8vo. *cloth*, 7s. 6d. 1857

Designed as a continuation of Abp. Wake's *Apostolical Epistles*, which are those of the first century.

Heathen Records to the Jewish Scripture History, containing all the Extracts from the Greek and Latin Writers in which the Jews and Christians are named, collected together and translated into English, with the original text in juxta-position. By the Rev. DR. GILES. 8vo. *cloth*, 7s. 6d. 1856

A Vindication of the Hymn "Te Deum Laudamus," from the Corruptions of a Thousand Years, with Ancient Versions in Anglo-Saxon, High-German, Norman-French, &c., and an English Paraphrase of the XVth Century; now first printed. By EBENEZER THOMSON. Fcap. 8vo. *cloth*, 3s. 1858

A book well worth the notice of the Ecclesiastical Antiquary and the Philologist.

Tonstall (Cuthbert, *Bishop of Durham*) Sermon preached on Palm Sunday, 1539, before Henry VIII; *reprinted verbatim from the rare edition by Berthelet, in* 1539. 12mo, 1s. 6d. 1823

An exceedingly interesting Sermon, at the commencement of the Reformation; Strype in his "Memorials," has made large extracts from it.

Common Prayer—Discourse of the Troubles begun at Frankfort, in the year 1554, about the Book of Common Prayer and Ceremonies, reprinted from the black letter edition of 1575, with an Introduction. Post 8vo. *cloth*, 2s. 6d. (original price 6s.) 1846

Sacred Music. By the Rev. W. SLOANE-EVANS, M.A. Roy. 8vo. *Third Edition, sewed*, 1s. 6d. (original price 6s.) 1847

MARTIN MAR-PRELATE CONTROVERSY.

An Epiſtle to the terrible Prieſts of the Convocation Houſe. By MARTIN MAR-PRELATE (1588), with Introduction and Notes, by J. PETHERAM. Poſt 8vo. 2s. 1842

Cooper (Bp. of Wincheſter) An Admonition to the People of England againſt Martin Mar-Prelate, 1589, with Introduction. Poſt 8vo. pp. 226, 3s. 6d. 1847

Pap with a Hatchet, being a Reply to Martin Mar-Prelate (1589), with Introduction and Notes. Poſt 8vo. 2s. 1844

Hay any Worke for Cooper? Being a Reply to the Admonition to the People of England by Martin Mar-Prelate, 1589, with Introduction and Notes. 8vo. 2s. 6d. 1845

An Almond for a Parrot; being a Reply to Martin Mar-Prelate, 1589, with Introduction. Poſt 8vo. 2s. 6d. 1846

Plaine Percevall the Peace-maker of England, being a Reply to Martin Mar-Prelate, with Introduction. Poſt 8vo. 2s. 1846

The Church of our Fathers, or St. Oſmund's Rite for the Church of Saliſbury, from a Manuſcript in the Library of that Cathedral. Printed for the firſt time, and elucidated with Diſſertations on the Belief and Ritual of the Church In England before and after the Coming of the Normans. By DANIEL ROCK, D.D. 4 vols. 8vo. illuſtrated with many engravings on wood and copper, cloth gilt, £4. 4s. 1849-53

Vols. 3 and 4 may be had to complete ſets, 2s. 24s. each.

Did the Early Church in Ireland acknowledge the Pope's Supremacy? anſwered in a Letter to Lord John Manners. By DANIEL ROCK, D.D. 8vo. bds., 2s. 6d. 1844

The Myſtic Crown of Mary, the Holy Maiden-Mother of God, born free from the ſtain of original ſin; in Verſe, with Notes. By DANIEL ROCK, D.D. Poſt 8vo. 2s. 6d. 1837

Calendar of Iriſh Saints; the Martyrology of Tallagh, with Notices of the Patron Saints of Ireland, and Hymns from an Ancient

Life of St. Laurence O'Toole, Archbiſhop of Dublin, 1132-1180; with copious Hiſtorical Notes. By the Rev. JOHN O'HANLON. 12mo, cloth, 1s. 6d. 1857

Prophecies of Saints Columbkille, Maeltamlacht, Ultan, Seadhna, Coireall, Bearcan, &c.; with the Iriſh Text, literal Tranſlations and Notes, by N. O'KEARNEY. 12mo. cloth, 3s. 1856

Saint Patrick's Purgatory; an Eſſay on the Legends of Hell, Purgatory, and Paradiſe, current during the middle Ages. By THOMAS WRIGHT, M.A., F.S.A. &c. Poſt 8vo. cloth, 6s. 1844

"It muſt be obſerved that this is not a mere account of St. Patrick's Purgatory, but a complete hiſtory of the legends and ſuperſtitions relating to the ſubject, from the earlieſt times, referred from old MSS. as well as from old printed books. Moreover, it embraces a ſingular chapter of literary hiſtory omitted by Warton and all former writers with whom we are acquainted; and we think we may add, that is forms the beſt introduction to Dante that has yet been publiſhed."—*Literary Gazette.*

"This appears to be a curious and even amuſing book on the ſingular ſubject of Purgatory, in which the idle and fanciful dreams of ſuperſtition are ſhown to be firſt narrated as tales, and then applied as means of deluding the moral character of the age in which they prevailed."—*Spectator.*

Miſcellanies. By JOHN AUBREY, F.R.S., the *Wiltſhire Antiquary.* FOURTH EDITION with ſome Additions and an Index. Fcap. 8vo. portrait and cuts, cloth, 4s. 1857

CONTENTS:—Day Fatality, Fatalities of Families and Places, Portents, Omens, Dreams, Apparitions, Voices, Impulſes, Knockings, Inviſible Blows, Prophecies, Miracles, Magic, Tranſportation by an Inviſible Power, Viſions in a Cryſtal, Converſe with Angels, Corpſe Candles, Oracles, Eccſtaſy, ſecond Sight, &c.; with an Appendix, containing his Introduction to the Survey of North Wiltſhire.

Remarkable Providences of the Earlier Days of American Coloniſation. By INCREASE MATHER, of Boſton, N.E. With Introductory Preface by George Offor. Fcp. 8vo. portrait, elegantly printed, cloth, 3s. 1856

A very ſingular collection of remarkable ſea deliverances, accidents, remarkable phenomenons, witchcraft, apparitions, &c. &c., connected with inhabitants of New England, &c. &c. A very amuſing volume, conveying a faithful portrait of the ſtate of ſociety, when the doctrine of a peculiar providence and perſonal interpoſition between this world and that which is unſeen was fully believed.

Hymns and Songs of the Church. By GEORGE WITHER. Edited, with Introduction, by EDWARD FARR. Alſo the Muſical Notes, compoſed by Orlando Gibbons. Fcp. 8vo. with portrait after Hole, 3s. 1856

Mr. Farr has added a very intereſting biographical introduction.

Hallelujah ; or, Britain's Second Re-
membrancer, in Praiſeful and Penitential
Hymns, Spiritual Songs, and Moral Odes.
By GEORGE WITHER. With Introduction
by EDWARD FARR. Fcap. 8vo. *portrait,*
cloth, 6s. 1857

Wither's this intereſting volume has only been known to the public
by extracts in various publications. So few copies of the original are known to exiſt, that the copy from which this reprint
has been taken coſt twenty-one guineas.

Poetical Works of ROBERT SOUTHWELL,
Canon of Loretto, now firſt completely edited
by W. B. Turnbull. Fcap. 8vo. *elegantly*
printed by Whittingham, cloth, 4s. 1856

His piety is ſimple and ſincere—a ſpirit of unaffected gentleneſs and
humilioris pervades his poems— and he is equally diſtinguiſhed by
weight of thought and freeneſs of expreſſion. — *Saturday*
Review.

Enchiridion, containing Inſtitutions—Di-
vine, Contemplative, Practical, Moral, Ethical,
Œconomical, and Political. By FRANCIS
QUARLES. Fcap. 8vo. *portrait, elegantly*
printed by Whittingham, 3s. 1856

" Had this little book been written at Athens or Rome, its author
would have been claſſed with the wiſe men of his country."—
Headley.

The Poetical Works of RICHARD CRA-
SHAW, Author of " Steps to the Temple,"
" Sacred Poems, with other Delights of the
Muſes," and " Poemata," now firſt collected.
Edited by W. B. D. TURNBULL. Fcap.
8vo. *cloth,* 5s. 1858

" His verſe is to have reſembled Herbert in the turn of mind, but
poſſeſſed more fancy and genius."—ELLIS.

Four Poems from " Zion's Flowers ;"
or, Chriſtian Poems for Spiritual Edification. By Mr. ZACHARIE BOYD, Miniſter in
Glaſgow. Printed from his MS. in the Library of the Univerſity of Glaſgow. With
Notes of his Life and Writings, by GAB.
NEIL. Small 4to. *portrait and facſimile,*
cloth, 10s. 6d. 1855

The above forms a portion of the well-known " Zachary Boyd's
Bible." A great many of his works and phraſes are curious
and amuſing, and the Book would repay a diligent peruſal.
Boyd was a contemporary of Shakeſpeare, and a great many
phraſes in his " Bible " are the ſame as in be found in the great
dramatic poet of Drummond.

A Little Book of Songs and Ballads,
gathered from Ancient Muſic Books, MS.
and Printed. By E. F. RIMBAULT, LL.D.,
F.S.A., &c., *elegantly printed in poſt 8vo.*
pp. 240, *half morocco, 6s.* 1851

" Dr. Rimbault has been at ſome pains to collect the words of
the ſongs which tend to delight the ruſtics of former times."—
Atlas.

Ballad Romances. By R. H. HORNE,
Eſq., Author of " Orion," &c. 12mo. pp.
248, *cloth,* 3s. (original price 6s. 6d.) 1852

Containing the Noble Heart, a Bohemian Legend; the Monk of
Swineſhead Abbey, a balled Chronicle of the death of King
John; The Three Knights of Camelott, a Fairy Tale; the
Ballad of Delora, or the Paſſion of Andrea Como; Bedd Gelert,
a Welſh Legend ; Ben Capſtan, a Ballad of the Night Watch ;
the Elfe of the Woodlands, a Child's ſtory.

" Pure fancy of the moſt abundant and picturesque deſcript. e.
Mr. Horne ſhould write us more Fairy Tales; we know none to
equal him here the days of Drayton and Herrick.— *Examiner.*

" The opening poem in this volume is a fine one, it is entitled the
' Noble Heart,' and not only in title but in treatment well illuſ-
trates the ſtyle of Beaumont and Fletcher."—*Athenæum.*

Wiltſhire Tales, illuſtrative of the Man-
ners, Cuſtoms, and Dialect of that and ad-
joining Counties. By JOHN YONGE AKER-
MAN. 12mo. *cloth,* 2s. 6d. 1853

" We will conclude with a ſimple but hearty recommendation of
a little book which is as humorous for the drolleries of the
future as it is intereſting as a picture of ruſtic manners."—
Tallis's Weekly Paper.

The Nurſery Rhymes of England, col-
lected chiefly from Oral Tradition. By
JAMES ORCHARD HALLIWELL, F.R.S., &c.
The SIXTH EDITION, enlarged, with many
Deſigns by W. B. SCOTT, Director of the
School of Deſign, Newcaſtle-on-Tyne. 12mo.
cloth, gilt leaves, 4s. 6d.

The largeſt Collection ever formed of theſe old ditties.

Popular Rhymes and Nurſery Tales,
with Hiſtorical Elucidations. Collected by
J. O. HALLIWELL. 12mo, *cloth,* 4s. 6d.
1849

This very intereſting volume on the Traditional Literature of
England is divided into Nurſery Antiquities, Fireſide Nurſery
Stories, Game Rhymes, Alphabet Rhymes, Riddle Rhymes,
Nurſery ſongs, Proverb Rhymes, Places, and Families, Super-
ſtition Rhymes, Cuſtom Rhymes, and Nurſery ſongs ; a large
number are here printed for the firſt time. It may be conſidered a ſequel to the preceding article.

The Dramatic Works of JOHN WEB-
STER. Edited, with Notes, &c., by WIL-
LIAM HAZLITT. 4 vols. fcap. 8vo., *elegantly
printed by Whittingham, cloth, £1.* 1857

*° A few copies printed on large paper, post 8vo., for the con-
venience of chroice books, price £1. 10s.
This is the most complete edition of Webster's works.*

The Dramatic Works of JOHN LILLY
(the Euphuift). Now firft collected, with
Life and Notes by F. W. FAIRHOLT.
2 vols. fcap. 8vo. *printed by Whittingham,
cloth,* 10s. 1858

° A few copies printed on large paper, post 8vo., price £1. 1s.

The Dramatic and Poetical Works of
THOMAS SACKVILLE, Lord Buckhurft, and
Earl of Dorfet. With Introduction and Life
by the Hon. and Rev. R. W. SACKVILLE-
WEST. Fcap. 8vo. *fine portrait from a
picture at Buckhurft, now firft engraved,
cloth,* 4s. 1859

The Poetical Works of WILLIAM
DRUMMOND, of Hawthornden. Now firft
publifhed entire. Edited by W. B. TURN-
BULL. Fcap. 8vo. *fine port., cloth,* 5s. 1856

*" The beauties of Drummond," fays Mr. Hallam, " are publifhed
and elegant, free from conceit and bad tafte, and in pure un-
blemifhed Englifh."*

The Works in Profe and Verfe of Sir
THOMAS OVERBURY. Now firft collected.
Edited, with Life and Notes, by E. F. RIM-
BAULT. Fcap. 8vo. *portrait after Pafs,
printed by Whittingham,* 5s. 1856

The Iliads of Homer, Prince of Poets,
never before in any language truly tranflated,
with a Comment on fome of his chief Places.
Done according to the Greek by GEORGE
CHAPMAN, with Introduction and Notes by
the Rev. RICHARD HOOPER. 2 vols. fquare
fcap. 8vo. *with portrait of Chapman, and
frontifpiece,* 12s. 1857

" The tranflation of Homer, publifhed by George Chapman, is one

Homer's Odyffey. Tranflated according
to the Greek by GEORGE CHAPMAN. With
Introduction and Notes by REV. RICHARD
HOOPER. 2 vols. fquare fep. 8vo. *with facfimile of the rare original frontifpiece,* 12s. 1857

Homer's Battle of the Frogs and Mice ;
HESIOD'S Works and Days; MUSÆUS'S
Hero and Leander ; JUVENAL'S Fifth Satire.
Tranflated by GEORGE CHAPMAN. Edited
by Rev. RICHARD HOOPER. Square fep.
8vo. *frontifpiece after Pafs,* 6s. 1858

*" The editor of thefe few rare volumes has done an incalculable
fervice to Englifh Literature by taking George Chapman's folios
out of the dust of time-honoured libraries, by collating them with
loving care and patience, and, through the agency of his enter-
prifing publifher, bringing Chapman entire and complete within
the reach of thofe who can beft appreciate and leaft afford to pur-
chafe the early editions."—Athenæum.*

Effay on Archæological Subjects, and on
various Queftions connected with the Hiftory
of Art, Science, and Literature in the Middle
Ages. By THOMAS WRIGHT, M.A., F.S.A.,
Corresponding Member of the Inftitute of
France, &c. 2 vols. poft 8vo. *printed by
Whittingham, illuftrated with 110 engravings,*
cloth, 16s. 1861

CONTENTS:—1. On the Remains of a Primitive People in the
South-Eaft corner of Yorkfhire; 2. On fome ancient Barrows, or
Tumuli, opened in Eaft Yorkfhire; 3. On fome curious forms
of fepulchral interment found in Eaft Yorkfhire; 4. Tongs, and
the large Tumulus at St. Weonard's; 5. On the Etymology of
South Britain at the period of the Eftablifhing of the Roman
Government in the Ifland; 6. On the Origin of the Welfh; 7.
On Anglo-Saxon Antiquities, with a particular reference to the
Faussett Collection; 8. On the True Character of the Biographer
Afser; 9. Anglo-Saxon Architecture, illuftrated from Illuminated
Manufcripts; 10. On the Literary Hiftory of Geoffrey of Mon-
mouth's Hiftory of the Britons, and of the Romantic Cycle of
King Arthur; 11. On Saints' Lives and Miracles; 12. On An-
tiquarian Excavations and Refearches in the Middle Ages; 13. On
the Ancient Map of the World preferved in Hereford Cathedral,
as illuftrative of the Hiftory of Geography in the Middle Ages;
14. On the Hiftory of the Englifh Language; 15. On the Abacus,
or Medieval fyftem of Arithmetic; 16. On the Antiquity of
Dates expreffed in Arabic Numerals; 17. Remarks on an Ivory
Cafket of the beginning of the Fourteenth Century; 18. On the
Carvings of the Stalls in Cathedral and Collegiate Churches; 19.
Illuftrations of fome Cuftoms relating to Architectural Antiquities—(a) Medieval Architecture illuftrated from Illuminated

The Social Hiftory of the People of the Southern Counties of England in paft Centuries illuftrated in regard to their Habits, Municipal Bye-laws, Civil Progrefs, &c. From the Refearches of GEORGE ROBERTS, Author of the "Hiftory of Lyme-Regis," "Life of the Duke of Monmouth," &c. Thick 8vo. cloth, 7s. 6d. (original price 16s.) 1856

An interesting volume on old English manners and cuftoms, mode of travelling, punifhments, witchcraft, gipfies, pirates, ftageplayers, pilgrimages, prices of labour and provifions, the clothing trade of the Weft of England, &c., &c., compiled chiefly from original materials, as the archives of Lyme-Regis and Weymouth, family papers, church regifters, &c. Dedicated to Lord Macaulay.

Chriftmaflide, its Hiftory, Feftivities, and Carols *(with their mufic).* By WILLIAM SANDYS, Efq., F.S.A. In a handfome vol. 8vo. *illuftrated with 20 engravings after the defigns of J. Stephanoff, extra cloth, gilt edges,* 5s. (original price 14s.)

"In this work that Chriftmaflide is germane to the day. Mr. Sandys has brought together, in an octavo of fome 300 pages, a great deal of often interefting information beyond the daily goffip about "Chriftmas in the olden time," and the thoufands make-believe of jollity and geniality which forwifh forth good books on the fubject. His carols, too, which include fome in old French and Provençal, are felefted from numerous fources, and competly many of the late known and more erudit knowing. His materials are profeffed with good feeling and maftery of his theme. On the whole the volume deferves, and fhould anticipate, a welcome."— *Spectator.*

Mufic and the Anglo-Saxons, being fome Account of the Anglo-Saxon Orcheftra, with Remarks on the Church-Mufic of the 19th Century. By F. D. WACKERBATH. 8vo. 2 plates, fewed, 4s. 1837

Reliquæ Antiquæ; Scraps from Ancient Manufcripts illuftrating chiefly Early Englifh Literature and the Englifh Language. Edited by WRIGHT and HALLIWELL. Parts 1 to 13, 8vo. fewed, odd parts to complete copies, 2s. each 1839-43

The Anglo-Saxon Epifcopate of Cornwall, with fome Account of the Bifhops of Crediton. By E. H. PEDLER. 8vo. cloth, 7s. 6d. 1860

Britifh Archæology, its Progrefs and

Autobiography of the Rt. Hon. Sir RICHARD COX, Bart., Lord-Chancellor of Ireland (1706), from the Original Manufcript. Edited by R. CAULFIELD. 8vo. fewed, 1s. 6d. 1860

St. Patrick's, Dublin.—Seven Copper-Plate Illuftrations of the Hiftory and Antiquities of St. Patrick's Cathedral, Dublin. By Revnov and GRATTAN. 4to. *in a wrapper,* 3s. 6d. 1860
The feries includes a fine whole length portrait of Dean Swift.

The Celtic Records and Hiftoric Literature of Ireland. By J. T. GILBERT, Author of the "Hiftory of Dublin," &c. 8vo. cloth, 5s. 1861

On an Oath taken by the Members of the Parliament of Scotland, 1641 to 1649, with Hiftorical Elucidations. By J. R. WALBRAN, F.S.A. *With a large facfimile of the original Record, with the autographs,* royal 8vo. *only 100 printed, bds.,* 5s. 1854
This curious document was lately difcovered in the Charter-cheft of Major Dunbar, of Blair Caftle, N.B.

A Hand-Book to Autographs, being a Ready Guide to the Handwriting of Diftinguifhed Men and Women of every Nation, defigned for the ufe of Literary Men, Autograph Collectors, and others. Executed by FREDERICK GEO. NETHERCLIFT. 8vo. parts 1 to 4, 2s. each. 1859-60
, A few copies printed upon one fide only may be had at 3s. each part.

The fpecimens contain two or three lines each befides the fignature, fo that to the hiftorian fuch a work will recommend itself as enabling him to teft the genuinenefs of the documents he confults, while the judgment of the autograph collector may be familiarly affifted, and his pecuniary refources economized by a judicious ufe of the "Manual." To the book-worm, whofe name is "legion," he would merely obferve, that daily experience teaches us the great value and fecurid attached to books containing "thoufand notes" and "fecund anda," when typed to be in front the pens of eminent perfons.

A Monograph of the Genus Bos. —The Natural Hiftory of Bulls, Bifons, and Buffaloes, exhibiting all the known Species (with an Introduction, containing an Account of Experiments on Rumination, from the French of M. FLOURENS). By GEORGE

Views of Labour and Gold. By the Rev. W. BARNES, B.D., Author of " Poems in the Dorset Dialect," " Notes on Ancient Britain," &c. Fcp. 8vo. *cloth*, 5s. 1859

" Mr. Barnes is a reader and a thinker. He has a third and a conspicuous merit - his style is perfectly lucid and simple. If the humblest reader of ordinary intelligence desired to follow out the process by which Society are built up and held together, he has but to betake himself to the study of Mr. Barnes's epitome. The title " Views of Labour and Gold,' cannot be laid to indicate the scope of the Essay, which opens with pictures of primitive life, and goes on, through an agreeably diversified range of topics, to considerations of the rights, duties, and interests of Labour and Capital, and to the enquiry, What constitutes the utility, wealth, and positive well being of a nation ? Subjects of this class are rarely handled with so firm a grasp and such light and artistic manipulation.' —*Athenæum.*

" The opinions of both a Scholar and Clergyman of the Established Church on subjects of political economy cannot fail to be both interesting and instructive, and it is originality of some of his views and expressions is well calculated to arrest and to repay the most careful attention.' —*Financial Reformer.*

Elements of Naval Architecture, being a Translation of the Third Part of Clairbois's " Traité Élémentaire de la Construction des Vaisseaux." By J. N. STRANGE, Commander, R.N. *with five large folding plates, cloth*, 5s. 1846

Lectures on Naval Architecture, being the Substance of those delivered at the United Service Institution. By E. GARDINER FISHBOURNE, Commander, R.N. 8vo. *plates, cloth*, 5s. 6d. 1846

Both these works are published in illustration of the " Wave System."

Buenos Ayres, and the Provinces of the Rio de la Plata, from their Discovery and Conquest by the Spaniards to the Establishment of their Political Independence ; with some Account of their Present State, Appendix of Historical Documents, Natural History, &c. By Sir WOODBINE PARISH. *Vice-President of the Royal Geographical Society, and many years Charge d'Affairs at Buenos Ayres.* Thick 8vo. *Second Edition, plates and woodcuts, also a valuable map by Arrowsmith, cloth*, 7s. 6d. (original price 24s.) 1852

" Among the contributions to the geography of the South American Continent, the work of our Vice-President, Sir Woodbine Parish, holds a very important place. Professing to be a Second edition of a former book, it is, in reality, almost a new work, from the great quantity of fresh matter it contains on the geography, statistics, natural history, and geology of that portion of the world." —*President of the Royal Geographical Society's Address.*

Colleccion de Memorias Cientificas. Por MARIANO EDUARDO DE RIVERO, *Cónsul del Peru.* 2 vols. 8vo. *plates and maps, sewed*, 12s. 1857

A valuable collection of Essays on the Natural History, Geography, Mineralogy, Climatology of Peru, Chili, New Granada, &c. &c. The author is well known as the discoverer and author of

Folious Appearances, a Consideration on our Ways of Lettering Books (a Curious Rhapsody). 8vo. *sewed*, 1s. 1854

History of Oregon and California, and the other territories on the North-West Coast of America, accompanied by a Geographical View and Map, and a number of Proofs and Illustrations of the History. By ROBERT GREENHOW, *Librarian of the Department of State of the United States.* Thick 8vo. *large map, cloth*, 7s. 6d. (pub. at 16s.) 1844

Historical Account of the Island of Saint Vincent, in the West Indies, with large Appendix, on Population, Meteorology, Produce of Estates, Revenue, Carib Grants, &c. By CHARLES SHEPHARD. 8vo. *plates, cloth*, 5s. (original price 12s.) 1831

History and Antiquities of Boston, the Capital of Massachusetts, and Metropolis of New England, from its Settlement in 1630 to the Year 1770 ; also an Introductory History of the Discovery and Settlement of New England, with Notes, critical and illustrative. By S. G. DRAKE. Thick royal 8vo. *portraits and plates, half-morocco*, £1. 11s. 6d.

Boston, U. S., 1856

The Ecclesiastical History of New England. By J. B. FELT. Vol. 1, 1517-1647 Thick 8vo. *cloth*, 10s. 6d. *Boston,* 1855

It every where disclaims a thoroughgoing of research and an accuracy of statement, in regard to matters of fact, which it early history of New England has never before had, and will never again need. Vol. 2 will appear immediately.

The Stranger at Rouen. A Guide for Englishmen. By M. A. LOWER. 12mo. *plates*, 1s. 1857

Mont Saint-Michel.—Histoire et Description de Mont St. Michel en Normandie. Text par Hericher, dessins par Bouet publiés par Bourdon. Folio, 130 pp., and 13 beautiful plates, executed in tinted lithography, *leather back, uncut*, £2. 2s. 1848

A handsome volume, interesting to the architect and archæologist.

Genoa, with Remarks on the Climate, and its Influence upon Invalids. By HENRY JONES BUNNETT, M.D. 12mo. *cloth*, 4s. 1844

On the March of Hannibal from the Rhone to the Alps. By HENRY LAWES LONG. 8vo. *map*, 2s. 6d. 1831

Copenhagen.—The Traveller's Handbook to Copenhagen and its Environs. By ANGLICANUS. 12mo. *with large map of Sealand, plan of Copenhagen, and views.*

The Scandinavian Question.—Practical Reflections. By ABELIOT GELLINA. Translated from the Swedish original, by an English Scandinavian. 8vo. 50 pp. *sd.*, 1s. 1857

Defence for the full Hereditary Right, according to the *Lex Regia* of the Kings and Royal House of Denmark, especially Prince Christian and his Spouse. By COUNCILLOR C. F. WICENER. Translated from the Danish. 8vo. *sewed*, 1s. 1853

Chelsea Athenæum Lectures.—No. 1, The Sources of English History. By THOS. WRIGHT, F.S.A. 8vo. 1s. 1859

——— No. 2, Ancient Egypt. By GEORGE FARREN. 8vo. 1s. 6d. 1860

Poems, partly of Rural Life, in National English. By the Rev. WILLIAM BARNES, author of " Poems in the Dorset Dialect." 12mo. *cloth*, 5s. 1846

The Rescue of Robert Burns, Feb. 1759.—A Centenary Poem. BY GEORGE STEPHENS, Professor of Old English in Copenhagen University. 8vo. 1s. 1859

Revenge, or Woman's Love, a Melodrama, in 5 Acts. By GEORGE STEPHENS, Professor of the English Language in the University of Copenhagen. 8vo. *sd.*, 3s. 1857
This play exhibits both originality and poetic feeling.

Mirrour of Justices, written originally in the old French, long before the Conquest, and many things added by ANDREW HORNE. Translated by W. HUGHES, of Gray's Inn. *A new edition.* 12mo. *cloth*, 2s. 1840
A curious, interesting, and authentic treatise on ancient English law. Andrew Horne, the editor, was Chamberlain of London A.D. 1328.

Saull (W. D.) On the Connection between Astronomical and Geological Phenomena, addressed to the Geologists of Europe and America. 8vo. *diagrams, sd.*, 2s. 1854

Dialect of Ulster. — Poor Rabbin's Ollminick, for the Town o' Bilfawst, con-

nies, are set forth. By JOHN D'ALTON, Barrister-at-Law, Author of the " History of the County of Dublin," " Drogheda," " Annals of the Boyles," &c, 2 thick vols. 8vo. pp. 1400, *cloth*, £1. 1s. 1860

Poems by PHILIP FRENEAU on Various Subjects, but chiefly Illustrative of the Events and Actors in the American War of Independence, *reprinted from the rare edition printed at Philadelphia in 1786, with a Preface.* Thick fcap. 8vo. *elegantly printed, cloth*, 6s. 1861
Freneau enjoyed the friendship of Adams, Franklin, Jefferson, Madison, and Monroe, and the last three were his constant correspondents while they lived. His Patriotic Songs and Ballads, which were superior to any metrical compositions then written in America, were everywhere sung with enthusiasm. See Griswold's " Poets and Poetry of America," and Duyckinck's " Cyclop. of American Literature."

Dr. COTTON MATHER'S Wonders of the Invisible World, being an account of the Trials of several Witches lately executed in New England, and of the several remarkable curiosities therein occurring. To which are added Dr. INCREASE MATHER'S Further Account of the Tryals, and Cases of Conscience concerning Witchcrafts, and Evil Spirits Personating Men. *Reprinted from the rare original editions of 1693, with an Introductory Preface.* Fcap. 8vo. *cloth*, 6s. 1861

Surtees (Robt.) History and Antiquities of the County of Durham. 4 vols. folio, *many fine plates, whole cloth, lettered, £18. 18s.* (pub. at £25.)

——— LARGE PAPER. 4 vols. royal folio, *bds.*, £20 (pub at £50.)

———Vol. IV., including a Memoir of the Author, by GEO. TAYLOR, Esq. Folio, *many fine plates,* £1. 4s. 1840
Containing the city and suburbs of Durham and Chester, Barnard Castle, Raintrop, and other Parishes in the Ward of Darlington (wanted by many subscribers.)

Raine (Rev. James) History and Antiquities of North Durham, as sub-divided into the Shires of Norham, Island, and Bedling-

Saint Cuthbert, with an Account of the ſtate in which his remains were found upon the opening of his Tomb in Durham Cathedral, 1827. By the Rev. JAMES RAINE. 4to. *plates and woodcuts, bds. (a very intereſting vol.),* 10s. 6d. (pub at £1. 11s. 6d.) 1828

"From the four corners of the earth they come,
To him this ſhrine—this mortal-breathing ſaint."

Hiſtorical Account of the Epiſcopal Caſtle or Palace of Auckland. By the Rev. JAMES RAINE, Author of the Hiſtory of North Durham. Royal 4to. *fine views, portraits and ſeals, cloth,* 10s. 6d. (original price £1. 1s.) 1852

Catterick Church, Yorkſhire. A correct copy of the contract for its building in 1412. Illuſtrated with Remarks and Notes by the Rev. JAMES RAINE. *With thirteen plates of views, elevations, and details, by A. SALVIN, Architect.* 4to. LARGE PAPER, *cloth,* 9s. (pub. at 18s.) 1834

St. Anſelme; Notice Biographique, Litteraire et Philoſophique. Par M. A. CHARMA, Profeſſeur de Philoſophie à Caen. 8vo. *ſewed,* 3s. 6d. 1853

A Hand-Liſt to the Early Engliſh Literature preſerved in the Douce Collection in the Bodleian Library, ſelected from the printed Catalogue of that Collection. By J. O. HALLIWELL. 8vo. *cloth, only 52 printed,* 16s. 1860

—— The ſame, of the Malone Collection in the Bodleian. 8vo. *cloth, only 52 printed,* 11s. 1860

Theſe Liſts compriſe the principal volumes of Early Engliſh Literature preſerved in the Douce and Malone Collections. They are priced for the uſe of thoſe ſtudents who do not care for the modern portions of theſe collections, and who find a folio volume is inconvenient for conſtant reference.

Curioſities of Modern Shakeſpeare Criticiſm. By J. O. HALLIWELL. 8vo., *with the firſt facſimile of the Dulwich letter, ſewed,* 1s. 1853

Obſervations on Some of the Manuſcript

The Reliquary, a Depoſitory for Precious Relics, Legendary, Biographical, and Hiſtorical, illuſtrative of the Habits, Cuſtoms, and Purſuits of our Forefathers. Edited by LLEWELLYN JEWITT, F.S.A. 8vo. *illuſtrated with engravings, publiſhed quarterly,* 2s. 6d. per No.

PUBLICATIONS OF THE CAXTON SOCIETY.

OF CHRONICLES AND OTHER WRITINGS ILLUSTRATIVE OF THE HISTORY AND MISCELLANEOUS LITERATURE OF THE MIDDLE AGES.

Uniformly printed in 8vo. with Engliſh Prefaces and Notes. Of ſeveral of the Volumes only 110 copies have been printed, and only three ſets can be completed.

Chronicon Henrici de Silgrave. Now firſt printed from the Cotton MS. By C. HOOK. 3s. 6d.

Gaimar (Geoffrey) Anglo-Norman Metrical Chronicle of the Anglo-Saxon Kings. Printed for the firſt time entire. With Appendix, containing the Lay of Havelok the Dane, the Legend of Ernulph, and Life of Hereward the Saxon. Edited by T. WRIGHT, Eſq., F.S.A., pp. 154 (*only to be had in a ſet*).

The only complete edition; that in the "Monumenta Hiſtorica Britannica," printed by the Record Commiſſion, is incomplete.

La Revolte du Comte de Warwick contre le Roi Edouard IV. Now firſt printed from a MS. at Ghent; to which is added a French Letter, concerning Lady Jane Grey and Queen Mary, from a MS. at Bruges. Edited by DR. GILES. 3s. 6d.

Walteri Abbatis Dervenſis Epiſtolæ. Now firſt printed from a MS. in St. John's College, Cambridge. By C. MESSITER, 4s. 6d.

Anecdota Bedæ, Lanfranci, et aliorum (inedited Tracts, Letters, Poems, &c., Bede, Lanfranc, Taiwin, &c.) By Dr. GILES. 10s.

Radulphi Nigri Chronica. Duo. Now first printed from MSS. in the British Museum. By Lieut.-Col. ANSTUTHER. 8s.

Memorial of Bishop Waynflete, Founder of St. Mary Magdalen College, Oxford. By Dr. Peter Heylyn. Now first edited from the original MS. By J. R. BLOXHAM, D.D., Fellow of the same College. 5s. 6d.

Robert Grosseteste (*Bishop of Lincoln*), "Chasteau d'Amour;" to which is added "La Vie de Sainte Marie Egyptienne," and an English Version (of the 13th Century) of the "Chasteau d'Amour." Now first edited. By M. COOKE. 6s. 6d.

Galfredi Monumententis Historia Britonum, nunc primum in Anglia novem codd. MSS. collatis. Edidit J. A. GILES. 10s.

Alani, Prioris Cantuariensis, postea Abbatis Tewkesberiensis, Scripta quæ extant. Edita J. A. GILES. 6s. 6d.

Vita Quorandum Anglo-Saxonum. Original Lives of Anglo-Saxons and others who lived before the Conquest (*in Latin*). Edited by Dr. GILES. 10s.

Scriptores Rerum Gestarum Wilhelmi Conquestoris. In unum collecti. Ab. J. A. GILES. 10s.

Contines : 1. Brevis Relatio de Willelmo Nobilissimo Comitis Normannorum. 2. Protestatio Willelmi Primi de Primis Cantuariensis Revisais. 3. Widonis Ambrianensis Carmen de Hastingeasi. 4. Charta Willelmi Bastardi. 5. Epistola Will. Conquestoris ad Gregorium Papam. 6. Excerpta de Vita Willelmi Conquestoris. 7. De Morte Will. Conq. 8. Hymnus de Morte Will. Conq. 9. De Morte Lanfranci. 10. Gesta Will. Ducis Normannorum. 11. Excerptum ex Cantuarion 8. Huberti. 12. Annalis Historia Brevis sive Chronica Monasterii S. Stephani Cadomonensis. 13. Carmen de Morte Lanfranci. 14. Charta a Rege Will. concessa Anglo-Saxonico scripta. 15. De Rei Guillelmo d'Angleterre, par Cretien de Troyes. 16. Le Dit de Guilleaume

Arundel : History and Antiquities of the Castle and Town of Arundel, including the Biography of its Earls. By the Rev. Canon TIERNEY. 2 vols, royal 8vo, *fine plates, cloth*, 12s. (original price, 2l. 10s.)
1834

Egyptian Mythology and Egyptian Christianity, with their Influence on the Opinions of Modern Christendom. By SAMUEL SHARPE, Author of the "Ancient History of Egypt," &c. Post 8vo, *with* 100 *engravings, cloth*. 3s. 1863

The Pharaoh of the Exodus. An Examination of the Modern Systems of Egyptian Chronology. By D. W. NASH, Author of "Taliesin," &c. 8vo, *with frontispiece of the Egyptian Calendar, from the ceiling of the Ramesseum, at Thebes, cloth*. 12s. 1863

A Hand-Book to the Modern Provencal Language, spoken in the South of France, Piedmont, &c., comprising a Grammar, Dialogues, Legends, Vocabularies, &c., useful for English Tourists and others. By the Rev. J. DUNCAN CRAIG, M.A. Royal 12mo, *cloth*. 3s. 6d. 1863

"This little book is a welcome addition to the literature of comparative philology in this country, as we have hitherto had no grammar of the sweet lyrical tongue of Southern France."—*Mirror*, May 8.

Cornish Dialect and Poems, viz.—

1. Treagle of Doomary Pool, and Original oraish Ballads.
2. Cornish Thalia : Original Comic Poems illustrative of the Dialect.
3. A Companion to the Cornish Thalia. By H. J. DANIEL.
4. Mirth for "One and All." By H. J. DANIEL.
5. Humorous Cornish Legends. By H. J. DANIEL.
6. A Budget of Cornish Poems, by various authors.
7. Dolly Pentreath and other Humorous

The Sutton-Dudleys of England, and the Dudleys of Massachusetts, in New England. By GEORGE ADLARD. 8vo, *pedigrees, &c., cloth,* 9s.   1862

An interesting volume to the English genealogist.

A Collection of English Metrical Homilies, from Manuscripts of the 14th Century, with Introduction and Glossarial Notes, by JOHN SMALL, *Librarian, University of Edinburgh.* Small 4to, *elegantly printed, cloth,* 12s.   1862

Although the authorship of this interesting collection of Sermons is a matter of uncertainty, still there can be no doubt that it was composed in the North of England, at a very early period, when the Anglo-Saxon was being transformed into English, and when the use of the Anglo-Norman French was not uncommon amongst the educated classes of the people, as it is stated in the Prologue, the design of the author was to make the services of religion intelligible to the unlearned :—

"For al men was boht, I wis,
Understand Latin and Frankis."

Gesta Regum Britanniæ : a Metrical History of the Britons (in Latin). Now first printed from three Manuscripts, with Introduction (in English), by FRANCISQUE MICHEL. 8vo, pp. 256, *sewed,* 7s. 6d. 1862

Wales. Sixty-seven Views of the Antiquities of Wales and of the Marches, also some in Cornwall and Brittany. Extracted from the "Archæologia Cambrensis." 8vo, *sewed,* 7s. 6d.   1862

Notes of Family Excursions in North Wales, taken chiefly from Rhyl, Abergele, Llarddna, and Bangor. By J. O. HALLIWELL, F.R.S. Fcp. 4to, *with engravings, elegantly printed by Whittingham, cloth,* 5s.   1860

Names of the Roman Catholics, Nonjurors, and others who refused to take the Oaths to King George I., together with their Titles, Additions, and Places of Abode, the Parishes and Townships where their Lands lay, the Names of the then Tenants, and the Annual Value of them as returned by themselves. Collected by Mr. COSIN, the Secretary to the Commissioners of the Forfeited Estates. *Reprinted from the Edition of* 1745. 8vo, *cloth,* 5s. 1862

A curious book for the topographer and genealogist.

Brief Historical Notices of the Parishes of Hurst Bourn and St. Mary Bourn, in Hampshire. 8vo, *plate and pedigree of the Family of Oxenbridge, sewed,* 2s. 1861

The Dialect of Leeds and its Neighbourhood, illustrated by Conversations and Tales of Common Life, etc. To which are added a Copious Glossary, Notices of the various Antiquities, Manners and Customs, and general Folk-Lore of the District. Thick 12mo, pp. 458, *cloth,* 6s. 186

"This is undoubtedly the best work hitherto published on the dialects of Yorkshire in general, and of Leeds in particular. The author, we believe one of our fellow townsmen — for his introductory remarks are dated 'Leeds, March, 1861'—has used not only great industry but much keen observation, and has produced a book which will everywhere be received as a valuable addition to the archæological literature of England."— LEEDS INTELLIGENCER.

"His account of the various dialects of Yorkshire, as well as his statements respecting the manners and customs of its various classes and semi-barbarous tribes, are alike strange and instructive. He shows, at the same time, a desire to preserve what is of genuine antiquity, and points out the manner in which language becomes corrupted. His theory upon the latter point is worth listening to."— LONDON REVIEW.

Ten Years' Diggings in Celtic and Saxon Grave-Hills, in the Counties of Derby, Stafford, and York, from 1848 to 1858, with Notices of some Former Discoveries hitherto unpublished, and Remarks on the Crania and Pottery from the Mounds. By THOMAS BATEMAN, *Author of the "Vestiges of Derbyshire."* 8vo, *numerous woodcuts, cloth,* 15s.   1861

The Reliquary : a Depository for Precious Relics, Legendary, Biographical, and Historical, illustrative of the Habits, Customs, and Pursuits of our Forefathers. Edited by LLEWELLYN JEWITT, F.S.A. Vols. 1, 2, and 3, 8vo, *illustrated with many engravings, cloth,* 11s. 6d. *each.* 1861—3

Publishing in Quarterly Parts, at 2s. 6d. each.

Of Anagrams : a Monograph of their History from the Earliest Ages, with an Introduction containing numerous Specimens of Macaronic Poetry, Punning Mottoes, Rhopalic, Shaped, Equivocal, Lyon, and Echo Verses, Alliteration, Acrostics, Lipograms, Chronograms, Logograms, Palindromes, and Bout-Rimes. By H. B. WHEATLEY. 12mo, *elegantly printed, a curious and interesting volume, half morocco,* 6s.   1862

History of Taunton Priory, in the County of Somerset. By the Rev. THOMAS HUGO. Impl. 8vo, *plates and woodcuts, cloth,* 9s.   1860

www.ingramcontent.com/pod-product-compliance
Lightning Source LLC
Chambersburg PA
CBHW030951110726
47900CB00004B/1216